Mínima Cuba

SUNY series in Latin American and Iberian Thought and Culture

Jorge J. E. Gracia and Rosemary Geisdorfer Feal, editors

Mínima Cuba

Heretical Poetics and Power in Post-Soviet Cuba

MARTA HERNÁNDEZ SALVÁN

SUNY PRESS

Cover photograph: *Untitled*, Lissette Solórzano, from Ferro Carril Series, 2002.

Published by
STATE UNIVERSITY OF NEW YORK PRESS
Albany

Printed in the United States of America

For information, contact
State University of New York Press
www.sunypress.edu

Production, Laurie D. Searl
Marketing, Anne M. Valentine

Library of Congress Cataloging-in-Publication Data

Hernández Salván, Marta, 1970- author.
Mínima Cuba : Heretical Poetics and Power in Post-Soviet Cuba / Marta Hernández Salván.
pages cm. — (SUNY series in Latin American and Iberian Thought and Culture)
Includes bibliographical references and index.
ISBN 978-1-4384-5669-0 (hardcover : alk. paper)
ISBN 978-1-4384-5670-6 (pbk. : alk. paper)
ISBN 978-1-4384-5671-3 (e-book)
1. Cuban literature—20th century—History and criticism. 2. Irony in literature. 3. Poetics. 4. Cuba—History—Revolution, 1959—Influence. I. Title.
PQ7378.H48 2015
860.9'97291—dc23 2014027654

10 9 8 7 6 5 4 3 2 1

To my mother, Elvira, and Marc

Contents

Acknowledgments

This book, and my scholarly endeavors in general, would not exist without the help of my mentors and dear friends Alberto Moreiras and Teresa Vilarós who believed in me and transformed my exile into the most thrilling intellectual adventure of my life. I hope that my love of Cuba will come out of the many pages of this book, especially as a tribute to all of the friends who have offered their hospitality, their invaluable knowledge and help during my travels: Carlos A. Aguilera, Araceli Carranza, Caridad Cumaná, Ambrosio Fornet, Jorge Fornet, Víctor Fowler, Juan Carlos Flores, Caridad Tamayo, Mayra López, Pedro Marqués de Armas, Desiderio Navarro, Antonio José Ponte, Omar Pérez, Ricardo A. Pérez, Soleída Ríos, Reina María Rodríguez, Rafael Rojas.

Also, I am deeply indebted to my dear friends and mentors who have patiently read and commented on chapters, offered their support, and written letters on my behalf: Ben Heller, Juan Carlos Quintero-Herencia, Ernesto Laclau, Jacqueline Loss, Juan Pablo Lupi, César Salgado, Enrico M. Santí, Gabriel Trop, Gareth Williams, Esther Withfield, Raúl Fernández. Throughout the years, my project has taken shape thanks to intellectual exchanges with friends and colleagues Susan Antebi, Sonja Bertucci, Oscar Cabezas, Alessandro Fornazzari, Erin Graff, Kate Jenckes, Toby Miller, Vorris Nunley, Rachel Price, Juan Carlos Rodríguez, Freya Schiwy. Many of them have also provided helpful feedback of my work.

I extend my deepest gratitude to my editor Alex Martin for his infinite patience, careful editing, and beautiful translations of the poems. It has been extremely gratifying to work with Beth Boulokos and production editor Laurie Searl, the editors at SUNY Press. I am really thankful for their diligence, patience, and assistance throughout the editing process. I would also like to thank Lissette Solórzano for the cover picture that so hauntingly speaks to my book.

A different kind of acknowledgment goes to my family: my mother Elvira, who taught me resilience, and my father Rodolfo, my brother Javier, and my nephews Elvira, Guillermo, Jorge, and Pablo, without whom nothing would be worth it. To Marc, I owe it all.

I thank the publishers for permission to republish the following essays, which appeared previously as follows: An earlier version of chapter 2 appeared as "A Requiem for a Chimera: Poetics of the Cuban Post-Revolution," in *Revista de Estudios Hispánicos* XLIII, no. 3 (2009): 149–69. Portions of chapter 1 were originally published in "Heterodox Marxism," in *The New Centennial Review* 12, no. 2 (Fall 2012): 151–82. A short section of chapter 4 appeared as "Out of History," in *Revista hispánica moderna* 64 (June 2011): 81–96.

Introduction

In October 1988, as part of a larger performance (9 *Alquimistas y un ciego* [9 *Alchemists and a Blind Man*]), the art group Arte Calle spread out a large portrait of Ernesto Che Guevara that covered most of Havana's L Gallery floor. On each side of the painting were written the words: "Hecho historia o hecho tierra [Victory or Defeat]." Right above the painting, there was another inscription reading: "¿Dónde estás Caballero Bayardo? [Where are you, Sir Bayard?]." This work, one of the bravest and most critical examples of the period, presupposes and calls into question the dominant ideological tendencies of the visual arts during the eighties in Cuba. In point of fact, the painting was challenging the legacy of the most popular and beloved revolutionary hero, and by extension the revolution and the fatherland. In addition, it was also criticizing one of the mythical poems written in homage to Che Guevara. "Where are you, Sir Bayard" was the first line of "Canción antigua a Che Guevara [Old Song to Che Guevara]," a conversationalist poem written by Mirta Aguirre one month after Guevara's death on October 9, 1967 (Aguirre 1979, 9). The fact that it had been written to commemorate the first month of his death sought to render its own subject just as iconic as the hero to which it alluded. Pierre Terraill de Bayard, a sixteenth-century French knight, was the subject of a popular legend, "Chevalier sans peur et sans reproche [Caballero sin miedo y sin tacha, Fearless Knight beyond Reproach]"—a title that was included by Aguirre as the poem's second line.

Let us shift the focus to nine years later. In 1997, Tania Bruguera—one of the iconic artists of the earlier generation—gives her first performance of *El peso de la culpa* (*The Burden of Guilt*). She had begun her career by making a very engaged form of art, *Memoria de la postguerra*, consisting of a collage of news from all types of sources, even Miami papers such as the *New Miami Herald*. The second issue, which was published in 1994, raised the sensitive topic of migration (especially referring to the *balseros*, or rafters, who had left the island by the thousands that same year). The paper was censored before it could be distributed, and Bruguera resumed her artistic activity by shifting to solo performance, transforming her body itself into a site of suffering (Weiss 2011, 232–33). In her open house, for a piece entitled *Estadísticas* (1996–98), Bruguera posed in front of a twelve-foot Cuban flag made out of human hair. A slaughtered lamb hung from her body, and she consumed small balls of moist soil taken from dishes filled with salted water. These actions actually refer to a legend in which the indigenous Cuban population ate soil to commit suicide and thereby performed an act of passive resistance against the Spanish invaders (Mosquera 2009).

We have here two very different performances with similar resonances. Both of them respond to the heroic mythology present in the revolutionary poetry of the sixties and seventies, a mythology exemplified by Aguirre's poem. The ironic and comic tone of the Arte Calle's performance poses a stark contrast with the poignant agony of Bruguera's actions. Bruguera embodies the revolutionary idea of sacrifice. She not only reenacts the gesture of suicide as self-immolation or resistance, but also takes the sacrifices of others upon her like a burdensome weight, initiating a never-ending cycle of guilt and responsibility. Aguirre's and Bruguera's representations of sacrifice speak of two different temporalities and understandings of violence and power, the complexity of which is the subject of this book. Whereas Aguirre's sacrifice consists in a bloody, raucous, and imposing trauma, Bruguera's appears submissive and silent. Aguirre's poem demands that revolutionary blood provide water for the soil, ultimately culminating in the life of a new fatherland: "Dónde estás, caballero el más fuerte/ . . . /En la sangre, en el polvo, en la herida/ . . . /Hecho saga en la muerte que muero;/ hecho historia, señora, hecho historia" (Aguirre 1979, 9).[1] For Bruguera's generation, however, the source of blood has dried up; it can no longer flow and give rise to filial relationships. Indeed, the performance, as well as Bruguera's generation's relation to sacrifice, culminates in a form of abjection, as Bruguera's performing an ingestion of soil indicates. "Comer tierra" (eating soil) not only alludes to the indigenous population's legend, it also points to its meaning in Cuban slang "to suffer hardship" (Mosquera 2009). The suffering in this case is double, since the ritual also alludes to the rituals of Passover, one in which salt water stands in for the Jewish slaves' tears in Egypt. In "Canción antigua a Che Guevara," the knight responds confidently to the question where he is: "hecho historia, señora, hecho historia" (Aguirre 1979, 9). Thus, if Guevara represents history in Aguirre's poem, in Arte Calle's ironic version, the narrative of history has turned into one of defeat: "hecho tierra." On the one hand, "defeat" is what the expression means, but taken literally, it designates the transformation of the hero into soil. In other words, the seeming birth of a new fatherland is resignified as defeat. In Bruguera's version however, "comer tierra," as a metaphor, becomes literalized, culminating in self-destruction. The soil of the fatherland becomes the site of a self-imposed death—one chokes on one's own earth—which in turn marks the transformation of the nation from a locus of freedom to one of subjugation.

These two examples articulate a critique of the national ideology of revolutionary heroism, and in so doing, may serve to frame the main concerns of this book. On the one hand, *Mínima Cuba* investigates the transformation of the sixties and seventies heroic "organic" intellectual—if there was ever one—into the apostate intellectual and antihero of the eighties and nineties. On the other hand, the book wants to capture the contradictory and yet simultaneous emotions of hopefulness, melancholy, and irony that coalesced during the latter decades as a result of those two eras' political turmoil.

This book aims to analyze the reconfiguration of aesthetics and power in Cuba throughout three different periods: the early revolutionary years (from the sixties until the "Five Gray Years"); the eighties (with an emphasis on the Rectification Process of Errors and Negative Tendencies that began in 1986); and the postrevolutionary transition (1989 to 2005, the conclusion of the "Special Period"). *Mínima Cuba* addresses trauma and ideology, a previously unexplored dyad in Cuban and postsocialism studies. The book places special emphasis on a form of cultural production from the island—mostly poetry and samizdats from the eighties and nineties—that has received little or no scholarly attention. *Mínima Cuba* studies the transformation of emancipatory politics, cultural production, state power, and the subjectivity of the revolutionary hero in a period that extends from the early sixties to the first decade of the twenty-first century.

This book offers an alternative reading of contemporary Cuba, one that shifts the focus to rhetorical and symbolic discursivity as opposed to cultural identity and experience. Analyzing the rhetorical tropes of revolutionary and postrevolutionary discourse in their political and aesthetic rather than ethnographic forms of representation, this book addresses the following issues: the transformation of an allegorical and utopian representation of the Revolution into its antirepresentational and dystopian antithesis in the eighties and nineties; the influence of the melancholic nature of Guevara's social construct of the New Man in the works of the eighties and nineties;

the passage from a cultural policy based on antagonistic politics to a biopolitical paradigm; the humanist and antihumanist political division between intellectuals during the eighties and nineties; the exhaustion of literature as a state-sanctioned bastion of official rhetoric in the nineties; and finally, the exhaustion of the political for the intellectuals born and raised after 1959.

The post–Cold War period that begins with Mikhail Gorbachev's perestroika in 1985 and ends with the so-called "Periodo especial en tiempos de paz [Cuban Special Period in Times of Peace, 1989–2005]" marks the beginning of the current Cuban transition. This period of hope, uncertainty, and economic hardship is the time span covered by this book. It was, as it seems, the best of times and the worst of times for the Cuban Revolution. The period began with perestroika and the hope of change for Cuba, only to end with the fall of the Berlin Wall and the subsequent economic and political crisis. While this development might seem paradoxical, it is in fact perfectly intelligible: what initially made Cubans hopeful about political change (the Soviet perestroika) also brought about the worst economic backlash of the Revolution. Culturally speaking, political hope triggered a desire to question all the grand narratives that had inspired the cultural production of the Revolution. This hope nevertheless simultaneously concretized the existence of a utopian desire that needed to be fed new ideas. Politically speaking, there was a disavowal of a partial capitalization of the economy, although capitalization was simultaneously desired. Although there was never *perestroika* on the island, in 1986, the government initiated the Rectification Process of Errors and Negative Tendencies (Proceso de rectificación de errores y tendencias negativas). These policies, characterized by a return of Guevarian ethical principles, contributed without a doubt (whether intentional or not) to the eighties' cultural and critical ebullience. Intellectuals recall the space for dissent and debate that emerged at the universities as a result of the weaker political control of the state: "Entre los años 1989 y 1994 hubo una situación de titubeo ideológico en las instituciones docentes y culturales del país. . . . Fue un período de confusión para unos y de libertad para otros. . . . En las aulas, entonces, se podía hacer y hablar de lo que uno estimara, era lícito invitar a cuanto intelectual de extramuros se deseara [Between 1989 and 1994 the state relaxed its ideological control over learning and cultural institutions. . . . It was a confusing period for some, and a period of freedom for others. . . . One could talk freely in class and have foreign—and also exiled—intellectuals from abroad]" (Ichikawa 2001, 134). From the eighties until the mid-2000s, all the arts were in one way or another focused on the Cuban Revolution and its leaders. This was a period of a major upheaval whose anxieties were reflected in all forms of cultural production, whether critical, melancholic, ironic, or hopeful.

When I first began thinking about this project in 2002, I wanted to discuss works emerging from the nascent civil society of 1989. Scholars have argued that underground movements such as hip-hop or the performing arts were the first expressions of an emerging public sphere that initiated a new movement of revolutionary critique (see Sujatha Fernandes, *Cuba Represent! Cuban Arts, State Power, and the Making of New Revolutionary Cultures*). Similar arguments are being made about the recent Cuban blogosphere and new technological interventions (see Katrin Hansing, "Changes from Below: New Dynamics, Spaces, and Attitudes in Cuban Society"). Poetry had its own critical groups and movements, and while some of them tried to open a conversation, others had to remain in the shadows. Discovering the poetry of the past three decades, changed the nature of my research, especially because I perceived that these works were speaking about the traumatic experience of revolutionary failure like no other genre. I was not interested in analyzing such works as modes of resistance to hegemonic ideology, because, as I will explain later, they are part of our postideological society. The notion of a public sphere in its Habermasian version as the constitution of a collective group where ideas are exchanged and discussed articulated an idea of clarity and transparency that resonated with revolutionary, rather than postrevolutionary, poetry. Postrevolutionary poetic works focus on the limit of language's representation, which is a notion that actually challenges the idea of public sphere itself. If the notion of the public sphere entails a discursive relationship between the state and interest groups, what is the margin of critique that the state will be willing to tolerate? This question becomes particularly important considering that official cultural politics are still defined by Fidel Castro's 1961 famous dictum "This means that within the Revolution, everything; against the Revolution, nothing." (Castro 2001, 81).[2]

The intellectual group of poets and essayists that this book considers first were gathered under the name of Proyecto Paideia. After the members of this group had been denied an official space to meet, read their works, and hold conferences, they began to meet regularly on the poet Reina María Rodríguez's rooftop (*azotea*). Some of these writers included: Víctor Fowler, Rolando Prats, Omar Pérez, Antonio José Ponte, Alessandra Molina, Rolando Sánchez Mejías, Pedro Marqués de Armas, Carlos A. Aguilera, Francisco Morán, Ricardo Alberto Pérez, and Almelio Calderón among others. In 1988 a group including Rodríguez, Fowler, Prats, Ernesto Hernández Busto, and Radamés Molina organized Proyecto Paideia, which proposed a cultural reform for the integration of independent intellectual ventures as part of the state's official cultural program. They had envisioned a framework encompassing several working groups, a lecture series, and a creative writing mentoring group. After several years of failed attempts to convince cultural authorities, and after receiving dissuasive governmental signals, the group dissolved and regrouped in Rodríguez's house.

In 1993, a few poets including Sánchez Mejías, Aguilera, Marqués de Armas, Ricardo Alberto Pérez, Rogelio Saunders, Ismael González Castañer, and José Manuel Prieto separated from the larger intellectual project to form Proyecto Diáspora(s), and in 1997 they launched *Diáspora(s)*, a print journal of no more than two hundred mimeographed copies distributed as a samizdat. They were radical, antireformists, poetically vanguardist, and critical of baroque and neobaroque poetics. *Mínima Cuba* focuses mainly on poetic and philosophical works, which are the genres that these writers cultivated. Poets altered the forms and ideological patterns of canonical national literature in a way that no other genre was able to do. Thus, the name of my book refers to poetic language as the less discursive and more concise expression of that which escapes the arena of civil society subsumed under state control. The cultural production that arose under Reina María Rodríguez's aegis and that was introduced by the generation of the "children of the revolution" is the subject of this study. Through a psychoanalytical reading of the traumatic transformation of the sixties melancholic hero into the New Man, finally becoming the nineties *homo sacer* (a figure divested of subjectivity) or schizo, I claim that a distinct body of literature from the eighties and nineties represents the political violence of a failed socialist imaginary on the body of the nation, giving rise to a poetics whose immanence performs at times the same negation that it tries to resist.

More specifically, this book seeks a deeper understanding of the complex and contradictory cultural and political representations triggered by utopia's imaginary. *Mínima Cuba* addresses the cultural meaning of revolutionary ideology understood not according to its political definition, but rather in its imaginary sense as utopia (etymologically meaning "no place," lack or absence of place). It focuses on the initial revolutionary utopian imaginary, as well as its symbolic "death" after the disintegration of the Soviet bloc in 1989. Scholars have rightly argued that "bitterness and melancholia were going to be the dominant themes of Cuban literature and arts at this point," but why melancholia and not hostility, for example? (Quiroga 2005, 20). After all, intellectuals had sufficient reason to be outraged by their powerlessness. If melancholia was indeed one of the dominant moods, what exactly had been lost? Was it hope or any concrete historical period or event? My main thesis is that melancholia was a paralyzing response to a political loss that could not be recovered, rather than a response to the withering of socialism.[3] These melancholic regressive forces were already ingrained in the revolutionary project itself, and the events of 1989 reignited what had been repressed until then.

To demonstrate this hypothesis, the book goes back to the sixties, and looks specifically at two of the founding works of revolutionary ideology: Ernesto Guevara's "El socialismo y el hombre en Cuba" and Fidel Castro's *La historia me absolverá*. The analysis of those two texts leads me to two different conclusions. First, I show that the revolutionary project's melancholic nature is already present in Guevara's discussion of the New Man (the revolutionary intellectual subject). Second, I argue that the experience and rhetoric of violence, as well as its sublimation, were the main *topoi* of revolutionary discourse. More than a concrete political program (or lack thereof), the initial revolutionary rhetoric was based on the melodramatic exaltation of violence and heroism, a cohesive narrative of nation formation. If utopia (the object of desire) remained unattainable, violent insurrection had been indisputably successful: the rebel insurgency had resulted in the triumph of the revolution. According to official discourse, however, it was not the 26th of July Movement but the people who had won the war. For all these reasons, the rhetoric of violence appeared to be the natural continuation of the process of insurgency itself. The rhetoric of war and heroism was more prevalent than a discourse about utopia. For example, in the sixties' cultural production, the destruction of the old order was never followed by its construction. A vast array of revolutionary works, including Tomás Gutiérrez Alea's *Historias de la revolución* (*Stories of the Revolution*), Luis Rogelio Nogueras's *Y si muero mañana* (If I Die Tomorrow), and conversationalist poetry, center on war, heroism, and sacrifice, ending with the Revolution's triumph. In the melodramatic rehearsals of war victories, utopia was constantly deferred. Aesthetically speaking, this also pointed to the political failure and contradictions of socialist realism, as I discuss in the polemic stirred by Mirta Aguirre's famous article "Apuntes sobre la literatura y el arte" (Notes on Literature and Art). All these works revealed the primary obstacle on which the revolution stumbled, that is, the belief that utopia had to be created anew and that history should be erased.

What was the fantasy that future generations would inherit, then? For them, utopia was an undefined and unattainable object of desire for which they nonetheless had to fight. Moreover, the New Man's Guevarian tropology had actually replaced utopia (an object or a place) with a subject (the revolutionary New Man). The symbolic loss of that object, which resulted from the end of socialism, was indeed the loss of the subject himself as we see in the early poetry of the nineties, as well as in Enrique Álvarez's film *La ola* (*The Wave*), and Antonio José Ponte's short story "Un arte de hacer ruinas" ("An Art of Making Ruins"). This melancholic crisis resulted from the loss of a self who was the ghostly image (an undefined, subjectless presence whose subjectivity, had been, like the nature of utopia, forever deferred) unknown to begin with.

But melancholia was not the only ethos of post-Soviet Cuba. Gorbachev's perestroika inspired some hope for change on the island, which translated into the critical and politically engaged cultural production of the early eighties. This production included the alternative cultural and political program of Proyecto Paideia. The symbolic death of the revolutionary project at the end of the nineties, as well as the repressive policies of the *quinquenio gris* (five gray years), resulted in the state's loss of ideological legitimacy. The state made some ideological concessions, the beginning of timid reforms, since as Castro repeatedly emphasized Cubans had to fight to save the conquests of socialism. In cultural production, the political imaginary lacked its initial utopian impulse and presented not an alternative ideology but a rejection of the former one. Realizing the ensuing loss of political legitimacy, the state resorted to increasing its control over the lives of its citizens. Biopower is a way of exerting power more in consonance with the needs of a country that, on the one hand, is now taking part in global capitalism, but that, on the other hand, also wants to preserve its singularity as a socialist nation. The film *Boleto al paraíso* (*Ticket to Paradise*) as well as the Elián González affair show how market ideology can be kept at bay with a politics that, instead of repressing, "lets live" and controls by creating docile subjects. This politics inaugurates the end of the Cuban utopian imaginary as shown by the ironic antiheroic figures that populate Proyecto Diáspora(s) samizdat's poetics, and finally with the end of the lettered city represented by Juan Carlos Flores's poetics.

Understanding the ideological and affective complexity of this period requires two different methodologies: psychoanalysis and power discourse analysis. A psychoanalytic reading is necessary to understand the ideological power of the revolutionary imaginary, which resulted from its transformation into a fantasy, more specifically understood in its Lacanian sense. The construction of fantasies about the object of desire represented by the revolution offsets the impossibility of reaching the full object, as shown in Ernesto Guevara's writings. As I explain in this introduction's final paragraph, I understand fantasy in its Lacanian sense as a narrative that allows us to mask the kernel of our desire. The book is simultaneously ingrained in historicity, and it could not be otherwise since my argument takes the narration of the revolution as the project's point of departure. What can literature, or art in general, tell us about the ideological and emotional trauma left by the withering of "real socialism," and how can we understand the relationship linking history, literature, and theory? These questions are what my next paragraphs discuss.

History and Literature

Above all, language is matter; it is also what engenders discourse, and what concerns this book. Words, the building blocks of discourse, are held together by rhetorical figures, producing edifices that, in turn, create discursive imaginaries. Discourses do not stand alone, however, since they are deeply ingrained in historical facts that they in turn inform. Historical events and historical discourses are thus inextricably linked, though they are not determined by each other. Instead, they are produced through uneven, loose, and unstable relationships. To say that history is a discourse, however, is not to claim that everything is fiction. Certainly, historical events and material conditions also exist that are bound together in complex webs of mutual determination and indetermination.

The historical referent, however, is not simply another text that can be subjected to hermeneutic scrutiny. It is, instead, history materialized as what Louis Althusser termed the "absent cause." That is, grounding ourselves in a materialist conception of history, we postulate a system not as one in which the economic levels determine the composition of the different ideological structures but rather as one whose units are semiautonomous, not determined from the outside but with a causality that is both inherent and, nonetheless, absent (Althusser 1971, 186–89). History as absent cause, according to Althusser, is not teleological and has no concrete subject. Therefore, if history can only be considered as absent cause, it cannot be inscribed within the symbolic order and must belong to the order of the Real. History is thus configured as a process that resists symbolization, one we can only access through its textualization, in order to unravel its narrativization through what Fredric Jameson has called the "political unconscious" (Jameson 1981, 35).

This book examines the political unconscious through a main focus on literature. I have just argued that literature, and art in general, are deeply ingrained in a temporal and political context, and this book does not ignore that fact. How then should we understand the complex relationship between literature and history? Is literature one more discourse, one more way of fictionalizing the world? Is it part of the world, or does it stand by itself, petrified in its own materiality? Literature has no goal other than itself, but it does not exist as an autonomous phenomenon. Literature is the creation of a phenomenological and intrinsically aesthetic rapport with the world, and as such it materializes as a mode of representation. Yet literature is not only an aesthetics, nor is it an anti-aesthetics. It is not a symptom of history, nor is it directly determined by it. As I have already argued, literature, or aesthetics, and history are necessary linked in complex and uneven relations that produce and inform each other. Perhaps then, one should ask not "what is literature?" but rather "why literature?" The book focuses on literature and art because, like trauma and utopia, they also approach the world with a language that defies a rational explanation. Literature is also key to understanding trauma and utopia because these two phenomena materialize in the world as artistic representations. That is, in Lacanian terms, trauma and utopia cannot be symbolized, but they come to pass as literary imaginaries masking the Real of our desire. In sum and above all, what matters is language.

Historical representations are part of the discursive strategies producing the context for literature's very complex production. This book seeks therefore to understand contemporary Cuba by analyzing various representations of the world, among them literature and history. In the case of Cuba, in particular, official historical accounts have often been instrumental to politics. Historiography has ceased to be an inquiry into reality and has become instead an ideological discourse. These are the historical discourses that this book discusses, and revolutionary rhetoric is one of them. In this regard, this book argues that revolutionary rhetoric has always represented utopia as an emotional ethos more than as a clear political goal.

Power and Biopolitics

Social malaise and affect are also deeply political, and ideology is always articulated through power, be it private or public. Like history, power, even in its most repressive form, is above all implemented through discourse. This is Althusser's point with respect to ideological state apparatuses, the myriad specialized institutions (religious, educational, familial, etc.) that *function by ideology* (Althusser 1971, 145). Utopian ideas in all their forms (repressive and liberating) hail individuals through political and social control. Thus, in addition to psychoanalysis, the analysis of governance and the rhetorics of power (as discourses) is also instrumental to understanding the utopian ethos, in Cuba and elsewhere. On April 19, 1986, the Cuban government launched the "Proceso de rectificación de errores y tendencias negativas" ("Rectification Process of Errors and Negative Tendencies"), which was supposed to lead to the abandonment of past repressive policies. In culture, these changes resulted in the celebration of authors previously forgotten (including José Lezama Lima and Virgilio Piñera), the acceptance of queer culture, and some leniency toward political disaffection. Far from setting in motion new forms of tolerance, however, these changes became a more effective form of control. What changed was the form with which control was imposed, not the ideology. This new form of control, what Michel Foucault calls biopolitics, took place as the rhetoric of violence was replaced by a discourse of the conservation and reproduction of life. Foucault's theory of biopolitics is relevant to this book for two main reasons. First, it illuminates the regressive nature of a policy that is apparently moving away from the repressive policies of the seventies. For example, it reveals that the sudden acceptance and recognition of previously repudiated authors such as Lezama Lima is a way to resignify their work according to state ideology. Second, it explains that the ambiguities of aesthetics, such as that of Proyecto Diáspora(s), configure a new type of opposition in which citizens devoid of subjectivity can, paradoxically, feel fee.

This book shows that a vast array of cultural production and cultural policies articulated this narrative of the reproduction of life, as well as many alternative and critical views on the subject. The study of this cultural production is crucial because it speaks of the regime's ideological immobility in spite of its claims to flexibility, as well as the consequences of this on the political unconscious of those years.

Periodization

The book looks at the political rhetoric that constituted revolutionary power, and the ideological evolution that formed its hegemony from the sixties until the present. It does not cover all these decades, however, because the question that interests me involves the early revolutionary years and the decade that preceded socialism's symbolic death. In that context, I am interested in looking at the first and last generation of revolutionary intellectuals, that is, the heroes who won the revolution, and the antiheroes who witnessed its withering. The first generation of intellectuals created the revolution's utopian imaginary, and the last generation (the first intellectuals born within the revolution) questioned that utopia's teleological aspect. Socialism's withering symbolically begins in 1989 with the period of political and economic crisis resulting from the fall of the Soviet bloc, and the end of the economic ties between Cuba and the Soviet Union. The year 1989 marks the beginning of the so-called Periodo especial en tiempos de paz (Special Period in Times of Peace), an official euphemism pointing to the end of the Cold War, and to the beginning of a new stage in the teleological history of the Cuban Revolution. This new stage was perhaps considered as a hiatus in the construction of socialism, but it was never seen as socialism's end. It was a period of profound economic crisis resulting in the partial and very slow economic reform of the last two decades. It is clear that both the symbolic death of socialism and the economic hardship initiated a new period of ideological and emotional convulsion, which is why most scholars rightly consider 1989 as the beginning of a new era deserving to be studied as a cohesive historical period.[4] The fact that my study of the post-Soviet era begins in 1986 instead does not override or question the former periodization, because the notion of "periodization" itself is one that my book questions.

Too often, history has been analyzed in ways that seek only to rigidly periodize the past in support of an ideological agenda. Such studies have often limited themselves to debating and delineating the period itself. This is why I do not want to start a debate about whether the so-called post-Soviet era began in 1989 or in 1986, when Gorbachev announced the reforms of perestroika and glasnost, inaugurating the island's partial capitalization.

Each "new" period has produced a discourse treating the past as "dead" while simultaneously dealing with a "past" already characterized by previous breaks. The break is thus the postulate of the interpretation. The problem with such method, as Michel de Certeau points out, is that the work determined by such a break is voluntaristic. This break selects between what can be "understood" and what can be forgotten to achieve the representation of a present intelligibility (de Certeau 1975, 10). In Cuba, state political rhetoric and its historical renderings provide a very good example of the type of historiography that I have just described. In other words, scholars have analyzed the Special Period as a historical event that created an epistemological break with the past, instead of taking into account that history is also a representation of a selective memorialization of the past that represses and silences social practices and ideas. The willingness to trace the symbolic nature of utopia throughout the years is what explains the leaps of time from the sixties to the nineties and the lack of chronological sequencing in the book's structure.

Blood and Sacrifice in the Sixties

To understand this period and what comes after, it is necessary to analyze the emotional ties with the revolution.[5] To fully comprehend the events of the eighties and nineties, one must examine the political rhetoric of the sixties; symbolically speaking, some of the political zeal and utopianism of the sixties was reenacted in the eighties, although most of it died in the late nineties and early 2000s. This is, in a nutshell, the cultural history of utopianism that fluctuates throughout the whole period. Desiderio Navarro argues that there is an attempt to erase the memory of preexisting intellectual practices during the revolution, and that the critical spaces of the sixties were erased in the seventies. He thus argues, "It is not by chance, then, that the 1980s critical interventions struggled to rescue the memory of their 1960s precedents as an interrupted tradition" (Navarro 2002, 198). This insight leads us to ask the question: What were the symbolic differences between metaphors of soil, blood, sacrifice, and heroism that appear in the sixties and that then resurface in the eighties and nineties? What do they tell us about the political unconscious and the libidinal economies of these years? How do they inform our reading of the Cuban Revolution's legacy for the future to come?

In order to explain the current impasse of state ideology, the book begins with an analysis of the sixties revolutionary imaginary, specifically as it pertains to the subjectivity of war and intellectual heroes (Ernesto Guevara's New Man). I analyze this trope as a signifier at three different levels that determine each other: as national subjectivity of Cubanness (heroism and violence), as a rhetorical ethos (melodrama), and as a form of affect (melancholy). The same analytical structure can be found in each chapter. At the first level I explain the essentialist nature of revolutionary subjectivity; at the second, I explore the relationship between aesthetic representation and politics; and at the third, I analyze their affective reflection of the country's unconscious imaginary.

The Critical and Mythical Eighties

During the early eighties, Cuba completed the strongest economic liberalization since the prerevolutionary period. These reforms also brought with them the first signs of corruption of many state employees. The loss of socialist ethics and the worsening conditions of the external markets on which Cuba relied caused Castro to launch a campaign of Rectification of Errors and Negative Tendencies during the Third Congress of the Communist Party in 1986 (Pérez-Stable 1993, 255). While Fidel Castro's program was contemporaneous with Mikhail Gorbachev's reforms, Cuba did not adhere to the policies of perestroika or glasnost. Gorbachev's program was a set of reforms aimed at opening up the country to the market economy while maintaining a centralized and planned economy and the control of power. The Rectification Process, on the contrary, promoted a return to the politics of ethics sustained by Guevarista principles that encouraged revolutionary spirit, revolutionary work, and voluntary labor (Eckstein 1994, 64). The program's goal was to strengthen the importance of social consciousness over material values and, most importantly, to encourage political commitment among the youngest population: "The main question was knowing whether the citizenry—the great majority of which was born or grew up after 1959—would become committed to socialism. This was precisely the goal of the process of rectification" (Pérez-Stable 1993, 260).

In fact, at the Fourth UNEAC (National Union of Writers and Artists of Cuba) Congress held in 1988, Minister of Culture Armando Hart expressed his concern at the critical spirit shown by the young artists formed by the Revolution: " 'I have talked to many young people, and the problem is that they want to be critical. They want to be close to reality. The new generation of artists and young artists is very critical,' said the Party's Politburo member" (*Granma* 1988, 4). Arte Calle's performance was only one example of the abundance of critical visual arts from the eighties. As Navarro argues, however, the spirit of such works exemplified the general attitude among the young intellectuals born and educated in the Revolution: "It was precisely at the beginning of the 1980s that new critical voices began to be heard, this time stronger and in greater numbers. They belonged to young intellectuals . . . the majority being plastic artists, though there were also fiction writers, dramatists and stage directors, filmmakers, and essayists" (Navarro 2002, 191). These rebellious attitudes were met with repression on the part of political authorities, who, over and over again, blamed and punished cultural officials. Sometimes exhibitions were closed, such as the famous Proyecto Castillo de la Fuerza in 1989, or films were only shown for a few days, like *Alicia en el pueblo Maravillas* (*Alice in Wondertown*, 1990), and most of the times, the Ministry of Culture made it impossible for artists to travel abroad. The latter happened, for example, in the case of many of the symposiums seeking to include both inland and exiled artists; intellectuals in Cuba were met with all sorts of bureaucratic difficulties to obtain a "permiso de salida [departure permit]."

In 1996, for instance, after a failed symposium in Madrid between writers from the island and the diaspora, Rolando Sánchez Mejías, one of the writers that this book analyzes, published a "Carta abierta a los escritores cubanos [Open letter to Cuban Writers]" in *Encuentro de la cultura cubana* (Sánchez Mejías 1996, 90).[6] In his letter, Sánchez Mejías defines Cuba as a totalitarian state and accuses the Ministry of Culture of absolute ideological control over culture. Responding to Sánchez Mejías's claim that Cuba no longer had intellectuals, Minister of Culture Abel Prieto published in the same journal "Ser (o no ser) intelectual en Cuba [To Be or Not to Be an Intellectual in Cuba]," a reply defending the free and plural nature of Cuban culture (Prieto 1996, 94).[7] Dissidents were met with "actos de repudio, [acts of rejection]" and films such as *Techo de vidrio* (*Glass Ceiling*, 1981) were removed from the theaters because they depicted acts of corruption in the workplace. Those totalitarian measures challenged what many scholars have viewed as the revitalization of civil society and the formation of interest groups.

The Poetry Boom of the Eighties and Nineties

Literary scholarship on this period of the end of a purported revolution has been growing steadily in the United States, but until now, its main focus has been on literature, especially fiction, written for the transnational market. This is understandable given the large amount of Cuban fiction that was published abroad during the nineties. This editorial and creative phenomenon is what Esther Whitfield calls the literature of "the new Cuban boom," whose emergence, as her book explores, is due to the Cuban dollarization of the economy (Whitfield 2008, 13).[8] But poetry, especially the books published for the island's internal market, has not received that much attention, in spite of its large production. As a matter of fact, Idalia Morejón Arnáiz indicates that there were at least thirty anthologies and a large number of anthologies and poetry books that garnered awards both in Cuba and abroad from the nineties until the first decade of the twenty-first century. Notwithstanding the long and rich poetic Cuban tradition, it is still puzzling that poetry played such an important role during those two decades. No other generation has been as heavily anthologized as this one. While Alberto Abreu Arcia refuses to venture an explanation for this phenomenon, José Quiroga suggests that poetry was able to articulate ideas in more covert and surreptitious ways. He also points out the lack of paper and difficulties with printing (Abreu Arcia 2007, 190; Quiroga 2005, 128). We can also venture a further hypothesis. Cultural officials had managed to keep at bay the works of the Frankfurt School, but in the eighties postmodernist theory came to the island in somewhat random ways. Young writers began to discuss works by postructuralists Maurice Blanchot, Roland Barthes, Jacques Derrida, and also political theorists, especially Michel Foucault, Gilles Deleuze, and Félix Guattari. They also read conceptual or philosophically inclined foreign authors such as Thomas Bernhardt, Milan Kundera, and Peter Sloterdijk, among others. Like all these authors, young Cubans condemned grand narratives, especially because the latter continued to determine the country's *realpolitk*. For example, in 1998 in the Sixth Congress of the UNEAC, Minister of Culture Abel Prieto still felt the need to defend Cuban national culture against hegemonic cultural globalization, instead encouraging the nation to continue creating a different sort of modernity. There was also the trauma caused by the political turmoil of the times. In this regard, poetry was the ideal genre that could combine a highly conceptual vocabulary with an intense emotional experience.

Certainly, the combination of abstraction and affect did not define the poetry of these decades as a whole, because a large group of writers, such as Liudmila Quincoses, Frank Abel Dopico, Nelson Simón, and Sonia Díaz Corrales, had a more lyrical—rather than conceptual—approach to poetry. Yet, regardless of their level of conceptuality, they were also exposed to the new trends set by poststructuralism. For example, as Osmar Sánchez Aguilera points out, in addition to their sociopolitical concerns, the works of this generation were defined by their intertextuality and formal innovations (Sánchez Aguilera 1993, 60). Poststructuralism was in the air, and it influenced all genres in general, as well as criticism. One of the most iconic examples is probably Margarita Mateo's *Ella escribía postcrítica* (*She Wrote Postcriticism*), a part-novel, part-theoretical essay where she discusses and performs a postmodernist style.

The Poetics of Samizdats

The samizdat of Proyecto Diáspora(s), *Diáspora(s) Documentos* (1997–2002), like many of the works that I examine in this book, was critical of state ideology, and it happened to be marginally produced, poorly distributed, and infrequently read. Its marginality was not social or economic but solely ideological; in this regard, apostasy would be a better term for its specific ideological position. That is, this movement was composed of an unorthodox generation wanting to change or challenge revolutionary parameters, a fact that can be seen by their decision to struggle with cultural institutions and open up cultural spaces wherein they might develop their programs. In one way or another, all the authors that this book explores were heretical, and therefore prone to censorship or rejection. Most of the times, direct censure was not an option, because cultural institutions such as UNEAC, Casa de las Américas, ICAIC, and so on would support the artist vis-à-vis the Ministry of Culture, finally publishing and distributing the work. *Proyecto Diáspora(s)* had a very tense and ultimately impossible relationship with cultural institutions, and this is what prompted them to go underground.

The poets who formed Proyecto Paideia and Proyecto Diáspora(s), two of the movements that this book explores, went even farther. Their work questioned revolutionary power as well as the poetics articulating state ideology. More important, as I will explain later, their work reveals the traumas that the dreamlike appearance of revolutionary rhetoric was occluding. This dreamlike appearance of revolutionary discourse appeared in the poetics of Proyecto Diáspora(s) as what Víctor Fowler has termed "una enunciación romántica inversa [an inverted romantic enunciation]" (Fowler 1999, 14). For Fowler this poetic enunciation recognizes "un ethos político que le niega a la nación como destino ideológico [a political ethos that denies a historical destiny to the country]." What has been actually occluded—such is my thesis—is the real antagonism between reality and utopian thought. How did this utopia fail and why did it fail? That is what is at stake in these works—as well as in the nation as a whole—but it also happens to frame itself as that which cannot be confronted directly (and therefore approaches the Real in Lacanian terms). In these works the Real, in this Lacanian sense, is articulated through the figure of the New Man and the way in which the works that I have studied reveal the transformation of this discursive mythology. The critical attitude of these works toward totalitarian politics has led Morejón Arnáiz to argue that they are still embedded in the dialectics of revolutionary literature: "Doesn't critically placing the literate citizen in a totalitarian space (not through topics . . . , but through writing itself) continue to be a rhetorical exercise that maintains poetry as a question of 'engagement,' in fact the great rhetorical nucleus of Cuban poetry since 1959?" (39).

If it is true, as Fowler and Morejón Arnáiz claim, that this movement is simply the antithesis of revolutionary poetics, and that it has not been able to move outside of this dialectic, how can one read their gesture to stay at the margins of the political by representing an ironic poetics of *pathos*?

These writers worked in precariousness. I do not mean that they aimed at a material precariousness, but rather, at a poetic precariousness reflecting the problematic nature of poetic representation. Words are considered insufficient means to represent the ontological crisis of ideology: "In other regions of the world this type of crisis of the word (language/discourse) is not a new matter; in Cuba, thirty years after 1959, it is, and very symptomatically. Crises unfold or begin to be recognized as such only when words have proved their impotence" (Sánchez Aguilera 1993, 60). These movements also thematize the regime's own cultural dearth. Ana Belén Martín Sevillano argues, for example, that Diáspora(s) is against the concept of popular culture promoted by the revolution: "Díaspora(s) displays an elitist understanding of literary activity that can be explained as a reaction to the cultural populism imposed by the revolution" (Martín Sevillano 2008, 99).

As a result of a self-imposed alienation from contemporary Cuban culture, literature for these young authors became cosmopolitan and stretched the boundaries of the nation. For once, the nation was not opening outward to external influences, nor was it extending its territory to different geographical spaces through exile and diaspora; rather, there was a movement coming from inside the nation that resulted in the implosion of the revolutionary literary canon. Intellectuals themselves sought new ideological sources, and remarkably, they did not only come from the Peninsula, but also from the United States and Europe.

A Melancholic Revolution

"We do not only work with signs. Not everything is a text. We also fight for our dreams." So reads an axiom of samizdat *Diáspora(s) Documentos* 1. In 1997, the poet Rolando Sánchez Mejías put in a nutshell the two aspirations of his generation: intellectual and political change. It seems that change was in the air, above all when one takes into account that these two wishes were coming from the children of the revolution. Indeed, this group of intellectuals was what Iván de la Nuez called "a monstrosity . . . that was once called the New Man" (de la Nuez 2001, 10). Namely, they were the first generation of revolutionary writers formed by the revolution, and in the words of Ernesto Guevara, they were the New Men uncontaminated by bourgeois culture. Guevara's New Men were in charge of constructing the socialist Cuba of the future by continuing the revolutionary struggle of their progenitors.

Contrary to Guevara's expectations, however, the children of the revolution "were responsible for the most radical break . . . in Cuban history" (ibid.). Given this genealogy, it was not odd that the New Man's two virtues consisted primarily in his intellectual and political prowess. This generation was clearly haunted by the figure of the New Man, and specifically, with his revolutionary attributes: sacrifice, heroism, and violence.

In the aftermath of the fall of the Soviet Union, the Cuban regime embarked on a slow economic transition, but cultural critics have argued that it kept the political reforms at a standstill. I argue instead that the traumatic impact of the withering of socialism produced an ideological transformation in Cuba: the acceptance of capitalism and its paradoxical and simultaneous denial (a disavowal, in psychoanalytic terms). The origin of this disavowal can be traced back to the melancholic nature of revolutionary ideology, that is, to the desire for a utopian objective that can never be fulfilled. Ana Serra's *The New Man in Cuba: Culture and Identity in the Revolution* shows the tensions in early revolutionary ideology through a cultural analysis of the discursive figure of the New Man. Drawing on her work, I argue that the New Man's subjectivity cannot be defined a priori; it exists in Guevara's melancholic discourse as an empty signifier that paradoxically seeks attainment. The logic of destruction with which he describes the relationship between intellectuals and bourgeois art was characterized by a melancholic conception of art, as I show in the debates about socialist realism in the sixties.

Chapter 1 focuses on the affective impact of the revolutionary ideology of the sixties on the cultural production of the nineties. I argue that the trauma caused by the fall of the Soviet Union resuscitated the spirit of the sixties. The poetics of the nineties were influenced by the melancholic nature of the Guevarian discursive configuration of the intellectual as the New Man. The Guevarian subjectivity of the New Man is achieved through an economy of restoration that offers the possibility of a liberation from the idealism of bourgeois art, and, after the liberation from an alienating past, the new Cuban being emerges also as a revolutionary New Man. In order to regain self-consciousness, intellectuals must negate their own ego and strive to embrace a new consciousness. The emptiness left after the negation of the ego produces a melancholic process, which leads to a total loss of subjectivity. Intellectuals from the eighties and nineties also responded to Guevara's celebration of war and violence, with an aesthetic violence. Both melancholy and violence haunted the cultural production of the eighties and nineties at different moments. For example, melancholy can be seen in an extensive body of poetic works of the eighties, as well as in Antonio José Ponte's "Un arte de hacer ruinas" (2000), and in the film *La ola* (1995). Aesthetic violence for Proyecto Diáspora(s) furnishes the means through which they attempt to escape the revolution understood as the sublime (absolute pleasure or utopia). Violence is, however, not simply a negation of pleasure. I argue that the understanding of violence as an experience of dread lies at the basis of what I call their "poetics of defacement."

Biopolitics

At the beginning of the nineties, the revolutionary dream became a capitalist one. This desire was both present and repressed and denied. Citizens' increasing economic independence impelled the state to resort to new strategies of power in order to retain political control over the population. This marked the beginning of a shift toward a biopolitical administration of power, especially in cultural politics. Following Foucault, I interpret biopolitics as the subjection of man's natural life to the mechanisms and calculations of power. Thus emerged an ideology that privileges the control of both subjectivity and the body, as opposed to a form of politics in which the right over the death of subjects determines the outer limit of the law. Biopolitics and the importance of the body manifest themselves in the literary apparition of the bare life, a figure understood in Giorgio Agamben's sense as a being who has been divested of subject position. By looking at the representation of the body in the criticism about José Lezama Lima, I examine the seventies' cultural politics of silencing intellectuals (as an exercise of sovereign power) and the reasons for Lezama's œuvre's official recuperation in the nineties, which, I argue, follows as a result of this shift toward biopolitical power. I interpret the intellectual revival of Lezama as the result of a cultural biopolitics that is aimed at the reproduction of life in the face of a dying ideology. The complexity of Lezama's ontological system facilitates its reappropriation as a grand narrative. I finally ponder the engagement of Proyecto Diáspora(s) with Lezama's work. The representation of the body in the works of these authors illuminates a form of political subjugation that nullifies individual subjectivity. Whereas in Lezama the body is a source of pleasure, in Proyecto Diáspora(s) it is represented as a disembodied being who could be Agamben's bare life, or a Deleuzian-Guattarian schizo (moved by concurrently positive and negative flows of energy created by desire).[9] It is at this point that their poetics become problematic. Is the schizo the embodiment of resistance against state violence, or does it construct the citizen as a docile body, as they also seem to suggest?

Humanism, Irony, and the End of Literature

The second consequence of the simultaneous affirmation and disavowal of capitalism plays a role in the transitory disappearance of the law (in its form as revolutionary ideology). By "law" I designate the ideologies legitimating the policies of the state. The law becomes an empty signifier because it no longer points to a specific political imaginary. The result of this ideological void reinforced the confusion between what was revolutionary or counterrevolutionary. I am not suggesting that this was a new phenomenon, what I am saying is that this confusion became even more acute. The popular song that I cite below is a very good example of such a phenomenon. This confusion between what is permissible (or ethically acceptable) and what is not is reflected in the emergence of a literary trend that problematizes—if not collapses—the distinction between freedom and coercion. This political or ethical confusion becomes a rhetorical irony in poetry, that is, a statement meaning the contrary of what it says. The resulting irony is a trope that both shows this ethical differentiation and, paradoxically, falls prey to it by becoming one more example of biopolitics. In sum, in the last chapter I argue that according to government rhetoric, "revolutionary ethos" becomes an empty signifier, a signifier without content, which is therefore no longer articulated according to a law. As a consequence, ethical principles have collapsed, resulting in a schizophrenic rule of sorts. The lack of this law is what pushes poets to inquire about the relationship between ethics and literature. If traditional ideologies are exhausted, can literature still have an ethical function? Paideia struggled to articulate a humanist cultural project as a way to suture itself back into an ethical framework. The failure of the project that I discuss in the context of an emergent theoretical shift in favor of civil society drew the group to cultivate irony as a literary practice. In poets such as Carlos A. Aguilera and Rolando Sánchez Mejías, the subject is represented as a disempowered victim, but the irony of the idiom can also serve humoristic ends, culminating in a liberating practice that extracts subjects from the oppressive voice of judgment.

Drawing on Blanchot's "writing of disaster," this concluding chapter finally ponders the limits of aesthetic representation. It asks what becomes of literature once its revolutionary potential becomes exhausted. If cultural representation is a symptom with its own historicity, can it also function as a defensive mechanism against the illness that it announces? As I claim in the first chapter, allegory becomes the trope of a revolutionary politics that aims to emancipate what it represents. At the same time, allegories can only freeze time in an ideal past or future; they cannot represent the present. By looking at what I call the "poetics of thought" and "circular poetics," I show that the poetry collections *Cabezas* (*Heads*, 2002) by Marqués de Armas and Juan Carlos Flores's *Distintos modos de cavar un túnel* (*Different Ways to Dig a Tunnel*, 2003) expose and concurrently challenge the limits of representation.

Ideology and Psychoanalysis

I. ¡Amigos, qué confusión,
qué confusión hay formada!
Yo no entiendo nada, nada
de "Santa Revolución"
Patriotismo . . . Religión . . .
Ya aquí no se sabe bien
si aplaudir a Dios o a quién
y ya no sé de esta suerte
si hay que decir "Patria o Muerte"
o debo decir "Amén"

II. Ahora la iglesia es la "onda"
y hay navidades felices;
si ya hay hasta quien dice
que la tierra no es redonda;
y que aunque Cristo se esconda
el líder máximo es "él"
y así en este enredo cruel
yo no sabré en adelante
si Fidel es comandante o
si es el "Padre Fidel."[10]

This popular song became one of the most widespread melodies in 1998 as people were anxiously awaiting the first papal visit to Cuba. The ironic song pointed out the government's ideological contradictions. After so many years of state-imposed atheism, the Cuban government invited Pope John Paul II, the highest authority of one of the most conservative religious institutions, to the island. The lyrics refer to the state's political double standard by making clear that the population cannot be duped, since they are aware that the new alliance between church and state responds to mutual economic and political interests. They know that as a result of these new relations, for which Fidel is willing to abandon his principles and even his place as the most powerful leader, the Catholic Church may become an important ally: "yo no sabré en adelante / si Fidel es el comandante o / si es el 'Padre Fidel.'" This example shows both what Peter Sloterdijk calls kynicism, and what he defines as political cynicism. Ideologically speaking, kynicism refers to the ironic dismissal of official culture by the popular classes, which is what the song clearly shows. But it also shows the people's cynicism: in spite of having informed suspicions, people still celebrate the pope's arrival in large numbers.

How can one best understand this contradiction? It seems, as Žižek claims, that psychoanalysis represents the best theoretical and practical approach to analyze authoritarian populism (1994, 29). Authoritarian and totalitarian regimes interpellate citizens through emotional rather than political principles. Purely emotional notions devoid of political rationale—such as "cult of personality," "mass," "sacrifice," or "fatherland"—are best explained as what they are. This indicates that, while not pretending to unveil any hidden "truth"—a psychological or psychoanalytical explanation could at least guide us to understand their mechanics. Understanding the libidinal economies of these regimes is tantamount to explaining their ideological dynamics, as I will explain shortly. I am, however, not claiming that psychoanalysis will reveal a truth nor simply posit a false truth. To claim that a psychoanalytical perspective could reveal the truth, would actually go against the postulates of Lacanian or even of Freudian theory. In addition, we would be also accepting the idea that we can still think in ideological terms, and, as I will discuss, ideology does not constitute an adequate category to describe our contemporary world.

It is, above all, necessary to define the notion of ideology that I use throughout this book, because I use it in two different senses. The first sense refers to the broader notion of ideology as a group of political or spiritual ideas or the beliefs shared by a group, an individual, a class, or a culture. The second sense of ideology refers to a sort of theoretical matrix that I use to analyze a body of works. Let me then explain what I understand by this notion of ideology and how I can see it applied for the analysis of cultural production. From a Marxist perspective, ideology is the set of beliefs or perceptions that make us see the world in a "mystified" way. The "mystification" of commodities is a process inherent to the capitalist mode of production, and it has to do with the value of commodities. Commodities are "mystified" when they are not valued according to the labor put into their production, but rather through market exchange (Marx 1990a, 126). When confronted with this reality, subjects can recognize the "truth" and struggle to change it, but they can also act with false consciousness by disregarding this truth in such a way that their own interests are served. *False consciousness* is a term coined by Georg Lukács to define a subordinate class that subjectively accepts its situation as "true" (i.e., according to the historical time period), but cannot express the objective essence of society. In other words, he is alluding to the misrepresentation of dominant social relations in the consciousness of the working class. The mental representations of society in the consciousness of the subordinate classes conceal the realities of exploitation. It is important to note that Lukács insists on the necessity of bypassing the true/false dichotomy since the goal is to understand the relations of society *as a whole*: he notes, "However, the dialectical method does not permit us simply to proclaim the 'falseness' of this consciousness and to persist in an inflexible confrontation of true and false" (1968, 50). I am emphasizing this point because this is also the interpretation of ideology that I will privilege: namely, as a set of strategic maneuvers that nevertheless do not permit of a facile resolution into the terms of "truth" and "falsehood."

Given the dedifferentiation between culture and economy that characterizes postmodernism, Žižek is right to wonder if "this concept of ideology as a naive consciousness still applies today" (Žižek 1989, 29). Glossing Sloterdijk, Žižek argues that in our contemporary society, we are all aware of the Marxian notions of value and exchange, and therefore, we can no longer speak about a perspective holding a naive conception of the world. For this reason, Sloterdijk claims that ideology operates in a cynical mode. The cynical subject is aware of the "mystification," but still insists on acting as if it did not exist. Contrary to "false consciousness," cynicism is usually the prerogative of the ruling class, who is aware of "the distance between the ideological mask and the reality, but it still finds reasons to retain the mask" (ibid., 29). In the opposite realm, there exists what he calls *kynicism*, which refers to the ironic and sardonic rejection of official culture by the popular classes, as we can observe in the epigraph above.

To sum up, the traditional concept of ideology as a naive perception of reality is no longer valid, but that does not mean that unequal social relations have disappeared. The difference is that now we as a society know about this fundamental inequality, but have decided not to act upon it. Given this state of affairs, it remains clear that we can no longer study social reality as a mere textual symptom.

Let us now return to the subject of this book, namely, how ideology as defined above provides a critical tool for an understanding of Cuban cultural production. As we have observed in the epigraph, subjects in general are not duped by state rhetoric. That is, they recognize the cynicism of a ruling class that is aware of the distance between the socialist system as a universal source of normativity and the inadequate or immoral application of these norms, and yet, they still impose this system on the population. On the other hand, the people respond with an ironic popular culture—or through other forms of representation, such as conceptual poetry, as we will see in this book. As I have argued, the naive concept of ideology no longer applies to this situation, but once more, following Žižek, I think that ideology could be replaced with fantasy in its Lacanian sense as a "construction which enables us to mask the Real of our desire" (Lacan, qtd. in Žižek 1994, 323).

Above all, when we examine authoritarian societies such as Cuba, it may be useful to go back to Althusser's notion of interpellation and his analysis of Ideological State Apparatuses. Ideology, like culture, becomes part of our belief system up to the point where it is no longer distinguishable from the reality we inhabit. This is precisely what we need to unravel. What Žižek adds to this scheme is a framework that allows us to analyze the dynamic of desire played out in this process by deploying the concept of the Lacanian Real. To put it in broad terms, the Real is what holds desires and fears that resist symbolization. From an Althusserian point of view, ideology is a dreamlike construction that does not allow us to see the "real" state of things, as I was arguing before. In idealist relativism this argument means that there is not one reality; there are various realities. At this point, psychoanalysis becomes useful, allowing Lacan to conceptualize the space that separates the Real from our dreamlike construction of the world by bypassing the distinction between materialist realism and idealist relativism. Žižek argues that the reason we are trapped in our ideological prejudices or dreamlike realities is that we do not dare face our genuine fears and desires. Thus, the Real is what we need to confront if we want to break away from our ideological prejudices.

To summarize, Žižek argues that even if we try to break free by opening our eyes and see reality as it is, as subjects of a postideological world free of all the ideological prejudices, we still remain in the "consciousness of our ideological dream," and the only way to break its power is to confront the Real of our desire which appears in this dream (Žižek 1994, 325–26). Precisely this process may be illustrated in the case of Cuba. For example, Chinese culture is a regular topic in the works of Carlos A. Aguilera, Rolando Sánchez Mejías, and Pedro Marqués de Armas, and it has a double valence. On the one hand, they seek to reveal Asian culture in Cuba, and on the other hand, their goal is to construct an ironic parallelism between the Marxist Chinese legacy and the Cuban Revolution with all its flaws.

Aguilera's "Viaje a China [Trip to China]" is a travel journal written from the point of view of the "Westerner" observing the "Oriental" in postcommunist China. The text produces an ironic critique of the false consciousness of the "Westerner," something that becomes apparent as he describes Beijing: "From a tall building one can see almost all the buildings, and seen in this way it appears like some cities in Northern Europe. This appearance is misleading. Beijing is a caricature and seems to be less a city than a mockery machine" (Aguilera 1999, 14). That is, the text offers a critique of the foreigner who can only make a description of otherness by applying his own ideological framework to this otherness. The implications of this limitation are also political, since the foreigner cannot understand the absurdity of an ideology turned into derision, a "mockery machine [*máquina de burla*]." The text thus advances a traditional Marxist interpretation of ideology, especially because it is trying to emphasize the false consciousness of the "Westerner." The reference to the traditional concept of ideology is extremely important to take into account, as it is this detail that gives away the fantasy upon which the text is constructed. We observe in this story an ironic and critical look at orientalist constructions: Beijing is described as a "trompe l'œil," whose orientalist description by the Westerner is then replaced with yet another Orientalism. In other words, it is our vision of Beijing which is a "mockery machine," and not the city itself. The critique is actually targeting the reader who identifies himself or herself with the narrator, who in turn makes an ironic description of the city. As Žižek would put it, the ideological description of the city as a "mockery machine" covers up the inconsistency of our own ideological system. Such inconsistency is the dreamlike fantasy that allows us to avoid a confrontation with the Real, which in this case might refer to the fear of an otherness that inhabits one's own space (i.e., Cuban Chinese culture).

Let me add one more note. What interests me in this study is not to gauge whether or not these figures speak the truth. Rather, I'm interested in "*the way this content is related to the subjective position implied by its own process of enunciation*" (Žižek 1994, 8; italics in original). Ultimately, I think that the generation under investigation in this study cannot simply divest themselves of the burden of the revolutionary struggle that was imposed upon them. If at all, one should begin by asking first if their poetics have established the conditions of possibility to confront the Real of revolutionary politics. In other words, can the political confront its own failure? The same could be said about literature, although it seems that the last generation of poets has already abandoned literature as the only mode of representation. In "Persistent Matrioshkas," Jacqueline Loss looks at hybrid representations by Cuban-Soviet female authors who live in between two different imaginaries. For poets such as Polina Martínez Shvietsova (1976) or those in the Omni Zona Franca group, these two different spaces also collide in experimental modes of representation that combine written word with visual and musical elements and performance.

The reality, however, is that the discursive construction of intellectuals as New Men already exhausted its political and aesthetic symbolic value in the cultural production of the past two decades. While the works from the eighties and nineties were in dialogue with revolutionary politics, the aesthetics of younger generations, however, do not have similar ideological intentions. They were raised in the hardest years of the Special Period, and most became disenchanted intellectuals with no sense of any debt toward the revolution. In contrast, their predecessors were still haunted by a sense of indebtedness to the revolution, and therefore plagued by a sort of guilty conscience that had been inculcated in them by revolutionary culture—whether or not they chose to recognize this debt.

As a result of the refusal of these intellectuals to act as revolutionary artists, the state put forward a biopolitical cultural politics whose goal was to give momentum to the revolutionary imaginary by reviving the ideology of the New Man. What emerged then was a spectral appearance from past generations, which ended up being a return of the Real in terms that have been articulated by Žižek, and "it is this real, foreclosed from the symbolic fiction that returns in the guise of spectral apparitions" (Žižek 1994, 26). These specters that returned from a site of repression resurfaced as a positionless nonsubject, a bare life turned into a rhetorical figure. It is in fact this figure that Diáspora(s) combats with the schizo as a trope, which in turn ends up embodying a metaphor as ambiguous as the state-sanctioned biopolitical ideology itself.

In the eighties, there were also humanist cultural groups with emancipatory ideas like Paideia, but their political failure showed the limits of the humanistic approach to civil society, approaches characterized primarily by a Habermasian interpretation of the public sphere. The group both enabled the emergence of a civil movement that posited itself as a new hegemonic bloc and simultaneously was able to expand (or perhaps even transcend) its utilitarian political nature with an even stronger intellectual agenda. Proyecto Diáspora(s), on the contrary, developed an antihumanist perspective that derided both the state and emancipatory politics, advocating instead a disengagement with the political. Yet, as Morejón Arnáiz shows, their critique of totalitarianism is a political gesture. What is more, their ideological attitude is still articulated by the desire to demythologize the main symbols of revolutionary struggle. Might it not be the case, after all, that this radical negation of revolutionary ideology generates a negative dialectic of sorts, that is, an act whose refusal attempts to construct a space of alterity and thereby gains weight as an alternative political gesture? Or is this form of poetics indeed simply a radical negation of the political as such?

This group perhaps embraces irony as an aesthetic recourse to avoid a prolonged confrontation with a traumatic Real—a haunting of the present that is, for example, the main subject of the poetry of Juan Carlos Flores. In the work of Proyecto Diáspora(s), however, writing and aesthetics risks a sublation into a mere detached and ironic mode, and thereby might be regarded as simply another expression of "*choteo*."[11] In contrast to this ironic and ludic idiom, in Juan Carlos Flores's writing, the trauma of the repressed emerges through words, which is, as was the case for Piñera, the only medium through which one could effectively confront a horror that goes beyond political oppression. Thus, for Flores, writing, more than ever, becomes absolutely necessary. Such a form of poetry has neither any relationship with civil society, nor with resistance as such, and therefore represents a rhetorical gesture that is, strictly speaking, neither negative nor affirmative, neither ironic nor utopian. Indeed, this poetry is not even redemptive in the sense of trying to recuperate memories that have been lost. Instead, it circles around what might perhaps be the most terrifying prospect that can be faced: the horror of the void, or of a world in which all struggles, be they political or personal, confront an even more primordial nothingness.

I

Sovereignty of Violence

> Oh, joven héroe arrebatado por los dioses,
> palmo a palmo ha crecido tu hondo rapto
> y ya tiene el tamaño de la isla,
> el sabor de nuestro aire y nuestro mar!
> iremos por las playas caminando entre tus dedos;
> escalaremos las montañas recordando tu rostro.
> no surcaremos las olas, sino tu ardiente pecho
>
> [Oh, young hero snatched away by the gods,
> inch by inch, handful by handful, your abduction has deepened
> until it now is the size of the island,
> the taste of our air and our sea!
> We will walk the beaches between your fingers;
> we will climb the mountains remembering your face.
> We will ride not the waves but your burning breast]
>
> —Cintio Vitier, "Camilo Cienfuegos"

In a poem dedicated to Camilo Cienfuegos, Cintio Vitier addresses him as the mythical hero of Antiquity's epics who has been abducted by the gods. Cienfuegos and Guevara were, according to Gott: "The two rebel *comandantes*, perceived as the most heroic, charismatic and romantic figures in Castro's army" (Gott 2004, 167). Cienfuegos, commander-in-chief of the army in the Sierra Maestra and always loyal to the revolution, was lost in October 1959, as he was flying over Camagüey where he was to replace

Huber Matos. He was never found, nor were his remains. Much like in Guevara's case, Cienfuegos's sudden disappearance confirmed him as the mythical hero he had already become during the armed insurrection. These, at least, are the type of metaphors that circulated in political discourse and culture during the first two years of the Cuban Revolution. After the radical shift of governance, it became imperative to look for new forms of nation building. The revolution took form by bringing into play a new citizen with a new identity. Until then, Cubanness was defined by discourses of cultural miscegenation; with the revolution, national identity was transformed by a new revolutionary ethos. The discourses of racial and cultural difference that were part of the national imaginary during the Republic became political discourses of heroism, sacrifice, and patriotism. The new revolutionary citizen was a hero whose sacrifices would help build the nation. Central to this was the notion of violence.

Following the victory of the Cuban Revolution—and perhaps also influenced by the "silenced" event of the Haitian Revolution in 1791—Roque Dalton published an essay in the Cuban journal *Casa de las Américas* calling for armed struggle against capitalism (1963, 20). José Martí had already argued a century before that it was time for Latin Americans to begin struggling for their second independence from the political and economic influence of the United States ("Congreso de Washington"). Like Frantz Fanon, Aimé Césaire, or Ernesto Guevara, other Latin Americans and revolutionary intellectuals of the sixties, Dalton argued that El Salvador needed to be liberated from its subjugation to the inequitable, corrupt, and bloodthirsty governments that had led it, from colonialism to the postcolonial period. While all these writers felt that armed struggle was the only means to achieve liberation, they had different reasons to make that claim. For Dalton a revolutionary had to take the same risks with weapons that a poet took with language, since both shared the same ethical responsibility. As the theoretical architect of *foquismo* and an advocate of guerrilla warfare, Ernesto Guevara believed that only an armed struggle would lead the masses to power. Indeed, Fanon's theory of violence was very influential on Guevara's thought.

This chapter looks at the deployment and interpretation of the ideological fantasies at play in the revolutionary process of the early 1960s, when the political foundations of the revolutionary movement were established. More specifically, I analyze the ideological legacy of the intellectual production of the 1960s—the first decade of the Cuban revolutionary period. The chapter deals with the ideas of novelty that arose to represent the new political ideology, as well as the cultural forms associated with it. It is important to note that revolutionary insurgence was postulated on its exceptionality. This originality was based on the concept of warfare and on political improvisation. What made the revolution a unique event was that it had *not* followed a theoretical program, which is why it did not lend itself to easy systematization and codification. In a letter written in 1960 to Argentinian writer Ernesto Sábato, Guevara explained that, in Cuba, revolutionary theory was codified after the revolution's exploits, and not vice versa: "This Revolution is a genuinely improvised creation. We are thus also speaking with a new language, because we walk much faster than we think and structure our thoughts. We are in constant movement, whereas theory goes at a slower pace" (Guevara 2003, 269–70). This also means that the "new" was not easily identifiable. The desire to create and articulate the idea of novelty recurs in many of the essays from the sixties. The revolution was the culmination of the long-standing aspiration for political autonomy and independence. This meant that nationalism and patriotism became two key defining aspects of the "new." In that regard, the Cuban Revolution was no different from any other political project of national liberation, or process of decolonization, for that matter. The consequence was the renaissance of an epic memorialization of war and the representation of Cuba as a nation under siege. This idea permeated all cultural production in the revolution's early years. During this period, attacks by counterrevolutionary and U.S. forces justified for the revolutionaries a rhetoric of war and heroism. But as the years went by, the rebels who took power continued to cultivate the same imaginary of the Sierra Maestra. The tropes of heroism, sacrifice, war, and violence were the essential *topoi* of revolutionary rhetoric, and they became the values that every Cuban citizen needed to embrace.

Revolutionary subjectivity was characterized by the self-sacrificing attitude of the hero or guerrilla fighter. Many soldiers gave their lives for the country, and the government felt always indebted to them. In return for this sacrifice, other citizens also had the duty to sacrifice themselves for the nation: "Para ello, la Unión de Jóvenes Comunistas alza sus símbolos, que son los símbolos de todo el pueblo de Cuba: el estudio, el trabajo y el fusil [For this, the Union of Young Communists raises its symbols, which are those of the entire Cuban people: study, work, and the rifle]" (Guevara 2009, 353). Most importantly, armed struggle was justified as the only possible means that could lead to a revolutionary transformation and a just society. The rhetorical mirage that led to the legitimization of violence was articulated, I argue, through the sanctification and martyrdom of the revolutionary hero, who became the country's only possible political Messiah. One can observe this logic at play in Fidel Castro's thought and in Ernesto Guevara's works, both deeply rooted in Fanon's theories of decolonization. Fanon argued that the colonized had a legitimate reason to rise in arms against the colonizers' oppression. His arguments were decisive in the struggle for decolonization. He refuted Octave Mannoni's theory of the colonized dependency complex, giving agency to colonized subjects with his arguments on racial difference (see Fanon 1963). Drawing on existentialism and his reading of Sartre, as Rojas rightly points out, he was also the first to articulate the dynamics of oppression and alienation in the colonial process. Did these theoretical premises establish the conditions of possibility for a new and radical way to conceive of liberation? I will address this question by looking at early revolutionary discourse, social poetry, and three key revolutionary works. First, I analyze Castro's justification of armed struggle in his self-defense narrative *La historia me absolverá* (*History Will Absolve Me*, 1954), and I analyze the logic of sacrifice by looking at Cintio Vitier's poems "Cruz" (Cross) and "Cara o cruz" (Head or Tails). Second, I consider the Guevarian theories of liberation and revolutionary subjectivity in *La guerra de guerrillas* (*Guerrilla Warfare*, 1961) and "El socialismo y el hombre en Cuba" ("Socialism and Man in Cuba," 1965). Among the numerous works about revolutionary heroism, I have chosen to look first at Tomás Gutiérrez Alea's earliest film, *Historias de la Revolución* (*Stories of the Revolution*, 1960), and then at Luis Rogelio Nogueras's detective novel *Y si muero mañana* (*If I Die Tomorrow*, 1978). Nogueras's novel, which is from a later period, shows that the representation of heroism and violence that dates back to the early sixties remained a key aspect of revolutionary subjectivity until the eighties. It is my contention that the rhetoric of violence was at the core of revolutionary discourse during the first revolutionary decade and that political change (or construction) was based on destruction. More important, this discourse radically laid the ideological foundations of subsequent Cuban revolutionary rhetoric. The dogmatism that constrained cultural production during the "five gray years" (*Quinquenio gris*,[1] 1971–76) was a direct consequence of these premises.

In addition to looking at the different articulations of the new ideology, I also examine the aesthetic debates surrounding it. More specifically, I study the debates around socialist realism, especially Mirta Aguirre's defense of it, as well as the conversationalist social poetry of the period. My argument is that—contrary to Guevara's claim—Cuba produced its own version of socialist realist literature and that the social strand of conversationalist poetry was a good example of this. As a matter of fact, I believe that Guevara's melancholic rendering of the New Man was also the model that inspired the heroic figures of these poems. Firmly anchored in the belief that form and content mirrored each other, materialist thinkers proposed socialist realism as the only form able to convey dialectical materialism. These aesthetic views emerged in opposition to idealism, the philosophy of the bourgeois representation of reality. This theoretical debate ultimately reintroduced the question of the national autonomy of the Cuban literary canon. In other words, at stake was the validity of the Western literary tradition and its ability to convey an objective and truthful representation of reality. Once more, the question of aesthetics was a question of national identity, as it had been for the literary tradition of the Republic. Most important, however, were the ideological interpretations of the claims to truth of two philosophical traditions, materialism and idealism, and how they were used to justify modes of governance. Scholars have pointed to the dynamism and transparency of these public debates to argue that that there was a space for political dissent and discussion.[2] Whereas these claims were certainly true, state apparatuses were already imposing a rigid hegemonic state discourse in the 1960s.

Divine and Ethical Violence

The 26th of July Movement (the rebel leaders) that brought down the Batista government conceived of revolution in an Arendtian sense, that is, as a new and radical political process leading to freedom.[3] Here is how Fidel Castro defined it in his December 24, 1955, speech "¡Frente a todos!" ("Against All!"): "The Cuban people want more than a change of leadership. Cuba yearns for radical change in all fields of public and social life" (Castro 1972a, 78). More specifically, Castro laid out the uprising's objectives in a speech that he delivered in his own defense while on trial for the first failed attack on the Moncada barracks in 1953,[4] where he also defended his use of armed struggle. Most revolutions are associated with violence, but not all revolutions need be violent. For Cuban revolutionaries, however, revolution and armed struggle were inseparable concepts. Violence can only be instrumental if it is not an end in itself, and Cuban revolutionaries knew they had to justify their use of violence as a means to liberate the country. According to revolutionary discourse, the armed uprising was the last resort to fight Batista's regime, but the repressive nature of Batista's rule demanded and justified it.

The 26th of July Movement came together on the grounds of a common belief in revolutionary action. As a matter of fact, in a replica from *Bohemia*, where he addressed Ortodoxo party's moderates, Fidel Castro argued that revolutionary action was not just an option, but rather a necessity: "El Movimiento Revolucionario 26 de Julio no constituye una tendencia dentro del partido: es el aparato revolucionario del chibasismo [The 26th of July Movement is not a tendency within the party: it is Chibasismo's revolutionary apparatus]" (Castro 1972b, 87). Unlike *History Will Absolve Me*, however, this letter, as well as subsequent ones that were also published in *Bohemia* in 1956, did not make a direct apology for armed struggle. The message was very clear: the revolutionaries would not strike first, but they would not tolerate Batista's repression either: "No amamos la fuerza; porque detestamos la fuerza es por lo que no estamos dispuestos a que se nos gobierne por la fuerza. No amamos la violencia; porque detestamos la violencia no estamos dispuestos a seguir soportando la violencia que desde hace cuatro años se ejerce sobre la nación [We don't like violence: it is because we dislike violence that we won't put up with the repression that's been devastating the nation for four years]" (Castro 1972b, 91). Fidel Castro's nonviolence claims gave the 26th of July Movement the moral ground over the Batista regime's brutal treatment of political opponents, as well as a legitimate right to self-defense and the political legitimacy that his nascent movement needed. When Fidel Castro confronted the Batista regime directly, for example, as he did in his famous 1953 discourse *History Will Absolve Me*, he justified violence as a right to self-defense.

The advocacy of violence as a means to a just end is precisely the type of argumentation that Fidel Castro used in order to differentiate two types of violence: that of the Batista government, on the one hand, and that of the 26th of July Movement, on the other. Whereas the people had the right to rise in arms against the oppressive regime, Fidel Castro argued, the Batista government's use of force was arbitrary and unjustified. In Cuba, the attack on the Moncada barracks was Fidel Castro's first, albeit unsuccessful, armed action. Initially, he was condemned to twenty-seven years in prison, but he was then given the possibility of a trial. Being a lawyer, Castro decided to defend himself. He laid out the political goals of the insurrection and also deployed a defense of armed struggle in his speech *History Will Absolve Me*.[5] One of the argumentative strategies of Castro's famous self-defense narrative was to assert that the assault of July 26, 1953, was a justified use of violent means to attain just ends: "¿Con qué derecho enviar a la cárcel a ciudadanos que vinieron a dar por el decoro de su patria su sangre y su vida? ¡Eso es monstruoso ante los ojos de la nación y los principios de la verdadera justicia! [By what right do you send to jail citizens who have just given, for the glory of their country, their blood and their lives? This is monstrosity before the eyes of the nation and before the principles of true justice!]" (Castro 1972c, 69). Castro accused his opponents of an unjust use of violence and, hence, of an unjust use of the law. In contrast, the 26th of July Movement's use of violence was just because it was founding a new law, a new type of legality. This strategy allowed Castro to argue that the ends to justify his means were just, a way of understanding violence that did not differ much from that of his opponent.

Once the rebels were in power, however, the use of violence became more difficult to justify. Yet, the government kept reinforcing the discourse of war. As Hugh Thomas points out, in 1961 Cuba was a militarized society full of aspiring soldiers (Thomas 1971, 1321). State rhetoric was influenced by Marxist ideas, but it also included a new doctrine: the worship of warfare. I take this argument farther and say that it used war, and especially its aesthetization, as the discursive core of revolutionary ideology. The aesthetic representation of violence was instrumental in creating popular support for the increasing militarization of society: it had to embody appeal, necessity, and above all, justice. This explains why, as Rojas eloquently puts it, revolutionary exploits were represented in a theatrical manner, and leaders were portrayed as religious saviors: "Las vidas ejemplares de la élite y el líder, como las de los santos del cristianismo, debían conformar la trama de una obra de teatro moralizante, que lograría la cohesión de la comunidad y, sobre todo, su involucramiento en la epopeya [As with Christian saints, the exemplary lives of the elite and the leader were represented in morality plays producing social cohesion, and above all, the people's involvement in the epic]" (Rojas 2007, 44). Many of the revolutionary accounts given by Fidel Castro and Ernesto Guevara illustrate this idea. In "Episodes of the Cuban Revolutionary War"'s description of the final revolutionary battle in Santa Clara, for example, Guevara talks about the suffering of the soldiers when the leader dies. Surprisingly, however, the soldiers do not cry for the dead leader, instead, they suffer because they cannot take his place: "Era curioso ver a los curtidos y nobles guerreros, mostrando su juventud en el despecho de unas lágrimas, por no tener el honor de estar en el primer lugar de combate y de muerte [Every time one of its men died—and this happened during every combat—and a new candidate was accepted, those who were not chosen could not hide their disappointment nor hold back their tears]" (Guevara 1977b, 264 [1968, 252]). As this example shows, most dramatizations of the revolutionary epic foreground a heroic death, which promises at the same time to be the conquest of justice. The hero fights in the name of universal justice, and the closer he gets to violence, the faster he can approach justice.

Making reference to Benjamin's concept of mythical violence, Rojas argues that these episodes have the "sentido mítico y teatral de la violencia y la moralización de la economía [mythical and theatrical sense of violence and the moralization of economy]" (Rojas 2007, 45). Yet, this violence was certainly not mythical; it was, rather, represented as a Benjaminian divine form of violence, and this also explains its religious connotations. For the sake of my argument, let me briefly elaborate on Benjamin's well-known essay "Critique on Violence" and, most specifically, on the difference between mythical and divine violence. After analyzing the role of violence within legal theory, Benjamin abandons the secular domain to look at violence in the mythical and religious spheres. Mythical violence, according to him, works very much like legal violence in that every act of power to establish the law is in itself an act of violence (Benjamin 1986, 296). In this regard, legal or mythical violence operates in the same fashion in democratic and nondemocratic regimes. Divine violence, however, is the opposite of mythical violence, because it destroys the law instead of founding it (Benjamin 1986, 297). Benjamin's discussion of divine violence is certainly the most metaphorical and complex fragment of the essay, among other things, because Benjamin refers to Talmudic law, and his example is underdeveloped and unclear. This being said, I think that it is a key passage to understand the question that Benjamin addresses: Is it possible to solve a conflict without resorting to violence? At the beginning of the essay, he partially responds to this question by invoking the power of language and communication, and most scholars have followed this interpretation. Yet, in my opinion, the more abstract and metaphorical response to his question is to be found in his discussion and critique of divine violence. As a matter of fact, divine violence can, according to Benjamin, put an end to mythical violence.

The understanding of this idea is crucial for my argument, because I contend that, in the name of divine violence, the state justified armed struggle, as a just means to attain ethical Justice. Unlike mythical violence, Benjamin argues in a rather poetic form, that divine violence destroys the law, that it expiates instead of demanding retribution, and that it is lethal without being bloody (Benjamin 1986, 297). Most importantly, his essay argues that only divine violence can be a just means to a just cause, because its goal is moral universal Justice, as opposed to legal justice. The relationship between the divine and universal Justice is key to understanding why Cuban revolutionary violence was divine and not mythical, and why revolutionary rhetoric was enunciated as a religious allegory. The religious undertones of revolutionary discourse were due to the understanding of armed struggle as ethical crusade. It was by appealing to a universal understanding of ethics that revolutionary rhetoric justified state violence. The implication was that the revolution would save people through armed struggle. Moreover, it also indicated that the state was acting in the fashion of the sovereign (understood as the monarchical figure endowed with godly powers). Thus, violence in the hands of the sovereign (qua divine violence) would be the means to eliminate the law (as a repressive instrument of power). In a way, this discourse was repeating the old patterns of the political theology of royal sovereignty. A state that justified violence in the name of Justice, as Fidel Castro did in *History Will Absolve Me*, acted like the sovereign endowed with the power to annihilate history and reconstruct it in the name of ethical Justice.

Understood in Benjaminian terms, this type of violence, far from representing a new, radical way of understanding governance, still followed the theological and metaphysical structure of sovereignty and divine violence. According to this logic, the revolutionaries were acting as Messiahs who had the power to annihilate the past in order to create a new law. The revolutionary hero sacrificed his life to follow the unwritten laws of the Messiah (Benjamin 1986, 320). In other words, for Castro, guerrilla warfare was understood in its Clausewitzian rendition as a continuation of politics by other means. According to this logic, partisans (guerrilleros or irregular soldiers) were fighting for a political objective and to achieve Justice. In *History Will Absolve Me*, Fidel Castro used constitutional law from different centuries and countries to justify the right to rise up in arms against a tyranny. He famously finished his discourse with a defense of armed struggle articulated as a religious metaphor addressed to future generations: "Condenadme, no importa, la historia me absolverá [Condemn me, it doesn't matter, history will absolve me]" (Castro 1972c, 71). That is, future generations would not condemn his sins (the use of force), because his cause was led by the moral imperative to attain universal Justice.

Violence and the Trope of Blood

As a result of the assimilation between violence and Justice, violence always had to be represented in an aesthetically pleasing form. The ethical purity of this type of violence demands that, unlike legal or mythical violence, sovereign or divine violence may always be represented as a bloodless action: especially because, as we perceive it in the cultural production of the sixties, a resurrection of sorts is always involved in the process of death. In the sixties, imageries about the telluric power of blood abounded in cultural production. In social poetry, Gutiérrez Alea's film *Historias de la Revolución* (*Stories of the Revolution*), and Castro's speech *History Will Absolve Me*, blood is the epic symbol of victory. José Baragaño's poem "Himno a las milicias" ("Anthem of Militias"), for example, repeats this metaphor in an elegy where poetry, war, and the people are represented as a unity. The poem's third stanza is a call to arms where blood symbolizes the people:

> ¡Milicianos del alba y de la sangre!
> Sin fuentes ni riberas
> Nuestro ojo ve la imagen abierta de las revoluciones
> Bajo un viento que quiere cantar
> Nadie sabe dónde se juntan esos ríos
> Nuestra sangre no se detiene
> Comunica a un nivel de libertad
> La creciente del pueblo
> En la estación profunda de la sangre.[6]

The reference to blood, especially in the first and last lines, is reminiscent of the Catholic representation of Christ's crucifixion. In particular, the words "en la estación profunda de la sangre" allude to his suffering in the cross (the Spanish *estación* can mean both "season" and "station," as in "stations of the Cross"). In the context of the poem, blood represents the soldiers, in the line "Nuestra sangre no se detiene." But in a different context, the same expression could refer to a group of people belonging to the same social class or ethnic group. Blood represents interrelated elements that always point to a sense of belonging and possession, which is related to the nationalistic nature of the revolutionary process. Étienne Balibar argues that for nationalism to be effective it needs to prove, for example, that there are no natural or hereditary differences among men who belong to the same nation. This results from the inherent impossibility of nationalism to be scientifically justified (Balibar 1998, 99–100). In this regard, the shedding of blood was the element literally uniting all Cubans as a nation. With the goal of producing an idea of nationhood, the revolution was represented as an old system of kinship in which what mattered was blood identity, and sacrifice was the rite of passage that created the mythology of Cubanness. This explains the symbolic importance of the concept of blood, and, in particular, its telluric aspect. Blood meant destruction, but its shedding also produced a cathartic sense of purification, and renewal. The shedding of blood was part of a ritual of passage into a decolonized imaginary space. I am using the concept of "decolonization" because the cultural production of this era reflected the desire to create a new voice divested of discursive and ideological elements from the past. In other words, the revolution was not only conceived of as a process of disrupting power and passing it from one hand to another. Guevara, like Fanon, knew how important it was to create a postcolonial subject and a nation-state, and blood symbolized the need to find commonality and pointed to the notion of "purity of blood": "Decolonization unifies that people by the radical decision to remove from it its heterogeneity, and by unifying it on a national, sometimes a racial, basis" (Fanon 1963 [1961], 46).

Blood's idealization, and the religious references of sacrifice, is precisely what we see in the cultural production of those years, specifically in Gutiérrez Alea's *Stories of the Revolution*. Unlike most of Gutiérrez Alea's films, which are characterized by an ironic look at revolutionary politics, his first film is a eulogy for the 1958 revolutionary war. It was the first feature film produced by the Instituto Cubano del Arte e Industria Cinematográficos (ICAIC) and a commemoration of the second anniversary of the Cuban Revolution. It was also one of the earliest examples of revolutionary film and as such featured actors who had been real combatants in the Sierra Maestra (Canel 1960). Revolutionary film or new Latin American Cinema originated as a film movement that opposed the main aesthetic goals of Hollywood film (i.e., entertainment and visual beauty) and supported the pedagogic and political function of film to create social consciousness. *Stories of the Revolution* is a chronological recounting of the struggles that led to the revolution. Three distinct episodes evoke the early fifties' urban armed struggle, the Sierra Maestra insurrection, and the final taking of Santa Clara, the strategic bastion that led the rebels to eventual victory.

The film adheres to the neorealist aesthetics of the new Latin American film of the 1960s, and as such it proposes a transparency of the image and its unmediated impact on the viewer, which is why the film's narrative arc conforms to the conventions of mythical epic poems: it has heroes and despicable soldiers, it has sustained dramatic tension, and it has victories and defeats. *Stories of the Revolution* is certainly an action film, yet the most dramatic scenes in two of the vignettes do not feature crude, gruesome, or tragic representations of violence. In this regard, the film follows all the conventions of melodrama. It is a black and white film with stereotyped scenography, but most strikingly, although an action film, it also conveys sentimentality through its many close-ups and medium long shots. Death imagined as a necessary religious ritual points to this type of sentimentality. For example, the section depicting the assault on Santa Clara begins by showing the popular celebration after the surrender of Batista's National Guard. In these scenes, Teresa, the working-class hero's girlfriend, played by Miriam Gómez, suddenly discovers the death of her beloved, whose dead body evokes a crucified Christ, much like the iconic image of Ernesto Guevara taken after his death.

"*Historias de la Revolución* (Tomás Gutiérrez Alea, 1960). Teresa's dead boyfriend.

The final close-up of the girlfriend's gaze even more clearly foregrounds the religious analogy. The take follows the slow transformation of her gaze until it finally acquires a martyr's quality. Silence plays a very important role. This halt in the narration gives the audience an opportunity to empathize with the character. It is also the moment to conquer popular taste. This is accomplished through a close-up showing Teresa's exaggerated feelings, as her hopelessness suddenly becomes strength and determination. After looking up to the sky, she looks forward again with a certain pride and honor, indicating the transformation of her identity.

Teresa is no longer in the background of the revolutionary insurrection; she has now become the last heroine of the uprising as she understands that, with his death, the hero has redeemed the community by attaining justice, and thus he has not been completely annihilated. Thus, in spite of the hero's death, as in melodrama, the film wraps up with a conventional happy ending. The woman's gaze encapsulates all the values of the revolutionary nation.

Sentimentality, more than any other factor, accounts for the representation of violence, which, far from being crude, gruesome, or tragic, is depicted as a ritualistic pantomime. There is another violent but bloodless scene in the film where death symbolizes rebirth rather than destruction. The second vignette reaches its climax with this scene, which lays out the strong symbolic power of sacrifice. The rebels are fighting Batista's troops in the Sierra Maestra. One of the younger soldiers lies on the floor, severely

"*Historias de la Revolución* (Tomás Gutiérrez Alea, 1960). Teresa's close-up.

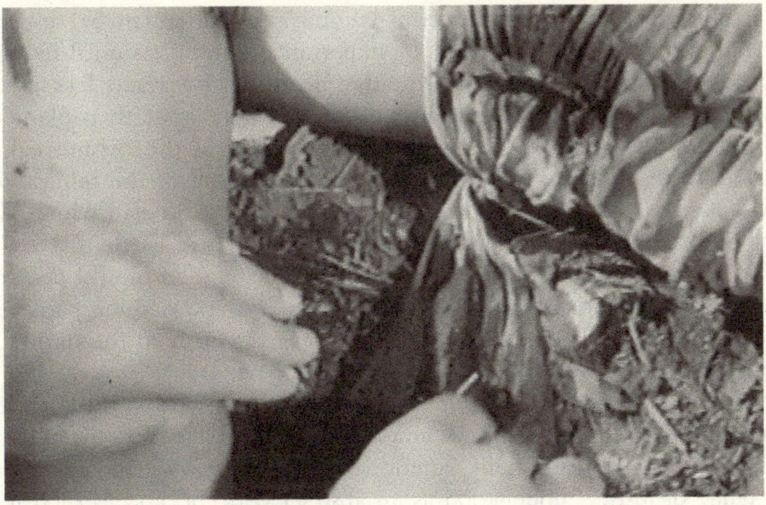

"*Historias de la Revolución* (Tomás Gutiérrez Alea, 1960). Piece of bloody shirt.

wounded by the enemy. The rebel's life is close to an end, and he is being watched by one of the older rebels. At one point, the older rebel kneels down and cuts a little piece of cloth from the young soldier's shirt. The rebel takes the piece of cloth, which is red with blood, and buries it in the ground next to the prostrate soldier.

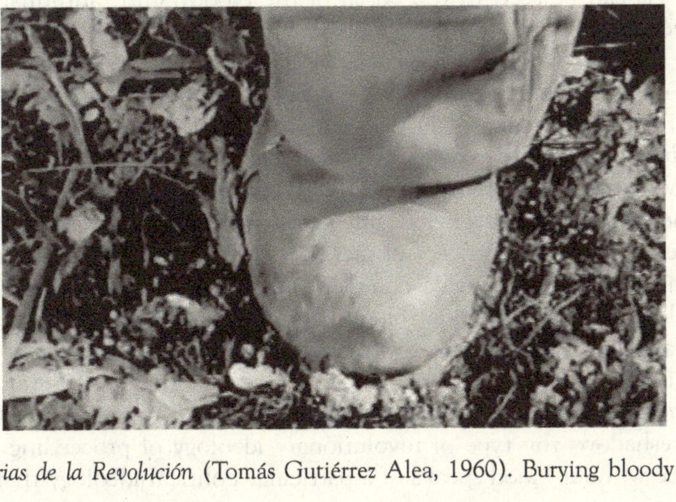

"*Historias de la Revolución* (Tomás Gutiérrez Alea, 1960). Burying bloody shirt.

The rebel has no intention of burying the dying man because he is just one more expendable body. His importance diminishes until he finally disappears. But the blood signifies neither death nor the tragic loss of a life; it signifies, rather, a new beginning of life. The bloody cloth is planted in the ground, revealing the strong telluric character of the Schmittian partisan and the revolution. We find the same metaphor of the telluric force of violence represented in Peter Weiss's essay on Guevara, in which Weiss attributes to him the following remark: "The patch of earth that I water with my blood is the only piece of land that belongs to me [El pedazo de tierra que riego con mi sangre el único trozo de tierra que me pertenece]" (Weiss 1968, 83). The spilling of blood that gives birth to the nation also represents the purification of the revolutionary hero.

By eschewing gore and idealizing blood, these two scenes create an imaginary where violence is sanctioned by justice (an abstract type of legality that transcends institutionally sanctioned law). It is a violence exercised in the name of justice, understood as an abstract concept, and as such it can only be imposed by a higher power that has authority over positive law. Whereas institutional law seeks retribution (in the form of a violent act) for an offense committed against the written law, the revolutionary logic at play in the film shows that a violent act committed in the name of justice seeks rebirth. Precisely because there is no blood or gore in the scene, violence is not avenged legally or personally. Rather than focusing on the heroes' desire for vengeance against Batista's troops for killing their comrades, the narrative emphasizes the ritual of the burial of the dead. As such, the film idealizes revolutionary violence, because rather than being destructive, death symbolizes radical change and redemption. What do I mean by this formulation? As can be seen in the burial of the bloody shirt, annihilation does not necessarily imply absolute destruction. The destructive force in this case is actually transformative because, as Castro argues, it is a means to a just cause, and therefore it should not be legally punished. It is a violence committed in the name of justice, which is what Castro argues in *History Will Absolve Me*. This explains why this blood is not corporeal but rather ideal. Violence is represented as the redemptive power of justice. This is why there are so many religious allegories in the film, as well as in official rhetoric, and why the concept of sacrifice is so prevalent in both. In *Politics of Friendship*, Jacques Derrida comments on the wars waged with the new technologies: "To kill without bloodshed, with the help of new techniques, is perhaps already to accede to a world without war and without politics, to the inhumanity of a war without war" (Derrida 1997, 130). *Stories of the Revolution*'s bloodless image of violence neutralizes the existence of politics and foreshadows the type of revolutionary ideology of proceeding decades. Violence without blood speaks of a particular political ideology that doesn't define war as its goal. Yet, although war is not the aim of revolutionary politics, it always looms in the background as a real possibility.

Sacrifice and the Logic of Exchange and Heroism

Guerrilla warfare was one thing; institutionalized violence was another. What type of violence was culture promoting? Violence is the driving force of sacrifice, the act that dictates revolutionary rhetoric's spiritual nature. Revolutionary sacrifice has the same mythical qualities as its religious counterpart. Throughout the revolutionary period, sacrifice has always been a condition of possibility for revolutionary change. In Cuba, the notion of sacrifice has longstanding religious connotations. In general, sacrifice is understood as an offering that does not necessarily require blood. In early revolutionary rhetoric, however, sacrifice always involved the spilling of human blood and, ideally, the loss of human life. The sacrificial demand was inherently perverse, because its symbolic value increased with each new offering. But the idea of value in revolutionary rhetoric functions paradoxically. In sacrifice one gives something of a greater value to receive something of a lesser value or no value at all. In sixties poetry, however, sacrifice was both rewarded with immortality (as the warrior's apotheosis) and demanded by the revolution (as the collective duty of all members of society). Intellectuals must sacrifice their aesthetics, workers must do extra hours of volunteer work, and soldiers must give their lives. But the individual was not to be rewarded for these sacrifices, for they were made on the community's behalf. The same was true from a sociological perspective. The rhetoric of sacrifice sought to create a sense of identity and equality among the people. Sacrifice also became the homogenizing element of a period, which, according to Fernando Martínez Heredia, was an era of radical patriotism (Martínez Heredia 2007, 149). As Ernesto Guevara pointed out in "El socialismo," the goal of homogenization was to produce a society in which differences between the leader and the masses disappear[7] (Guevara 2007 [1965], 5).

The following poems show how the trope of sacrifice becomes a homogenizing element of the revolutionary process. This idea is articulated in "Cruz" and "Cara o Cruz," two poems with religious undertones written by Catholic Origenista Cintio Vitier. These poems are dedicated to the sacrifices of a Guevarian hero. In "Cruz," the first poem, he is represented as an omnipresent and ever-agonizing figure for whom men sacrifice themselves: "Estás en el trabajo / en la atención, / en el juego de los niños. . . . En el esfuerzo de los hombres de buena voluntad"[8] (Vitier 1976a, 81). The Christlike man is also the Guevarian New Man, which indicates that secularism and sacredness have become one: "Los que piensan en el prójimo / y lo ayudan y trabajan para él / son tus discípulos"[9] (ibid., 82). "Cruz," is a reinterpretion of Christ's crucifixion. Whereas the signifier "cruz" is a cross, "cara o cruz" is an idiomatic expression for calling "heads or tails" on a coin toss. This means that, as a signifier, "cruz" takes on a double meaning. It can refer to sacrifice, but it can also be the other side of the coin. What follows from this ambiguity is that "cruz," or sacrifice, can represent fate (of the soldier as a man) or salvation (of the soldier as a hero). But "cruz," like a coin, may also represent both at the same time, and thus neither of them in particular. This explains why, as a signifier, sacrifice does not point to either fate (secular) or salvation (sacred) but to both. The signified of destiny and salvation are as arbitrary and necessarily bound as those of tails and heads. Sacrifice is simultaneously fate and salvation. This means that any man can be a hero (a sacred figure), and thus that the sacred and the secular are one and the same.

Unlike a divine figure, however, the hero does not demand sacrifices, nor does he need to be recognized. He only asks for men's work and endurance. In Vitier's words, religious symbolism or idealism is replaced by the work of the people or materialism: "en el sudor, / en la ignorancia, / en el Olvido de Ti Mismo / que es la Materia de la Realidad"[10] (Vitier 1976a, 82). The poem represents work as a material and tangible action, whereas Catholic rituals are only ideals. In "Cruz" it is clear that neither does God demand a sacrifice, nor do men ask for salvation: "In the efforts of men / of goodwill, / unaware of the treasure / that they bear to your breast" (ibid., 81). Paradoxically, the following verses show that the poet refers to the hero as a martyr: "del aire que te dan, del poco alivio / que traen sus manos rudas, ciegas, / al horror de tu agonía / que no acaba."[11] The hero does not demand recognition or sacrifice, but would men still be punished for their misdeeds? If sacrifice is no longer a ritual to venerate and recognize God's deeds, does that mean that the concept of sacrifice has been transformed? Since heroism has replaced religiosity, let us look farther into the representation of the hero's identity and its relationship to sacrifice.

In Vitier's "Camilo Cienfuegos," an excerpt of which serves as this chapter's epigraph, the hero has become the island and vice versa (Vitier 1976b, 78–79). The hero is the representation of a homogenous notion of the nation, but he is not given a voice. Instead, the poet speaks for him and reifies his identity. The soldier should be described as a political figure who becomes one with nature. The natural subjectivity bears a strong resemblance to José Martí's "natural man." By acting like the natural man, the soldier becomes unpredictable, organic, and part of a system that regulates itself. The natural, unlike the political or the cultural, is transcendental, which is why the hero is a sacred figure.

In "Cruz" and "Camilo Cienfuegos," nature is threatened with destruction because of the disappearance of Jesus Christ. It is no longer God who runs nature. The order of the world is orchestrated, instead, by men and their work. The world follows a certain order due to the materiality of men's work, and the hero has taken Christ's place. The limit between the profane and the sacred has been breached, but the idea of the divine persists. We thought that all differences between men and divine figures had disappeared, but another sacred figure has taken God's place, and men are still under his aegis. As an ideal figure, however, he still has a presence in the world as the one who sacrificed himself for the revolution. As Vitier writes in "Cruz," "En verdad te gustaría, / mientras mueres, / que todo fuera muy bien hecho"[12] (Vitier 1976a, 81). Thus, his sacrifice is not seen as a gift. It had a purpose and was not in vain. The fact that sacrifice is still attached to the idea of purpose actually reestablishes anew the economy and logic of exchange, of a compensated heroism. Namely, if the deed has a goal, it is because this goal accomplishes something with value. In this case, an exchange as such does not take place, but because the logic of exchange still exists, this means that men's deeds must also have a purpose. Men's sacrifices must also have a purpose, but they cannot bear the trace of the "exchange." That is, the ideology of exchange is what rules, but out of ignorance or false consciousness, men conceive sacrifice as a gratuitous act, as "Cara o cruz" shows: "Los que piensan en el prójimo / y lo ayudan y trabajan para él / son tus discípulos: / no importa que lo ignoren"[13] (Vitier 1976a, 82).

What are the implications of the sacrifice as an ideology of exchange? If we go back to the idea of nationhood, the purpose of sacrifice becomes even clearer. Men are united by the idea of a shared ethic. Social and economic heterogeneity, in the aftermath of the revolution, was a threat to nation building; it was erased by a common ethic beyond social, gender, ethnic, or economic differences. Precisely because of the ideology just described, sacrifices did not have the appearance of exchanges. As gifts they could be of different value, because they had no exchange value. They were not commodified by a society that would have to compensate citizens for their work. By establishing an apparent ethos of equality among people, sacrifice kept its ritualistic nature, and it also erased social difference. At the same time, however, the hero retained his status as both the common man and a divine figure. The meaning of sacrifice did not change since it signified salvation and fate, the biblical paradox. Sacrifice would not be compensated, but the logic of exchange remained. The discourse of sacrifice was thus articulated by two contradictory arguments. On the one hand, the redemptive Christian logic had disappeared, which meant that men did not need to atone for their sins. If sacrifice was not atonement (performance of a good deed to atone for a sin), then what was left was a type of sacrifice that was no longer religious. The notion of sacrifice thus took on the significance of the "good deed," an action whose goal was not salvation.

On the other hand, the divine figure was transformed but not eliminated, since the hero took the place of the Christian God. The divine therefore did not lose its transcendental nature, nor did the divine figure cease to be someone who had sacrificed himself through his willingness to die for the revolution. In other words, the logic of exchange had never disappeared, but it was ideologically hidden by the philosophy of the good deed. The soldier's representation as a hero and as a divine figure reintroduced the conceptual divide between the secular and the religious, and between the divine figure (the hero) and man (the masses). This idea also contradicted the representation of a classless society that both poems defend. These paradoxes were not only ideological; above all, they concealed a sense of dread. This fear was produced by the same idea that the poems vindicate: the threat of a classless society.

Out of Bondage and the New Consciousness

In advocating violence as the only means to freedom in the struggle for national liberation, the philosophy of the revolution was very much in line with state discourse and with other postcolonial thinkers, such as Fanon, who argued that the colonized had to fight the colonizers with the violence that the oppressors had instilled in them.[14] Revolutionary leaders claimed that like other revolutions of national liberation, the Cuban Revolution was above all a process of decolonization, especially because it wanted to transform a double relation of dependency: the vertical, interdependent relationship between the oligarchy and popular classes within the country and a horizontal, interdependent relationship between third world countries and first world capitalism. As such, the goal of the revolution was to eliminate the economic, political, and cultural control of U.S. neocolonialism, and to put an end to Batista's brutal dictatorship. In the *Segunda declaración de La Habana* (*Second Havana Declaration*), Fidel Castro expresses these ideas with a Marxian vocabulary. He declares that the revolution's goal is to transform the motor of the capitalist class dominance: private property. He argues that the nineteenth-century bourgeois revolution built the new society over the ashes of the feudal order: "The bourgeoisie took political power and established on the ruins of feudal society its capitalist mode of production [L]a burguesía conquistó el poder político y estableció sobre las ruinas de la sociedad feudal su modo capitalista de producción]" (Castro 2008, 244 [1962,13]). The bourgeois revolution did not eliminate the real causes of the old order: private property and class dominance. The Cuban Revolution, however, transformed the capitalist system with the destruction of its structural premises: "But Cuba rose up. Cuba was able to redeem itself from the bastard tutelage. Cuba broke the chains that tied its fortunes to those of the imperial oppressor, redeemed its riches, reclaimed its culture, and unfurled its banner of Free Territory and People of the Americas [Pero Cuba se levantó, Cuba pudo redimirse a si misma del bastardo tutelaje. Cuba rompió las cadenas que ataban su suerte al imperio opresor, rescató sus riquezas, reivindicó su cultura, y desplegó su bandera soberana de Territorio y Pueblo Libre de América]" (2008, 242 [1962,12]). It was a violent revolution that sought the restoration and renaissance of the nation: "Revolution historically is like the doctor who assists at the birth of a new life. It does not needlessly use the tools of force, but will use them without hesitation whenever necessary to help the birth—a birth that brings to the enslaved and exploited masses the hope of a new and better life [La revolución es en la historia como el médico que asiste al nacimiento de una nueva vida. No usa sin necesidad los aparatos de fuerza, pero los usa sin vacilaciones cada vez que sea necesario para ayudar al parto. Parto que trae a las masas esclavizadas y explotadas la esperanza de una vida mejor]" (2008, 249 [1962, 17]). This was also Fanon's idea of revolution: "National liberation, national renaissance, the restoration of nationhood to the people . . . decolonization is always a violent phenomenon [Libération nationale, renaissance nationale, restitution de la nation au people . . . la décolonisation est toujours un phénomène violent]" (Fanon 1963 [1961], 35 [2002, 39]). The logic of violence was precisely determined by two contradictory ideas. On the one hand, the idea of restoration; on the other hand, that of renaissance. The people had to reclaim their country that had been seized, yet at the same time they also had to rebuild it. In other words, the revolution was conceived as a process to seize the past in order to destroy it. That is, unlike the bourgeois revolution, these processes of decolonization sought to annihilate the ruins of the past: "The destruction of the colonial world is no more and no less than the abolition of one zone, its burial in the depths of the earth or its expulsion from the country [Détruire le monde colonial c'est ni plus ni moins abolir une zone, l'enfouir au plus profond du sol ou l'expulser du territoire]" (1963 [1961], 41 [2002, 44]). In Cuba's case, it meant creating a new history that would represent revolution as the degree zero of history. It was not a mode to affirm the negation (destruction) and build from its ruins; it was a theological gesture of creation.

The concept of revolution as a process of annihilation was precisely what triggered the rhetorical emphasis on violence. Inspired by the Hegelian master-slave dialectic, Fanon argued that the colonized had to curse the colonialist with the language they had learned from him. The violence of colonization's "civilizing" mission was now the asset of the colonized people. Guevara also believed that capitalism's violence could only be fought with violence: "Violence is not the monopoly of the exploiters and as such the exploited can use it too, moreover, [they] ought to use it when the moment arrives" (Guevara 1997 [1961], 74). In his well-known essay *Calibán: Apuntes sobre la cultura en nuestra América* (*Caliban: Notes on Culture in Our America*), Roberto Fernández Retamar reads Shakespeare's *The Tempest* as an allegory of colonial oppression. He interprets Caliban's education as the cultural imposition that resulted from the colonizer's civilizing mission in the Caribbean. Prospero imposes his culture and his language on Caliban, who realizes he can use the master's language to curse him back. Likewise, it can be argued that violence became the language of the colonized, because that is what they learned from their masters: "He of whom *they* have never stopped saying that the only language he understands is that of force, decides to give utterance by force [Lui à qui on n'a jamais cessé de dire qu'il ne comprenait que le langage de la force, décide de s'exprimer par la force]" (Fanon 1963 [1961], 84 [2002, 81]). Thus, they cursed their masters back with the use of violence and strove to take their place (Fanon 1963 [1961], 53). But in order to fight back, the colonized need to be aware of their own agency as subjects. This moment of self-recognition is key in Fanon's theory, and it can only happen through struggle. In other words, the colonized do not become subjects until they confront the master. Subjectivity or the possibility for emancipation only materializes through struggle. Hence, the struggle between colonized and colonizers was above all a battle for self-recognition. What is required, then, is to understand the ontological implications of this struggle for the colonized. Basing his approach on Alexandre Kojève's materialist reading of Hegel's dialectic, Fanon clearly reinterprets Hegel's ontological model of the self-recognition process by assimilating it to the process of decolonization. Hegel argues that self-consciousness only exists after the subject is acknowledged by the other (Hegel 1997 [1807], 105). In order to illustrate this idea and the dialectical power relations that take place in this process, he represents it allegorically as the relation between a master and a slave. This is precisely the model that inspires Fanon to understand the relationship between colonizers and colonized.

For Hegel, self-consciousness requires consciousness of the other's recognition of oneself. In other words, if I cannot recognize that the other is recognizing me, I cannot recognize my own existence. Negativity is key in the dialectical process, for only its sublation into positivity can bring about transformation and eventually freedom. In Hegel's allegory, the bondsman and the lord face each other in a struggle to death, as both try to attain self-consciousness. Since the moment of negativity is necessary for the completion of the dialectic, they can only attain self-sufficiency by dreadfully risking their own lives. The master wins the battle because he chooses to risk his life in spite of fear. He gets his self-recognition from the bondsman, who prefers to be objectified by the master and stay in fear. But because the master depends on the bondsman to attain self-consciousness, he does not actually become independent (Hegel 1997, 114). The bondsman cannot break free of his bondage to the lord, who needs him for his self-recognition. So he only possesses his independence in thinghood, not manhood (ibid., 115). By choosing to be free of attachments, however, the slave steadily gains his self-consciousness through work, as he sees himself mirrored in what he produces. To conclude his story, Hegel repeats the importance of dread. He says that men need to live in dread and anxiety in order to become self-conscious. If the individual has not really felt deep fear, self-recognition will not occur: "If it has not experienced absolute fear but only some lesser dread, the negative being has remained for it something external, its substance has not been infected by it through and through" (ibid., 119).

This feeling of dread is also key to understanding the rhetoric of Fanon and Guevara, as dread triggers the people's will to revolt. Both writers choose violence as a means to gain self-consciousness and eventually freedom: "The colonized man finds his freedom in and through violence [L'homme colonisé se libère dans et par la violence]" (Fanon 1963 [1961], 86 [2002, 83]). For Fanon and Guevara, the people or the colonized are bondsmen. They are objectified by the lord, who needs their recognition to attain self-consciousness. Whereas in the Hegelian model, the bondsman becomes self-conscious through labor, for Guevara and Fanon the bondsman attains freedom by winning the struggle with the lord and taking his place. "The guerrilla is the combat vanguard of the people . . . willing to carry out a series of warlike actions for one possible strategic end—the seizure of power," Guevara writes (1997 [1961], 71). ("La guerrilla es la vanguardia combativa del pueblo armada, dispuesta a desarrollar una serie de acciones bélicas tendientes al único fin estratégico posible: la toma del poder [1977a, 204].) This is the most important difference between their theory and the Hegelian model, and it also explains why Fanon's and Guevara's models are not dialectical. In their theories, the bondsman surpasses the moment of negativity or dread, but instead of sublating this negativity into positivity, he falls back into positivity: "Decolonization is truly the creation of new men. But this creation does not receive its legitimacy from any supernatural power: the colonized 'thing' becomes a man through the very process by which it frees itself [La décolonisation est véritablement création d'hommes nouveaux. Mais cette création ne reçoit pas sa légitimité d'aucune puissance surnaturelle: 'la chose' colonisée devient homme dans le processus même par lequel elle se libère]" (Fanon 1963 [1961], 36 [2002, 40]). That is, the colonized reach self-consciousness when they eventually win the battle, and not through work. In other words, the slave ceases being a bondsman and thus becomes a lord. As a result, he never becomes independent or free. He attains self-recognition but not independence, because he always depends on the gaze of a bondsman for his self-consciousness. Instead of becoming truly free, the colonized repeat the cycle of violence indefinitely. In other words, Fanon's and Guevara's propositions might be doing away with the teleological nature of Hegel's theory of self-recognition, but they are still embedded in the onto-theological foundations of Hegelian thought. The structure of power remains the same. And since the relationship of codependency between the lord and the people remains the same, no real freedom or change is achieved. The logic of violence also articulated the theory of the New Man as an intellectual, especially in Ernesto Guevara's thought. Guevara's theory contains no idea of intellectual organicity. Intellectuals are and were society's vanguard, having been educated and brought up to be so. They do not need to go through a process of transformation to be leaders. But they do need to break with the bourgeois ideology that formed them as intellectuals. Intellectuals need to negate their bourgeois ego and regain a new consciousness in the new society through work and sacrifice. For Guevara, this new intellectual is the New Man or the hero and the warrior. The New Man thus has to restore himself through work and sacrifice by negating the bourgeois consciousness and sublating it into positivity as a new hero and warrior. How can intellectuals find self-consciousness by negating their own ego? This is the question that Guevara addresses through the allegory of the New Man. Warfare ideology gained prominence after the institutionalization of the revolution. The guerrilla warfare hero, the defense of the fatherland, and armed struggle became the three fundamental principles articulating the discourse of national liberation on which the new society was constructed. Warfare came to symbolize progress, modernity, and construction rather than destruction, and the subject whose identity embraced all these values was the warrior or the New Man. The New Man was the revolutionary hero, with whom all Cubans born within the revolution had to identify: "The Revolution began to be identified with the Sierra Maestra and the people with the Rebel Army, while the United States and those Cubans without national dignity represented the enemy" (Pérez-Stable 1993, 134). Guevara developed the concept in his description of revolutionary intellectuals' goals and values in "El socialismo y el hombre nuevo en Cuba" ("Socialism and the New Man in Cuba"). In this, one of his most paradigmatic essays, Guevara argues that only the generations formed in the new revolutionary society would be free of temptation from capitalism. The younger generations were made out of "malleable clay" from which Cuban socialism would create the New Men of the Revolution, the intellectual vanguard that would lead the masses.

The Melancholic Tropology of the Guevarian New Man

> Decolonization never takes place unnoticed, for it influences individuals and modifies them fundamentally. . . . It brings a natural rhythm into existence, introduced by new men, and with it a new language, and a new humanity. . . . Decolonization is the veritable creation of new men. But this creation owes nothing of its legitimacy to any supernatural power; the "thing" which has been colonized becomes man during the same process by which it frees itself.
>
> —Frantz Fanon, *The Wretched of the Earth*

Ernesto Guevara's essay on the "New Man" has come to define models of nationalist and revolutionary subjectivity through the figure of the guerrilla hero, thus becoming one of the most influential allegories for the state-promoted discourse of revolutionary emancipation. The Guevarian historical subject must negate his past and let his subjectivity emerge anew through the synthesis of work and a new conscience. The New Man's subjectivity is the product of a restorative economy where men are liberated from the alienation of a capitalist past and then given the possibility to arise as new revolutionary subjects by regaining a lost identity that had been soiled by capitalism. Revolutionary subjectivity is essentiality heroic and can only be articulated through sacrifice: "El individuo de nuestro país sabe que la época gloriosa que le toca vivir es de sacrificio; conoce el sacrificio [People in our country know that the glorious period in which they happen to live is one of sacrifice; they are familiar with sacrifice]" (Guevara 1977c, 269). Revolutionary rhetoric is formed through the creation of a new ontology characterized by the transformation of the Cuban subject into a heroic subject. This entails the fusion of a heroic subject with the vanguard or the state through a sacrificial relationship whose object is the creation of a utopian community. The utopian nation can only arise through the sacrifice and the martyrdom of the hero. By becoming a martyr, the hero becomes an embodiment of the fatherland. This fiction of restoration is articulated through a cultural production developed and promoted by official state institutions.

The melancholic ethos of the Cuban revolutionary project materialized through Guevara's work, which inscribed an inherent loss as the ideological basis of the Cuban Revolution. This could not have been otherwise given the profoundly melancholic features of Guevarian theory that are present in a text as paradigmatic as "Socialism and Man in Cuba."[15] This text is also important because it is the first document that defines the New

Man's intellectual background and the development of his political ethics, and all these ideas were key for the development of the revolution's political project. This essay played a very important role in the political unconscious of the revolutionary intellectuals, and especially for the intellectuals of the nineties who, according to Guevara, were going to be the real New Men of the Cuban Revolution: "Resumiendo, la culpabilidad de muchos de nuestros intelectuales y artistas reside en su pecado original; no son auténticamente revolucionarios. . . . Las nuevas generaciones vendrán libres del pecado original [The guilt of many of our intellectuals and artists lies in their original sin; they are not authentically revolutionaries. . . . The new generations will emerge free of this original sin]" (Guevara 1977c, 267–68). In Guevara's socialist construction of history, the figure of the New Man is the link to the formation of the superstructure in society. Following his Leninist distinction between the vanguard and the masses, Guevara makes a distinction in this essay between the transformation of intellectuals and that of workers. Like the Hegelian slave, workers gain self-consciousness through labor. Intellectuals, however, need to indoctrinate and educate the masses and thus be free of any idealist or bourgeois influences.

What are the new values that the vanguard must instill in the common man? Guevara draws a parallel with art in order to clarify his point. According to Guevara, his fellow intellectuals had not been liberated from their original sin because their ideology was ingrained in idealism. Intellectuals had to be formed in a revolutionary society free of any trace of the capitalist world. Only the new generations formed in the new revolutionary society would be free of temptation from capitalism. The younger generations were made of the "malleable clay" from which Cuban socialism was going to create the New Men of the twenty-first century, the intellectual vanguard that would form the masses: "La arcilla fundamental de nuestra obra es la juventud [The fundamental clay of our work is the young]" (Guevara 1977c, 272). Guevara's accusations followed on a debate about socialist realism from the early sixties. As we will see, intellectuals from various artistic disciplines were involved in a debate about the formal structures of revolutionary aesthetics. Was socialist realism the only style that could analyze social and economic conditions, or could there be universal artistic values? Guevara's intention was to put an end to the debate by arguing for an aesthetics that rejected both options. He called for an aesthetic free of bourgeois idealism and mechanistic depictions of reality. Instead of defending nineteenth-century realism for its scientific analysis of social structures, as advocates of socialist realism did, he proposed a historicist argument to invalidate past and present aesthetic theories in the name of their presumed bourgeois ideology. Bourgeois art was limited in that it could not represent human alienation; instead, it could only offer escapism from human existential angst. The solution was to look at the future and abandon past and present aesthetics. Intellectuals must emerge as New Men in the present, in their revolutionary and socialist present, with a subjectivity restored in their new transitional present. Cuban intellectuals therefore could not recover their identity until they moved away from their past, which was marked by a capitalist mode of production.

Using the same idealist formulations that he was criticizing, Guevara accused contemporary intellectuals of sin. Offering no path to redemption, he simply condemned them to disappear: "Podemos intentar injertar el olmo para que dé peras, pero simultáneamente hay que sembrar perales. Nuestra tarea consiste en impedir que la generación actual, dislocada por sus conflictos, se pervierta y pervierta a las nuevas [We can inject the elm tree to make it give pears, but at the same time we must plant pear trees. Our task is to prevent the current generation, dislocated by its conflicts, from perverting itself and generations to come]" (Guevara 1977c, 267–68). Unlike workers, Cuban intellectuals were not able to gain self-consciousness. Their own process of recognition could only follow the logic of destruction that Guevara proposed for war fighters. According to Guevara, intellectuals are alienated, having lost their egos through the temptations of an alienating intellectual tradition. Only the intellectuals who would be formed in a revolutionary society free of bourgeois idealism could undertake the task of creating a new art. This meant that intellectuals who were born before the revolution had to negate their ego and adopt a subjectivity that was yet to be determined. This theoretical gesture was caught in an antinomy as it strove to locate consciousness in a temporality outside of history. How can one represent a time to come out of sheer nothingness? What is a history without a past other than atemporality? The New Man's subjectivity cannot be defined a priori, and it looms in Guevara's discourse as an empty signifier that, paradoxically, needs to be attained. The logic of destruction with which he describes the relationship between intellectuals and bourgeois art was plunged in a melancholic conception of art. This melancholic ideology would structurally mark the epistemology of the New Man in times ahead.

Why define it as melancholic process? Intellectuals were no longer recognized by others and had thus lost their self-consciousness. The future (new and revolutionary) consciousness became the object of desire, because only the new can lead to the other's recognition of oneself. In order to assume the new ego, the old one needs to be negated. Yet, when this moment of negativity occurs, there is no sublation into a positivity, because the negation must be a complete destruction. Let us think about this relationship in terms of the Hegelian master-slave narrative, the model followed by Guevara himself. According to that logic, the third world intellectual has adopted Western aesthetics and created a relationship of dependency on

Western thought. In order to regain self-consciousness, the third world intellectual must negate his own ego and strive to embrace a new consciousness. The emptiness left after the negation of the ego produces a melancholic process because the subject cannot abandon the object of desire (his own self-consciousness or recognition). The impossibility of reaching the new subject position produces hatred, but the desire has not receded. What is more, because the subject never abandons a libidinal position, he continues to desire the object until he incorporates it into his own ego. When this incorporation takes place, a cathexis occurs from the object to the subject, and the subject himself becomes a hated object. The result is the objectification of the ego and a total loss of subjectivity (Freud 1963 [1915], 241). The subject is condemned to reside in a historical limbo: in the transitional period between capitalism and pure socialism (freedom).

The Guevarian subjectivity of the New Man is achieved through an economy of restoration that offers the possibility of a liberation from the capitalist mode of production, and, after the liberation from an alienating past, the new Cuban being emerges also as a revolutionary being. The Cuban being or, what amounts to the same thing, the revolutionary being can only be defined through heroism. In turn, heroism can only be defined through sacrifice: "Sabemos que hay sacrificios delante nuestro y que debemos pagar un precio por el hecho heroico de constituir una vanguardia como nación. Todos y cada uno de nosotros paga puntualmente su cuota de sacrificio . . . conscientes de avanzar con todos hacia el hombre nuevo que se vislumbra en el horizonte [We know that sacrifices await us and that we must pay a price for the heroic deed of constituting a vanguard as a nation. . . . All and each of us promptly pay our share of sacrifice . . . conscious of advancing all together toward the new man who can be glimpsed on the horizon]" (Guevara 1977c, 271). The revolutionary rhetoric is formed through the creation of a new ontology characterized by the transformation of the Cuban subject into a heroic subject. The fusion between the heroic subject and the state through a relation of sacrifice will result in the production of the utopian community. We thus have a subject who is not only identified as a Cuban national subject but also becomes a historic subject, since the state is also hypostasized in his person. This fiction of the restoration of the lost object was developed through a genre amply promoted by the institutional and official channels of the Cuban state.

The new detective novel of the seventies was one of the genres that best exemplified the use of this fiction and its allegorical function. The detective novel by poet Luis Rogelio Nogueras, *Y si muero mañana*, illustrates this idea paradigmatically. Nogueras's novel—published in 1978 and awarded the prestigious Unión de Escritores y Artistas Cubanos (UNEAC) prize for best novel—is one of the best examples of the new detective novel, or what some termed the revolutionary detective novel. The Cuban publishing industry privileged this genre by promoting and financing it through the Interior Ministry (MININT). The genre was also promoted through the creation of a national competition for detective novels one year after the Padilla affair.[16] This novel was exemplary of the cultural politics of the "five gray years," during which Cuba experienced the worst censorship and political dogmatism of the revolutionary period. This resulted in the ostracism, imprisonment, and exile of many authors, as well as the banning or silencing of their works.[17] Genres such as the detective novel, however, were privileged because, as Leonardo Padura claims, they had a "filiación revolucionaria y socialista que quedaba establecida desde las bases de la convocatoria del concurso y, por tanto, traía como marca de nacimiento la función ideológica reafirmativa [revolutionary and socialist affiliation established beginning in the competition's invitation for submissions and, therefore, bore as a birthmark the ideological function of reaffirmation]" (150). This type of style gave birth to what José Antonio Portuondo calls the official repetition of the "same old tune" (*teque*) that is "la exposición apologética de la ideología revolucionaria, la propaganda elemental y primaria, el elogio desembozado de los procedimientos revolucionarios [the apologetic exposition of revolutionary ideology, basic and primary propaganda, open praise of revolutionary methods]" (qtd. in Padura 2000,152).

Like most detective novels, *Y si muero mañana* is articulated according to a Manichean representation of the forces of good and evil. The official organ of the Cuban State Security represents the good and the U.S. Secret Services of Intelligence incarnate the evil of imperialism. Ricardo Villa, the novel's hero, is a Cuban spy infiltrated in the Anti-Castroist groups of Miami, and his mission is to inform the Cubans of the terrorist acts that his group prepares. Ricardo Villa is the hero par excellence because he lives for the cause. The novel's temporal structure advances in a dialectical manner toward "Life," the final chapter where the revolutionary heroism reaches its climax. The novel ends with the paradigmatic sacrificial act, represented by Villa's death for the revolution. Villa dies precisely at the same moment he is transmitting a telegraphed message to Havana that is going to save the revolution: "He began to send toward them, over the warm blue Caribbean, his own life" (Nogueras 2001 [1978], 120). The revolutionary hero becomes objectified when he loses his ego and then turns into a revolutionary link. There is, however, the possibility of the restoration of the lost ego through a revolutionary fight that will make the hero "immortal" because of his fight for the revolution. In other words, the death of the hero creates what Jean-Luc Nancy calls the possibility of a superior union through a relation that transcends individual existence (Nancy 1991, 17). Human sacrifice restores lost individuality through its transcendence in a communal union.

The symbiosis between the individual and the masses is the condition of possibility for the creation of the utopian community. That is why the narrator in Nogueras's novel says that "there is spasmodic movement in the disconcerted masses in exile and, for an instant (a month, a week, maybe a day) hope is reborn of a proud return [*por la puerta grande*]" (ibid., 57). This offbeat rhythm is opposed to the diapasonic rhythm that, according to Guevara, occurs between the applause of the masses and those of their leader, Fidel Castro: "En las grandes concentraciones públicas se observa algo así como el diálogo de dos diapasones cuyas vibraciones provocan otras nuevas en el interlocutor. Fidel y la masa comienzan a vibrar en un diálogo de intensidad creciente hasta alcanzar el clímax en un final abrupto, coronado por nuestro grito de lucha y de victoria [In the great public gatherings you can observe something like the dialogue of two tuning forks, whose vibrations provoke new ones in each other. Fidel and the masses begin to vibrate in an increasingly intense dialogue, until they attain the climax in an abrupt finale, crowned by our shouts of struggle and victory]" (Guevara 1977c, 256).

This new melody is the product of the attunement of all the voices to the rhythm of the leader's voice. Thus emerges a community formed out of the dissolution of individuality and the creation of an absolute that becomes a common being. The New Man is also the Cuban par excellence, whose individuality needs to be sacrificed and then restored through what I would call the "being-in-common."

Conversationalism was the other style glorifying the image of the revolutionary hero, and it was also the poetic style closest to the socialist realism Guevara criticized. Perhaps one of the most illustrative poems of this movement is "Isla" by Rolando T. Escardó, in which the poet says: "Pero lo que importa es la Revolución / lo demás son palabras / del trasfondo / de este poema que entrego al mundo / lo demás son mis argumentos"[18] (Escardó 1980, 359). "Isla" is a poem that, like many other poems from the Cuban tradition, begins with the genesis of the Cuban nation. The poem symbolizes a new becoming of Cubanness whose new horizon is defined by a revolutionary utopia and not by a transculturated nature. The poetic voice is also the voice of the sun as an irreplaceable witness of the unfolding of history, whose beginning is also the genesis of the world: "*planeta ardiendo en el cielo* / llega la hora de mi nacimiento / y también la de mis muertes / pues al mundo he venido a instalarme / feliz de esta Revolución que me da dientes"[19] (Escardó 1980, 358). Utopia can only arrive through the revolutionary praxis, and the ideal community that comes with the arrival of socialism will give cohesion to the essence of Cubanness. The new ideological paradigm of the revolution is explained as the beginning of a history whose essence is an object of desire ready to be discovered. The ideological paradigm of national identity was conceptualized since Martí as an anthropological idealization characterized by a humanistic viewpoint. This type of ideology equates the ontological being through the identity of being as a political or civil subject. According to this ideology, the national subject was defined through a hegemonic trope representing Cubanness as the hypostasis of a dialectical conjunction between a cultural and a racial heterogeneity. The revolutionary paradigm of the New Man emphasizes this anthropological conceptualization with a similar argumentative twist. In the tropology of the New Man, to be Cuban is to be revolutionary. The singularity of a Cuban being is defined no longer culturally or racially but politically. This is what allowed the official ideologues of the Cuban regime to read the Cuban Revolution as a degree zero of Cuban history. And, it is also why in the conversationalist style, exoticism was replaced by heroism. From the sixties onward, the essence of national identity began to be defined in terms of heroism. If before the revolution, the object of desire was represented by the archetypical race or culture, after the revolution, the object of desire became the ideal of the perfect hero. In both cases, the paradigm spoke of the yearning for the recovery of a lost being.

Cultural Debates of the Sixties

Mirta Aguirre's seminal essay "Notes on Literature and Art" (1963) is part of an ongoing cultural debate about revolutionary aesthetics and the relationship between art and ideology. This debate, triggered in part by Fidel Castro's controversial 1961 speech "Palabras a los intelectuales" ("Address to Intellectuals"), produced numerous essays roughly representing two contrary positions: art seen as universal or art seen as social practice. In 1965, Guevara also referred to this debate in "El socialismo," when he defined what revolutionary art ought to be. Guevara did not want the new revolutionary art to be influenced by socialist realism, but he also rejected capitalist art:

> Los hombres del Partido deben tomar esa tarea entre las manos y buscar el logro del objetivo principal: educar al pueblo. Se busca entonces la simplificación, lo que entiende todo el mundo, que es lo que entienden los funcionarios . . . se reduce el problema de la cultura general a una apropiación del presente socialista y del pasado muerto (por tanto no peligroso). Así nace el realismo socialista sobre las bases del arte del siglo pasado. . . . El capitalismo en cultura ha dado todo de sí y no queda de él sino el anuncio de un cadáver maloliente. . . . Pero, por qué pretender buscar en las formas congeladas del realismo socialista la única receta válida?" (Guevara 1977c, 266)[20]

Citing and reversing the surrealist "*cadavre exquis*" (exquisite corpse) to eliminate "bourgeois art," Guevara undermined his own cause. By rejecting historical art, Guevara and Aguirre set the conditions for an expression that could only lead to socialist realism. Not surprisingly, then, socialist realism soon made its presence felt in Cuban letters.

To understand the full scope of the controversy about socialist realism, let us return to Mirta Aguirre's essay. In the 1960s, partisans of culture as universal did not support a social understanding of art whereby form was determined by class. For them, there was no ideological divide between form and content. Advocates of art as social practice, in contrast, thought socialist realism was the genre best suited to representing the objective social conditions of reality.[21] In 1963 a group of ICAIC cinematographers raised the issue again in a letter-manifesto defending art as the representation of a universal reality not simply and necessarily determined by social classes (Molina 2006, 22).[22] Aguirre's essay was an indirect response to the letter and in turn triggered a chain of consecutive responses (Aguirre 2006, 17–126).[23] The extensive reaction to the essay resulted in part from its ambition to define socialist realism as a materialist practice in which aesthetics is defined by knowledge.[24] In reaching that goal, Aguirre argued that materialism has surpassed idealism in art. Thus, more than a defense of dialectical materialism, her essay is above all an effort to demystify canonical Western culture. Although the responses to her article deal with many other issues, I am primarily interested in the debate between materialism and idealism.

While Aguirre claims that dialectical materialism is not a political imperative, she condemns idealism in art. Materialism needs to take idealism to task: "[un] apresurador recurso marxista de la derrota del idealismo [[an] urgent Marxist appeal for the defeat of idealism]" (Aguirre 2006, 43). An important part of her argument consists in demonstrating that idealism is a bourgeois ideology. The essay, however, does not successfully provide a rigorous definition of idealism as an abstract theoretical concept. Disregarding its highly philosophical complexity, the essay only conceives of idealism as a political and aesthetic signifier. By opposing it to materialism, Aguirre only defines idealism as an equivalent of capitalist European culture. She maintains that Cuba needs to create its own literature, one suited to the advancement of revolutionary ideals (not necessarily dialectical materialism). Basing her argumentation mostly on formal elements, Aguirre claims that a culture based on idealism does not produce knowledge. Instead it only fosters escapism, sentimentalism, and aesthetic pleasure.

The works that Aguirre demonizes are all foreign, mostly European. In spite of this, she devotes part of her essay to discussing the formal elements that socialist realism can borrow from European art.[25] Thus comes the crux of the argument in all its contradictions. If idealism and materialism are opposed philosophies, and Marxist-influenced works need to combat idealism, how can socialist realism adopt formal techniques from European art inspired by idealism? Aguirre does clarify that form and content do not always correspond, but if socialist realist form takes after idealism, why does it not become idealist, too? This is what she fails to explain rigorously, a failure that results from the conceptual vagueness of her understanding of idealism.

This contradiction, and the theoretical fuzziness of idealism, determines her discussion of socialist realism as the dominant style of sixties and seventies poetry. As the form privileged by Marx and Engels, realism becomes immediately and by default the style that can re-create and transform the conscience of objective reality (Aguirre 2006, 44). Dialectical materialism has revolutionized art by surpassing the idealist abstraction of reality and its decorative aesthetics. In order to show the latter, the essay fights against the three chief criticisms of Soviet socialist realism: its dogmatism, its dull aesthetics, and its lack of argumentative complexity. First, Aguirre elaborates on two of the characteristics of dialectical materialism: the subordination of aesthetics to ideas and the rejection of obscure language.[26] Thus, for example, Aguirre recognizes the importance of art's aesthetics but privileges its ideas: "En el arte, el sentimiento estético, la apreciación de lo bello, su producción, tiene una importancia de primer orden. . . . Pero no por eso el arte deja de tener por finalidad algo más alto: la revelación de la esencia a través del fenómeno que con mayor perfección la exterioriza entre todos los que la contienen [In art, aesthetic feeling, the appreciation of the beautiful, its production, is of primordial importance. . . . But art nonetheless has a higher purpose: the revelation of essence through the phenomenon that most perfectly expresses it, among all those phenomena containing that essence]" (ibid., 57). Then, she sets forth her article's three premises. First, she posits realism as the style best suited to dialectical materialism. Second, she asserts that realism is not a method or a historical style but on the contrary the artistic channel to the scientific truth of dialectical materialism. Most important, she claims that realism can be articulated through different stylistic forms, as long as they provide clarity. Third, she argues that dialectical materialism has debunked idealism.

To explain the first point she argues that from a materialist perspective, art must have the transformation of reality as a goal and clarity as a necessary condition: "Lo que en los hechos supone que, a mayor necesidad de comunicación—comprensión—, mayor necesidad de claridad. . . . El realismo socialista, que no menosprecia en el arte la belleza, lo entiende como vehículo de la veracidad, como camino del conocimiento y como arma para la transformación del mundo [Which in practice implies that, the greater the need for communication (comprehension), the greater the need for clarity. . . . Socialist realism, which does not undervalue beauty in art, understands it as a vehicle for veracity, as a path to knowledge and as a weapon for the transformation of the world]" (Aguirre 2006, 52–53). Once Aguirre has established these premises, she attempts to refute the critiques of socialist realism. She first acknowledges that aesthetics is what distinguishes art from the sciences, as we saw above in her discussion of the importance of aesthetics art and art's "higher purpose" of revealing "essence." "Lo bello [The beautiful], she adds, "es la manera intrínsicamente propia de existir que tiene el arte, a diferencia de la ciencia" "[is art's intrinsically characteristic mode of existing, in contrast to the sciences]" (ibid., 57). Second, and most important, she argues that realism can be rich in form and complex in thought. A Hegelian interpretation of mediation allows her to advance her argument: "El dogmatismo es tan enemigo del arte como de la ciencia. La verdad es multiforme y multiformes son los procedimientos que permiten encontrarla. . . . Si una de las grandes riquezas del marxismo-leninismo, uno de los secretos de su inagotabilidad es el flexible y cambiante encadenamiento que establece entre la verdad absoluta y la relativa, ¿por qué tender, en arte, a dar carácter de metafísicas verdades absolutas a ciertas técnicas, estilos, géneros o escuelas? [Dogmatism is as great an enemy of art as it is of science. Truth is multiform, as are the means that enable one to find it. . . . If one of the great assets of Marxism-Leninism, one of the secrets of its inexhaustibility, is the flexible and changing linkage it establishes between absolute and relative truth, why the tendency in art to give certain techniques, styles, genres, or schools the character of absolute metaphysical truths?]"[27] (ibid., 47). If aesthetics is the essential characteristic of art and the differentiating element between art and sciences, how is the beautiful determined? Following Aguirre's train of thought, it seems that content and form are equally important when it comes to art. Drawing on Lenin, Aguirre argues there is an absolute objective truth and a relative truth conditioned by history. Is there also and absolute and relative aesthetics? To answer this question, Aguirre demonstrates that the revolution has put in place the ideological conditions of possibility for an open dialogue concerning aesthetics. To support her argument, she indirectly refers to Fidel Castro's famous declaration from "Palabras a los intelectuales" (1961): "Dentro de la Revolución: todo; contra la Revolución: ningún derecho [This means that within the Revolution, everything; against the Revolution, nothing] (Castro 2001 [1961], 81). As Aguirre puts it, "Las contradicciones estéticas son inevitables en el camino hacia el comunismo, y el reconocimiento de ellas y su libre elucidación ayudan mucho, entre otras cosas, a que el dogmatismo no enraíce con facilidad en lo artístico [Aesthetic contradictions are inevitable in the path toward communism, and the recognition of these and their free elucidation contribute greatly, among other things, to preventing dogmatism from easily rooting itself in the artistic]" (Aguirre 2006, 60). In spite of this claim, one of the essay's main goals is to prove that realism is the style best suited to re-creating and transforming reality, and reflecting the consciousness of objective reality.

Finally, Aguirre tackles the crucial discussion of form and content, by offering a broader philosophical reflection about materialism and idealism, in which she reductively associates the first one with content, and the second one with form. This argumentative logic thus posits that idealism is concerned with aesthetics, whereas materialism deals with content. The implication of this reasoning is the undermining of aesthetics, at the expense of content. This is indeed the main idea of the type of socialist realism that she defends, and it is also the untenable position that her entire essay conceals. One of them has to do with realism. By becoming materialist and scientific, realism has revolutionized art. Aguirre analyzes several other styles, such as surrealism, *culteranismo*, and abstract art, but she measures their political effectiveness by comparing them to realism, the model of dialectical materialism. Thus, by subordinating all the other styles to realism, she simultaneously posits the latter as the socialist poetics par excellence.

Paradoxically, Aguirre's Leninist understanding of realism is far from being Marxian, since for Marx and Engels, realism has its roots in the nineteenth-century bourgeois novel, whereas Aguirre thinks that nineteenth-century realism has deep roots in philosophical idealism. Jean Renoir's film *La bête humaine* (1938), inspired by Émile Zola's novel of the same title, offers perhaps one of the best visual examples of nineteenth-century realism. The film opens with a long sequence of a train at full speed. The frame of the first scene is engulfed by the train, which like a beast is being fed charcoal by a machinist covered in soot, played by Jean Gabin. In Marxian terms, we can argue that the machinist's existence is determined by his social relations to the forces of production. He is more like an animal than a machine, as Marx argues: "In his human functions he no longer feels himself to be anything but an animal. What is animal becomes human and what is human becomes animal" (Marx and Engels 1978, 74). As a result, he is barely visible and moves as in a perfectly choreographed dance to the rhythm of the machine. Naturalist realism such as Zola's is precisely the style that can present an objective exploration of social issues, as it specifically focuses on the representation of the working class. Marx and Engels, who were the point of reference in the Cuban debates about aesthetics during the 1960s, praised nineteenth-century realism for its truthful representation of reality.

Although they did not produce an aesthetic theory per se, Marx and Engels wrote a great deal about realism, and about literature in general. In an 1888 letter to Margaret Harkness, for example, Engels calls Honoré de Balzac's *La Comédie humaine* one of "the greatest triumphs of realism" (Marx and Engels 1947, 42).[28] Marx and Engels see the writer as a thinker, an educator whose role is to unveil social truths and reveal the inner workings of society: "Realism, to my mind, implies, besides truth of detail, the truthful reproduction of typical characters under typical circumstances" (ibid., 41). In his writings about literature, Marx comments on several genres and historical periods and shows admiration for the Western classics. In addition to French realists such as Balzac and Zola, he admires Shakespeare, Shelley, and the realists Charlotte Brontë and Charles Dickens.

The fact that Marx admired these works is very relevant to understanding Aguirre's position. Marx commended realism for its depiction of social conditions, but he also praised the elaborate metaphors and rhetorical word play of Shelley and Shakespeare. Aguirre, on the contrary, rejects formal complexity on the grounds that it obscures ideas: "La metáfora, el tropo, el lenguaje figurado, en literatura o en cualquier arte, valen como instrumentos de comunicación. Cuando se convierten en verdaderos enigmas no facilitan ya la comprensión sino que, por el contrario, hacen oscuro lo que por lo general podría ser dicho con claridad; y lo que es más, al obligar a inútiles ejercicios descifradores niegan su propia naturaleza [The metaphor, the trope, and figurative language, in literature or in any art form, are valuable as tools of communication. When they become true enigmas, they no longer facilitate comprehension but rather, on the contrary, obscure what could in general be said clearly; furthermore, by requiring pointless exercises in code-breaking, they deny literature's very nature]" (Aguirre 2006, 50).

Unlike Marx, Aguirre rejects Balzac and nineteenth-century realism in general for its idealism:

> Pero hasta la aparición del materialismo dialéctico en el siglo pasado y, más aún, hasta su histórico triunfo práctico en este siglo, el arte—inclusive el realista—había reflejado el mundo metafísicamente, en estática; o había "inventado" el mundo en forma fantástica. . . . En los casos mejores, como el de Balzac, formidables observaciones realistas debidas al método, se maridaban con utópicas, fatalistas, reaccionarias conclusiones debidas al sistema de ideas del autor. Gracias a Marx, la filosofía . . . comprendió que había que explicarlo [el mundo] de otro modo y que, además, se planteaba a ella el deber de impulsar, por todos los caminos, su transformación.
>
> [Until the appearance of dialectical materialism in the last century, however, and especially until its practical historical triumph in this century, art (including realist art) had reflected the world metaphysically, statically; or it had "invented" the world fantasti-

> cally. . . . In the best cases like that of Balzac, wonderful realist observations resulting from the method were paired with utopian, fatalistic, and reactionary conclusions resulting from the author's system of ideas. Thanks to Marx, philosophy . . . understood that it had to explain [the world] in another way and that, furthermore, it was up to philosophy to drive, by all means, the world's transformation.] (Aguirre 2006, 55)

Whereas Marx and Engels applaud Balzac for transcending his class and creating ideological alliances with the proletariat, Aguirre sees Marx's epistemological system as key to unveil the flaws of idealist writers such as Balzac.

But Aguirre is intent on showing that socialist realism is not dull. Given the poor ideological and aesthetic reputation of Soviet-style realism, and given that she supports socialist realism's ideology, her only convincing argument rests in aesthetics. Her criticism of formal complexity notwithstanding, she therefore insists that Cuban socialist realism could borrow sophisticated formal techniques: "Lo mismo que existe un romanticismo bien llevado con el realismo socialista, puede existir un impresionismo—u otra cosa—que le sea útil. Las diferencias de enfoque ideológico no constituyen un obstáculo insuperable para la apropiación de técnicas o rasgos estilísticos [Just as there exists a romanticism that pairs well with socialist realism, there can exist an impressionism—or any other thing that might be useful to [socialist realism]. The differences in ideological focus are not insuperable obstacles to the appropriation of stylistic techniques and traits]" (ibid., 65). Her lengthy discussion of style weakens her point that form matters less than content, and reveals the internal contradictions of her argument, which could be summarized as follows: Art is essentially defined by its beauty, but it must be ideologically useful and clear, and socialist realism is the best poetics for that purpose. Since form and content do not determine each other, socialist realism could be as stylistically diverse as any other form. Style, however, is always ideologically determined, thus any stylistic form coming from a European tradition of philosophical idealism cannot be considered a "useful type of realism." What seems like an open-minded way to conceive of socialist realism in fact contradicts one of her premises. If form matters less than content, and does not determine it, why would she discuss it at such length? She does because this argumentation allows her to defend the regime's ideology as nondogmatic. This is why, in her discussion of the political potential of different historical artistic movements, Aguirre defends Cuban socialist realism, while simultaneously frowning on the Western realist tradition for its idealism. The difference between socialist realism and classical realism is that the former seeks a transformation of reality, whereas the latter is still determined by idealism: "Hay que tener presente que todas las maneras, desde Homero hasta nuestros días, sin excluir el realismo crítico del XIX, el naturalismo, el objetivismo y todo el realismo no socialista del presente siglo, son abierta o subrepticiamente idealistas y están determinadas o influidas por el idealismo [We must bear in mind that all styles, from Homer to our day, including the critical realism of the nineteenth century, naturalism, objectivism, and all the nonsocialist realism of the present century, are openly or surreptitiously idealist and determined by idealism]" (ibid., 54). By assuming that only socialist realism can produce a materialist explanation of reality, Aguirre contradicts herself. First, by positing style as a historically determined form, she forecloses the possibility of borrowing from artistic forms that come from a tradition of philosophical idealism. Second, and in opposition to what the essay claims, Aguirre acknowledges form as a primary component of ideology. In other words, her lengthy discussion of form reveals the latter's importance in conveying meaning, her previous statements notwithstanding.

But, although Aguirre criticizes past realisms for their idealist roots, she is simultaneously willing to accept formal techniques that, like impressionism, have been conceived within equally idealist societies. In addition, if, as she has previously stated, the two philosophies are absolutely incompatible ("no hay conciliación posible entre el materialismo dialéctico y el idealism [there is no possible reconciliation of dialectical materialism and idealism]" (ibid., 60), how can idealist aesthetics be suitable for socialist realism? Aguirre claims that romanticism and other styles can lend their techniques to realism even if their ideological stances are different. This is because, according to her, form and content are independent of each other. What, then, is the function of form in art? If art needs clarity, why would impressionist techniques serve a purpose for realism? If form is meaningless, what is its purpose? If any form can articulate different ideas, why does realism have to be the style best suited to dialectical materialism? Does this not indicate that form and content are related? The question then is, Is Aguirre really accepting a manifold way to conceive of socialist realism, or is she just petrifying it much more than she is willing to admit?

Following Marx, Aguirre conceives of knowledge as a truth of metaphysical and teleological characteristics. She posits realism, and more specifically socialist realism, to be the bearer of that truth. And she also acknowledges realism as a rhetoric that can be complemented by other formal techniques. Unlike Aguirre, however, Marx posits style as a personal idiosyncrasy. When writing about censorship, Marx describes truth in a Platonic way as the truth or Idea that transcends our perception of it. In his view, however, truth is not determined by form or subordinated by it. In other words, expression is not subordinated to realism as the socialist poetics par excellence: "Further, truth is general, it does not belong to me alone, it belongs to all, it owns me, I do not own it. My property is *form*, it is my spiritual individuality. *The style is the man*. And how! The law allows me to write, but on the condition that I write in a style other than my own, I have the right to show the face of my spirit, but I must first set in the *prescribed expression*!" (Marx and Engels 1947, 60).[29]

Interestingly enough, however, Marx also argues in different works that form and content are indivisible. The relationship between content and form is thus unlike the one between money and value. The value of money fluctuates, changing the nature or essence of the commodity. Language, however, does not change the essence of an idea:

> To compare money with language is not less erroneous. Language does not transform ideas, so that the peculiarity of ideas is dissolved and their social character runs alongside them as a separate entity, like prices alongside commodities. Ideas do not exist separately from language. Ideas which have first to be translated out of their mother tongue into a foreign language in order to circulate, in order to become exchangeable, offer a somewhat better analogy; but the analogy then lies not in language, but in the foreignness of language. (Marx 1973, 162–63)

In other words, for Marx, an idea can be expressed in different styles, but the style does not change the idea. Aguirre, in contrast, conceives of form as a fluctuating value capable of transforming the idea that it articulates. Paradoxically, as we will see, this conception of style leads her to embrace idealism.

Idealism and Materialism

Aguirre's criticism of idealism evidently stems from the Marxian critique of German idealism. In this context, idealism is understood in a broad Kantian way, as an epistemology whereby thought or concepts define objects, and not one where objects define thought. As is well known, Kantian epistemology seeks to explain how we make rational sense of the empirical world. Kant by no means holds the premise that the world is not real, but he argues that in order to understand it, we have to presuppose a transcendental consciousness uniting our intuitions and perceptions. Generally speaking, Kant's ultimate philosophical objective is to link epistemology (the understanding of reality) and reason (an ethical praxis whose goal is freedom). Marxist theory is partly based on the rebuttal of German idealism's response to bridging these two faculties (understanding of the world and reason). What Marx and Lenin criticize—addressing Hegelian philosophies in particular—is twofold. On the one hand, they oppose the Kantian epistemological premises of idealism. On the other hand, in Marxism the unifying principle is praxis, rather than theory as in idealism. For Johann Gottlieb Fichte, for example, this unifying principle is the subject and his self-consciousness to reach freedom. For Marx, in contrast, "the nature of individuals [thus] depends on the material conditions determining their production," and only through praxis can they attain freedom (Marx and Engels 1999, 42).

In 1980, and in commemoration of the Second Congress of the Cuban Communist Party, Aguirre edited *Poesía social cubana*. Although not exactly an anthology, the book is a selection of political or civil poems that begins with José Martí and concludes with Ángel Escobar. The book opens with Martí's poetry because, per official history, he represents the degree zero of the Cuban revolutionary process. This and the introduction set the book's patriotic tone. A year before, Aguirre published *Dice la palma: poesía*. Although thematically and ideologically similar, the first book was less ambitious in scope and only included poetry from 1959 through 1977, which is the period that concerns us. These are epic war poems that celebrate the victory of the revolutionary rebels while mourning the loss of heroic lives in combat. They are conversationalist poems, the decade's prevailing style, which as its name indicates, imitates prosaic language. As we have seen, clarity of expression is a necessary condition of social poetry, but not the only one. Elegiac in tone, these poems perform a laudatory function rather than a social one. The question, then, is how to consider these poems from a stylistic and an ideological point of view. Do they conform to the requirements of socialist realism, or are they elegies rather than social poems? This is an important question to consider given Aguirre's ideological agenda and the crucial political role of literature. The exaltation of heroism and the celebration of war victories common in social poems had been a subject of controversy among intellectuals. Whereas some thought that the distance between the hero and the people could inspire the latter, others argued that people could not identify with figures so romanticized. Julio García Espinosa, for example, expresses his doubts about the pedagogical function of these idealized versions of war: "Hace poco se hablaba en una reunión del papel del héroe positivo en las películas socialistas. Nosotros pensábamos en el daño que la mayoría de esas películas han hecho a los verdaderos héroes positivos. ¿Puede plantearse como una dominante en la expresión artística la exaltación del héroe positivo con el cual apenas puede identificarse el hombre común, el hombre lleno de contradicciones? ¿Ayuda más a la evolución de este hombre de todos los días la contemplación pasiva del ejemplo excepcional, ejemplo incluso que puede aplaudir pero como algo que le es ajeno? [Not long ago we were talking in a meeting about the role of the positive hero in socialist films. We were thinking of the damage that most of these films have done to true positive heroes. Should we have as a dominant trend in artistic expression the exaltation of a positive hero with whom the common man, full of contradictions, can scarcely identify? Is the evolution of this day-to-day man further advanced by the passive contemplation of the exceptional example, one he might even applaud but that is foreign to him?]" (García Espinosa 2006, 12).

What is of interest for our argument, however, is that, whether they are heroic or not, pedagogy was the mission of all these poems. In that regard, they conformed with the rules of socialist realism. As an example, let us reconsider "Himno a las milicias," Baragaño's poem written in 1961, a year before his death (Baragaño 1979, 14–17). It is one of the most obscure poems of the book, as the metaphors refer indistinctly to language and war.

Like many of the other poems in the collection, "Himno a las milicias" is a patriotic celebration of warfare and above all a reflection on the relationship between praxis (warfare) and pedagogy (poetry). How can art imitate warfare? Or, how can poetry, like warfare, perform a revolutionary action leading to freedom? Writing is key in this poem, which begins with its personalization: "Escribo: / Muerdo la soga gris de la palabra / . . . / Sepan los condenados y recuerden / El hombre no es un adjetivo / En el lenguaje de la guerra"[30] (ibid., 14). In this poem, language is personified, and also about to die as it is strangled by the writer's hand. War also has a vocabulary, which is precisely the theme of the poem. That is, these verses explain the meaning of war in the rest of the poem. The subject of this war is the soldier, but the function that the poem emphasizes is not so much his power to kill as his duty to die. Both language and men must endure a sacrifice: "En nuestro cuerpo a cuerpo / Con esta muerte de hombre / Con nuestra nada dilatada hacia la gloria / La herramienta verde de la vida / No es la pala que abate la hojarasca. / Del enemigo ahogado en su sangre podrida / En sus cuarenta y ocho estrellas de vómito / Nuestras palabras son como nuestras herramientas / No son del futuro son el futuro."[31]

The death of the soldier is also his rebirth and the rebirth of language. But language ceases being a word, and it becomes an action of the people. Does this idea mean that idealism is being replaced by materialism? If we follow the logic of socialist realism, the idealist representation of creation becomes a materialist event in which the Christian idea of creation disappears. Christianity, one of the idealist doctrines par excellence, posits a transcendental idea of creation as the result of a divine power that predicates its own existence: "In the beginning was the Word, and the Word was with God, and the Word was God" (John 1:1). In opposition to this idea, the poem proposes a materialist ontology based on the immanent relationship between work as creation and the people as creators. This is why the poetic voice transforms Protagoras's famous dictum, "Man is the measure of all things" into "El pueblo es la medida de todas las cosas" "The people are the measure of all things." In other words, the people create the world by transforming nature. But the poetic voice advises the reader not to confuse the people with the masses: "No la masa no es un nudo de insectos."[32] Instead, they are the word, the creator, and its creation: "Un límite del hombre su palabra"[33] (Baragaño 1979, 16). That is, the people exist through their work and are transformed by it, because work is their means of expression, "su palabra."

In the poem, nature takes on a new signifier. It is represented by the hero and the people, because they create it with their deaths. Every time a hero dies, he comes to life again by transforming nature. Men transform nature with their work and their lives:

> No la masa no es un nudo de insectos
> Ni la calzada negra de los grandes
> Es una aurora violenta
> Un árbol de alas y banderas
> Un límite del hombre su palabra
> Tendido arco de esperanzas
> Árbol para que el que no hay tempestad
> Siempre verde
> Mezclando la tierra con la sangre.[34] (Baragaño 1979, 16)

This material act of transformation takes on a metaphorical quality through the blood that drenches the soil: "mezclando la tierra con la sangre." This act transforms nature, which becomes a fatherland. This is how men engender the fatherland that will in turn "father" them. Unlike in idealism, in materialism there is a dialectical relation of transformation between the creator and creation as they feed each other. As in idealism, however, this process culminates by reaching freedom. Revolutionary men attain freedom when they become one with the people by conquering nature. The people transform nature with their work, and the revolutionaries give their lives to conquer the land in the name of the people, and then become one with it. This is how the fatherland rises and freedom is attained: "Miliciano del alma / No hay muerte para ti . . . / Tu mano arranca la cabellera del enemigo / Hace ceder su puesto / . . . / Avanza / Como un contingente de estrellas jóvenes / Traza las líneas de la mano / Del sueño de los hombres / Y articula el lenguaje profundo de los pobres en un tiempo de gloria"[35] (Baragaño 1979, 16). Thus, in both instances, the process of transformation has a goal to attain. In the Christian doctrine, men have to attain moral perfection to be free of sin, and in materialism men have to attain freedom by becoming one with nature.

The poetic voice thus indicates that only death and sacrifice lead to the making of the fatherland. War and work are acts of creation, whose goal is to reach freedom: the Idea. In other words, there exists a divinity of sorts, made up of the hero and the people, that is immanent instead of transcendental. In the poem, war and work are the Idea or the Christian Word that finally frees the people: "No tengo más grado que mi pluma / Y mi arma / Canto contigo miliciano / Me disuelvo en guerrillas batallones / Renaciendo mis sangres mutiladas / En un mañana verde mi mañana"[36] (Baragaño 1979, 17). The word coincides with the people and the Revolution; there is an absolute identity between áll of them, which is why the poem is written with a metaphysical vision imbricated in idealism. In other words, as Ernesto Laclau argues, the correspondence between the thing and the idea is objective thought for idealists. "Idealism, in its sense of opposition to materialism and not to realism, is the affirmation that they do not exist objects external to the mind, but rather that the innermost nature of these objects is identical to that of the mind—that is to say ultimately thought. (Not thought of individual minds, of course; not even of a transcendent God, but objective thought)" (Laclau 1990, 106). The word is prior to all creation; it is the divine and eternal creator of the world. That is, most of the poems in this collection follow a realist style grounded on idealism, which is, paradoxically, antithetical to the realism that Aguirre defends in her essay.

Conclusion

In this chapter I have looked at sixties revolutionary imaginary, specifically as it pertains to the subjectivity of war and intellectual heroes (Guevara's New Man). This trope functions as a signifier at three different levels that determine each other: as national subjectivity of Cubanness (heroism and violence), as a rhetorical ethos (socialist realism and melodrama), and as a form of affect (melancholy). Far from setting the conditions of possibility for the development of citizenship, the rhetoric of violence and heroism imposes a revolutionary subjectivity grounded on an onto-theological metaphysics. That is, it replicates a Christian model of subjectivity. As a divine force, the revolution creates the word and the man, he who is predetermined to follow a path of salvation to regain the fatherland. Fanon's model of self-recognition supports this idea because the colonized subject never becomes really free. He is destined to always depend on the recognition that comes from the other. This dependence on the other is partly what determines the melancholic condition of the Guevarian New Man. Intellectuals must negate their own egos to be independent and become the New Men. Their ego simultaneously becomes an object of desire they will be unable to reach and the hated object they want to negate. The tropology of the New Man haunts all future cultural production, especially for intellectuals who, as Guevara observes, were born and formed within the revolution.

From a rhetorical point of view, this dilemma resurfaces again as the debate between idealism (bourgeois culture) and materialism (socialist culture). What is ultimately at stake in this dispute between idealism and materialism, however, is actually the question of nationalism. It is Martí's problem that resurfaces anew. Is it possible to create a Latin American (Cuban) identity while acknowledging the European heritage? Martí yearned for a model of identity that could combine the European, African, and indigenous influences on the Cuban heritage: "El genio hubiera estado en hermanar con la claridad del corazón y con el atrevimiento de los fundadores, la vincha y la toga [True genius would have laid in pairing (*hermanar*), with clarity of heart and the daring of our founders, the headband and the toga]" (Martí 1997, 41). Socialist realism, on the contrary, is a philosophy that rejects the European heritage on the grounds of its capitalist origins. The stereotyped hero becomes the model of Cubanness, for reasons that are clear. To avoid cultural or psychological complexity, Cuban socialist realism reverted to the typology of heroes from classical literature. These intellectuals wanted to create particularism (revolutionary Cubanness), yet they actually reverted to the universalism of Western heroic literature. Like the Western literature they rejected, their types were grounded in idealism.

As Guevara saw it, intellectuals who have a bourgeois literary background are sinners and must atone by negating their egos. This lack of life or subjectivity is precisely what we see in the cultural production of the time. That is, the characters portrayed in the works that we have studied are Manichean representations of good and evil and incarnations of moral vices or virtues rather than complex subjectivities. Their melodramatic representation is an attempt to attract a popular readership or audience. Most important, however, it marks the end of the sacred symbolized by the values of the Church and the old regime. Drawing a parallel with the French Revolution, we can argue with Peter Brooks that the traditional truth values and ethics get thrown into question. This "dissolution of a hierarchically cohesive society" brings with it "the invalidation of literary forms" (Brooks 1976, 60). The old values have lost their validity, and the new regime is eager to establish the new set of truths and ethics. These two factors explain the use of melodrama, a style that can both articulate clear and simple truth values and speak to larger audiences. The consequence of this, however, was an aesthetization of politics. Armed struggle was both aestheticized and stylized. As a result, the political was "culturized." In other words, it was not that culture became political, as one would expect, but that politics became cultural. The theoretical foundations of revolutionary epic poetry are also a product of the aesthetization of poetry. They are perfunctory litanies to the soldiers that do not articulate a Lukácsian conception of art. In other words, these poems do not convey any ideas for a utopian configuration of society. In this regard, their scope is idealist in nature since the political and the aesthetic are one and the same.

In his short poem "Arte poética 1974," Roque Dalton defines the aesthetics of the revolutionary poet: "Poesía / Perdóname por haberte ayudado a comprender / que no estás hecha sólo de palabras"[37] (Dalton 1978, 34). The poem begins as a contradiction. That is, the poetic voice apologizes (to a personalized poetics) for having helped to unveil a truth. By thematizing praxis and art, the poem alludes to the main paradox of social poetry. Namely, how can social poetry create praxis as a real political transformation? For Dalton there is only one possible answer to this conundrum: the creation of a poetics that can sustain such contradiction. That is, a poetry that can represent reality and show the limits of language to apprehend reality. This could seem like an essentialist gesture because Dalton is indicating that poetry has a residue that resists language. In other words, one could think that he is defining poetry as a genre with a unique ineffable core. Yet, this is not the case, because of the contradictory gesture that the poem performs. On the one hand, the poem is mourning the death of a belief, and on the other hand, it is celebrating it. What exactly is the poem mourning? The poetic voice is mourning the end of realist poetry. That is, a poetry able to apprehend objective reality and the truth. The poem mourns because the consequences of this disappearance could also lead to the end of poetry. If poetry cannot represent reality in its entirety, what purpose does it serve? Yet, at the same time, the poem offers a gift: some unsolicited help. This gift appears in the form of an opening, which is represented by a grammatically negative affirmation: "que no estás hecha sólo de palabras." In other words, negativity (the possibility of death) is also an affirmation of life, one indicated by the last word of the poem: "palabras." That is, the negation of a realist poetics does not result in the end of poetry. On the contrary, it reaffirms poetry's potentiality as the words (*palabras*) that are yet to come. This word is not pointing to the limits of language to apprehend reality. It is, rather, opening up to the possibility of an aesthetics that can combine the sublime (revolutionary zeal) with the profane (critical thought about the real conditions). This "word" to come did not have to negate its own recurrent trajectory. Instead, it had to resist the impending force of dogma.

2

Violence and Melancholia in the Eighties and Nineties

As we saw in chapter 1, melancholia and violence were the affective and ideological legacies of the sixties' revolutionary rhetoric. In the first part of this chapter, I show how I understand the melancholic poetics of the eighties by analyzing the work of different authors, including Pedro Marqués de Armas, Antonio José Ponte (especially his short story "Un arte de hacer ruinas"), Emilio García Montiel, and Juan Carlos Flores. In the second part, I introduce the Diáspora(s) iconoclast group and its samizdat *Diáspora(s)*, and demonstrate their relationship to the recurrent theme of violence. I argue that violence is one of Diáspora(s)'s main themes, and that it offers a critique of sixties rhetoric.

This chapter explores Ernesto Guevara's understanding of how revolutionary ideology can create the New Man as intellectual and soldier. The two cultural symptoms that I analyze in this chapter (melancholia and violence) are a result of this legacy and its impact on the first generation of intellectuals formed by the revolution. It is important to remember that these writers had been intellectually formed during the years of the Rectification Process, during which Guevarian ethical principles were advocated as a means to overcome economic challenges. Hence, they were the heirs of his ideas, and as the first generation free of bourgeois ideology, they also incarnated the "New Men." The intellectuals of this period were influenced by both this legacy and the end of the socialist utopia.

On February 25, 1986, during the Twenty-Seventh Congress of the Soviet Communist Party, Mikhail Gorbachev proposed a radical reform of his country's economic and political life. Thus began a long process that culminated in the fall of the Berlin Wall and the disintegration of the Soviet Union. Although the Cuban government did not welcome warmly the Soviet reform plans, this did not keep Cubans' political imaginary from doing so. In a now classic essay on the revolution's cultural and ideological politics, Desiderio Navarro underscored, like Gerardo Mosquera before him, the emergence of new critical voices among the plastic artists and writers from the youngest generation born under the revolution (Navarro 2002, 192). For a few years, the island experienced a collective euphoria directly related to the hopes created by Gorbachev's Soviet reforms and the change that these might bring to Cuba. These hopes for change also explain why the late eighties were dominated by social protest in the visual arts. Thus, for example, in 1994 at the Fifth Havana Biennial a group of artists showcased a José Martí whose ears had been transformed into the national flag. Another group had showcased a 1953 Cadillac with the motto, "Nobody gives up here." In popular music, the lyrics of new hip hop artists such as Obsesión and Papá Humbertico contested the revolution's status quo. In the social sciences and humanities, scholars expressed a growing interest in other forms of Marxism. They discussed widely the significance for Cuba of Antonio Gramsci's notion of civil society, and the Paideia Project was conceived of as a Gramscian initiative for cultural reform. Like-minded cultural forums appeared in spaces such as the Fundación Alejo Carpentier and Reina María Rodríguez's azotea.

Simultaneously, some other works whose emotional economy was not articulated by euphoria and revolt began to emerge. Other works were tainted instead by nostalgia and even melancholia. Thus, in the Fifth Havana Biennial, Kcho's installation *Regata*, showcased in the Tres Reyes del Morro Castle, was made out of old shoes, tires, skiffs, planks, corks, chocolate boxes for tourists, and candles, a myriad of objects evoking the new desire to belong to a market economy. At the same time, they also suggested the desire frustrated by disenfranchisement from this economy. This frustration was symbolized by the diaspora rafts that *Regata* invoked spectrally. In a similar manner, Fernando Pérez's *Madagascar*, one of the most interesting films of the period, pointed to a different ethos. Through metaphors of deafness and muteness, the film ominously suggested that familiarity was haunted by horror, and that the trauma affecting the fathers of the Cuban Revolution was also leaving its sons and daughters without speech. The affective economy of the country appears to be much more complex than Mosquera and Navarro have shown, and cultural critics must take into account the prevalence of nostalgia and melancholia.

This melancholic crisis also targeted the first generation of artists formed by the revolution. Since this generation had the mission to incarnate the revolutionary New Man, its works were marked by the Guevarian tropology. This generation had been educated to bear the brunt of sacrifice and to imagine new paths to utopia; an endeavor symbolically truncated by the fall of socialism. For '80s and '90s young intellectuals, the utopia that their elders had imagined was not theirs, however. Their object of desire was a very different one. But, symptomatically speaking, their generation was also a victim of the loss of the object of desire. The response to this loss was a return to the Grupo Orígenes,[1] which is what earned them the label of "postorigenistas." As I explain in chapter 3, official cultural policies also revived critical interest in Origenista poets. The official discourse on Origenismo, however, followed a very different approach. As a state practice it can be read as one of the cultural strategies of biopolitical rule, whereas in the works of young poets the return to the Grupo Orígenes typified the decade's melancholic cultural turn.[2] The young poets no longer identified with revolutionary conversationalism and were in search of a different language. Their Origenismo was part of the resistance against conversationalism, but it also had a melancholic imprint. It was a gesture to rescue a buried past, which was irretrievable by definition. This repressed history of an era became an object of desire in which contemporary poetry perceived its own reflection. For the young poets, the loss became the melancholic loss of their own being. Thus, their thought begins with an imaginary that they inherited from the Grupo Orígenes, and José Lezama Lima in particular. These intellectuals were the leading figures of the postmodern, cosmopolitan, and nonconformist turn of culture. I explain in the second part of this chapter that their works, and especially the samizdat *Diáspora(s)*, retake the notion of heroic violence and transform it into antiheroic power.

One of the works that captures this melancholic reaction most accurately is Enrique Álvarez's film *La ola* (*The Wave*, 1995). The most unsettling characteristic of this decade's cultural production is that the object of desire is never specified, and the film offers an interesting take on this. Although the film's characters and poetic voices cannot define their desire, their anxieties are always related to their lost sense of space and time. The film depicts the idle wanderings of two nameless lovers as they go through a process of self-recognition in order to deal with the void in their lives symbolically produced by the end of socialism. This very lyrical recounting of the lack of time and space symbolizes the spirit of the nineties, as an era that, José Quiroga argues in *Cuban Palimpsests*, seems to recoil from history. The film, which, according to Álvarez, was inspired by the 1994 Cuban raft exodus ("crisis de los balseros"), focuses mostly on the experience of exile, but the inquiry is more inward and psychological, rather than historical (Álvarez 2005, n.p.). Exile is represented as an experience of split desire for the outside world and a desire for permanence. The film thus thematizes the split subjectivity that results from all processes of transition.[3] In this case, this fracture is symbolized by the Platonic concept of subjects as incomplete beings who have to find their other half to recover their primal nature. The film begins and ends with two variations on this idea: "Sí, yo es otro, porque es el otro quien no puede completar [Yes, *je est un autre*, because it is the other that cannot complete itself]."[4] The fissure is ontological but fundamentally existential. That is, while the male lover in the film says he wants to stay, the female lover wants to leave. Like Lezama Lima, he travels vicariously through literature, whereas she desires a real escape. While he represents the "insilio," she represents exile. But her desire to leave is only existential, and like the waves it goes back and forth, between the future and the past. The narration of these events is interrupted by footage with a nondiegetic voiceover reciting a poem at three different moments in the film. The three poems by Origenista poets appear in the following order: first, "Oda a la joven luz" ("Ode to the Young Light") by Eliseo Diego, then "Noche insular: jardines invisibles" ("Insular Night: Invisible Gardens") by Lezama Lima, and finally Gastón Baquero's "Testamento del pez" ("The Fish's Testament"). Lezama Lima recites a fragment of his own poem in a voiceover, while simultaneously the camera shows a scene of popular dance and music taken out from fifties footage. Oddly enough, this scene and the previous one thematize light, like the poem, despite the dance's taking place

La ola (Enrique Álvarez, 1995). Woman peeking oculus.

La ola (Enrique Álvarez, 1995). Couple walking.

at night. In the previous scene the couple strolls around the ruins of the unfinished original project of the Instituto Superior de Artes (ISA) at the Universidad de las Artes de Cuba. When the woman admiring the light coming from an oculus says: "Look how lovely the light is down there," there is a cut to a scene showing the couple strolling down through the space from where the light comes.

The following cut takes us to the fifties footage as we hear Lezama Lima's "Noche insular: jardines invisibles," a poem whose verse coincidentally mentions the dancing light: "dance la luz ocultando su rostro."[5] The poem's mythological scene announces the crepuscule and the awakening of the natural and animal world that culminates in the union between gods and human beings. Following the same idea, the couple's stroll through ISA's arcades and into the light invokes the utopian possibilities of art.

La ola's recurring theme of light, a topic also present in Diego's poem, evokes the light and heat of Cuba, the eternal presence that never disappears. While Diego recites his poem, the film introduces footage of the masses as they celebrate and chant to the revolution in a scene of beaming light, which represents revolutionary fervor and utopia. According to the young man, the light that gives Cuba its identity also disturbs Cubans, not allowing them to think. But the light is also the ontological light of truth, and its incessant but unproductive search. In Diego's poem, the light also represents the Cuban nation, a reality whose permanence transcends history and time.

In Baquero's "Testamento del pez," a poem presumably inspired by the vision of a fish jumping off the water, as the author and Lezama Lima were strolling around the Malecón, the poet adopts the voice of a fish that contemplates the city (Zamora Céspedes 2002 n.p.). Baquero recites the poem in a voiceover, during a scene of a stormy sea. The footage thus progresses in a non-chronological sequence that goes from the revolutionary decades of massive revolutionary support, back to the Havana of the fifties, and finally to the city's decay during the nineties. These three events involve people and nature: light, darkness, dance, revolution, and natural destruction. They also punctuate the rhythm of the film with a tempo marked by the cycle of both, a doomed revolution and a failed Republican era, which lead to the historical catastrophe of the nation.

Breaking this cycle to introduce a notion of permanence, however, is the continued reference to light. In both poems, Lezama Lima's and Diego's, light is the force that can restore order and combat evil. As such, light symbolizes national unity and its teleological goal to reach the absolute: "Dance la luz reconciliando / al hombre con sus demonios desdeñosos. / Ambos sonrientes, diciendo / los vencimientos de la muerte universal / y la calidad tranquila de la luz"[6] (Lezama Lima 1975, 742). Light is purity; it represents lightness, truth, revelation. "En mi país la luz / . . . / La luz / en mi país resiste a la memoria . . . Y es que ciega la luz en mi país deslumbra / su propio corazón inviolable / sin saber de ganancias ni de pérdidas"[7] (Diego 1973, 351). Instead, in works from the sixties such as Humberto Arenal's *El sol a plomo*, light is associated with the burning and unbearable Cuban heat that, as the film's male protagonist complains, makes it hard to think.[8] In this regard the Grupo Orígenes represents some order, brilliance, and depth. The Orígenes's poems are about the nation's unity and grandeur, just as it is about to crumble. Likewise, in the film light is the shining object of desire that may be able to fill the empty page of young writers like the protagonist: "I know, the blank page is to blame for everything. The problem is that if you can't express yourself, you have to hide it, because nothingness is something shouldn't be seen. . . . But a blank page, it confesses this to you; it remains a mystery, an uncertainty. Desire, impossibility." This lack as well as the unachievable nature of desire must be disavowed. And yet, the light's strong presence as a discourse gives a name to that desire and a theme whose narration may save the nation. As a natural force, the light clashes with the wave, going back and forth, creating an imaginary of disarray as the couple becomes the island: "The island is ourselves."

Álvarez's intellectual generation shares a common and historical experience determined by the political and economic consequences of the collapse of Soviet socialism. While the more tangible consequences of the fall of the Eastern Bloc were economic, there is no doubt that as Odette Casamayor-Cisneros argues: "la crisis socialista, acaecida tras el derribo del Muro de Berlín en 1989, asest[ó] un duro golpe—¿mortal?—al ideal revolucionario [the socialist crisis provoked after the fall of the Berlin Wall in 1989 (was) a—mortal?—hard hit for revolutionary ideals]" (Casamayor-Cisneros 2013, 59). Yet, this historical event also symbolized the end of an impending and long awaited demise, because in Cuba, the loss of socialism as a libidinal object was not a phenomenon exclusive to the nineties. The Cuban critic Jorge Fornet claims that the emergence of postrevolutionary disenchantment among Cuban intellectuals dates back to 1968, after the death of Ernesto Guevara. Fornet, however, also differentiates between two generations: the "disenchanted" (desencantados) and the "newest" (novísimos). The disenchanted were disillusioned with the revolutionary project, yet remained loyal to utopia. The newest, instead, had lost their trust in utopia (Fornet 2001, 20–25). In a response to Fornet's article, Ambrosio Fornet contradicted his son by arguing that the last generation of writers had not lost faith in utopia (Fornet 2002, 20). Interestingly enough, in spite of their disagreements, both critics concurred that the term *disenchantment* did not refer to an emotional state, but rather to a rational understanding of history. This coincidence between the two critics speaks more than their disagreements, since it actually points to the limits of a critique whose stumbling block is the emotional aspect of ideology. That is, it is important to note the refusal to address the emotional consequences of ideological transformations, and to ask what is at stake in this refusal. Especially, because in a different context, Quiroga makes a similar denial. While referring to nineties Cuban cultural production in *Cuban Palimpsests*, he argues that "melancholia may be the most crucial element in terms of the disenchantment that haunts the survivors of a nation," but then he refuses to look at this phenomenon from a psychoanalytical perspective (Quiroga 2005, 22).

Thus, while it has become commonplace to claim that the nineties was an era of disenchantment and melancholia, there has been a reluctance to substantiate that claim with a psychoanalytical argument. Yet, I think that only by looking at this problem from a psychoanalytical perspective can we understand why scholars are talking about melancholia in the first place. Indeed, the complexity of this matter resides in the object of melancholia itself. That is, what is complicated, especially from an ideological perspective, is to be able to name the object that has provoked the emotional attachment and consecutive loss. Is that object imaginary or real? Is it historical or abstract? As I've already argued elsewhere, the main difficulty we face is that we are actually dealing with the object of desire, which is, as we know, as elusive as what produces it. Indeed, this is why this object should be studied both at historical and abstract levels. Since the triumph of the revolution in 1959, the excess of the revolution (as an object of desire) was suspended by the operations of bureaucratization and repression as immanent operations of the state. To be more precise, this excess was suspended because of the melancholic character of the revolutionary project since its inception, as I have shown in my analysis of Ernesto Guevara's "El socialismo." Thus, melancholia about the revolutionary object of desire doesn't appear in the nineties, it is, rather, ingrained in the nature of the revolutionary project itself.

The Revolutionary Legacy

Debts

Some intellectuals of the first generation of the revolution, among whom were Heberto Padilla and Guillermo Cabrera Infante, were the first to be haunted by this inherent loss that was inscribed within Guevarian thought, at the ideological basis of the Cuban Revolution. It is thus clear that the disappointment with the revolution was present throughout the revolutionary period. Yet, it's also true that, while many intellectuals lost their faith in utopian politics as a result of this, many others never lost their belief in emancipatory politics. This is actually the case with Padilla, whose collection of poems *Fuera del juego* (*Outside the Game*) still had a utopian ethos, despite their also manifesting a disappointment with the revolution. *Fuera del juego*'s "El discurso del método" ("The Discourse on the Method"), for instance, advises people to escape the island to avoid the errors caused by revolutionary reason. The poem also contests the main premise of the Cartesian cogito, which argues the epistemological dominance of reason over the senses. According to the poem, the arbitrary nature of revolutionary reason demonstrates that the Cartesian premise is false. No argument can prove that reason has primacy over the senses, nor are there arguments that can prove that revolutionary reason is arbitrary. The falseness can only be proven by the intuition of the senses: "Si después que termina el bombardeo . . . / eres capaz de imaginar que no estás viendo / lo que se va a plantar irremediablemente delante de tus ojos . . . / yo te aconsejo que corras enseguida"[9] (Padilla 1971, 11). The poem thus favors a metaphysical destabilization of reason to prove that reason should not be the only foundation of rationality and that senses should also be taken into account when establishing a revolutionary logic. The Padilla scandal notwithstanding, *Fuera del juego* belongs to a generation whose cultural production still reflected the general belief in the revolutionary project as a utopian possibility. The same was also true of the poetics of the eighties, of which Reina María Rodríguez's work is one of the best examples.[10]

"Deudas" ("Doubts"), one of the representative poems of this period, retakes the idea of the debt articulated in Roberto Fernández Retamar's conversationalist poem "El otro" ("The Other"), as I will explain below. As we will see, in "El otro" a political and historical debt to the first revolutionary heroes remains to be settled through the sacrifice of the newer generations. "Deudas," in contrast, speaks from a gendered perspective and cares not about what is owed but about what women are lacking. The poem is concerned not with political debt as much as with individual and feminine lack: "hoy quisiera escribir lo que me falta . . . / bajar a mis profundidades sola y desnuda"[11] (1982, 46). If feminine subjectivity is no longer attained through heroism, what defines it? Certainly not heroic virtues but only nondescript characteristics and possessions: "soy sencillamente fea / con pecas, sueños y dolores"[12] (ibid.). Contrary to revolutionary decorum, the pictures of the heroes that the revolution has traditionally commodified, such as Martí and Ernest Hemingway, are considered in this poem to be trivial possessions. This gesture desacralizes the two heroes. It is only at the end of the poem that feminine subjectivity asserts itself by claiming its existence through the notions of debt and life: "y muchas deudas / infinitas deudas con la vida"[13] (1982, 47). In other words, if revolutionary and masculine subjectivity can only be attained through the hero's sacrifice (death or destruction), women are claiming a nonheroic subjectivity articulated through the natural evolutionary phases of life (progress or construction). As we can see in this example, in the poetics of the eighties, the revolution, as in the case of Padilla, is still the only historical referent. The cultural and gender practices of revolutionary rhetoric need to be transformed, so subjective feminine practices will turn them upside down, the way Marx turned Hegelian dialectics on its head.

The Eighties

In the late eighties, the contradictions posed by the beginning of a new economic structure in a stagnant political realm stirred anew the question of the revolutionary ethos. How to define a revolutionary ideal according to the new times? This question was particularly pertinent for the heirs of Guevara's New Men, who were supposed to be the first truly revolutionary Cubans. The demise of real socialism also decreased Ernesto Guevara's popularity as a revolutionary ideologue. Promoted by the state as the ideological mentor of younger generations, Guevara's fallen myth would eventually leave young intellectuals fatherless. Aware of this, the state fought to keep alive the myth by bringing his mortal remains for burial to Havana in 1997.

Confronted with the ideological void left in front of them, many intellectuals clung on to the Guevarian model. After all, they had been brought up with a revolutionary ideology, and they had suffered the consequences of the sixties' utopia debacle. As Iván de la Nuez says, "They are irredeemably marked as subjects of the hammer and sickle [están irremediablemente marcados como sujetos de la hoz y el martillo]" (de la Nuez 2006, 118). They have all suffered the consequences of the sixties utopia's debacle, but only the group of young writers that this book studies has set itself the task of reflecting on this historical event. This generation engendered by an ideological ruin cannot be anything else but a ruin: "Somos más bien los infaltables infusorios, el toque final que hace caer con estrépito el ruinoso edificio. Porque el edificio es ruinoso y seguirá siéndolo, al menos durante un tiempo. [We are, rather, the inevitable microorganisms, the finishing touch that brings the ruined building crashing down. Because the building is a ruin and will remain one, at least for a while]" (Sánchez Mejías 1999, 5). If they can only conceive of language as one more ruin, this is because they still have a relationship of debt to the Guevarian New Man. They long for a word that was never given to them, and they can only speak with the forlorn language of defeat because the image of the New Man still haunts them and because they have not let go of the object of desire as utopia.

Narcissus in the Presence of the Specular Abyss

The Guevarian New Men had inherited the paternal sacrifice, as if they were the hypothetical sons of Oedipus. They had to recover their lost ego through revolutionary sacrifice. The open wounds left after the revolutionary disillusionment of the seventies, which could never heal, opened again after the fall of the Berlin Wall and the end of economic relations between the Soviet Union and Cuba. Oedipus blinds himself as punishment for not having seen the truth. Blindness becomes the only possible sacrifice that can conjure guilt and recover the loss. The melancholic tropology of the New Man imposes the restitution of the socialist utopian horizon through revolutionary sacrifice. The young intellectuals of the nineties were destined to become the Guevarian New Men, and they had to take over and continue the sacrifice for the homeland. They had inherited the paternal debt, which they had to repay. This debt is what Fernández Retamar calls "sobrevida" in "El otro," dated January 1, 1959: "Nosotros los sobrevivientes, / ¿A quiénes debemos la sobrevida? / ¿Quién se murió por mí en la ergástula, ¿Quién recibió la bala mía, / la para mí en su corazón?"[14] (1959, 385). This poem narrates the feeling of debt of those who did not have to make a sacrifice for the revolution. According to the poem, survival depends on the sacrifice of others' lives without which the revolution would not have happened. The younger generation of intellectuals from the nineties did not feel guilty for not assuming the paternal law of sacrifice. They had to expiate the paternal guilt but the sociopolitical transformations from the nineties paralyzed them. The antinomies produced by the simultaneous official will to preserve socialism and embrace capitalism produced a radical transformation in the social conscience of the new generations. The New Man's restitutive melancholy no longer made sense to them. In spite of their revolutionary education, socialist utopia was not their object of desire. On the contrary, the fall of the Berlin Wall produced a sense of loss and lack that materialized in the empty shelves of Havana's stores, but that did not point to a specific object. These intellectuals, had not lost a dream, and as a result, this loss became a loss of their own ego. The most powerful fiction of those years was not the loss of the object, but rather the loss of the self. The ego objectified itself and became irrecoverable. Like Narcissus, they lost their own sense of self-recognition as the desired Other faced them from the mirror. The thought was that they could recover their lost ego, but unlike previous generations, they did not believe in the possibility of restitution, so they accepted the loss of their own egos. The search for the self became this generation's fundamental trope.

Postorigenista Poetry

The poems I discuss in this section are examples of what, following James Buckwalter-Arias's denomination for contemporary fiction, I call postorigenista poetics.[15] They present the same symptom: a belief in the loss of the word and of memory. They also share a double debt: to the writing of José Lezama Lima, on the one hand, and to the conversationalist poetry of the seventies, on the other. Postorigenista poetics draws its complexity, furthermore, from its refusal of the limits of this double legacy and from its melancholic and obsessive fixation on the past. The works of Pedro Marqués de Armas and Juan Carlos Flores are those in which the postorigenista symptoms of post-Soviet Cuba reveal themselves with greatest intensity and pain. They also show the emotional web in which the young people of this generation found themselves caught, in both their attraction to paradigms that had led them to the search for a national identity and their desire to reject these paradigms. This is why neither of these two poets abandoned the trope of the island, behind which hid the anxiety-filled question of national identity. In this sense, I disagree with Rolando Sánchez Mejías's view that the poetics of these authors do not speak from what he calls "the Origin or the nostalgic pathos for the Island and its past" (Sánchez Mejías 1995, 7). On the contrary, Marqués de Armas and Flores display a deep concern with the quest for a reestablished memory.

Spurned Love: Memory, Dialectics, and Insularism

The most significant aspects of Nicolas Abraham and Maria Torok's analysis of melancholia are their characterization of it as an open wound and their emphasis on its paradoxical nature. The melancholic, according to Abraham and Torok, fights a merciless battle between love and death. Abraham and Torok's reading underscores something that Freud noted, but not with great emphasis. In their extreme emotional condition, melancholics are prisoners of two contradictory desires that they feel simultaneously and with the same force. Melancholics loathe the object that eludes them and that has abandoned them, but they also desire it with an absolute passion, and in fact they have never ceased desiring it.

Marqués de Armas's *Los altos manicomios* (*The Upper Asylums*) (1993) is a book on the alienation and abandonment felt by postrevolutionary men and women. It also stresses the increasingly complex alienation between the individual being and the political being. But it is above all a book about the impossibility of delineating a memory and a utopian horizon. "Habría más memoria si no asomara tanto ciervo entre láminas de humo,"[16] writes Marqués de Armas in "Monólogo de Augusto" (1993, 5), echoing these famous lines by José Martí: "Mi verso es de un verde claro / y de un carmín encendido: / mi verso es un ciervo herido / que busca en el monte amparo"[17] (Martí 2007, 307). Martí's poem draws a parallel between nature and the spiritual state, both of which appear wanting and above all painful. The poem is wounded because it cannot express national unity. Marqués de Armas's poem exhibits a desire to reconstruct a history that is mortally wounded, but not exactly by the trauma Martí describes.

Memory and the Fantasy of Its Loss

In the poems of this generation, we find a great anxiety to decipher memory, simultaneously accompanied by the impossibility of approaching the past. In Marqués de Armas's "Leda," the wife of Tyndareus and lover of Zeus also represents the mysterious and desired city of Havana before which others must metamorphose themselves, but which does not allow itself to be mastered. Like Leda, the city has been taken: "Rompo el aliento de los caballos briosos. / Rompo el pan, el ombligo."[18] And yet the poet finds himself before the inhabitants of a city that, like Leda, will not accept madness: "Temen las turbias galerías. / Temen mi alma que anilla los fulgores."[19] The poet thus withdraws, changing himself in turn into the island of forgetting: "Soy el ojo. / Acaso esta isla que piso sin memoria."[20] Cuba is an island whose memory does not exist for the youngest generations. In "Las palomas de mi madre" ("My Mother's Doves"), the poet is also a being without memory: "Entonces soy un niño y lo confundo todo / o soy un rey que olvida"[21] (1993, 15). The poet struggles between ignorance and conscious forgetting, a struggle associated with a profound sense of guilt for not having paid the debts of past mistakes. And there is no possibility of building a future because the past is an opaque zone. Marqués de Armas's work encloses itself circularly in "El avestruz y yo" ("The Ostrich and I"), a poem that reflects on the creation of historic memory. To this end, the poem deploys the tropology of the sacrifice of divine progeny. As in "Monólogo de Augusto," "El avestruz y yo" refers to the desire to flee the island and especially the desire to escape a history based on sacrifice: "Yo te lo pido, padre. / Vamos a la terraza a ver los barcos."[22] The hope remains that if flight from the island is possible, one will be able to create a different memory: "Dime si lo eterno no es un sueño—Dime si la memoria no es un dios, / el frío banco de remero, el remo roto."[23] Memory has been made into an elemental sacrifice as weighty as the Cross of Christ, which is why the historical being wonders, "¿Por qué ahora peso como la cruz que alguien puso en el poniente?"[24] The historical being cannot conceive that a new history might emerge that would make us remember everything with nostalgia: "No vuelve la canción. / No vuelve el pájaro de ozono. / Mi realidad no vuelve"[25] (ibid., 23). As in Jorge Luis Borges's *El hacedor* (*The Maker*, available in English as *The Dreamtigers*), in this poem, the poet realizes that there is no distinction between his own, subjective memory and the memory objectified by official history: "Ahora me cuesta ser el inventor de esta memoria."[26] And yet he continues to suffer at the thought that he cannot remember everything: "Cómo fugaron las primeras cosas al conocimiento"[27] (ibid., 24). This is the reason for the poem's ironic ending, in which the Maker wonders about the validity of his dream. Thus becomes obvious the confusion in Cuban historiography between utopia and the historical record, the narration of history and its possibilities. The narration of history is impossible because there is a void that cannot be filled.

This is also expressed in several poems by Antonio José Ponte, including "Antes de releer la Ilíada" ("Before Rereading the *Iliad*"), in which, through another allegory from Greek mythico-literary history, we read of the unease caused by the inability to understand the tragedy that created the need to conquer Troy: "Dientes, huesos, cenizas, sal antigua: / yo busco un signo que aclare aquella historia"[28] (1997, 39). If there is no memory, this is because a part of history has been forgotten or ignored. The poetry of this period by Marqués de Armas and Flores, together with some of the poems and essays by Ponte and José Manuel Prieto, displays this restlessness with their alienation from the past. In some cases, such as that of Ponte, the writer chooses to rewrite "another" history, as happens for example with the other history of the Grupo Orígenes, the history established in opposition to the myth of Orígenes and published under the title *El libro perdido de los origenistas* (*The Lost Book of the Origenistas*). Marqués de Armas also rewrote some important essays in which he revised the official reading of Piñera and Lezama, but it is poetry that best resists the assimilation of history. In the case of *Los altos manicomios*, this alienation prevents a relationship with the past, and thus also renders impossible a relationship with the present. The past constitutes itself as an object of desire, whose inaccessibility simultaneously limits access to the present. This creates a purely immanent situation in which what is most unreachable is also what one most longs for, and therefore in addition to being unable to attain what one desires, one also cannot distance oneself from it.[29] For Marqués de Armas, the present cannot emerge because, for this to be possible, the new historical era would have to emerge out of the spectralization of a preceding knowledge. As in the Lezamian gnoseological tradition, in Marqués de Armas's poetry it becomes obvious that new historical eras cannot be consolidated without the knowledge of preceding eras. If it could be named, this previous knowledge would remain as a site of mourning that could be resisted. If, however, the past cannot be named, the operation of mourning must be suspended. All that remains is an interminable agony caused by the open wound produced by the originary lack. Given this unnamed suffering, the fantasy of the impossibility of naming the past is created.

"La canción de Visotski" ("Vysotsky's Song"), is a poem where Emilio García Montiel, who like many of his peers studied in the USSR in the mid- to late 1980s pays homage to "Fastidious Horses," the song by Russian songwriter and poet Vladimir Vysotsky. In spite of his popularity, Vysotsky was critical of the Soviet regime, and "Fastidious Horses" is a clamor to freedom on which García Montiel's poem elaborates. In Vysotsky's poem, the horses represent a life out of control that carries the subject, and for García Montiel, the movement that impulses comes from a utopian dream that cannot be halted: "lo arrastran sus caballos/. . . . / sólo al sueño obedecen [His horses drag him/. . . . / only to dreams do they obey]" (Ponte and Fowler 56–57). To the horses led by the utopian dream, García Montiel opposes a horseman whose dream is a prosaic enjoyment of the passing moment: "su sueño/ es una hoguera al tanto de la noche [His dream/ is a bonfire up-to-date with the night]" (ibid., 57). The pace of history leads subjects through a life devoid of individual memory: "dónde está la memoria / dónde está el que va a ser y es inocente / del olvido que tramas al que fuiste / ¿será otra guerra y tú el que ya estás muerto?"[30] (ibid.).

Juan Carlos Flores's *Los pájaros escritos* is a collection of poems that also speaks out of a radical suffering that seems to be caused by the impossibility of reconciling oneself with the past. The line that gives the book its title refers to the Lezamian paradox defining writing as a force at once liberating and oppressive. A direct consequence of this idea is the creation of a means of escape that does not necessarily entail flight from the island. In "Dios y el paraíso" ("God and Paradise"), for example, we read of a world without hope because it has been abandoned by God. This world, whose inhabitants await the Apocalypse, can no longer recover the past. "Descendí a los helados túneles de la memoria / sólo una araña tejía y destejía un paño gris"[31] (Flores 1994, 52). "El ojo de la aguja" ("The Eye of the Needle") is a poem about travel, or rather about the impossibility of going through the eye of the needle—or the past—to get to a present. As in Marqués de Armas's "Monólogo de Augusto," the journey is the desired and the impossible, but also the unnecessary. In both poems history reveals itself to be implacable, as something against which it useless to struggle: "El tiempo es una larga cetrería / que hasta en la armadura del mejor caballero / deja grietas"[32] (ibid., 52). The angel in Flores's poem symbolizes the rejection and the impossibility of transmitting the legacy of the past: "El ángel era tirando para el fondo, / extraña heredad la que me dieron."[33] The poem displays an absolute disdain for those who chose to have faith in the present's course of history: "A los beatos cedo el sitio."[34] Nevertheless, Flores concludes with a hopeful force lacking in the poems of Marqués de Armas: "Yo vine para sembrar tomillos en las frentes,"[35] expressing a utopian personal mission (70). An angel also appears in "El guardián del trigal" ("The Guardian of the Cornfield"). This time the guardian angel is a mistreated being unable to fulfill his mission as messenger. The disruption between past and present makes the existence of bridges impossible: "En cada serenidad / hay un golpe anunciando la penúltima calle / Si los puentes fueran / hoy no veríamos el rostro del ángel maltratado."[36] Like "El ojo de la aguja," this poem refers to a history that becomes misery: "quienes iban a incendiar las altas torres / siguen subiendo al pedestal minucias,"[37] and the poem concludes with the same disdain for "beatos": "Yo escupo el rostro de todas las comparsas"[38] (37). In the "Apocalipsis según San Juan" ("Apocalypse of John"), in contrast, the angel is the herald who comes to bring the utopian good news (82).

The Horizon, the Black Sun, or the Utopia of the Melancholic

That in black ink my love may still shine bright.

—Shakespeare, Sonnet 65

pero en el reino de la muerte también rompe la luz.[39]

—Flores, *Los pájaros escritos*

As is well known, melancholia is a serious state of depression. For melancholics, their passion is absolutely tragic since their final destiny is clear and ineluctable. For Julia Kristeva, however, melancholia is also the Nervalian black sun. The image of the black sun can refer to a force that is luminous but also bears its own tragedy, its death.

The metaphor of the black sun attains its full force in the work of Jean Starobinski, in which the effect of melancholia appears in turn as the ink with which it extracts its reflection. The reflection of the ink is the black sun of the soul and of writing. Both reflect the same contradiction: melancholia as an at once destructive and hopeful passion. This is the same contradiction we find in the Saturnine condition of Lezama Lima's work: Kronos's merciless struggle against himself; the inclemency of time devouring creatures that he himself has conceived, as we see in the disturbing painting by Goya—the paradox of Kristeva's black sun and Starobinski's brilliant ink. For Abraham and Torok the reflection of ink is just this, the patina of the shine after which there can only be shadows, shadows or fantasies that the melancholic incorporates in order to close and encrypt the open wound, the lack. This fantasy is thus a delirium, a hallucination. But its paradoxical nature results in its being at the same time hope and death, terminus, end.

Without a past, no history can be established. If there is no memory this is because an alienation exists with respect to it. This happens as a consequence of a process of interrupted mourning that has not allowed for an adequate transition, or because official history is not part of a personal patrimony. Marqués de Armas's poem "Antígona" ("Antigone") is a reflection on the historical suffering brought about by not having been able to bury the dead in accordance with the unwritten laws of the polis. Why, for example, was it impossible to commemorate Origenismo without having to fall into officialist and nationalist exaltation? This desire to experience a different history is symbolized in the poem through the creation of an Antigone who, unlike in the myth, is described as an erotic woman. Antigone furthermore surrenders to a man's desires: "fue mío el casto pie de Antígona."[40] Antigone's eroticism, her otherness, expresses the hope of fulfilling a desire through a different writing of history. And yet this possibility is quickly extinguished: "porque ya nadie alza el cuerpo claro de un destino / blandamente cayendo en estas islas. [Because nobody raises the clear destiny's body / gently falling in these islands]" (Marqués de Armas 1993, 6). No epistemological possibilities exist that would allow us to rewrite history. Antigone cannot contravene written laws. What remains is therefore a pure, unfulfillable desire: "Hoy me he tendido entre las flores bajas. / Una y otras canción son a la noche / como un mar de Antígonas, lleno de pies desnudos, / de vagos cuerpos que avanzan hasta confundir sus ganas" (ibid.).[41] In other poems, this frustrated desire is also associated with the New Man, as in "Tu no irás a Troya" ("You won't go to Troy"). The conquest of Troy cannot cause Achilles's being to burst forth, nor will the ship anchor offshore. Nor will the New Man find his being through war: "No irás a Troya a desmentir su sombra /

Como el amor, sólo ese cuerpo gotea y se recoge y en él yaces tendido sin despertar."[42] Achilles's being will not emerge through the struggle, but the journey or flight from the island will not conclude with a promise either, since there are "mil puertas que no fugan."[43] The desire for the object exists, but the possibility of reaching it does not: "De pronto la ciudad no signa con tu fiebre / Pero no vale el amor / no vale la angustia de los días / que van sajando el alma."[44] Thus, the longing for conquest, like the desire for another future, symbolized by the arrival at another shore, remains drifting, unattainable, awaiting the promise that can fill their void. And yet this promise and this desire lack a referent; they are pure affect without specific object. Desire is as empty as a night without stars: "Esta noche sin astros / imita a mi deseo / carne de lo imposible / Esta noche yo me pregunto / cuánto pie de Antígonas / alcanzaré a besar ante mi muerte"[45] (ibid., 8). Nonetheless, in some poems desire is incarnated in the sea as in poem "II." In a clear gesture against nationalist insularism, the sea is outlined as an object of desire. This sea to which one aspires is not synonymous with conquest, as in Homer's epic: "No es el mar de Odiseo, es la extensión."[46] Nor is it the nostalgic sea of Martí: "No es el mar de Martí, es el júbilo."[47] This is a sea as symbol of the infinite: "Es el no mar huidizo, errante / Mi fuga"[48] (20). Desire is defined as the unlimited and the pleasurable—as the vast and jubilant sea—and yet it represents the most absolute suffering as in "II (Variante de Antígona o El cuadrado amarillo)" ("II [Antigone's Variation or the Yellow Square]"): "Cuánto mar de pies desnudos / cuánto de cuerpo o bruma / hacia otro límite imparable / y acabado como el deseo / La angustia es el deseo. / Es la mujer que se abre por la herida, / —lo que no alcanza el deseo / mientras me ocultan a los ojos / el cuadrado amarillo"[49] (21). In these lines reminiscent of Luis Cernuda, desire is defined as what cannot be satisfied, and what therefore can only be suffering. "La paradoja lamentable / A su regla otra vez te pliega: 'Conocer lo que no conoce / Desear lo que no desea' "[50] (Cernuda 1993, 543). As for Cernuda, the object of desire is always absent because by definition the lack can never be filled. This is the great paradox of desire, and, as a result, the final refusal of any approach to a utopia.

Flores's poem "Naturaleza muerta con albatros" ("Still Life with Albatross") clearly evokes Julián del Casal's poem "Nostalgias," in turn influenced by Charles Baudelaire's "L'Albratros" and "L'Invitation au voyage." The poem refers to a still life depicting birds that are as dead as everything surrounding them. It thus alludes sardonically to insularity as a myth of national identity. In this way it ironizes on the appearance of still lifes that exotic islands take on in certain orientalist poets such as Rimbaud, Casal, or Baudelaire. Thus, instead of appearing as a liberating paradise, the exotic island to which Casal would escape becomes in Flores's poem an apocalyptic place: "He visto a la ciudad quemada y a los cuerpos / quemándose / eran desiertos los pechos, eran cisternas las bocas / de acordeones"[51] (Flores 1994, 22). The island is demystified and ceases to be an exotic landscape symbolizing flight. The insularist utopia is now a dystopia. Like Marcabru, the Provençal troubadour whom he claims as a literary ancestor, Flores refuses to approve and venerate the feats of recent history. Flores denounces the feats of history in an enigmatic and metaphysical poetry that could easily be compared to Marcabru's *trovar clus*: "Escribo estas ponzoñas y es como si llevara / pleamares a una ermita / Pero soy el escollo, eunuco si queréis y no lo que / se suponía / no el cantor de ferias, el que reparte el vino y recibe / otras monedas"[52] (ibid., 22). One also finds here a critique of the revolutionary utopia. Desperation arises from a vision of history's contradictions, as in "Defensa del olvido" ("Oblivion's Defense"), where those who fought for the coming of the utopia know that utopias also become ominous nightmares: "Los que vieron al pez en la terraza / ya vieron un oasis en medio de la guerra"[53] (ibid., 81).

In spite of everything, Flores appears to lament the lack of a new Messiah, an absence that leads to the truncating of words: "labios míos, puertas del país, la lengua no es un lago / es como un cepo / porque nos falta el grande, el curador."[54] Asking to be protected by the mother or the nation is like asking to die, so the paternalist figure of a redeemer is rejected. Like Marqués de Armas's sea, the open ocean appears here as an allegory of utopia: "Ayer, mientras recogía guijarros en la playa vi / a dos aves / ardiendo, el polen del mar en sus pupilas"[55] (Flores 1994, 7). As in Ponte's poems, ruins also speak to us of an object of desire: "Un barco. Un barco. Límites / Ciudades que se nombran con el mismo amor / con que se nombran las ruinas en la infancia / No sólo queda quien mira el fin"[56] (ibid., 39). Unlike for other poets of his generation and for Julián del Casal's "Nostalgias," for Flores exile and travel are not thematized as a horizon, or as a desire. Instead, his work proposes the agonistic experience of the limit as a source of knowledge: "No es partir sino tañer el agua con que aliviar / los límites, tañerla para que el fiel se alce y haga un nido / en la madera."[57] On the one hand, "Naturaleza muerta con albatros" is a clear critique of Casal's exoticism. The Casalian paradises are places ravaged by war, and in that regard they are no different than the place inhabited by the poetic voice. On the other hand, the city in ruins also evokes the crisis of the subject, which is why the poem says that the differences between exteriority and interiority have collapsed: "¿Te has detenido tú, entre el bullicio de las puertas / que ya no significan nada, no has borrado el afuera / y comprobado la ausencia de esos pájaros?"[58] (23). The power of the subject does not reside in movement or escape, but in his ability to experience the uneasy and painful space of the lack. There's no outside to this immanent structure, but the poetic voice does not choose annihilation, instead it offers the movement of a "mano de ovillo" (skein's hand), which is the paradoxical movement that can be found in the action of recoiling: "El movimiento de mi mano de ovillo tiene la belleza/ que no tiene el movimiento de la mano hacia la sien" (ibid.)[59]

In Flores's poetry utopia is ultimately incarnated in the word, in the poetic substance, as we see in the final stage of Lezama Lima's work. Flores's poem "Idea de la poesía" ("Idea of Poetry"), evokes Lezama Lima's reflection on the Saturnine or melancholic quality of poetry: "La poesía en el duermevela / como el ave de la resurrección / a cada instante nace, se aniquila."[60] He also repeats the vanguardist idea of the transformative dialectic between poetry and reality: "La libertad, timón hacia la poesía / la poesía, timón hacia la libertad"[61] (Flores 1994, 57). This idea recurs in "Destino de la ninfa" ("Fate of the Nymph"), a poem in homage to Garcilaso de la Vega that establishes a parallel between the aesthetic and transformative power of the sea nymph Galatea (who turned her lover into a river) and the power of poetry: "la poesía es capaz de transformar la memoria, la memoria es capaz de transformar la poesía."[62] The answers to truth are found in poetry: "Hombre, mujer, isla o coágulo que anuda el paraíso: entre líneas andamos buscando, preguntándonos"[63] (ibid., 21). Truth is not found in the transformative capacity of a politics isolated in its governmental praxis, which is why the concluding line of "Idea de la poesía" shows the death of this type of power: "El cadáver de un rey flota en el pasto"[64] (57).

Return of Melancholic Utopia amid the Ruins of Socialism in Pedro Marqués de Armas's Poetry and Antonio José Ponte's Fiction

Many poems of the nineties are formulated from a mythical story of the sort found in the Greco-Roman or biblical traditions, as in the works of Antonio José Ponte, Juan Carlos Flores, and Pedro Marqués de Armas. The allegorical form of mythical history is characteristic of the poetry of José Lezama Lima, and in the poetry of the nineties it is a way not only to circumvent censorship but also to express the need to build and imagine a different destiny for the nation. "Monólogo de Augusto" ("Augustus's Monologue") by Marqués de Armas is an allegory based on Roman mythical history. The poem begins by evoking the reflections of Augustus as he prepares to pacify the Republic after the fall of Julius Caesar's dictatorship. This allegory about the imperial renaissance of Rome should be read on a second level as a poem about the Cuban Revolution. Like Augustus, the generation of Marqués de Armas is the heir of the ruling class. Not finding this function appealing, many members of this generation leave the country. This parallelism justifies the desire to travel that initiates the poem: "Aquí yo escucho el soplo de los barcos pasar y no pretendo volarme los ojos como Edipo"[65] (Marqués de Armas 1993, 5). Despite Guevara's predictions, the New Man no longer believes in revolutionary sacrifice, and his desire to leave the island has to be read as a transgression against the law of the father. Unlike the first inheritors of the revolution such as Fernández Retamar, the New Men do not feel indebted to it. These New Men, like Augustus, had the mission to create a new beginning for history, but the New Men can no longer emerge from Guevara's heroic sacrifice. That is why the New Man can only be present as a statue, such as the ones commemorating Augustus as a pacifier: "Desde los pies me alzo como estatua"[66] (ibid., 5). For the New Men, history is no longer unfolding and the Cuban Revolution has reached its end: "Veo caer el tiempo piedra a piedra: brumosa percepción es el destino que se hunde"[67] (ibid.). The New Men, like Augustus, are powerless because they face the catastrophe of history as well as an uncanny revolution. Yet the New Men, like Augustus, are also ready to fulfill their duty to pacify the Republic through a new reformist project: "todo lo que pude contra el tiempo es una hoja de laurel"[68] (ibid.). This reformist political praxis, to which the previous stanza alludes, refers to a real project undertaken by a group of Cuban intellectuals between 1986 and 1993. Marqués de Armas and Ponte were among the artists who launched the Paideia Project, which, as its name suggests, was a program of cultural action influenced by the Gramscian ideal of cultural praxis as an active social reform. One of the project's most challenging claims was that artistic practices could no longer be developed without taking into account the country's new economic and social realities that those practices represented. As I will show in the final chapter, the goal of Paideia intellectuals was to establish a dialogue with the state to fight for their artistic autonomy.

Returning to the poem, we notice that although the poet wants to attempt a reformist project within the revolution, his yearning to escape the island is even stronger. The existence of an outside symbolized by the arrival of the boats awakens a very last hope for all those who want to abandon the island: "Con vehemencia estrujaría esa hoja, pero se escucha el soplo de los barcos últimos. El horizonte es una línea, otra serpiente se abre en mil cabezas"[69] (Marqués de Armas 1993, 5). As the New Man considers leaving the island and thus taking on a new identity, the horizon soon becomes a fate rendered unattainable by the mythological monster that blocks his departure from the island. The poem tells us that there remains one alternative, since the New Man may destroy his work before it can destroy him. The poem reminds us that this is what Virgil was going to do with the *Aeneid* before Augustus decided to publish it. Thus, if we follow the allegory, Virgil could have destroyed the *Aeneid*, and the New Man could have given up on a Paideia project that could not fulfill its promise:

"Quemó Virgilio su Eneida, quemaría yo mi Roma o no tendremos el valor de Edipo que nos apunta con su báculo ciego"[70] (ibid.). As we all know, however, neither the *Aeneid* nor the Paideia project were burned, and the New Men could not alter the revolutionary course of History, since in both cases the hegemonic ideological power banned it. That is why the New Man can predict his new future in an island in turmoil, as was Rome when Augustus took power: "Arde la ciudad y estoy al centro"[71] (ibid.). Preventing the burning of the *Aeneid* helped achieve the goals of the hegemonic power that the epic poem was defending. It also helped Augustus to become the emperor who achieved the *pax romana.* Why can the New Man not burn the city and end the revolutionary dream? Because there is no outside to the ideology of the Cuban Revolution. This is why when the city burns it generates a new image replicating the old order: "Pero el humo también crece. Allá arriba dibuja una ciudad semejante"[72] (ibid.). The revolutionary order has an infinite temporality like the mythological serpent whose heads appear again every time they are severed. We thus see that the poem reveals a melancholic internal logic. In the paradigm of this logic, intellectuals still believe that the revolutionary order can transform itself ideologically from within. That is why the object of desire is the arrival of a different revolutionary order such as the one proposed by Paideia. This order would not be defined through a cultural exceptionalism in the vein of Martí, as Marqués de Armas's intertextual reference to one of his poems indicates: "Habría más memoria si no asomara tanto ciervo entre láminas de humo"[73] (ibid.). As we have already seen, the deer is a reference to one of Martí's most famous poems: "Mi verso es de un verde claro y de un carmín encendido: / Mi verso es un ciervo herido / Que busca en el monte amparo"[74] (Martí, 2007, 307). In Martí, national identity is defined through the fantasy of an original materiality. Marqués's poem refers ironically to this ideological Cuban history to show how it prevents the emergence of a historical memory. For Marqués, the new era emerging with a different historical sense is symbolized by the arrival of the other deer: "Tras las huecas cañas otean otros ciervos, avanzan presurosos como las llamas por la noche"[75] (Marqués de Armas 1993, 5). This desire closes the poem, however, as a fantasy for restitution of the lost object, which is also a different revolutionary order amid the Cuban Revolution of the present: "En mis manos una hoja de laurel"[76] (ibid.). As we know, Lacan argues that desire only exists as a lack, and Abraham and Torok characterize this lack as an open wound. Melancholics, according to Abraham and Torok, tend to close this wound by incorporating a fantasy (Abraham and Torok 1994, 135). The delirium thus translates into the notion that the lack, the void, can only be avoided by holding on to the lost object: the revolutionary order, which is symbolized by the bay leaf that Augustus holds as the city burns. This fantasy is of the possibility of changing the revolution from within, as the Paideia project endeavored to do. The poem's rhetorical choices also tell us that one of the goals of Marqués de Armas's poetry is to recover and reuse the Lezamian metaphor. After the silencing of Lezama Lima's works during the seventies and the hegemony of conversationalist poetry, many works of poetry revived Lezamian baroque style.[77] The dense Lezamian metaphors allowed these works to acquire a philosophical and spiritual depth that the conversationalist poetry lacked. This stylistic choice meant two things. On the one hand, it indicated that the New Man was no longer willing to sacrifice his future for the revolution. On the other hand, it implied that the New Man, like Fernández Retamar's Caliban, was going to use the revolutionary language of his masters to fight against them. In the poem it becomes clear that Marqués de Armas's style both points to these two goals and, simultaneously, reveals a lack that the New Man cannot confront. It is "the void" that appears after the destruction of the city and its infinite replica: "Entre ambas está el vacío y los cuerpos que giran sin tocar la sal"[78] (Marqués de Armas 1993, 5). The only thing left is a void, the horror, and there is nothing worse than approaching a (w) hole. This void is there to show that the poem still longs for a melancholic restitution of the past symbolized by a Lezamian approach to the revolution from within the revolution itself. The New Man is left with a history that is a fantasy and with a void he dares not approach. This (w)hole symbolizes the absence of the New Man's own language. No longer wanting to be Caliban, the New Man needs to find his own voice.

A similar uncanny reproduction of the lost object occurs in Ponte's fantastic short story "Un arte de hacer ruinas" ("An Art of Making Ruins"). This Borgesian story narrates a conspiracy in present-day Havana, but in allegorical terms it is a story about memory. The story explores one of Ponte's most recurrent and Benjaminian metaphors, the representation of history and memory through architectural spaces. In this case, the story addresses the architectural decay of Havana, as well as the social problem created by the lack of housing, with the consequent need to build new living spaces. As I will explain, these two opposing forces—destruction and construction—are the two key concepts on which the allegorical meaning of the story is deployed. More specifically, the story uses the *barbacoa* as a spatial metaphor, because it conveys both ideas in a paradoxical manner, as we shall see. *Barbacoas* have become a very typical way to cope with the housing problem. Cubans take advantage of the high ceilings of their colonial houses to build newer rooms or *barbacoas* in the underused space of the ceilings. This means that Cubans can only solve their housing problem by contributing to the decay of the city and the destruction of its buildings. This is the paradox that the narrative will emphasize by creating a plot where two professors and a doctoral candidate in civil engineering are caught up in a conspiracy imagined by evil creatures, the *tugures*, who plan to destroy all the buildings in the city. *Tugures* are fictional characters whose name comes from the word *tugurio*, which in Spanish refers to a small, cheap place. The story takes place in an unknown time and place that the reader easily associates with contemporary Havana. Thus, in Havana, buildings are ruined by their excessive interior changes, and by urban policies that fail to plan newer constructions. In this context, *tugures* occupy buildings to turn them into ruins. *Tugures* do not intend to live in the buildings, which they ruin because their real objective is to build downward. Thus, the first allegorical level of the story has to do with construction, as I will explain below.

The story ends when the narrator finally finds his way into Tuguria, the underground city that the *tugures* have been constructing. When he reaches the entrance to Tuguria, he discovers to his horror that before him lays an exact replica of Havana. After the buildings collapse in the real city, the *tugures* rebuild them underground: "Y frente a un edificio al que faltaba una de sus paredes, comprendí que esa pared, en pie aún en el mundo de arriba, no demoraría en llegarle [And facing a building that was missing one of its walls, I understood that this wall, still standing in the world above ground, would soon arrive here]" (Ponte 2000, 39). This reproduction is indeed the only memory of the city as it used to be in the past, before buildings began collapsing, thus turning the city into a wasteland: "Sólo así . . . habría llegado a Tuguria, la ciudad hundida, donde todo se conservaba como en la memoria [Only thus . . . would I have arrived in Tuguria, the sunken city, where everything was preserved as in memory]" (ibid.). Tuguria is a boundless space, but it is also a place without exit. Tuguria is the simulacrum of the old city of Havana, and that is why it is a dead city whose uncanny appearance inspires both horror and familiarity. This mix of love and horror, recognition and alienation, produces in the narrator an infinite nostalgia.

Slavoj Žižek agrees with Graham Greene who, in *The End of the Affair*, claims that the protagonist's sorrow at the death of his wife should be less painful than his sorrow for her absence while alive. Žižek finds the protagonist's rummaging through his dead wife's belongings unrealistic. While she was still alive, the husband felt her unexplained absences, when he might imagine she was with her lover; but after death she cannot be anywhere: "Because she's always away, she's never away," Žižek writes. "You see, she's never anywhere else. She's not having lunch with anybody, she's not at a cinema with you. There's nowhere for her to be but at home" (Žižek 2001, 144). For Žižek, this episode perfectly illustrates the logic of the melancholic identification, because the object is overrepresented in its unconditional and irrecoverable loss.

This is exactly what occurs in Ponte's story, because Tuguria the city is overrepresented in its unconditional and irrecoverable loss. Tuguria and Havana are inversely proportional, and that is also how nostalgic identification works, which is why Tuguria grows at the same pace as Havana deteriorates and crumbles. Havana's decadence and the projection of its well-known disappearance augment its spiritual image. The narrative thus expresses the impossibility of getting rid of the lost object and of Havana's need to become "la ciudad hundida, donde todo se conserva como en la memoria [the sunken city, where everything was preserved as in memory] (Ponte, 2000 39). The melancholic never lost anything, because he never had it. He never possessed Havana, which explains why, through his unconditional fixation on the city, he can possess what he never had. It is only at the end of the story that the narrator understands the melancholic investment that so many Cubans—including Reina María Rodríguez, to whom the story is dedicated—have had in the revolution. All of them have been *tugures* at some point in their lives: "Entonces las circunstancias hacen de ti un tugur [So the circumstances make you into a *tugur*]" (Ponte 2000, 34). Their blind and intense belief in the revolution made them all desire the restitution of an object that they thought was lost but that never existed, as the narrator discovers at the end of the story. This explains why he suddenly recalls and understands the enigmatic meaning of the Lord Dunsany story that his grandfather used to tell him: "Mi pensamiento está muy lejos, en la soledad de Bethmoora, cuyas puertas baten en el silencio, golpean y crujen en el viento, pero nadie las oye. . . . No hay luces en sus casas, ni pisadas en sus calles. Está muerta y más allá de los montes, y yo quisiera ver de nuevo a Bethmoora pero no me atrevo [My thoughts are very far away, in the solitude of Bethmoora, whose doors swing in the silence, slam and creak in the wind, but no one hears them. . . . No lights are on in its houses, no footsteps in its streets. It is dead and beyond the hills, and I wish I could see Bethmoora again but I don't dare]" (ibid., 40). The narrator finally understands that the melancholic memory can only lead to a pathological re-creation of a revolution that was never there to begin with.

As I have indicated, the destruction of the city inaugurates the second level of the allegory. If we measure history in spatial terms, as in the story, we realize that history does not progress toward the future, since the city grows inward. Like space, history and time do not progress. They can only go in circles accreting wreckage upon wreckage. The wreckages of history pile up, arresting its course. As a result of the city's spatial extension, one can live in different ages simultaneously, among ruins each from its own historical period. The narrator tells us that because of the city's present condition, its destruction is imminent. How does one interpret the ruins of the city? In Havana, as in Benjaminian German and baroque drama, fragments superimposed upon one another to create new metaphors and meaning. The result is a whole that is more perfect in its destruction than the ruins of the past to which it refers. History slips through the interstices of the ruin, and what appears through those ruins is the decadence of history. History can come into existence only as a ruin and never as the hope for a different future.

Yet the Benjaminian city, like Havana, miraculously resists: "Una ciudad con tan pocos cimientos y que carga más de lo soportable, sólo puede explicarse por flotación . . . Estática milagrosa [A city with so few foundations and that bears more than is bearable can only be explained by floatation . . . miraculous statics]" (Ponte 2000, 30). What makes the city resist is the complex dialectics to which it is subjected: "podía entenderse como la lucha entre tugurización y estática milagrosa [It could be understood as the struggle between *tugurización* and miraculous statics]" (ibid., 31). This constant tension between these two forces is never resolved, and this is also what makes it so crucial, since what it is telling us is that any possibility for a future or a progress will be foreclosed unless our memory of history achieves this particular balance between destruction and reconstruction. In other words, although the Cuban Revolution will not be forgotten, we can no longer ask it to deliver the promise we once thought it would bring. Thus, we must listen to what the ruins are telling us about history and understand that history has been defeated. Like the Benjaminian angel of history, we cannot forget to look back at the ravages of the past when we are being pushed by the winds of progress. Yet we should not wish to inhabit the past either.

If the ruins reflect the state of history, the allegories reflect the state of language or form. We know that, according to Benjamin, "Allegories are in the realm of thought, what ruins are in the world of things" (Benjamin 1998, 178). But if the ruins of the city make us think of baroque German drama, Ponte's language does not. Ponte's metaphors are not knotty; they do not arise out of a conglomerate of diverse signifiers, as happens in the baroque prose of Lezama Lima or in "Monólogo de Augusto." Ponte's metaphors do not dwell on parody, and, in contrast to a predominant pattern characterizing his generation, his style does not convey the idea of a language that is in ruins and that reflects on its own impossibility to speak about history. On the contrary, following the Benjaminian tradition, Ponte speaks through allegory. In this sense, allegories help us understand the materiality of thought and its possibility to speak about the historical in an ontological manner, transforming things into signs. For Benjamin, the allegory is an experience of the world, but it is always a fragmentary and incomplete one. This is exactly what happens in Ponte's story, which gives us an unfinished image of what the future and the work of memory could be. The emphasis in Ponte's prose is articulated through the choice of certain signs that speak to us about the world. For Ponte, language does not evoke history through its ruins; it evokes history through its allegorical power.

The conversationalist poetry and the detective novels of the seventies best symbolize the national allegories of closure and plenitude promoted by the state. As we have seen, however, all of them are haunted by the melancholic rhetoric of the New Man. This melancholic force returns again in many of the works of the early nineties, as "Monólogo de Augusto" exemplifies. There is a substantial difference, however, between the works of the early nineties and those that preceded them. While "El otro" by Fernández Retamar demands a sacrificial act and the restitution of an imagined revolution, "Monólogo de Augusto" is an allegory about the scarcity of the revolution. Yet the poem is still anchored in a revolution that believes in its ability to reform. This fantasy is precisely what turns the scarcity into a void. In the later poetics of Marqués de Armas, we will see how this lack is articulated through a language that is in ruins and can no longer speak about history.

This void also symbolizes Cuba's ongoing historical crisis, which is reflected by the historicity's disavowal in contemporary Cuba, as I argued in the introduction. "Un arte de hacer ruinas," however, unveils the melancholic attachment to the revolution and its hopeless political results. Its allegorical nature is not an attempt to create a vicarious system to compensate for the lack of a historical totality, as was the case with much conversationalist poetry. Instead, it opens up history to a future whose condition of possibility is the remembrance of the wounds of the past. In other words, Ponte's prose tells us that history can only unravel through a process that will foster progress (expenditure or construction) through a politics of memory (scarcity or destruction). Unfortunately, the allegorical nature of Ponte's work also leads to the creation of images, such as the ruin, that like the "imago lezamiana" lend themselves to easy ideological appropriation by official state discourse and to commodification by a neoliberal world market whose machinery of production cannot survive without constantly creating desires and needs.

The Cultural History of the Eighties and Nineties

The Azotea and Proyecto Diáspora(s)

As Rojas (2009, 69) points out, in the eighties there was more room for dissent in theater, cinema, and the visual arts than in literature and thought. Films by Andrei Tarkovski or Andrzej Wajda, to name just two directors, were usually playing at the movie theater, and Desiderio Navarro's theoretical journal *Criterios* included articles by Mikhail Bakhtin and Yuri Lotman;

meanwhile, intellectuals Milan Kundera, Octavio Paz, and Michel Foucault, among others, were not published in the island (ibid., 70). But the interest in postmodern literature and theory was such that young writers exchanged books brought to the island by friends and family. This is how books by Derrida, Deleuze, Lyotard, and the like changed hands, "as if in a theoreticians' cooperative" (ibid.). Rojas's social metaphor seemingly describes the atmosphere of the azotea (rooftop), a cultural space that the poet Reina María Rodríguez created in her home in 1991. It became a bastion of intellectual independence where intellectuals discussed texts that often questioned orthodox Marxism and the national canon of Cuban literature. Rodríguez was instrumental in creating what critics have called the "cultural center of Havana" during the late eighties and nineties. It all began with Paideia in 1989, a cultural project organized by Rodríguez and other young writers. As I will show in more detail in chapter 4, Paideia was an interdisciplinary cultural project opposed to the increasing institutionalization of culture.[79]

A *salon littéraire* of sorts, the azotea emerged as Paideia began to wither, and it played a pivotal role in creating the first autonomous, vanguardist, and theoretically sophisticated generation of writers of the revolutionary period. In homage to Virginia Woolf and the Bloomsbury group, Rodríguez organized meetings every Thursday and gathered large groups of young writers at her house for readings, discussions, and lectures. The group hosted highly regarded writers such as Henri de Louis or Daniel Samoilovich (Real Arcia). During its decade of existence, the Azotea established a reputation on and off the island. Poets of that period remember it as a space of comfort that shielded intellectuals from the most difficult material conditions of the so-called Special Period. During these years, the end of economic ties with the Soviet bloc deprived the government of all its suppliers of affordable food. The resulting period of hunger affected the entire population. This explains why intellectuals in Rodríguez's circle mystified that period by understanding it as the result of their hunger. As the poet Flores has said, they experienced two types of hunger: one intellectual and the other physical (Real Arcia). Rodríguez refers to it as a period of intellectual plenitude despite the scarcity of means and food. In sum, this period has remained in their memories as the most stimulating and formative years in their careers. There is a certain nostalgia and idealization of those years that seems connected to the dwindling of the group until it eventually disintegrated, as writers began going into exile between 1995 and 1998.

In this space, Diáspora(s) read their first works and became a radical, avant-garde group regarded by many as rarefied and exclusive. Rodríguez, who was not invited in spite of her willingness, considered the project as "the doors to heaven" (Real Arcia). Diáspora(s)'s first idea was to create an interdisciplinary journal that went against the grain. They wanted to create an alternative space to official publications (*El caimán barbudo*, *La unión*, *Gaceta de Cuba*, etc.), which would not publish polemical or ideologically independent articles. To understand how the project came to fruition, it is important to recall these writers' formative years and the always complicated ties that Cuban intellectuals develop with cultural institutions. Like most writers of this generation, Diáspora(s)'s members met each other in *talleres literarios* (literary workshops) during the early eighties. The *talleres*, a key institution of revolutionary cultural policy created in 1961, were devised as a space to form future writers, who would eventually join Asociación Hermanos Saíz (AHS), and then the Unión Nacional de Escritores y Artistas Cubanos (UNEAC).[80] The *talleres* were organized by the Unión de Jóvenes Comunistas (UJC), whose role was the formation of new revolutionary intellectuals. In the late eighties, Sánchez Mejías, one of Diáspora(s)'s founding members, was a UJC member and taught classes in the *talleres literarios*. The second half of the eighties witnessed the beginning of a cultural renaissance led by all these young intellectuals. By then, Víctor Fowler and Jorge Yglesias who supported these young writers' cultural initiatives, were in charge of restructuring AHS. They realized that by increasing AHS's membership, they could also bring in new young writers and transform its ideology. At the time, AHS enjoyed support from *El Caimán Barbudo*, which in contrast did nothing to promote the *talleres literarios*.

As a result of AHS expansion, many writers from the *talleres literarios* became members of the association, which is how they began meeting each other. The state was still providing generous funding for cultural activities, and the group began taking shape. The most interesting events were organized by such poets as Ernesto Hernández Busto or Rolando Prats. This intellectual dynamism was a result of the socialization between poets, and also with ISA artists, especially Grupo Arte Calle. For example, they organized performances or disruptive impromptus, as when Arte Calle interrupted official UNEAC functions. As a result of the intellectual euphoria of those years and the opening of the Centro Cultural Alejo Carpentier in 1989, a new cultural production emerged in spite of material difficulties. The state reduced its publishing rates due to the lack of materials, but in 2000 the government passed a law to allow small independent presses in the provinces (the Sistema de Editoriales Provinciales [SEP]). These presses were very efficient thanks to "risografía," a low-cost method based on the use of Riso computers and duplicating machines. There were also more creative solutions, including the making of artisanal books. Ediciones La Azotea, created by Reina María Rodríguez, began publishing a literary journal of the same name, as well as first translations of otherwise unavailable works. The most creative and resourceful publisher was Ediciones Vigía (in Matanzas), which printed small numbers of artisanal books made from cardboard.

The publication of small books or *plaquettes* became another option, which helped emerging writers and those from smaller cities. In spite of the paper shortages and other material hardships, writers managed to publish, which says a lot about the intellectual fervor of those years.[81]

A new period of cultural dynamism began when Rodríguez opened the azotea, which became the most cutting-edge and dynamic cultural space in Havana. Intellectual gatherings were organized in a private space and without any state intervention, and poets organized performances, poetry readings, and intellectual discussions. It was then that most of these poets began to publish their first books, including Marqués de Armas's *Los altos manicomios* (*The Upper Asylums*) (1993), Flores's *Los pájaros escritos* (*The Written Birds*) (1994), Sánchez Mejías's *Derivas* (*Drifts*) (1994), Ponte's *Asiento en las ruinas* (*Seat in the Ruins*) (1997), and Carlos Alberto Aguilera's *Das Kapital* (1997).

As young authors, they had written for *El caimán barbudo*, the supplement of *Juventud rebelde* (*Rebel Youth*) and the UJC and AHS ideological platform. Most were still members of the AHS, but many wanted to distance themselves from it. The answer was the creation of an alternative journal, *Naranja dulce* (*Sweet Orange*), which became the literary supplement of *El caimán barbudo*. The editorial board consisted of young writers from the same generation: Víctor Fowler, Ernesto Hernández Busto, Omar Pérez, Luis Felipe Calvo, Emilio García Montiel, Atilio Caballero, Antonio José Ponte, and Abelardo Mena. In the words of Gerardo Fernández Fe, *Naranja dulce* was "elitist, frívola, diferente (¿alguien dijo coqueta?) [elitist, frivolous, different (did anybody say coquettish?)]"[82] The journal's interest in sexuality (not the topic for debate that it is now) caused considerable ideological controversy and condemned it to a short life. It celebrated erotica as a genre and non-heteronormative sexual behavior. One issue included articles about homosexuality and homoeroticism, heterosexuality, and erotic literature, many of which were written from a Freudian perspective.

In sum, since this generation was the children of the revolution, as Guevara proclaimed, its members wanted to reform the system from within and obtain some intellectual autonomy. As Norge Espinosa put it, "Creo que nosotros queríamos discutir la Revolución, exigirle desde la voz de los hijos que somos un reajuste que nos dejara un espacio propio, una autonomía que renovara los mecanismos de la propia Revolución [I think we wanted to discuss the Revolution, to demand from it, with the voice of its children that we are, an adjustment that would give us our own space, an autonomy that would renew the Revolution's own mechanisms]" (Cabezas 2012, 469). This was not the political position embraced by members of Proyecto Diáspora(s), who instead used official institutions as a platform for their own agenda. Aguilera, Marqués de Armas, Ricardo Pérez, Sánchez Mejías, and Rogelio

Saunders created Diáspora(s)'s group in 1993. By the time the first issue of their samizdat *Diáspora(s)* came out in 1997, they had already organized numerous cultural events (performances, talks, videos, courses, etc.) (Aguilera 2003, 7). For example, in April 1994 Aguilera gave a reading and performance of his poem "GlaSS," and in October 1994 Marqués de Armas and Sánchez Mejías read their polemical essays about Orígenes.[83] In the nineties, they began publishing their own books, mostly essays, poetry, and short stories, and they were awarded national prizes. As essayists their main subjects were the totalitarian state and Cuban national discourse. They all had many theoretical readings in common (Derrida, Foucault, Deleuze) and, in addition to Lezama Lima, they were particularly fond of Lorenzo García Vega and Virgilio Piñera, the bêtes noires of Orígenes.

The more active members of Diáspora(s) were Sánchez Mejías, Aguilera, Marqués de Armas, and Ricardo Pérez; the first three were also leading poets from that period. Like any other published Cuban writers, they had been members of AHS and then UNEAC. Sánchez Mejías had even been a UJC member. He had been in the army as a subcommander and then had become a high-ranking civil servant in the Department of Culture's National Center for Community Culture between 1987 and 1988. As a teacher in the *talleres literarios*, he was able to create a type of intellectual environment that exceeded the expectations of official institutions. As a result of ideological disagreements, Sánchez Mejías decided not to become affiliated with the Party. He nevertheless was awarded the Premio Nacional de la Crítica in 1993 and 1994. He also defied the UNEAC's ideological pressure, such as when he and other writers were ostracized for attending the "Encuentro de Estocolmo" conference, which produced the "Stockholm Declaration" on May 27, 1994.[84] During the next decade he, Aguilera, and Marqués de Armas won important literary awards and had their works published. In addition to Sánchez Mejías's Premio Nacional de la Crítica, Aguilera won the Premio Calendario de Poesía in 1996 (the beginning of his career), and Marqués de Armas received the Premio UNEAC Poesía in 2001. Given their iconoclastic views, it is not surprising that within a decade two of the three, Sánchez Mejías and Aguilera, had gone into exile, with the help of European grants.[85] Their common intellectual project nonetheless lasted until 2002. Marqués de Armas finally left Cuba the following year.

The three poets, along with many other writers of their generation, came to the fore when Fowler was asked to reform the Brigada Hermanos Saíz (BHS), which until then had only promoted "anticonversacionalista poetry." When Fowler became the BHS's vice president in 1986, he invited younger poets to submit their works, enabling them to join the BHS (Fowler 2006). The idea was to offset the conversationalist poetics developed by the previous generation, *El Caimán Barbudo*'s second generation of poets.

The latter cultivated a nonconversationalist poetics that can be found, for example, in the early works of Rodríguez or Ángel Escobar. Rejecting the sixties and seventies conversationalist poetics that I analyzed in chapter 1, their self-referential poetry foregrounded voices (especially those of women and Afro-Cubans) that had been silenced by the New Man's white and male-oriented culture of conversationalist poetry. The new younger poets cultivated a more abstract and hermetic style that brought them closer to Orígenes than to the previous generation. Their coming together in the BHS was key to the development and official recognition of late eighties postorigenista poetry as it materialized in the early works of Almelio Calderón, Ismael Castañer, Juan Carlos Flores, and Marqués de Armas.

Most of the poems included in Aguilera's anthology *Memorias de la clase muerta*, share Diáspora(s)'s aesthetic. The "clase muerta" ("dead class") of the title emphasizes the group's marginality vis-à-vis the revolutionary cultural project. Theirs is a group that has no place in the teleological revolutionary history, or in Cuban social stratification. It is a group without a relation and place. These poets were the heirs of a sublime revolutionary ideal that never materialized, and that existed only as an object of desire. But this group was not only a product of its time, it was, in general, a group that existed in a permanent state of exile. Diáspora(s) were never welcomed by official cultural institutions, but they also marginalized themselves politically and aesthetically from most writers of their generation. Marginality was, as a matter of fact, part of their aesthetic and their ethos.

DIÁSPORA(S) AND VANGUARDISM

In the nineties Diáspora(s) represented the coming into being of a new aesthetics that rejected postorigenismo. But Diáspora(s) was much more than that, which is why official institutions dismissed it. In 1993, after Minister of Culture Abel Prieto rejected Sánchez Mejías's ideas for an interdisciplinary journal, the group decided to launch *Diáspora(s)* as a samizdat.[86] In spite of their somewhat different poetics, the founding members of the project had many other traits in common. Most of them did not come from careers in the humanities, and their interdisciplinary work was largely influenced by poststructuralism. In spite of the fact that Sánchez Mejías, Aguilera, and Marqués de Armas are poets, their work belongs in a liminal, hybrid space, which does away with the concept of genre altogether. Writing is no longer defined by genres. It is instead based on the high conceptual power of words and the most economical use of syntactical patterns, in a minimalist use of words and a maximalist approach to conceptual abstraction.

Above all, the three writers shared ideological views. First, they rejected the idea of a national canon and a national identity. They took issue with the official Orígenes revival of the eighties and nineties, specifically the ideological capitalization on that group's take on the relationship between national identity and literature. Instead of seeking to rescue Grupo Orígenes's writing from oblivion, they engaged it critically. They were especially interested in Virgilio Piñera and Lorenzo García Vega, whose poetics they embraced as their own. The Proyecto Diáspora(s) shared Piñera's and García Vega's irreverent attitude and their antibaroquism. Sánchez Mejías, Aguilera, and Marqués de Armas shared a sardonic outlook on social mores and a nonutopian view of history. Their poetics were aggressive, ironic, and devoid of sentimentality. Second, Diáspora(s)'s rejection of totalitarianism fed their interest in Central European authors such as Walter Benjamin, Theodor Adorno, Friedrich Nietzsche, Ror Wolf, and Franz Kafka, all of whom had been critical of absolutist systems of thought. To publish and discuss literature that disrupts state-sponsored culture was one of the aims of *Diáspora(s)*.

Like the members of the Grupo Orígenes, they had a more internationalist approach to literature, and in addition to reading the French symbolists and the Spanish Generation of 1927, they also explored works by authors who had never been published in Cuba, such as Boris Pasternak, Milan Kundera, Michel Foucault, and Jacques Derrida. Their understanding of literature clearly went against the sixties ideological remnants that rejected European and Western literature, in general, for their roots in philosophical idealism.

They were also very interested in poststructuralism and questions of postmodernity, and they were the first to organize a panel on modernity and postmodernity, which took place in October 1996 at the UNEAC. As Hans Magnus Enzensberger says in his text "America," they also argue that literature saved their lives (1999, 64). The samizdat was also committed to publishing *auteurs maudits* whose ideology and aesthetics went against the grain and who were silenced by the regime (Lorenzo García Vega, Virgilio Piñera, etc.). From an ideological point of view, for example, the journal reprinted polemical articles by dissident authors from the Eastern European bloc, pieces that could not have circulated in any of Cuba's official cultural journals.[87] They also had anticanonical views about Cuban literature. Like many other intellectuals of the nineties, they conceived of themselves as the inheritors of a genealogy of *auteurs maudits* silenced by the national canon. Juan Zenea, Julián del Casal, Virgilio Piñera, and Ángel Escobar were relegated in the canon to the status of obscure or minor poets, and the samizdat *Diáspora(s)* contributed to the dissemination of their work. In "El arte de graznar" ("The Art of Squawking"), Sánchez Mejías criticizes Cintio Vitier's *Lo cubano en la poesía* (*Cubanness in Poetry*) for its agenda to construct a canon that fits the teleological narration of the nation in cultural terms (2002, 27).

Sánchez Mejías's point is that Virgilio Piñera's poetics does not contribute to that narration, and as a result is excluded from the canon. The nation thus understood arises with the project of modernity and its cultural construction. Such a national discourse takes shape in the works of José Martí and Rubén Darío, the two major modernists who advanced the values of modernity and shaped the vanguardist projects of the beginning of the twentieth century. It is thus not farfetched to compare both movements (modernism and the vanguardism represented by anticanonical authors) as the two major turning points of the twentieth and twenty-first centuries.[88] Not only are these two movements crucial, but they are also antithetical. More than establishing a new anticanon, however, the Diáspora(s) was interested in creating a poetics against the grain of modernity. The ideological and formal premises of Darío's work, for example, were antithetically debunked. If Darío's poetics attacked capitalist utilitarianism with the excess of beauty, *Diáspora(s)* attacked violent totalitarian discourse with more violence and "feísmo" (the aesthetic of ugliness). Actually, Enrique Saínz calls it "dirty writing": "Escritura en ocasiones sucia (en el sentido de objeto estéticamente sucio, no admitido por poéticas establecidas antes de la vanguardia) [Dirty writing (as in an aesthetically dirty object, not admitted by the poetics established before the vanguards)]" (Saínz 2013, 28). For Darío, aristocratic beauty was the space of lavishness and delightful waste; for *Diáspora(s)*, excessive ornament characterizes a political discourse that conceals an ideological lack. To such linguistic extravagance, *Diáspora(s)* responds with the abstraction and the rigor of philosophy. The swans that populate Dario's poetry become revolting animals in *Diáspora(s)* (rats, pigs, insects, etc.), and the harmonious relationship with nature turns into the alienation of beings from the space they inhabit. What about the social and political aims of the two movements?

This has been a controversial question in discussions of modernist writers, especially Darío, precisely because of the aesthetics of his poetry. Scholars have argued that while his work does not have a political agenda, its language is ideologically charged. There is a tension in Darío's work between the desire to guard the autonomy of art while simultaneously creating a language capable of challenging hegemonic discourse. This tension is also fundamental for Diáspora(s), because of these writers' attack on linguistic tropes, especially metaphor and allegory. In sum, Diáspora(s) rejects baroque language because its numerous metaphors can be co-opted by official political rhetoric. They also reject the social poetry of the seventies for its doctrinaire nature. Their goal, then, is to create a language not determined by a political cause, a language that attests to its ideological and formal withering, and that accounts for state violence. Their style is a direct consequence of the emergent interest in poststructuralist and post-Marxist theory as a new way to experiment with language and thought, as I argue in the introduction. Although these considerations were true for most poets of this decade (Omar Pérez, Emilio Sánchez Montiel, Alessandra Molina, etc.), Diáspora(s) was more radical than the rest.

As its name indicates, *Diáspora(s)* was first and foremost a publication that sought to deterritorialize power and language. To publish and discuss literature that disrupts state-sponsored culture is one of the aims of *Diáspora(s)*. On some occasions, however, this gesture, which in fact is not grandiose, results in the fetishization of the Diáspora(s)'s work. The journal shared some of the characteristics of a minor literature, and the work of Deleuze and Guattari clearly influenced its mission. This is a useful category for a first approximation to their poetics, but like most literary classifications, it lacks complexity. I will, nonetheless, approach their poetics by discussing their work as a minor literature, especially because of their own interest in Deleuze and Guattari.

Minor literature is the denomination Deleuze and Guattari use to describe Franz Kafka's work in *Kafka: Toward a Minor Literature*, as their attempt to cut through the debate over the distinction between highbrow and lowbrow literature. Their ideologically framed discussion aims to demonstrate the revolutionary potential of experimental literature. In this sense, the contextual framework of this discussion stems from the debate between Bertolt Brecht and Georg Lukács about the avant-garde and its revolutionary potential. For Deleuze and Guattari, however, a minor literature can be "experimental" (highbrow) or "marginal" (lowbrow), but it must above all be a form of deterritorialization of a major language. Linguistically speaking, a deterritorialization is the destruction of a standard language, that is, the expression of a minority who uses a major language (Deleuze and Guattari 1986, 16). In the case of Kafka, they argue that his writing is caught between several languages (German, Czech, and Yiddish) and that he does not recognize any of them as his own. That is, Kafka (a minority writer) is writing in German (a major language). Minor literature can also be an "experimental" mode of writing, such as the high modernist rupture of style (as in Joyce or Beckett). Deterritorialization must also be political because it must destroy grand narratives, such as Freudian psychoanalysis and its imposition of Greco-Roman myths as a universal analytical matrix. Unlike major literatures that narrate individual stories, in minor literature there is no separation between the political and the personal. The destruction of those narratives must above all be a collective and revolutionary project that arises from an active solidarity and that produces alternative communities.

The collective role of literature also has an emancipatory function, and in this regard it blends with sixties revolutionary Cuban literature: "But above all else, because collective or national consciousness is 'often inactive in external life and always in the process of break-down,' literature finds itself positively charged with the role and function of collective, and even, revolutionary enunciation" (Deleuze and Guattari 1986, 17).

The journal *Diáspora(s)*, however, was not a project of resistance, as its classification as minor literature might lead one to think (Díaz Infante). This scholarly appreciation of *Diáspora(s)* as a "minor literature," is also how the works that the samizdat discusses have been defined. But the critics have fallen prey to the epistemological contradictions of "minor literature" as a notion that recreates the same premise it criticizes. That is, "minor literature" is a concept that seeks to disassociate certain authors from a hegemonic norm by affirming their particularities. But in so doing it reinscribes them into a category, since they still share their belonging to a group. The idea of a "minor literature" defeats its own purpose because any process of identification is necessarily also a process of differentiation, so the concept is recreating the same duality it wants to abolish. In this regard, instead of "minor literature" I prefer what Maurice Blanchot has called "a community without a community," a concept that points to the idea of group or ensemble in spite of its undetermined nature. To categorize *Diáspora(s)* as a systematic or asystematic literary endeavor goes against the nature of a project that is constantly calling into question the process of differentiation. In other words, this type of categorization not only goes against the intellectual project of *Diáspora(s)*, it also fetishizes the group's work. Ricardo Alberto Pérez, another member of the group, argues that Diáspora(s) never took a direct political position. The political nature of their work was actually articulated by their poetics, and is to be inferred from their writing, as Pérez seems to suggest.[89] In other words, in general they have an antisystemic view of the world, but this did not translate into a systematic political agenda. It did, however, create an iconoclastic poetics driven by antisystemic political ideology.

The editorial collective shared similar aesthetics and an antiestablishment position. Influenced by Eastern European dissident movements and by the belief that walls would fall in Havana as they had in Berlin, the journal attacked and analyzed totalitarianism. Most important, the journal was unique in condemning the understanding of literature as a national category. It was also one of the rare journals committed to the dissemination of foreign literature, and in that regard, it followed the mission of important journals such as *Criterios* and *Pensamiento crítico*. Moreover, the samizdat *Diáspora(s)* did away with the focus on national and cultural identity. In so doing, its endeavor radicalized minor literature's goal to decenter the nation, getting rid of national narrations altogether. The name of the journal also alluded to a spatial dispersion, to the narrowness of the nation and the need to embrace worldwide intellectual genealogies. During the Republic, the Grupo Orígenes noted for the first time how Mexico was debating the problem between nationalism and cosmopolitism. This debate is brought back to light now, after the anti-intellectualism and dogmatism that characterized the conversationalist poetic movement. In this sense, the parenthetical "s" in *Diáspora(s)* has two meanings that do not exclude each other. On the one hand, it refers to a retreat from hegemonic thought; on the other, it points to a place of isolation. The project thus alluded to a space of exile or dissidence that, paradoxically never points to a physical reality or a communal space. In other words, if what characterizes the journal is the idea of dispersion, then one cannot argue simultaneously that the project is defined according to the notion of collective action as the notion of minor literature implies. This type of politics keeps considering democracy as the attempt to achieve hegemony by wresting power from the elite rather than as the possibility of abolishing the relations of rule (Vatter 2011, 2). As we have discussed, politically speaking, *Diáspora(s)* was neither a literature of resistance (literature associated with the political struggles of national liberation) nor a minor literature, two categories that understand the political as emancipation. That is, the journal denounced intellectual projects, which in general understood literature as an instrument of political emancipation, regardless of whether they originated in the island or in the Cuban exile. As a matter of fact, it was as critical of emancipatory literature originating in the exiled community. *Diáspora(s)* clearly differentiated its tactics from those of different journals. For example, it implicitly criticized *Encuentro de la cultura cubana* (*Meeting of Cuban Culture*), a journal created by Jesús Díaz, an exiled intellectual who had been very close to the regime at the beginning of the revolution. The journal was based in Madrid and launched in 1996, three years before Sánchez Mejías wrote the following text:

> Ahora se sueña con una Cuba donde todos sus intelectuales serán como sus hijos soñados. Se habla del "encuentro," de la "confluencia," del estado final de gracia de todos—incluso los que nunca han tenido voz en Cuba—serán redimidos por la Nación. Los "cubanólogos" (esa nueva raza del intelectual cubano) inventan nuevas averiguaciones: construyen, producen, se adelantan a la futura máquina de producción de realidad. Se parecen al socialismo por su energía de organizar nuevos constructos de saber y de utopía nacionales en nombre de una epopeya insular.

> [Today people dream of a Cuba in which all the country's intellectuals would be like the children of its dreams. People speak of the "meeting" [*encuentro*], of the "convergence," of the state of final grace in which everyone—including those who have never had a voice in Cuba—will be redeemed by the nation. "Cubanologists" (that new race of Cuban intellectuals) invent new research questions, building, producing, pushing ahead of the future reality machine—They act like socialism in its endeavor of organizing new life simulacra, new constructs of knowledge and utopia in the name of an island epic.] (1999, 6–7)

The original mission of *Encuentro de la cultura cubana* was to create an intellectual space for debate between exiled intellectuals (dissidents) and those living on the island.[90] This explains why Sánchez Mejías clearly refers to it by apparently questioning the politics of ideological consensus between dissidents and the island's critical or official intellectuals. *Encuentro de la cultura cubana* was not the only journal that *Diáspora(s)* targeted. Sánchez Mejías was also alluding to previous attempts to create a dialogue between the Cuban and the Cuban American cultural productions, often metaphorically depicted as a "bridge" between Miami and Cuba.[91] That is, this argument replicated the paradigm of cultural exceptionalism as a way to define the nation in revolutionary official discourse. This is what Sánchez Mejías identifies as "the island epic." Hence, rather than national identity, literature needs to address the question of state intervention in culture. Namely, the writer has to fight for literature's autonomy. A literature at the service of a political idea of emancipation is bound to become the literature of the ruling class: "Porque el poder sueña con convertirse en Naturaleza. Finalmente el poder también sueña como un niño: aunque sueñe con la cabeza vacía. Su sueño es tan monstruoso como el de la literatura [Because power dreams of converting itself into Nature. In the end, power also dreams like a child, although it dreams empty-headed. Its dream is as monstrous as that of literature]" (ibid., 6).

Proyecto Diáspora(s) and the Poetics of Violence

The many different works that the samizdat *Diáspora(s)* reprints have the following characteristics in common: they are unmapped and mostly from Central European authors, many of them dissidents with similar conceptual and aesthetic perspectives. The most salient one is what I call the poetics of defacement. This poetics points (as it were in a deictic manner) to the contradictions of a normative regime of totalizing forms. The poetics of defacement mars heroism, sacrifice, and utopia in their construction of the revolutionary nation. More specifically, it questions the revolutionary understanding of violence as a necessary force for national reconstruction. The revolutionary rhetoric of the sixties and seventies conceived of violence as a materialist and humanist practice with Nietzschean undertones. That is, on the one hand, it calls for a Marxist socialist humanism and, on the other hand, it reminds us of the Nietzschean allegory of the eternal return. Cuban subjects can only become revolutionary through a sacrifice that requires them to give their lives for the cause. In this regard death becomes, as we saw in chapter 1, the way to build the nation, as individual sacrifice becomes a communal renaissance. This Cuban revolutionary logic is articulated as Marx's theory of socialist humanism in that man attains real materialization of his being by abolishing alienation: "*Abolition* as an objective movement *taking back* into itself what has been alienated—this insight expressed within the alienation is the *adoption* of the objective essence by eliminating what alienates it. . . . Only by first removing this interceding element—which, however is a necessary prerequisite—does *positive*, self-created humanism come into being" (Marx and Engels 1947, 62).

While in the Cuban revolutionary logic "man" creates himself through his own death (subjects become heroes), for Marx "man" attains "his" being through labor. It is precisely this difference that gives the revolutionary logic its Nietzschean undertones. Like the Nietzschean overman, the hero must have a will to power as if his life were to return anew. Death, in contrast, although not absolutely affirmed as a positive force in Nietzsche, also leads to the renaissance of life in the world as a consequence of the overman's deeds.

The poetics of defacement shows the contradictions of this humanist logic based on the building of the nation through sacrifice and death, that is, through violence in a more abstract sense. This poetics proposes an antihumanist ontology that can only be articulated through the death drive, and that unravels as a negative dialectics of sorts. Violence as a concept is a part of the Diáspora(s)'s theoretical vocabulary that articulates its poetics. Not only because this concept reappears in many of the theoretical pieces, but also because it is part of the Diáspora(s)'s aesthetics. The group's manifesto and some of its fiction articulate the idea that violence is aesthetic, and that aesthetics are violent. This paradox is precisely what hinders libidinal cathexis between aesthetics and the world, and creates an approach to reality mediated by the death drive. If there is no libidinal cathexis between these negative forces (namely, poetry and the world), can these forces be productive or are they simply nihilistic? This question cannot be posed without taking into account that the death drive finds pleasure in what is most perturbing, which means that the attraction to the negative perversely produces pleasure. If it is the case, then, that pleasure (affirmation) and displeasure (negation) are part of the same force, can this union produce any type of knowledge? Or, would it, like the Adornian negative dialectic, dissipate fundamental antagonisms? Is violence the creative and revolutionary part of negation? It is with these questions in mind that I will examine the Diáspora(s)'s understanding of violence, especially in its relation to aesthetics.

The Revolution as the Sublime

The journal's mission statement opens with several references to death, violence, and terror:

> Pero volvamos al uso de la libertad, en poesía / esta libertad tiene las mismas características que la / lucha política / se impone inspirando terror; redescubriendo el Deber (Pasolini).
>
> Acelerar el vector del imaginario en este sentido: "una violencia que debe ser tanto o más notable cuanto mayor sea el quantum que la imaginación comprende en una intuición" (Kant)
>
> [But let us return to the use of liberty, in poetry / this liberty has the same characteristics as / political struggle / it imposes itself inspiring terror; rediscovering Duty (Pasolini).
>
> Accelerate the vector of the imaginary in this sense: "violence must be the more significant the larger the quantum is that the imagination comprehends in one intuition" (Kant).] (Sánchez Mejías 1997b, 1)

"Presentación" by Sánchez Mejías, the text that opens the first issue, has become the group's poetic manifesto. The essay begins with two epigraphs embedded into the text announcing the intellectual project of the journal, as the relationship between aesthetics and political ethos. The citation of Pier Paolo Pasolini, which comes from his poem "La restaurazione di sinistra" ("The Restoration of the Left") is a critique of the Left as a constitutive power.[92] The Proyecto Diáspora(s) embraces Pasolini's heterodox views on the Left. The reference to Pasolini is extremely interesting indeed, not just because of his admiration for the younger generation's revolutionary zeal but also because of his critique of the eventual generational cycle of *embourgeoisement* (between revolutionary fathers and sons).[93] As a former member of the Partido Comunista Italiano (PCI), he became very critical of May 1968. But his allusion to "terror" is not to be taken literally, quite the opposite. "La restaurazione di sinistra" denounces the Left for ruling as reformists and abandoning its fight for radical change. The Left must embrace its "Duty" to bring about structural change through "revolution" (terror). A critic of the fierce repression by the Italian state during the sixties, Pasolini is not calling for armed political action. Instead, his aim is to reveal and denounce the practice of state terror through its representation qua terror. In other words, state terror has to be combatted with an aesthetic of terror carrying the intensity of political action. Above all, poetics have to move us by causing extreme fear, which will eventually create a political consciousness for revolution.

In spite of Pasolini's heterodox communism, it is clear that, like the conversationalist Cuban poets, he still believed in the emancipatory role of literature. Unlike them, however, he rejected the melancholic notions of heroism and sacrifice, and he called for a nonconversationalist type of poetry. Sánchez Mejías's manifesto clearly supports Pasolini's later convictions and poetics. The second quote that opens the manifesto comes from Kant's *Critique of Judgment*, and more specifically from a fragment in which he defines the sublime. Before explaining the sublime, let me summarily gloss the Kantian categories of cognition. Kant's cognitive process begins with intuitions, which are, phenomenologically speaking, the sensuous experiences that we have in our first apprehension of the world. Concepts help qualify and quantify those experiences, and the imagination is where concepts and intuitions meet. If we go back to the sublime, it is now easier to understand that, according to Kant, the sublime has magnitudes and qualities that challenge our cognitive capacities. In other words, the sublime is a form of cognition that short-circuits the imagination because it cannot be symbolized. The relation between the object of apprehension and thought breaks, causing in the subject a sense of powerlessness. As a result, the subject is at first shocked and anguished: "the mind feels agitated" (Kant 1987, 115). Yet the subject also feels pleased and fulfilled. Although this seems like a contradiction, Kant's rationalism does away with it. First, he argues that, subjectively speaking, the experience of the sublime produces pain because we cannot comprehend it, so it merely remains as an intuition. But, objectively speaking ("for reason's idea of the Supresensible" [ibid.]), it also provokes a feeling of pleasure because our striving for it is in harmony with rational ideas (but the judgment itself remains only aesthetic). This antagonistic feeling is very important for understanding one of the aesthetic goals of the Proyecto Diáspora(s) manifesto, as I will explain shortly.

Sánchez Mejías's citation of Kant thus alludes to the imagination's inability to capture the sublime. The quotation is just one clause in a longer sentence, but the entire citation reads: "Hence (since temporal succession is a condition of the inner sense and of an intuition), it is a subjective movement of the imagination by which it does violence to the inner sense, and this violence must be the more significant the larger the quantum is that the imagination comprehends in one intuition" (Kant 1987, 116). To measure the sublime from a temporal perspective, Kant argues that the imagination must be able to process a succession of temporal events at once. Our inner sense (our capacity to understand time), however, can only grasp events in succession. How, then, Kant asks, can the imagination comprehend successive events in one instant? To measure the sublime, we (our imagination) must wrestle with our limited capacity to understand time and with our limited perception of it (our intuition). Understanding the seemingly incomprehensible notion of the simultaneity of time requires a cognitive violence. That is, our imagination has to be disrupted with the same proportional force as our disturbing perception of violence. This means that mastery over the sublime requires the disturbing experience of the sublime. What Sánchez Mejías emphasizes, however, is that the representation of the world is the result of the sensuous experience of violence conveyed by the sublime (the Real). In other words, the experience of the sublime requires violence. But what is the origin of that violence? It could be the fear that overcomes us when we face it, as well as the pleasure that we experience when grappling with it: "The object is apprehended as sublime with a pleasure that is possible only by means of displeasure" (Kant 1987, 117). Violence is both pleasurable and disturbing.

In the context of the samizdat *Diáspora(s)*, Sánchez Mejías resignifies Kant's fragment, and what is a cognitive violence for Kant becomes aesthetic and political. The Kantian quote is also recontextualized to define or explain "the imaginary [*imaginario*]," that is, the weltanschauung or worldview advanced by the samizdat. One must experience violence in order to approach the sublime (the Real), and this experience can only be represented aesthetically through violence. Although Sánchez Mejías does not mention the sublime, it is obviously present between the lines and as subtext. I am arguing this because he places Pasolini and Kant side by side, and Pasolini's concept of revolution bears that quality of the sublime insofar as it is the most substantial event, that which cannot be measured or compared. But whereas for Pasolini poetics have an essential political function, for the Proyecto Diáspora(s) they bear no relation to a political project. Thus, while both Pasolini's and the Diáspora(s)'s sublime may be interpreted as the Lacanian Real, for Pasolini the sublime points to the notion of revolution, unlike for the Diáspora(s). For Pasolini a politics of terror leads to the creation of consciousness. Aesthetically speaking, he represents terror with a realist style. But this is not true of the Diáspora(s) and its poetics of defacement. The Proyecto Diáspora(s) responds to violence with more violence, but does it appear as an ontological notion in the Diáspora(s)'s works? This question is key to explaining their poetics, since we need to know the origin of the violence that the Diáspora(s) fights. To answer this question, it is important to discuss the Diáspora(s)'s choice of authors dealing with the same topic. One of the key essays featured in *Diáspora(s)* is a Thomas Bernhard speech.

Poesis of Thought

Bernhard's representation of the world belongs to the so-called aesthetic tradition of minor literature. It is pertinent to draw a parallel between Bernhard's work and the Diáspora(s)'s because the latter's view of the world stems from the same premise. The Diáspora(s)'s work originates from an antihumanist perspective and emphasizes the epistemological nature of language. In his speech "En busca de la verdad y de la muerte" (In Search of Truth and Death"), reprinted in the second issue of the journal, Bernhard argues that language is the privileged space for thought in a world that has succumbed to violence. This address was written in 1968 for Bernhard's reception of the Anton Wildgans Prize of Austrian Industry. Instead of following the stylistic conventions of acceptance speeches, his text symbolically negates the social and ethical value of the prize by showing the dismissal of History's atrocities that makes the prize possible in the first place. For him, communication in society is constantly hindered by an irrevocable misunderstanding: "Os agradezco por esta distinción, por el malentendido que constituye sin ninguna duda esta distinción, pues como sabéis todo es malentendido [I thank you for this honor, for the misunderstanding that this honor undoubtedly constitutes, since as you know everything is a misunderstanding]" (Bernhard 1998, 9). This misunderstanding occurs because there is no outside to ideology, which, like nature, represents an irrational force that leads to destruction: "Hablo ahora de la muerte, puesto que me habéis encargado un discurso, algo sobre la vida, es cierto, pero yo hablo, aún cuando hablo de la vida, de la muerte. . . . Todo lo que se dice es siempre sobre la muerte [I speak now of death, since you have commissioned me to give a speech, something about life, certainly, but even when I speak of life, I speak of death. . . . Everything that is said is always about death]" (ibid., 6). To be alive amounts to being dead because we are subjected to the dominant and deforming powers of society, which annihilate us.

Bernhard claims that one must use language to destroy hegemonic language. Despite our inability to escape the fundamental power of ideology by externalizing its effects and articulating the monstrousness that governs our consciousness, we can cope with the enemy within us. The externalization of such monstrousness, however, can only come from a place of negativity, and thus can only be articulated through the same negative rhetoric that produces it. This explains why Bernhard's speech is merely a list of

History's atrocities: "Podría también contar una historia. . . . hablo de la mentira y el ridículo y no cuento *El cuento de la profundidad*. . . . no hago más que rozar todo esto y arrojo a esta sala algunas palabras, por ejemplo la palabra "aislamiento," "degeneración," "vulgaridad" . . . y puesto que muy rápidamente nos cansamos de la comedia, del espectáculo de la existencia, de todo el arte dramático . . . un día, en un solo instante, en el instante decisivo, nos arrojamos de cabeza a la muerte [I could also tell a story. . . . I speak of lies and the ridiculous, and I don't tell *The Tale of Profundity*. . . . I simply mention all this in passing and throw into this room a few words, such as the words 'isolation,' 'denigration,' 'vulgarity' . . . and since we tire quickly of the comedy, of the spectacle of existence, of the whole dramatic art . . . one day, in a single instant, in the decisive instant, we throw ourselves headlong into death]" (ibid., 8). It also explains why he lists topics but never actually speaks about them. He develops this discursive strategy by affirming that his text doesn't speak about anything, which is a way to also express how power silences the narration of History's defeats: "Pero creo que he dicho bastante, o hablado, ¿no es así? Señalado, ¿no es así?, *pasado en silencio* muchos temas, como véis, pasado en silencio casi todos los temas [But I think I've said enough, or spoken (isn't that right?), pointed out (isn't that right?), *passed over in silence* many topics, as you see, passed over in silence almost all topics]" (ibid., 9). This is the rhetoric of an antispeech that constantly annihilates the truth at the level of discourse. The speech develops an argumentation to demonstrate that the search for truth is doomed to be a search for death.

Finding "the truth" is not the Diáspora(s)'s goal, either. In *Diáspora(s)*, the hegemonic rhetoric of violence is met with a poetics of violence. For the Diáspora(s), as for Bernhard, literature must confront the power that silences it, by exerting its own mode of violence: "El vigor de una 'literatura desplazada,' si no se produce una hecatombe que la borre, puede ser directamente proporcional a la violencia que se ejerce sobre ella. Puede decirse más: ningún abrazo se ha vuelto más prometedor que la estrecha acometida, que el empujón seductor entre la violencia del poder y la violencia con que la literatura intenta desplazar al poder [The vigor of a 'displaced literature,' if no disaster occurs that wipes it out, can be directly proportional to the violence exerted on it. We could say even more: no embrace has been more promising than the close attack, than the seductive shoving between the violence of power and the violence with which literature seeks to displace power]" (Sánchez Mejías 1999, 6).

This antithetical relationship between destruction and love posits power as a violent force that can only be counteracted with a violent literature. Literary destruction thus understood, however, does not point toward reconstruction. Since literature is no longer considered as an emancipatory project, Sánchez Mejías is not proposing the destruction of state power in order to establish a different type of power. What is the nature of this violence that must oppose the violence of power? It consists of a critical practice to debunk the onto-theological paradigm that underlies all structures of domination, like the sixties revolutionary rhetoric. It is actually a violence against the idea of literature itself, so far conceived of as an allegorical literature, as I argued in chapter 1. According to Aguilera, allegorical and canonical literature was born dead: "En una literatura 'muerta': que sublima y sublima constantemente lo mismo, que se estanca en malas ficciones, que no piensa [In a 'dead' literature: which sublimes and constantly sublimes the same thing, which mires itself in bad fictions, which does not think]" (Saunders 2001, 1). Sánchez Mejías repeats the same idea of a dead literature: "El sistema totalitario odia los huecos negros. No soporta las líneas de fuga. Todo debe adquirir la fijeza mortal de una realidad ordenable en términos de control [The totalitarian system despises black holes. It cannot tolerate lines of flight. Everything must take on the deadly rigidity of a reality that can be ordered in terms of control]" (Sánchez Mejías 1999, 3). To oppose this dead literature, the Diáspora(s)calls for the power of language: "Cuando nuestra generación organizó algunas tácticas de 'política literaria' (revistas marginales . . .) no lo hizo tanto en relación con el poder . . . como para preservar tozudamente el nervio de la literature [When our generation organized tactics of 'literary politics' (marginal magazines . . .), it did not do this so much with respect to power . . . as to stubbornly preserve the backbone [*nervio*] of literature]" (ibid., 6). Paradoxically, however, the language that the Diáspora(s) is claiming is illegible, and thus also dead: "Es una generación que supo resistir los sarcasmos embozados de la crítica oficial, que en ningún momento dejó de utilizar todas las palabras del mundo aunque sus poemas y relatos se volvieran ilegibles para el bien público y para la tradición literaria cubana [This is a generation that was able to resist the veiled sarcasm of official criticism, that at no point stopped using all the words in the world even though its poems and stories became illegible for the public good and for the Cuban literary tradition]" (ibid., 5).

Poetics of Defacement

It is in this sense that the members of Diáspora(s) escape a poetry of the sublime, of radical change, that is, one of total destruction (obliteration of aesthetics), as well as the poetry of absolute pleasure (national canonical Cuban aesthetics) that the group attacks for its archaic understanding of history and identity.

The emotional response of "dysfunctional delight" is key to understanding the type of affect that the Diáspora(s)'s work displaces. As we have seen, poesis comes from negativity, violence, or destruction. If we read it in psychological terms, it means that the poetic creation and experience mobilize the death drive. This intangible and metaphysical Freudian concept refers to our preorganic and chaotic past, and aims at unsettling the whole that is the organic system. The death drive finds pleasure in what is most troubling in the organism. It does not rebut but rather attracts the subject. As we know, libidinal cathexis creates attachments between objects and subjects, but the death drive destroys them by instigating conflict. Interestingly enough, this is exactly the goal of the Diáspora(s)'s "dysfunctional delight." This oxymoron thus indicates that poetic expression must be articulated as negative passion that takes pleasure in unsettling the system. In the Cuban case, "the system" refers to the hegemonic representation of the literary canon and the discourse of national identity on which it is based. Now comes a second question, however: How is the relationship between ideology and aesthetics played out in the creation of this particular affect?

Sánchez Mejías's "Violence and Literature" is one of Diáspora(s)'s iconic texts because it lays out their position on this issue. On the one hand, the essay posits the autonomy of literature in opposition to social poetics as they were practiced during the sixties and seventies. On the other hand, it assigns to literature the power to stand up to the ideological power of hegemonic official discourses: "¿Qué se le puede oponer al poder? . . . Pero lo que resplandece sin lugar a dudas es la idea de la literature [What can oppose power? . . . what shines forth without a shadow of doubt is the idea of literature]" (Sánchez Mejías 1999, 5). Both gestures negate what hegemonic literature affirms and embraces: harmony, social power, and clarity of expression. According to the Diáspora(s), conversationalist and nonconversationalist poetry put more emphasis on the social function of literature, while the members of the Diáspora(s) believe that language alone defines literature: "Si yo fuera a definir a mi generación literaria, la definiría con el siguiente lema: 'hijos de la palabra' [If I had to define my literary generation, I would do so with the following slogan: 'children of the word']" (ibid.). Does this mean that they conceive of literature as merely an aesthetic practice? The answer to this question has to do with the complexity of the relationship between ideology and the materiality of language. Let us remember that this was precisely the same question that the proponents of socialist realism addressed during the early stages of the revolution. How are we to understand the treatment of this complex and long-standing question for Cuban revolutionary literature in the work of the Proyecto Diáspora(s)?

The answer to this question is actually of an Adornian nature, and as one may suspect, it is related to Adorno's notion of negative dialectics. His materialist philosophy is a response to Hegel's idealism and the idea that there is an identification between referent and signified. In opposition to Hegel, he thinks that the a priori categories of understanding are nonconceptual, because otherwise they would be incomprehensible. With Marx, Adorno thinks that economic antagonisms structure the social, and that the identification between use value and exchange value is false. The theoretical problem that concerns Adorno has to do with the Hegelian notion of identification. He argues that the sublation of negativity in the dialectic conceals the singularities of each subject/object by wrapping them into a totalizing system. That is, in the dialectical synthesis of affirmation and negation, the absolute is always an affirmation. As a way to preserve particularities, Adorno suggests instead that identity should take the form of negativity. In other words, the dialectic would be a process of sublation between identity and nonidentity that would result in nonidentity. Against Marx, he does not believe that philosophy can have a direct access to what he calls the nonidentical. He argues, however, that reason can have access to the nonidentical through the conceptual criticism of "false identifications" (the ones that the social produces). What are the available resources to grapple with them? For Adorno, we can only access false identifications and their contradictions through language. These contradictions can only be represented via their *Darstellung* (presentation). Adorno's modified version of the Benjaminian *Darstellung* is the idea that philosophy has a rhetorical power to present concepts that enables it to say something that is itself nonconceptual: "Its integral, nonconceptually mimetic moment of expression is objectified only by presentation in language. The freedom of philosophy is nothing but the capacity to lend a voice to its unfreedom" (Adorno 1973, 18). In other words, language is reified by social discourses, but philosophy is able to recover the meaning of concepts and the representation of experience by means of the contextual meaning to be found between the lines and, especially with the discovery of what exceeds the meaning of a word.

Let me then rehearse the questions that I have raised by addressing them to the poetics of the Proyecto Diáspora(s). Given that the Diáspora(s)'s members do not believe in the emancipatory function of literature, what is the role of literature? Or does it even have one? Is literature only an aesthetic experience for them? We can indeed pose a similar question about the significance of violence. Do the members of the Diáspora(s) follow Bernhard's notion of violence as a form that externalizes the effects of the ideological trap in which we are caught? Is the symbolic power of violence creating an alternative narrative to Darío's? In other words, is it conceived as a form of liberation from hegemonic ideology? Does violence articulate a new language that opens up different paths to theorize? And, finally, does violence act like a *Darstellung*, enabling the presentation of what exceeds language? Only the texts themselves can unravel these questions, or entangle them further.

Like most Diáspora(s) pieces, "Un gato llamado Smith" (A Cat Named Adam Smith"), by Rogelio Saunders, resists all kinds of formal categorizations, whether of genre, style, theme, or plot. In what appears to be an adventure story the narrator, Jean-Paul Sartre, and Simone de Beauvoir embark on a trip deep into the jungle, which is at once a geographical, mental, and literary space. Abandoned by their Jeep driver, they walk until they bump into a Lewis Carroll Cheshire cat of sorts: " 'Bien dicho,' susurró el gato, apareciendo de ninguna parte, como un dibujo animado que brota de una gota de tinta ['Well spoken,' whispered the cat, appearing out of nowhere, like a cartoon sprouting from a drop of ink]" (Saunders 2002, 16). The piece is narrated as a Joycean stream of consciousness. What is relevant for our purpose, however, is how the poetics of defacement articulate the text. Before meeting the cat, the three characters get out of the Jeep and start walking until they reach a clearing that the narrator describes in awe:

> Llegada a un claro en medio de la inmensidad. . . . En medio del mayor espesor y de su transparencia. Arte del agrimensor sobre las hojas de silueta de venablo repetidas ad infinitum. Peso y densidad. Forma y volumen. Medir y volver a medir. Medirme a mi mismo. Pesarme a mi mismo. Y luego medir y pesar a la bella Simone. Tomar el peso de sus pequeñas nalgas *y sobre todo escapar hacia ese azul imponente atrayente erótico denso inmenso de una vez por todas*. ¿Perdidos porque (re)encontrados? ¿Dónde están las ciudades que nos prometieron? . . . ¿Dónde estaba lo nuevo (el *novum*), mi querida Simone?
>
> [Arrival in a clearing amid the vastness. . . . Amid the greater thickness and its transparency. The surveyor's art on the leaves silhouetted like darts repeated ad infinitum. Weight and density. Form and volume. Measure and remeasure. Measure myself. Weigh myself. And then measure and weigh the lovely Simone. Weigh her small buttocks *and above all escape to the impotent compelling erotic dense immense blue once and for all*. Lost why found (again)? Where are the cities they promised us? . . . Where is the new (the *novum*), my dear Simone?] (ibid.)

Interestingly enough, the narrator describes the impossibility of measuring what he sees. As he tries to compare himself to nature, he feels powerless and unable to do it: "Measure and remeasure." As if he had suddenly discovered nature as the sublime, the narrator is unable to measure the object of his contemplation. The image of femininity blends with nature and its sublime quality. But, contrary to what is common in Latin American modernist fiction, woman and nature do not form an allegorical representation of the nation. Quite the contrary, the characters are lost and without roots. In spite of this, they are not victims because the logical sequence between the actions of losing and meeting is reversed: "Lost why found (again)?" In other words, there are two different motions at play, one of dispersal and the other of attraction, and they are indistinguishable. As the characters walk through the jungle, they suddenly find themselves in indigenous territory. The two opposite forces reappear as the real (physical) and the unreal (fiction) merge, and space and time disappear:

> No era de noche ni de día. No había espacio o únicamente había tiempo. ¿Quién eres tú? Yo creé la figura horrenda. Yo sola le di a luz. A la figra mágica, horrenda, última. Me interné en el bosque (en el único bosque). No ha habido calavera más sórdida ni crimen más ejemplarizante. Creo en los niños del mundo, atentos y con terroríficos orificios a modo de ojos. Lo dice el gran bosque, cantando con el silbido profundo de los leñadores, que responden a otros silbidos iguales lanzados por otros leñadores en los confines rojos de Australia.
>
> [It was neither night nor day. There was no space or there was only time. Who are you? I created the horrendous figure. I alone gave birth to it. To the magic, horrendous, final figure. I went into the forest (the only forest). There hasn't been a more sordid skull, nor a more exemplifying crime. I believe in the world children, attentive, and with horrific holes by way of eyes, singing with the deep whistle of woodcutters, who answer other similar whistles from other woodcutters in the red depths of Australia.] (ibid., 17)

These two scenes are articulated through paradoxes that do not lead to a resolution. Deceptively caught by nature's sublimity, the narrator realizes the lack of novelty (*novum*). Thus, sublimity does not provoke, as it does in Kant, an undecipherable perception. In other words, there is no sudden shock because there is no separation between reality and fiction; the action occurs without logic. As a matter of fact, the narrator admits to being in a state of insanity, which of course makes him an "unreliable narrator."

Violence, whether real or not, is the fabric of the story. It is also the experience that creates it, its point of departure: "I created the horrendous figure. I alone gave birth to it." Clearly referencing Piñera's "La isla en peso [The Island by Weight]," the short story climbs to an anticlimactic end through an apocalyptic representation of nature defined by sex, bestiality, and excess. It is indeed reality in its entirety that short-circuits the imagination, transforming it all into "the sleepless moment of children" (ibid., 21). It is precisely the inversion that the Enlightenment saw in imaginary monstrosity, as it was, for example, represented by Goya's condemnation of irrationality: "La imaginación abandonada por la razón concibe monstruos imposibles [Imagination abandoned by reason conceives impossible monsters]" (Goya's *Caprichos*). As a matter of fact, the text frequently comments critically on Cartesian rationalism. What is more, violence is language, and above all writing: "Yo soy quien no escribe, porque quien escribe supongo que sufre (que sufre mucho) y yo no sufro nada. Nada de nada [I'm the one who doesn't write, because I suspect that a person who writes suffers (suffers a lot) and I don't suffer anything. Anything at all]" (ibid., 18). Writing is actually the source of violence and suffering. The word is violence, and the word qua violence is produced by the death drive that generates the text: "Si escribes (si de verdad escribes dit-elle), entonces no es cosa de mirar abajo, al borde de la página. Eres algo que se estremece, borracho, hurgando entre las heces [If you write (if you really write, dit-elle), then it's nothing to look down on, at the edge of the page. You're something that shudders, drunk, rummaging amid the feces]" (ibid.). That is, writing is not a fiction; it does not originate in the process of creation, by looking at the page as a blank source of possibilities. Instead, it comes from an inner darkness of the intoxicated subject (*borracho*), who once believed in political emancipation: "Where are the cities they promised us? . . . Where is the new (the *novum*)?" It is not by chance, of course, that the narrator is addressing Sartre with those words. Sartre's commitment to the Cuban Revolution, his endorsement of communism, which have been backed up by book-length essays such as *Sartre on Cuba* as well as numerous articles written for *Le Monde*, are the target of the narrator's sarcasm:

> No nos han (ni te han) dejado otra cosa. Ni ha habido ni hay otra cosa. Convéncete. Eres un puro oh humano detritus. Un coprolitus sagrado. Tu fineza (tu improbable y en todo caso espúrea descendencia aristocrática) es sólo el discurso delirante de un desencuadernado esqueleto no museable, un milisegundo antes de disolverse en polvo con o sin estruendo, más bello para siempre en la luz que dueño indiscutido de sus razones. La gesta es una mano que ondula en el sueño proa a la desaparición y pasto de horripilantes legiones. No sueño esto y sobre todo nunca lo escribiré.
>
> [They haven't left us (or you) anything else. There wasn't and isn't anything else. Be sure of it. You're a pure oh human detritus.

> A holy coprolite. Your finesse (your improbable and in any event spurious aristocratic lineage) is just the delirious speech of an unbound skeleton unfit for a museum, a millisecond before dissolving with or without making a clatter, forever more beautiful in the light than undisputed master of its reason. The saga is a hand that flutters in a dream prior to disappearing and food for hideous legions. I didn't dream this and above all will never write it.] (ibid., 18)

"The saga [*la gesta*]" obviously refers to the epic revolutionary literature that we discussed in the first chapter. The narrator, a son of the revolution, belongs to a generation disenchanted with it. His writing comes from the violence inflicted by a revolutionary epic that conceived of violence as a means of salvation. This explains why the story conceives of the Revolution as a defeat: "Nunca saldremos de aquí. Es mejor que lo sepamos (y sobre todo que lo aceptemos) de una vez por todas. . . . No hay regreso ni estela [We'll never get out of here. Better that we realize (and above all accept it) once and for all. . . . There is no return and no wake (*estela*)]" (ibid., 20). Since this literature creates an imaginary that cannot be deciphered, it resists the Symbolic and belongs to the Real: "Y en cuanto a la susodicha comprensión, ¿a quién le importa? . . . Nos espera el exceso y una desaparición tan antológica [And as for the aforementioned understanding, who cares? . . . What awaits us is excess and a disappearance for the history books]" (ibid.).

In the story, writing has the function of the death drive, because it disrupts the system by hindering communication and interrupting libidinal cathexis. As such it produces suffering, although paradoxically, this is not the only feeling that writing produces. In several instances, contentment and discontent are at the source of the same phenomenological perception: "¿O este divertirse hasta la locura (este amar hasta la locura y más allá de la locura, como cuando se dice: "era la locura") podría ser sufrimiento en estado puro? [Oh this enjoyment to the point of madness (this loving to the point of madness and beyond, like when they say, 'It was madness') could it be suffering in its purest form?]" (ibid., 18). The paradox is that the death drive finds pleasure in what is most troubling in the organism. How can we explain such paradox in political terms and how did it play out in the different authors we have discussed? In sixties and seventies epic poetry, violence produces fulfillment because it is a means for a just cause. In this poetry, the discourse of violence follows a Hegelian dialectic where life sublates into death and produces an affirmation in the form of salvation. For Pasolini, instead, the denunciation of terror as it is perpetrated by the state is presented (*Darstellung*) as a negative force whose goal is an affirmation in the form of destruction (i.e., elimination of state hegemony). This operation has the logic of Adornian negative dialectics. In contrast to these two logics (revolutionary ideology and Pasolini's terror), the Proyecto Diáspora(s) aims to produce a "dysfunctional delight":

> 7
>
> El placer del texto ya pasará. Entonces vendrá la época del displacer, de raspar el texto con los ojos, o de poner los ojos en blanco, frente al texto.
>
> 8
>
> Ojalá que al leernos sientan, ustedes, una fruición inespecífica, disfuncional.
>
> [7
>
> The pleasure of the text will pass. Then will come the era of displeasure, of scraping the text with one's eyes, or rolling one's eyes before the text.
>
> 8
>
> As you read us may you feel an unspecified, dysfunctional delight.] (Sánchez Mejías 1997b, 2)

The relationship between pleasure and displeasure needs to be read as a dialectical relationship between affirmation and negation. Displeasure is articulated by the death drive, a force that finds pleasure in what is most troubling. As I have shown, for the Diáspora(s) discontent does not come necessarily from disenchantment with revolutionary politics. In other words, there is no melancholic desire to recover the lost dream. Discontent comes from the Diáspora(s) members' epistemological disagreement with revolutionary ideology, and their cultural politics, which is what they want to "destroy." This destruction is a negation (displeasure), but it is also an affirmation (pleasure), because it is articulated by the death drive. That is, the affirmation (pleasure) of the negation (destruction of revolutionary ideology) produces "dysfunctional delight," but it does not propose a construction (affirmation). The lack of purpose in this dynamic means that there is no closure (neither affirmation nor negation). In this regard, the Diáspora(s)'s poetics is not based in the notion that philosophy can recover the "truth" of ideology (as a thought that has been reified). Does this "dysfunctional delight" produce a Kantian sublime? For Kant, the sublime has magnitudes and qualities that challenge our cognitive capacities. In other words, the sublime is a form of cognition that short-circuits the imagination because it cannot be symbolized. In Lacanian terms this can be read as the Real. The poetics of defacement originates in negativity, and if the creation of this negativity is based on pleasure (in the negative), its goal is the creation of a pleasurable experience in the reader. If we look at it from the perspective of reception, this poetics is asking the reader to think. Yet, as in Kant, one needs to experience dread in order to form a thought. This is precisely what Carmelo Bene argues in his essay about Deleuze reprinted in *Diáspora(s)* 3. Bene cites Foucault as he argues that the writer has to explore beastliness by incorporating it:

> La inteligencia no responde a la bestialidad: es la bestialidad ya vencida, el arte categorial de evitar el error. El estudioso es inteligente. Pero es el pensamiento quién desafía a la bestialidad, y es la filosofía quien la mira. A la larga, están cara a cara. Con la mirada inmersa en este cráneo sin vela. Es su propia cabeza de muerto, Su tentación, su deseo, tal vez su teatro catatónico. Al límite, pensar sería contemplar intensamente, desde muy cerca, casi hasta que no veamos más, a la bestialidad; . . ." [el filósofo] debe siempre poseer una dosis de "mal carácter" para enfrentar la bestialidad, para contemplarla sin un gesto, hasta la estupefacción, para poder acercarse bien a ella y mimarla, para dejarla montar lentamente sobre sí (es tal vez lo que eufemísticamente se traduce como 'Ser absorbido en los propios pensamientos.')
>
> [Intelligence does not respond to beastliness. It is vanquished beastliness, the categorical art of avoiding error. The studious person is intelligent. But it is thought that defies beastliness, and philosophy that gazes upon it. In the end they are face to face. With the gaze plunged in the candleless skull. It is one's own death's head, one's temptation, one's desire, perhaps one's catatonic theater. At the limit, to think would be to contemplate beastliness deeply, up close, almost until we cannot see anymore; . . . [the philosopher] must always possess a degree of "bad temper" in order to confront beastliness, in order to contemplate it without flinching [*sin un gesto*], to the point of stupefaction, in order to get close to it and mimic it, to let it climb up on oneself (this might be what is euphemistically translated as "being absorbed in thoughts themselves").] (Bene 1998, 20)

That is, first Bene argues that one must experience evil in order to think about it. Second, once a violent act has occurred thought is powerless. Evil cannot be thought a posteriori because it should have been predicted a priori. Third, in order to predict evil one must inhabit it and experience it, but one must not fall into the temptation to combat evil with one's own violence. Sánchez Mejías defies the reader to experience discontent and "scrape the text with [his] eyes." That is, he is literally asking the reader to remove the outer layer of the text, meaning not to focus on ornamentation. Readers must undertake reading as an operation to think, and their action must cause some damage. In other words, to begin thinking it is necessary to do away with language (the outer layer), the surface that disables our capacity to think. This action of thinking causes us to "roll our eyes" or look in astonishment, surprise, or dismay. Thought creates a "dysfunctional delight," and the aesthetic experience becomes a poetics of defacement. That is, a poetics that originates from an experience of dread, and a defacement of language articulated by thought.

3

Biopolitics and the Revival of José Lezama Lima in the Eighties and the Nineties

Issue 4/5 of the samizdat journal *Diáspora(s)* features on its cover a detail of "Film de estreno [Film Première]," a drawing by Eduardo Zarza Guirola, a visual artist who is a contemporary of the members of the Proyecto Diáspora(s) (1998). A mass of screaming skeletons fill the cropped image. They seem about to leap from the page, panicked, clearly fleeing an imminent danger. In her article about Zarza that accompanies the image, Carmen Paula Bermúdez notes the omnipresence of death in his work: "Death can be anywhere; Death is life asking to renew itself" (1999, 102). Zarza represents human beings as living in a liminal space between death and life. This space points to the eerie temporality of the so-called Special Period (1989–2005), when the demise of the Soviet bloc dragged Cuba into ideological and economic collapse, leading the island to a political return of the past, which José Quiroga calls the Special Period's "memorialization" (Quiroga 2005, 4). Zarza's drawing points precisely to this change and alludes to the biopolitical administration of power during that decade. Biopolitics is an ideology that privileges the control of subjectivity and the body, as opposed to a politics where the power to kill the subject regiments the law. It is the control of life and the subjection of individuals by state power and the market. Understood in juridical terms, in a disciplinary (or modern) regime the sovereign had the right to kill or let live. After modernity, however, Western societies became regimented by what Michel Foucault calls biopolitics, a more sophisticated form of power. The ideological subjection of the population that the government required for its legitimization was carried out through the control of the population by biopower (power over life). In most Western democratic regimes there has been a transition from sovereign power to biopolitical power. But in Cuba, sovereign power coexists with a biopolitical regime. In its most basic Foucauldian sense, a biopolitical regime exists where power maintains administrative control over the life of subjects, in contrast to a sovereign regime, in which citizens are subjected through the monarch's right to kill. In a biopolitical regime, political rule nurtures and protects life. That is, biopolitical control is achieved through a series of technologies of the self (discourses of truth) that create "docile bodies," and "by which processes of subjectivation [bring] the individual to bind himself to his own identity and consciousness and, at the same time, to an external power" (Agamben 1998, 5). As we will see in this chapter, the representation of the body as an aesthetic and ontological transformation of the New Man reveals the different strategies of state power and domination.

I begin by focusing on the cultural politics that strove to "revive," the literary importance of José Lezama Lima during the nineties, as well as on the effort to stultify Lezama's impact in the seventies. I advance this argument by analyzing the different power strategies that shaped cultural policies during the two eras. During the first two decades of the Cuban Revolution, government power was legitimized and enforced through a set of policies based on the right of the state to enforce the law through violent measures. This was made possible by the significant political role of the armed forces and the legitimization the revolutionary victory gave them. As is well known, these were the years of the draconian state measures to combat diversionary ideology and eliminate homosexuality. In 1968, for example, Heberto Padilla was targeted for the counterrevolutionary content of his poems collection *Fuera del juego*. The polemic that sparked off when José Antonio Portuondo attacked Padilla in the armed forces journal *Verde olivo* eventually led to Padilla's arrest and forced confession of errors. In 1963, the state had also waged a war against homosexuality by using the armed forces to "rehabilitate" gays and other "social deviants" with the Unidades Militares de Ayuda a la Producción (UMAP) (Domínguez 1978, 392). One more example of these repressive policies was the creation of the "ley contra la vagancia" (law against idleness) in the early seventies, a measure that gave the state leeway for indiscriminate arrest (Pérez-Stable 1993, 224).

In contrast, during the nineties, there was more room for disagreement, and it became more efficient to control the life of citizens by regulating it through norms. As a matter of fact, the strategies of state power had already changed with the process of liberalization of the early eighties, as I have already argued. Similarly to what happened in the nineties, at the end of the eighties the government launched the "Proceso de rectificación de errores y tendencias negativas" ("Rectification Process of Errors and Negative

Tendencies") on April 19, 1986, to recover socialist values lost with the liberalization reforms. Whereas sovereign power was still present in Cuba, the state developed new strategies of power more akin to those of the Soviet bloc. Although Cuba did not undertake any of Gorbachev's perestroika or glasnost initiatives, it developed new tactics to control the life of the population and ensure its support of a withering ideology. One of these new power tactics has been to argue that the country is reforming, and thus opening to the world. The control of the population does not change, however, what changes is the form of control. Instead of repressing and prohibiting, the rhetoric becomes "Live and let live." Moral values are again emphasized in the workplace; homosexuality and queer culture are gradually accepted. Yet the new rhetoric of acceptance of difference is paradoxically a new and more subtle tactic of control that Foucault calls biopower, a new form of subjection to the same regressive ideology. The government's claims notwithstanding, in other words, there is not really an ideological change but instead simply a new form of exerting control.

Cultural initiatives such as the revival of Lezama, for example, were biopolitical forms of power devised to maintain an ideological control. Among the upsurge of scholarly work about Lezama written during the eighties and nineties, I specifically focus on the reading of the sexualized body in Lezama's work. This official criticism of Lezama's work is key to understanding how his discourse became a dispositif of power intended to desexualize the body that vicariously represented the New Man. On the one hand, official criticism reinterpreted sexual jouissance as the culmination of the Catholic Lezamian *imago*. On the other hand, the intellectual group Proyecto Diáspora(s) destroyed the Catholic and baroque body to show the biopolitical transformation of citizens into docile bodies. In Diáspora(s)'s samizdat *Diáspora(s)* as in its members' poetry, these bodies are given an ambiguous political reading. The subjectivity of the characters these texts portray could be symbolizing a freedom of sorts. But these characters could also be representing citizens who have lost their subjectivity and the control over their lives. In order to fully understand this ambiguity, I reflect on emancipation through Gilles Deleuze and Félix Guattari's notions of "the schizo" and "becoming-animal," parts of a theoretical framework that has deeply influenced Diáspora(s)'s work. In my counterreading of these figures, I argue that some of these characters have in fact uncannily turned into Giorgio Agamben's "*homo sacer*," the docile body with no control over its own life.

The study of state power and its manifestations (sovereign or biopolitical) is crucial to understanding the poetics of Diáspora(s), because the group's understanding of subjectivity is a critique of biopower. As we saw with Zarza's "Film Première," the politics administering power over life dehumanize those subjected to them, and this is precisely what Diáspora(s) show in their work. This is why, before delving into Lezama, this chapter looks at the theoretical implications of biopower in the context of the "Special Period." To illustrate the deployment of biopower I look at *Boleto al paraíso* (*Ticket to Paradise*), a film depicting the segregation of HIV-positive patients in Cuba, and I analyze the Elián González affair. It is the dialectics between life and death that I seek to analyze in this chapter. First, I show how sovereign power (the right to kill with impunity) and biopower (the control over life and subjectivity) coexist. Second, I demonstrate how institutionalized culture deploys these two forms of power in silencing José Lezama Lima's work and sexuality (the right to kill), and how it revives them (control over subjectivity and body). Finally, I analyze Diáspora(s)'s focus on these two types of power through their relationship to Lezama's baroque language, and through their own poetry.

Biopolitical Policies

The sovereign has the power to kill or let live, and all other rights derive from it. The power of death and life has been exerted differently over the centuries, however. Premodern forms of power privileged the right to kill over the right to allow life, and the former has become, since modernity, the main form of power. How does the power to spare life manifest as a form of power or biopower (power over life)? Biopower is a form of control and subjection of the population to the law of the state. In Cuba, the two forms of power (the right to kill and biopower) coexist, but the latter has proven to be the most effective way to maintain the regime. During the seventies more emphasis was put on the right to sanction than on the right to let live. The first indication of biopolitical power's influence in the nineties came when the Cuban government dubbed the period as the "Special Period in Peacetime" ("Periodo especial en tiempos de paz")." In the aftermath of the Soviet bloc, the country sank into the worst economic and ideological crisis of the revolution. The government responded by taking drastic economic and social measures that put revolutionary ideals on hold. Since the Cuban Revolution was loosely based on Marxist doctrine, it was also conceived as a process whose different political stages would finally lead to a classless society. The revolution had indeed gone through different socioeconomic periods determined, unfortunately, by foreign policy rather than internal policies. As a consequence, the government had usually defined the different periods in relation to their antagonism to "imperialism." The Cold War was a period "en tiempos de guerra" but, for the first time, the crisis was so intense that the worst enemy became real socialism. In these circumstances, and unwillingly, the government had no choice but to rely on capitalism. Socialism was put at a standstill, and capitalism was given the role of savior. On the one hand, there was no war to be waged against capitalism; on the other, the government calculated that its adoption of a semicapitalist economy would be temporary, exceptional, and "special."

The eighties and the nineties could be a period of change and renaissance, or so everybody thought. Once the economy was reestablished, a new type of socialism could arise from the ashes. This explains why some scholars have argued that the state became more tolerant of criticism. During crisis periods such as the early 1990s, notes Susan Eckstein, "the arts . . . enjoyed [a] certain autonomy of expression, although explicit criticism of the regime was never tolerated and even allegorical criticism was not [permitted]" (Eckstein 1994, 25). In a debate about Cuban civil society—a hot topic during the period—Haroldo Dilla acknowledged that the role of the state had changed: "In truth, we were leaving a situation of the overpresence of the state; the news spread rapidly and everyone began clamoring for more civil society" (Dilla 1994, 165). Although the economic changes it made were not drastic, the government was forced to join the market economy.

Dollarization, the liberation of agricultural cooperatives, and the authorization of "cuentapropismo" (private business) and joint ventures with foreign companies were some of the government's market reforms. But it took these steps reluctantly. During the Popular Power Assembly held in December 1993, Fidel Castro "inveighed against capitalism, its 'excesses' and the 'profit motive'" (Pérez-Stable 1993, 294). Almost half the population lived from the "remesas" sent by their families abroad or from the tourist industry. Although the government insisted on subsuming economic interests to political choices, new political strategies were essential to mobilize an economically independent population: "The citizens had access to resources that did not come from the state, a situation that threatened the paradigm of mobilization so important for political control. If a significant number of citizens became economically independent, how could they be compelled to listen?" (ibid., 295). The use of biopolitical power was one of those strategies.

A good example of these practices was the way the state dealt with the arrival of AIDS on the island. Medical sources claim that AIDS was brought to Cuba by military personnel returning from Africa in the late eighties and early nineties (Cooper, Kennely, and Orduñez-García 2206, 821).[1] The first case was diagnosed in 1985. The government came up with different strategies to prevent and combat AIDS. One of the most widely criticized plans began with the arrival of the disease and lasted until 1993 (Sweig 2009, 146). After a mandatory test, people infected with HIV were quarantined in special health facilities, where they received medical treatment in complete isolation from the outside world. A vast array of cultural production has focused on this particular form of seclusion of those suffering from the pandemic. Foremost in this production are the testimonies, memoirs, and short stories written by the patients themselves. A quasi-paradoxical characteristic of the health facilities, as the recent film *Boleto al paraíso* (*Ticket to Paradise*) shows, is that although the patients were confined, their living conditions were much better than those of the average citizen. In a period characterized by the shortage of food and the deterioration of the material conditions of daily life, the AIDS sanatoriums seemed like a paradise. At least this is the premise of *Boleto al paraíso*, where a group of young friends without a clear future transmit AIDS to each other in the hopes of ending their lives in a state sanatorium. The scene of ritualistic bacchanalia in which the friends pass the virus to each other is one of the most revealing depictions of the era's biopolitical medical discourse. The viewer's gaze is directed toward the different moaning faces as the friends have sex with each other. The camera shows long slow close-ups of their faces lit with candles, composing a sacred space of sorts.

As bodies change and move, the spectator no longer knows who is who. The bodies lose their individual identity, becoming one and the same. One realizes that they have crossed the threshold that separates life from death. They have become expendable bodies that will be subjected to the incarcerating power of an institution that both makes them live and normalizes their life with a metaphoric discourse that qualifies the illness as a plague (Sontag 1989, 142).[2]

The medical practices and discourses identified AIDS victims as "risk groups," a denomination whose military allusions—conveyed in words such as defense, attack, invasion, etc.—cast them as a threat to society (Sontag 1989, 183). As we will see in this chapter, these types of normalizing

Boleto al paraíso (Gerardo Chijona, 2011). Candles.

Boleto al paraíso (Gerardo Chijona, 2011). Alejandro and Milena.

discourses, whose primary and paradoxical purpose was the administration and prolongation of life, became common in the cultural politics of the late eighties and nineties. Zarza's drawing captures the biopolitical nature of power discourses, an institutional rhetoric to keep alive those who are biologically dead. Biopolitical power is still present in our contemporary era. For instance, the daily column in *Granma* devoted to "Las reflexiones del compañero Fidel" accounts for this gesture, too, albeit in a more metaphorical fashion. While decision-making power rests in the hands of Cuba's current government presided over by Raúl Castro, Fidel Castro's image and discourse still has a fundamental presence in the media. The prolongation

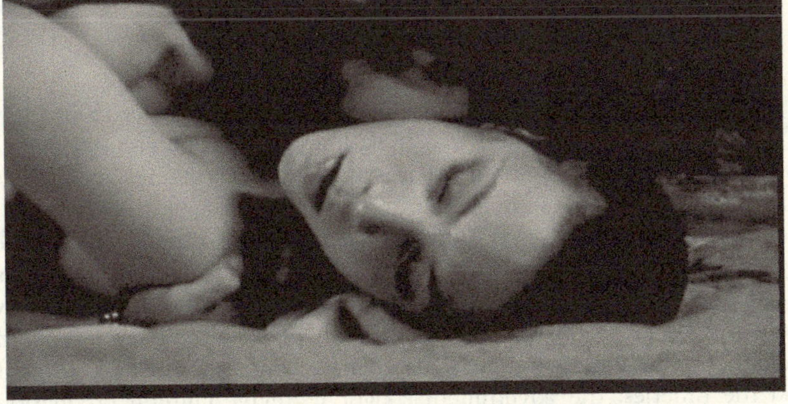

Boleto al paraíso (Gerardo Chijona, 2011). Alejandro and Lidia.

of his political life through mediatic power has been critical in preserving the socialist dream alive. When Fidel Castro's health forced him to withdraw from the public sphere, the country's anxious response made it very clear that a personalistic regime such as Cuba's could not afford to lose the leader's physical presence.

The uproar over the removal of the boy Elián González from Miami, in the year 2000, was another sign of the deployment of biopolitical power. This effort was part of the "Battle of Ideas" campaign, inspired by José Martí's affirmation in "Nuestra América" that "trincheras de ideas valen más que trincheras de piedras" [Trenches of ideas are worth more than trenches of stones], simultaneously an affirmation of life and a rejection of antagonistic political positions (Martí 1997, 37). Fidel Castro introduced this campaign in December 1998, at the end of the seventh congress of the Unión de Jóvenes Comunistas de Cuba (UJC). Intended as a campaign for revolutionary achievements and values, the "Batalla de Ideas" began during the international conflict with the United States that sought to have Elián González returned to Cuba. The aim, according to the government, was to deepen political consciousness among workers and young people. Symbolically, the fight for the child was a surrogate for the recovery of the body of the nation. Once Elián was won back by Cuba, he was given the same economic and social privileges of the apparatchik class, an effort to show that Cuba could also offer its citizens a prosperous and successful life. He was then made into a government media star, a leader of the Pioneers Movement, and the herald of revolutionary principles as he progressed through his military career. This is one the best examples of a power that exerts itself around the principle of life and that desubjectivates individuals by measuring life by its utility and its value, and not for itself (Foucault 1990, 144).

State Biopolitics and Representations of the Body in Lezama's Criticism

The nineties' biopolitics manifested itself in cultural politics as the *revival* of intellectual figures (rather than their life per se). The cultural measures intended to remedy the political mistakes of the seventies were exerted only as the negation of the latter, and not as meaningful changes of the ideological parameters of revolutionary practices. In other words, the disciplinary power of the seventies that regimented society had now become a biopolitical power. Whereas during the seventies the government was more interested in the metaphorical death of a cultural production that did not fulfill the government's ideological mandates, during the eighties and the nineties, the government sought to revive cultural production it had previously prohibited. During the seventies, which were defined by the political and intellectual dogmatism of the "five gray years" (*Quinquenio gris*) (1971–76), authors considered apolitical or counterrevolutionary were removed from state positions and their works were deemed unacceptable for publication. During the late eighties and nineties, however, the same authors were canonized, their works reprinted by publishers and reconsidered by scholars.[3] Several of these authors who returned to favor belonged to the Grupo Orígenes, a circle of poets that included José Lezama Lima and Virgilio Piñera.[4] The group, a major influence on Diáspora(s), took its name from a high modernist literary and cultural journal that Lezama and José Rodríguez Feo edited from 1944 to 1956. Discredited by the revolution's cultural apparatus during the seventies as hermetic and aesthetically ineffective (Salgado 2002, 201), the works of the Grupo Orígenes were republished during the eighties and nineties as part of a series of cultural measures aimed at rectifying the seventies' political errors.[5]

It is crucial that we analyze state power and look at the differences between its application as sovereign power or biopower. In order to understand the ideological complexities embedded in the critical configuration of official discourses and independent voices, we should now briefly describe the different approaches to Lezama's theories. We must begin by reviewing the first scholarly pieces written in the forties and fifties. If we did not, we would miss one of the most important aspects of this evolution: the fact that the same scholars who praised Lezama's poetics for their transcendentalism and for creating a national culture in the fifties, a decade later interpreted his work as an allegory of the revolution's teleological narration. In the seventies, the revolutionary reading no longer persuaded cultural authorities, who used Lezama's transcendentalism and his so-called idealism and antimaterialism to discredit his work. After his death, his work was institutionally restituted and his thought rearticulated in revolutionary terms. Some scholars have already noted the instrumentalization of Lezama's work for ideological purposes. For example, Enrico Santí writes that "the Revolution invented . . . José Lezama Lima, since it was during [the Revolution] that his work took on unprecedented projection. . . . I refer not only to the diffusion of this work . . . but to the creation of Lezama as an institution" (Santí 2002, 195–96).

In this chapter, I suggest that the different interpretations of Lezama during the past five decades have been instrumentalized for various political purposes. The changes result from the different modes of instrumentalization and their relation to different modes of governance. As is well known, there was an upsurge of Lezama studies in the eighties and the nineties, and official interpretations coming from the island widely discussed the role of sexuality in his work, especially his novels. In this chapter we will see that the understanding of sexuality has not changed that much. What have evolved instead are new discursive strategies, procedures, and mechanisms of power. The population is controlled more surreptitiously, through biopolitics, a power of subjection articulated through ideas affirming life instead of death. In the nineties, only the young writers of Diáspora(s) called into question the official revival of Lezama, but they also rejected his baroque style. What type of literature is left after the denial of the baroque body, and after the official discourse of life? We are left with a body without subjectivity, a hardly human one that Agamben refers to as bare life. The *homo sacer*, the "sacred" or excluded man, stripped of subjectivity is a product of biopolitical governance and also present in Diáspora(s) aesthetics. Bare life, as incarnated by *homo sacer*, is an emotionless body, apolitical and outside of history, yet in Diáspora(s) aesthetics it also functions as a political force because it represents what Deleuze and Guattari understand as a body without organs.

Prerevolution and Revolution

The Forties and Fifties: Cultural and National Readings of Lezama

The forties and fifties are the period when Orígenes developed and became an object of critical interest. Cintio Vitier, then part of the group, invented Orígenes and canonized it at the end of the forties: "Este carácter de grupo referido a Orígenes ha sido recientemente defendido. . . . Y ya estaba dicho en la página inicial del prólogo a la primera de las dos antologías, de 1948 y 1952, en que Cintio Vitier fijó el canon de lo que en cuanto a poesía, raíz de su tarea, iba a ser conocido como grupo Orígenes [This group known as Orígenes has recently been championed. . . . And the group was mentioned on the first page of the prologue of the first of two excellent anthologies, published in 1948 and 1952, in which Cintio Vitier set forth the canon of the poetry of what became known as the 'Grupo Orígenes,' the core of his work]" (Fernández Retamar 1994, 294). Although Vitier created Orígenes, Roberto Fernández Retamar was actually the first scholar who, in 1954, systematized the peculiarities of the Orígenes style, and more specifically Lezama style. For Lezama, poetry was an ethos, as well as a hermeneutic key to the world of aesthetics and knowledge. The abstract and highly allegorical nature of Lezama's poetics led Fernández Retamar to argue in 1954 that his poetry was "transcendental . . . in that it does not limit itself to verbal pleasures, or to considering the poem as an affective-conceptual exposition. Rather, it sees the poem as the possible capture of reality" (ibid., 86–87). If Fernández Retamar celebrated Lezama's poetry for its ontological qualities, Vitier praised its potential to express the essence of Cuban cultural and historical identity. In other words, Vitier believed that Cuba's future was predetermined and inscribed in Lezama's vision of history. His well-known analysis of Lezama's work comes out of a commissioned series of lectures on Cuban poetry delivered in 1957 and published in 1958 as *Lo cubano en la poesía*. As the title indicates, this study sought to construct a history of Cuban canonical poetry as a cultural compensation of Cuban national identity.

Vitier's narrative of national identity begins with "Espejo de paciencia" ("Mirror of Patience," the 1608 poem by Silvestre de Balboa) and culminates with Grupo Orígenes. The ideological metaphor that articulates the text posits that throughout history, the search for a poetic voice has been driven by the quest for a national identity informed by the singularities of ethnicity and land. The pinnacle of this quest is Lezama's work, and most specifically his "insular teleology": "Poetry does have its own finality, but this finality is all-encompassing. The devouring substance is necessarily teleological. This is how . . . Lezama attempts to conjure the absence of finality against which our republican poetry has struggled" (Vitier 1986, 396). For Vitier, poetry and history narrate the nation through a progress toward a parallel telos informed by the idea of an essential "Cubanness." Accordingly, Lezama's poetry is seen as the culmination of the nation's identity. Although Lezama coined the term "teleología insular," he never actually used it to characterize the goal of his work. Instead, Vitier reappropriated it to suit his nationalistic reading of Lezama. As Vitier recounts in an essay written for an international conference about Lezama held in Poitiers, France, he borrowed the term in 1939 from a letter Lezama wrote to him. Orígenes did not exist then, but it was beginning to develop at the poetry readings Vitier organized in his home. Lezama enthusiastically and ironically responded to one of those invitations by vowing to create a poetic mission: "Ya va siendo hora de que todos nos empeñemos en una Economía Astronómica, en una Meterología habanera para uso de descarriados y poetas, en una Teleología Insular, en algo de veras grande y nutridor [It is high time that we all set to work on an Astronomical Economy, on a Havana Meteorology to be used by wayward people and poets, on an Insular Teleology, on something truly grand and sustaining]" (Vitier 1984, 27). Although Lezama's proposal was obviously ironic, Vitier took it seriously and adopted it.

The First Revolutionary Years

When the revolution erupted, Vitier was one of the intellectuals who supported it most fiercely. He began embracing the revolution's social ideas from a non-Marxist perspective rooted in Catholic liberation theology. Whereas in *Lo cubano en la poesía*, Vitier gave the "teleología insular" a cultural connotation, once the revolution was in place, "lo cubano" (Cubanness) itself became political. From then onward, to be Cuban meant to be revolutionary, and this is how Vitier saw Lezama:

> El empeño fundamental de Martí había consistido en encarnar la poesía en la historia. Lezama en su visión de las eras imaginarias parece que quiere desencarnar la historia en la poesía. . . . Si en Martí el acto es el fecundador de la expresión, del verbo, de la imagen . . . en Lezama la imagen es la matriz de lo analógico, totalizadora de la realidad como verbo. Considerados separadamente, ambos mundos parece que se excluyen o contradicen, pero si los vemos dialécticamente . . . si comprendemos que el mundo verbal de Lezama corresponde a la frustración histórica del mundo de Martí . . . se nos hace más evidente una relación más profunda. A esa luz la obra de Lezama resulta una respuesta antifonal a la obra de Martí, el puente que lleva su ausencia a la otra orilla, mientras que por otros caminos los héroes y los hechos se dirigían al punto de la nueva convergencia de la imagen y la historia, de la nueva encarnación de la poesía en el acto.
>
> [Martí's fundamental effort was to incarnate poetry in history. Lezama, in his vision of imaginary eras, seems to wish to disincarnate history in poetry. . . . If in Martí the act is the progenitor of expression, of the word, of the image . . . in Lezama the image is the womb of the analogical, totalizing reality as the word. Considered separately both worlds seem to exclude or contradict each other, but if we consider them dialectically . . . if we understand that Lezama's verbal world corresponds to the historical frustration of Martí's world . . . a deeper relationship becomes evident. In this light, Lezama's work appears to be an antiphonal response to that of Martí, the bridge carrying its absence to the other shore, while on other roads heroes and deeds head for the new point of convergence of the image and history, the new incarnation of poetry in the act.] (Vitier 2001, 345)

According to Vitier, Lezama followed Martí's genealogy because for both authors poetry was as much a revolutionary act as a national allegory of redemption. That is, for Martí, poetry compensated for a failed revolution, whereas for Lezama the image could create an act. Paradoxically, while this interpretation would align Lezama with the cultural policies of the seventies, it also went against him. A poet who claimed that art could create a reality was immediately considered as an idealist for the seventies social poets. Revolutionary art could only exist on the basis of a materialist view of the world, which Lezama lacked.

Even Fernández Retamar, who had praised Orígenes for the transcendental nature of its poetics, began reading Lezama during the revolution as a messianic poet who had foreseen the 1953 Moncada barracks attack that would lead to the events of 1959:

> Innecesario subrayar la fecha: 1953. Cuando Cuba había sido metida hasta el cuello en la sentina descrita por Rodríguez Feo, Lezama, que nada tenía de poeta puro y muchísimo de poeta absoluto, llegando a serlo en una dimensión que entre nosotros solo sobrepasó Martí, lanzó a propósito de este, en su centenario una profecía que pocos meses, invocándose también a Martí, intentaría a fondo encarnar en la historia.
>
> [No need to underscore the date: 1953. When Cuba was up to its neck in the cesspool described by Rodríguez Feo, Lezama, who was in no way a pure poet and in many ways an absolute poet, to a degree that among us only Martí surpassed, issued on the centennial of the latter's birth, also invoking Martí, a prophecy that in a few months would attempt to fully incarnate history.] (Fernández Retamar 1994, 320)

In sum, whereas before the Revolution, critics had emphasized the cultural and ontological nature of Lezama's poetry, in the early sixties they ascribed a political meaning to it.

Deadening Lezama in the Sixties and Seventies

The cultural policies of the sixties and the seventies were mostly guided by Fidel's ominous pronouncement, "Con la Revolución, todo; contra la Revolución, nada" ("Within the Revolution, everything; outside the Revolution, nothing"). This injunction took on a ghostly power that presided over the creative process of every intellectual; it became the main ethical duty of the writer to practice engaged literature (*littérature engagée*). Castro's dictum reaffirmed the idea that under the Revolution, politics were defined in a Schmittian sense as the antagonism between friends and enemies. Those who did not follow Castro's directive were considered unethical counterrevolutionaries, enemies of the regime. Castro's injunction made an impossible demand of intellectuals: to obey a law whose limits were undecipherable and unknown. In other words, where did a revolutionary critique of the new existing order begin, and when did that critique become counterrevolutionary? Since the limits of the law were not clearly enunciated, there was ample room for arbitrary decisions.

This is why I posit that Castro's injunction was also the product of the sovereign regime of power, which, intellectually speaking, unfolded according to its right to *make die*, as it did with Lezama's work. Sovereign power also dictated arbitrary cultural policies establishing which intellectuals would be supported and allowed to thrive, and which ones would be silenced and repudiated. Critics rejected Lezama for not conforming to the norms of colloquialism. Scholars condemned his aestheticism, his metaphysical themes, and the autonomy of literature that his writing symbolized. Lezama's hermetism, which Fernández Retamar had praised, was no longer acceptable because it contradicted the social function of literature. As I discussed in chapter 1, contrary to Ernesto Guevara's claim in "Socialism and Man in Cuba," socialist realism had a significant presence in Cuban art, especially regarding poetry. One of the main premises of colloquialism was that form and content had to mirror each other. Colloquialism or social poetry loosely followed a number of rules devised by Jean-Paul Sartre, whose poetics had considerable influence among Cuban intellectuals in the sixties. These included the requirement that literature give an objective testimony of reality, which precluded a subjective and lyrical account of the world and led to the transformation of realism into social realism. For Sartre, theory and praxis were inseparable: the writer had to be a hero, in the mold of José Martí. As a poetic movement based on political imagery and direct language, colloquialism repudiated Lezama's writing.

In his analysis of the portrayals of Lezama and *Orígenes* published in the *Revista de Casa de las Américas*, Juan Carlos Quintero-Herencia quotes some of the most hostile ones, such as Roberto Branly's remarks in his appraisal of the poet Pedro de Oraá in *Casa de las Américas* 9:

> En ambas vertientes, Oraá trasluce su tiempo horadado por el cristal de la poesía, en imágenes fluyentes y acabadas, como surgidas del pincel barroco, donde una estética—que obviamente hoy día el propio autor no comparte plenamente—emerge con sus mitos de remanso quieto, fijo, atento y contemplativo. Es decir: esa mitología de la imagen "pura" traspasada por la espiral de pensamiento idealista que esplendiera en los poetas de la revista *Orígenes*. Verbigracia del círculo etéreo de la "insularidad," su paisaje venturoso y tenue y otras especies del diminuto universo criollo, vigente sólo en la visión parcial de los origenistas. Claro que es ahora, en la Nueva Cuba donde nuestro pueblo ejercita cabalmente su revolución patriótica, democrática y socialista, donde la realidad genuina—no afiebrada por "intuiciones"; sino

> eso: genuina—nos es dable aprehender, partiendo efectivamente de su interpretación raigal y exacta: el marxismo leninismo.
>
> [Oraá reveals his time transpierced by the crystal of poetry. In fluid and refined imagery, as if traced by a baroque brush, an aesthetics (which obviously the author himself no longer fully shares) emerges with its myths of a tranquil, still, attentive, and contemplative haven. That is, the mythology of the "pure" image shot through by the spiral of idealistic thought that flourished in the poets of the journal *Orígenes*, the verbal grace of the ethereal circle of "insularity," its happy and delicate landscape, and other matters of the diminutive *criollo* universe, which function only in the tendentious visions of the Origenists. It is clear that now, in the New Cuba in which our people fully wages its patriotic, democratic, and socialist revolution, in which we can perceive genuine reality—not feverish [*afiebrada*] by "intuitions" but, precisely, genuine reality—basing ourselves in its fundamental and precise interpretation: Marxism Leninism.] (qtd. in Quintero Herencia 1997, 94)

Branly's hostility is directed toward the poetics that Lezama shared with Oraá. Branly opposes revolutionary materialism to Lezama's idealism, which, like Vitier, he defines in its most vulgar sense as an idea that can create a reality. During the sixties and the seventies, revolutionary critics dismissed the hermetic and transcendental nature of Lezama's work because it could not materialize the political ethos that the revolution demanded. During the eighties and nineties, however, official critics began defending the transcendental nature of Lezama's poetics by interpreting his work as an allegory of the revolution's teleological project. Cultural policy privileged a certain interpretation of Lezama to ideologically reify his work. Like Santí, Antonio José Ponte alludes to this phenomenon in discussing the critical impoverishment of Lezama's scholarly criticism (Ponte 1998, 2–3.)

The Eighties and Nineties

Power practices shifted in the nineties with the emergence of a biopolitical regime. At the beginning of the so-called Special Period, Fidel Castro stated that Cuba could no longer construct socialism but had to save its achievements. His pronouncement "La cultura es lo primero que hay que salvar" (Culture is what must be saved) appears as the title of the Fifth Congress Proceedings of the National Union of Cuban Writers and Artists (UNEAC) in 1993 (*Memorias* 1993). These claims indicate that Fidel's political strategy following the crisis was articulated as the political necessity to *make live*. The intellectual voices that had been rendered invisible during the sixties had to be made visible anew. These policies responded to an erosion of national culture such as the one that had taken place during the Republic. The national building project of the revolution was based on culturally mediated forms that strongly articulated the social and the state, but during the nineties this paradigm collapsed. The crisis of this model put an end to the possibility of actualizing the myth of the New Man imagined by Guevara in "Socialism and Man in Cuba." According to Guevara's calculations, the New Man was to emerge in the nineties, but by then real socialism had collapsed and the ideological momentum that made the revolution possible had withered. These two facts explain why the generation of the nineties immediately identified with postmodernity and its lack of utopian desire instead of embracing the revolutionary enthusiasm represented by the New Man.

State officials were well aware of this. For example, Minister of Culture Armando Hart argued that "the generation of intellectuals formed in, and by, the revolution is interested in politics and desires to participate in it, but its members have felt the terrible impact of the socialist reversal of the eighties" (Hart 1988, 56). Indeed, since the beginning of that decade, postmodernist rhetoric and aesthetics had become pervasive in all cultural forms, especially written works. Margarita Mateo Palmer was the first scholar to theorize the rise of postmodernism in Cuban literature in *Ella escribía poscrítica* (*She Wrote Postcriticism*), a book of essays that won the Premio Nacional de la Crítica in 1996. The aesthetics of transgression that Mateo Palmer discussed was not necessarily at odds with revolutionary values. Postmodern trends included claims in favor of popular culture, marginal identities, and testimonial values. She failed to acknowledge, however, that recent fiction showed a general skepticism of utopian ideals, which is precisely the type of skepticism that government officials criticized in young writers: "Ahora ante la tragedia moral de la llamada postmodernidad, recuerdo otro pensamiento del Apóstol: 'No hay proa que taje una nube de ideas. Una idea enérgica flameada a tiempo ante el mundo, para, como la bandera mística del juicio final, a un escuadrón de acorazados' [Today, faced with the moral tragedy of so-called postmodernity, I recall another maxim of the Apostle [Martí]: 'No ship's bow can cut through a cloud of ideas. An energetic idea that flutters early enough before the world will halt, like the mystical flag of the final judgment, a fleet of battleships]'" (ibid., 60). Through his reference to Martí, Hart sought to emphasize the continuation of the revolution's ideological project. This gesture can only be read as an overcompensation for the regime's political and economic contradictions.

In a context where the grand narratives were being questioned, the revival of the Grupo Orígenes made much political sense. Since the unity of the nation was crumbling and the younger generation of intellectuals was contributing to this collapse, it became imperative to recover the works of writers, who, like Lezama, had focused on the crisis and construction of national identity. Two years after Batista's coup, in a letter addressed to Spanish philosopher María Zambrano, Lezama had bitterly denounced the disintegration of the nation during the Republic: "No parece alzarse nunca la recta interpretación, a la veracidad, todo para fruto de escamoteos, de sustituciones. Si los profetas le llamaban a Babilonia la gran prostituta, ¿cómo no llamarle a nuestra querida isla, la gran mentirosa? Se corrompe la palabra [Correct interpretation and truthfulness never seem to carry the day, all because of sleight of hand and substitutions. If the prophets called Babylon the great whore, how can we not call our dear island the great liar? The word is being corrupted]" (Lezama 2001, 550). This was a corruption that the Grupo Orígenes had fiercely criticized. During the Republic, the Grupo Orígenes, specifically Lezama, had been very critical of Fulgencio Batista's 1952 coup and the ensuing political unfolding of his kleptocracy. Lezama's concern about the national project of the literary canon was then appropriated by Vitier, who read his work as an allegorical representation of the nation's teleological destiny. Like Vitier, Abel Prieto stated that, for Lezama, the literary and political project of the nation during the Republic was exhausted. Prieto also drew a parallel between the cultural and ideological crisis of the Republic and that of the nineties. In his opening speech of UNEAC's Fifth Congress, Prieto called for the reestablishment of a national literature of resistance capable of articulating the revolution's teleological project: "Sabemos, aunque vale la pena repetirlo, que la cultura forma parte sustancial del esfuerzo de resistencia de la Cuba de hoy. También sabemos que es una de las formas de hacer visible ese ramo de fuego, de hacer cristalizar ese milagro, esa experiencia peculiar de sentir la 'historia de muchos en una sola visión,' la fórmula idónea para que el hombre fragmento encuentre la imantación para hacer avanzar el proyecto de todos [We know, although it is worth repeating, that culture is a substantial part of the resistance effort of today's Cuba. We also know that it is one of the ways to make visible this flaming branch, to crystallize this miracle, that particular experience of feeling the 'story of many in a single vision,' the proper formula allowing fragmented man to develop the magnetism necessary to advance the project of all]" (Prieto 1993, 53).

This cultural politics also aligned with the new ideological turn toward a Martian nationalist project that superseded the traditional emphasis on Marxism Leninism.[6] The nationalist emphasis on Martí's legacy actually revealed a political disavowal. That is, on the one hand, the country opened up to integrated world capitalism because the government recognized the economic impasse and took drastic measures to overcome it. On the other hand, the government refused to acknowledge the *political* crisis caused by the disappearance of socialism as realistic politics. As Rafael Rojas noted, "Paradójicamente, mientras el estado cubano flexibiliza su idea de sí mismo y cede una porción de la iniciativa económica a la sociedad, nuestra cultura política pretende definirse desde un nacionalismo cada vez más intransigente [Paradoxically, while the Cuban state is making more flexible its self-conception and ceding part of the economic initiative to society, our political culture is seeking to define itself through an increasingly intransigent nationalism]" (Rojas 1998, 53). The *revival* of Martí's legacy was one more consequence of biopolitics. Reviving Martí and Lezama was a purely instrumental gesture. The objective was the control of bodies, because these discourses were written from the emptiness of a body devoid of subjectivity. Lezama and Piñera were ostracized in the seventies above all because of their sexuality. Their bodies disappeared, as it were, and during the nineties they were brought back. The new discussion of Lezama took on transcendental and political overtones. Like many other writers from the nineties, the members of Diáspora(s) brought the body and sexuality to the fore. Pedro Marqués de Armas, for instance, wrote *Fascículos sobre Lezama*, a psychoanalytical interpretation of sexuality in *Oppiano Licario*. Diáspora(s) also sought to debunk the biopolitical revival of Lezama.

During the eighties and the nineties, two different and ideologically opposed recuperations of Orígenes emerged. First, a series of state-sponsored cultural events around the figure of Lezama generated a renewed interest in Orígenes among his first critics, especially Orígenes-affiliated critics such as Vitier and Fina García Marruz, as well as Fernández Retamar, whom Lezama had mentored. Second, the younger contemporary poets took increasing critical interest in Orígenes. Why were Orígenes's first critics involved in this new critical reawakening? Mainly because of the ideological proximity between them and cultural officials. During the eighties and nineties, intellectuals belonging to this older generation held important positions in cultural institutions and followed the ideological line of the Ministry of Culture and the government. Cultural officials looked on Vitier, Fernández Retamar, and García Marruz as the experts on Orígenes. The expertise of García Marruz and Vitier on Lezama was legitimated by their intellectual involvement in Orígenes. Above all, they won official support because, despite their Catholicism, they read Lezama teleologically, coinciding with the utopian version of the revolution as a historical process. Vitier, García Marruz, and future culture minister Abel Prieto were selected by the Ministry of Culture to attend the international colloquium on Lezama's work in Poitiers, France, in 1982. The degree of institutional involvement in this conference indicates the ideological importance of a topic that would not have received official support during the two previous decades. In the discussion of sexuality in Lezama's novels, these critics' interpretations contributed to the dissemination of a biopolitical discourse.

THE BODY: BIOPOLITICS IN OFFICIAL CRITICISM OF LEZAMA IN THE NINETIES

Once Lezama was rehabilitated by cultural policies, the topic of sexuality raised an enormous interest. In previous decades, his novel *Paradiso* had inspired polemics because of its explicit pansexuality (Triana 1998, 111).[7] It was thus logical that some critics and scholars were eager to reconsider the controversy and the novel's sexuality in a new light. The discussion of Lezama's sexuality was part of the state cultural project to rectify the sixties' and seventies' policies against homosexuality. But more was at play in this ideological gesture, which was also part of a larger political endeavor. As we will see in analyzing this critical revision of Lezama, sexuality was accepted as long as it remained true to a reproductive goal. That is, the control of discourses on sexuality was part of a set of governmental measures to regulate and control sexual conduct. It was a way of controlling sexual discourse without force. This type of control no longer required the eradication of evil or of the enemy. Instead, it manifested itself through a rhetoric centered on the conservation and administration of life. This type of rhetoric can be seen in many official discourses throughout the nineties. For example, in 1998, the journal *Trabajadores*'s headline about UNEAC's Sixth Congress read, "UNEAC Lives" (8). The journal then quotes keynote speaker Abel Prieto's citation of Fidel Castro: "Culture is what must be saved."

This rhetoric of life responded to the European and North American rhetoric about the death of socialism. It was also a governmental mode of subjection over a population whose desire to emigrate was increasing as rapidly as the ruler's political legitimacy declined. Whereas during the two previous decades policies censured and suppressed ideological dissent, during the nineties they emphasized the quality of life, as Prieto, again citing Fidel Castro, claimed: "El propio concepto de 'calidad de vida,' tan envilecido por el comunismo habría que asociarlo a la cultura: 'Las actividades culturales (dijo Fidel, esta vez en el IV Congreso de la UNEAC) pueden convertirse en una de las más altas expresiones del nivel de vida del pueblo' [The very concept of 'the quality of life,' so debased by communism, should be associated with culture: 'Cultural activities (said Fidel, this time in the Fourth UNEAC Congress) can become one of the highest expressions of the people's standard of living']" (8). Never had the Cuban economy suffered so much, and thus the government strove to convince Cubans that they should be able to sublimate their hunger into art in lieu of food. Not coincidentally,

Ponte wrote a very lyrical, evocative, and to a certain extent ironic book of essays titled *Las comidas profundas*. Ponte's book is a commentary on the opposition between lack and plenitude, where the association of the terms is reversed. Nationhood has always been represented by plenitude and exoticism. Reading the canon against the grain, however, Ponte argues that Cuban culture should be defined by the lack resulting from the unfulfilled promise of a continually deferred nationhood. Referring to the nineties, he inverts the state's biopolitical logic by asserting that human life is curtailed by the shortage of food. The lack of a national identity produced a cultural narration of Cubanness, which filled that void with words. This explains why the baroque became so prevalent in Cuba. Ponte closes the essay by arguing ironically that during the food shortages of the nineties, literature was offered as a substitute.

It was also no coincidence that the National Center for Sex Education (CENESEX, Centro Nacional de Educación Sexual) was created in 1989, a year after the reemergence of queer literature in Cuba (Alonso Estenoz 2000, 1).[8] The center announced its mission as "the application of the Cuban policy of Sex Education by coordinating the participation of entities and organizations devoted to social communication, community work and sex education, guidance, and therapy to help ensure that human beings can live their sexuality in a healthy, full, pleasing, and responsible way." Thus, the government no longer censored the practice of openly gay sexuality and its literary representation as in times past. Instead, as the CENESEX proclaimed, the strategy was to regulate sexuality through public discourses of utility.[9]

In scholarly work, critics from the fifties also discussed the reproduction of life from a sexual perspective, especially as a critique of homosexuality. In "Invitación a *Paradiso*," an essay written in 1989, Vitier erases the importance of homosexuality and offers a transcendental reading of *Paradiso*, specifically concerning chapter 8: "Este capítulo, por lo tanto, más allá de las argumentaciones contrapuestas en torno al tema de la homosexualidad, concluye visionariamente con una exaltación y apoteosis del culto a la fecundidad heterosexual, si bien en las páginas finales de la novela será completada o superada por el sentido egipcio original del culto fálico (mito de Isis y Osiris) como alusivo a la resurrección o fecundación trascendente [This chapter thus goes beyond the opposing arguments on the subject of homosexuality, concluding with a visionary exaltation and apotheosis of the cult of heterosexual fecundity, even if in the novel's final pages this view is completed or superseded by the original Egyptian sense of the phallic cult (the myth of Isis and Osiris) as alluding to resurrection or transcendental fertilization]" (Vitier 2001, 387). Vitier condemns the representation of an incestuous sexual relationship as a "repugnant account" (ibid., 391), and he warns the reader to go beyond the explicit sexual scenes of chapter 8 (the reason the book was poorly received when first published). He represents sexuality in the novel as an immoral stage that needs to be superseded by subsuming pleasure under knowledge: "Los que sólo leyeron el capítulo VIII y pasajes análogos (sorprendidos por una tendencia a la hipérbole que es constante en el estilo lezamiano), sin duda no entendieron nada porque ignoraron el contexto de una historia que le confiere a esas páginas su verdadero sentido: el del hitos de un camino que, al salir el protagonista del agridulce paraíso de la infancia, conduce del submundo de las pasiones tumultuosas a la pasión estelar del conocimiento [Those who only read chapter 8 and analogous passages (surprised by a propensity for hyperbole that is a constant of Lezama's style) will doubtless not understand anything not knowing the context of the story that gives these pages their true meaning: that of milestones along a road that, after the protagonist leaves the bittersweet paradise of childhood, leads from the underworld of tumultuous passions to the celestial [*estelar*] passion of knowledge]" (380–81). Vitier interprets the novel as a process of desexualizing pleasure arriving at a transcendental word: "El sexo, pues, aparece aquí primero, como concupiscencia sin amor, como derroche amoral de energía, en escenas simétricas mentalmente construidas o reconstruidas, y después de una torcida espiritualidad, como locura [Sex thus first appears here as lasciviousness without love, as amoral dissipation of energy, in symmetrical scenes mentally constructed or reconstructed, and later as deformed spirituality, as madness]" (384). For Vitier, then, Catholicism needs the presence of the body in order to reach the "truth." Vitier cannot make his argument without alluding to the body because the "imago" only comes from the union and division of body and soul. Instead of being repressed, this sexuality is brought up continuously in a discourse that at the same time negates it (Foucault 1990, 148).

Referring also to *Paradiso*'s chapter 8, Prats Sariol, another Lezama scholar, criticizes the Christian understanding of sexuality as a mere reproductive function, but he then contradicts his own position. Sariol argues that sexuality need not be justified: "Sex, like any other human reality, requires presences. Its discovery and knowledge do not require explanations. To require such explanations is a form of alienation, whether subliminally as described by orthodox Freudians or through repression, as in Judeo-Christian dogma. *Paradiso* is free of 'sin.' It enjoys perfect sexual health, in the manner of Vatsyayana's *Kama Sutra* or Kalyana Malla's *Ananga Ranga*" (Prats Sariol 1996, 661). By claiming that sex requires no justification, Prats Sariol is also arguing that no moral principle should censor it. He thus rejects Freudian analysis or Judeo-Christian religion. Both discourses describe sex according to their ideologies, and both judge certain sexual practices. Instead, he proposes that *Paradiso* displays "sexual health," valuing sex as a beneficial or nondiseased practice. But if we follow this argument to its logical conclusion, the proposition that characterizes sex as a healthy practice is based on an type of medical discourse, which regulates sexual behavior by classifying it as "healthy" or "unhealthy." Vitier's and Sariol's essays are examples of how power exerts itself around the principle of reproductive life. The control over the human body and its administration permits the calculating administration of life, so that life becomes useful and productive (Foucault 1990, 140). This explains why a discourse around sexuality is so important and was so prevalent in disciplines such as literary criticism: "It is through sex—in fact, an imaginary point determined by the deployment of sexuality—that each individual has to pass in order to have access to his own intelligibility (seeing that it is both the hidden aspect and the generative principle of meaning)" (ibid., 155).

The Revival of Lezama by the Children of the Revolution

How did the children of the revolution respond to Lezama's official revival? At the beginning of the eighties, the members of Diáspora(s) and many other intellectuals of their generation rediscovered Lezama's poetics. Lezama's language was a model for many of these young writers. The poets associated with Diáspora(s) maintained an oedipal attitude toward Lezama, adopting his poetics at the beginning of their careers and later rejecting them. (As a matter of fact, by the time the first issue of *Diáspora(s)* appeared, the founders of Diáspora(s) had already condemned Lezama's poetics of history.) Lezama's baroque language expressed a more complex aesthetic and ideological imaginary than did the realism of conversationalist poetics. Lezama thus represented an alternative to the watchful gaze of the prior generation's paternal figures, who disparaged Lezama's "apolitical" work (Marqués de Armas 1997, 20).

Diáspora(s) argued that the official reading of Lezama had obliterated the works that did not serve the state's ideological purposes.[10] In October 1994, one year after Diáspora(s) was created, Rolando Sánchez Mejías and Pedro Marqués de Armas gave two papers at the roundtable "*Orígenes* and Its Influences on New Writers" at a symposium about the journal organized by Casa de las Américas. Their interventions disrupted the ideological approach of the event and provoked an argument with other participants and bitter comments by Miguel Barnet, head of Casa de las Américas. From then on, Diáspora(s) was barred from freely participating in cultural events (interview with Marqués de Armas 2010).[11] The two papers Sánchez Mejías and Marqués de Armas read were subsequently published in *Diáspora(s)*.

At the beginning of the nineties, Diáspora(s)'s poets also began to be critical of the messianic aspects of Lezama's poetic theories about the telos of

History. They argued that this ideological aspect of Lezama's work was clear in essays he had written at the onset of the revolution. Indeed, in "A partir de la poesía" he interpreted the Cuban Revolution as a messianic force that brought the word that would save the nation: "La revolución cubana significa que todos los conjuros negativos han sido decapitados. . . . El hombre que muere en la imagen, gana la sobreabundancia de la resurrección (Lezama 1975, 840).[12] Lezama argued that there was a coincidence between the last "imagined era," its endless possibility in the Cuban Revolution, and the revolution's poetic hypostasis. In other words, the power of poesis is not only poetic but historical. For Lezama, the revolution was the result of a confluence between the material act and the idea that imagined it. This was the dialectical allegory whose telos was the Cuban Revolution and the essentialist idea that Diáspora(s) poets criticized, arguing that, "Aquello que para Lezama y Vitier fue un corte o fulminación o consecuencias de la Historia, fue para otros hombres el dolor de la historia en sus propios cuerpos [What Lezama and Vitier saw as a cutting or annihilation or consequence of History was for others the pain of history in their own bodies]" (Sánchez Mejías 1997, 19).

The Body, Pleasure, and Baroque: Lezamian Poetics of the Early Nineties

The children of the revolution also took part in the general upsurge of scholarship dealing with issues of sexuality and gender in Lezama's work. They did this for two reasons. First, they sought to challenge past scholarship, including of the kind we have just discussed. Second, they hoped to develop a new model of poetics that, like Lezama's, would focus on language. Until the eighties, Lezama had been studied in Cuba from social or philosophical perspectives, but issues of sexuality had remained taboo. The possibility of open debates about queer representations in *Paradiso* or *Oppiano Licario* marked a crucial ideological shift in Lezama studies. While these new critical perspectives were certainly welcome and well received, cultural officials were concerned that postmodernity, and especially the arrival of a market economy, would be accompanied by the wrong values.

In fact, young intellectuals had lost trust in the grand narratives of the Left and had turned toward postmodernism. Official cultural discourse, however, was still grounded in ideologies of emancipation. Both official and emerging discourses focused on the representation of sexuality in Lezama's work, which not only experienced a revival in the eighties, but also nurtured the discourse about life, reproduction, and sexuality that official ideology was so intent on promoting. This focus on sexuality was also very revealing because, paradoxically, both the newer and older generations of critics revived the fifties' view of Lezama as a transcendental writer. The generations took different political positions, however: official critics praised Lezama's transcendentalism, whereas younger poets were critical of it. Official critics used transcendentalism to disavow the presence of homosexual desire and *jouissance* in Lezama's writing. By opposition, younger intellectuals celebrated the inclusion of homosexual and sexual desire in *Paradiso* and *Oppiano Licario*. Marqués de Armas's *Fascículos de Lezama*, which offered a psychoanalytical reading of sexuality in both novels, was a good example of the latter. This debate demonstrated the importance attributed to life and reproduction, and the decisive role they played in shaping cultural policies geared toward the ideological control over life, as opposed to a repressive politics. Power had not relinquished its ideological manipulation of the population. What had changed was the way of exerting it. This debate had larger ideological implications for different interpretations of Lezama, and for the ethical understanding of power.

Lezama's baroque representations of the body were decisive in this debate about language and life, because the baroque is deeply ingrained in Christianity, a system of belief based on the relationship between the body and the word. As is well known, the body plays a crucial role in the symbolic representation of the Christian rituals. The word becomes flesh; that is, the Word of God is materialized through the body of Christ. We attain the word (truth) through communion with God and by incorporating His body through the sacred ritual of the Eucharist. By eating holy bread, Christians receive the body of Christ and become one with Him. The revelation of the word of Christ brings plenitude, bliss, or *jouissance*, because it also means truth. The debate about Lezama revolved around the relationship between truth (word) and pleasure (sexuality). Was Lezama's representation of sexuality a vindication of pleasure or Lacanian *jouissance*, or was it umbued with theological undertones? In other words, did it articulate an ideology motivated by the control and power over the body (or life), or did it, on the contrary, represent an affirmation of sexuality as pure desire? These were the points of contention at the heart of the debate between the generations of the fifties and the eighties.

Diáspora(s) rejected the transcendental representation of sexuality articulated by the baroque body. Whereas in the eighties, as we saw in the previous chapter, members of Diáspora(s) as well as other young poets reappropriated Lezama's baroque style in search of a more complex understanding of language, in the nineties they rejected the baroque and its concomitant transcendentalism.[13] Marqués de Armas took his generation of writers to task for adopting Lezama's transcendental, baroque style. In his assessment of Lezamian-influenced poetry of the early nineties, Marqués de Armas implied that Lezama was a transcendentalist poet because Lezama believed in the unity of word and spirit:

> Con Lezama se iba a producir una avalancha del signo, y una nueva puesta en escena del barroco. De modo que las tres "D" que le constituyen en tanto estilo, pronto cayeron sobre nosotros. Claro que hubo en la mayoría de los casos como era de esperarse, más "delicia" que "delirio y aún más que "derroche." La solución pues se abrió en lugar de hacia el verbo hacia el espíritu. Y puesto que el propio Lezama sostenía la unidad de ambos en vez de sus diferencias, el resultado fue, en la manera en que le asumimos, puro trascendentalismo.
>
> [Lezama created an avalanche of the sign and a new *mise en scène* of the baroque, such that the three D's that comprise it as a style would soon fall upon us. Of course, as one might expect, in most cases, this was more "delight" than "delirium" and still more than "dissipation." The solution, then, revealed itself not toward the word but toward the spirit. And given that Lezama himself argued for the unity of the two rather than for their differences, the result was, in the way we consider it, pure transcendentalism.] (Marqués de Armas 1997, 20)

Marqués de Armas offered here one of the main critiques of the baroque present throughout Diáspora(s)'s work. This view equates the baroque with Christianity, the spirituality that it represents, as well as the Aristotelian paradigm on which it is based. That is to say, this critique rejects the idea that conceives the body and the soul as a unity. The main goal of Christianity and the baroque is the knowledge of truth, whose revelation, Lacan argues, causes *jouissance*: "everything is exhibition of the body evoking jouissance" (Lacan 1998, 113). That is, in Christianity, truth can always be reached, and when that occurs, a feeling of plenitude ensues because the body and the soul become one. Lacan argues, however, that the union with the body of Christ may produce *jouissance*, but it does not produce knowledge. What produces *jouissance* is the phantasy of a union with God and the promise of bliss. If there is no knowledge, and the soul is one with the body, then the plenitude can only be expressed in sensual terms. Thus, according to Lacan, everything in baroque art is an exhibition of obscene bodies.[14] What is at stake, then, is the fact that, as in Christianity, baroque is a vehicle allowing the body soul, and the word to form a transcendental unity. In other words, this poetic language shows the quest for a transcendental otherness, which in Christianity is God qua truth.

Víctor Fowler, who was at the forefront of the nascent critical literature about homosexuality and pleasure, read sexuality in Lezama in the same Lacanian way. He was one of the first who debated and defended the sensual pleasure of the text. *La maldición: Una historia de placer como conquista* (*The Curse: A History of Pleasure as Conquest*) was the collection of essays that he devoted to that topic. One of the collection's essays dealt with the representation of sexuality in Lezama's *Paradiso*. In his interpretation of Lezama, Fowler went farther than Marqués de Armas because, like Lacan, he interpreted Lezama's writing as a symptom of Lezama's sexual fears. He did this by asking first why sexuality in Lezama never ends in the body and instead transcends the physical in search of a relationship with God. That is, for Lacan, sexual relations only happen as a phantasy, such as the Christian one in which the subject, by incorporating the body of Christ, becomes one with Him. Obscenity is what is "being said"—it corresponds to language. But why is the Christian passion represented by bodies instead of words? Lacan explains that this points to a lack, which needs to be filled with the word or truth that cannot be reached. Lezama's baroque language is, as Fowler indicates, a constant tropological amalgamation of words. It is the revelation that *jouissance*, in the form of truth incorporated as body, is sexual pleasure (hence the erotic undertones of Santa Teresa de Jesús's or Fray Luis de León's mystic poetry). For Lacan, "The baroque is the regulating of the soul by corporeal radioscopy [Le baroque c'est la régulation de l'âme par la scopie corporelle]" (1998, 116 [1975, 147]). The soul cannot be explained by the body. Instead, the soul "speaks" through the presence or absence of the body, that is, through a body that is present as phantasy but not in a symbolic form:

> Laberintos y citas eruditas, torcimientos tropológicos, enrevesada sintaxis, juego de los conceptos, acciones de los personajes, multitud de figuras míticas, difuminación del significado, todo está al servicio de la tarea escrita. Sorprende entonces, desde nuestra óptica, la violenta pureza que el cuerpo necesita para no despeñarse en lo que se imagina como abismo o caos. Fronesis acechado por Foción, pero salvado al transformar la cópula con Lucía en acto de poesía, posesión casi por imagen; Foción enamorado de Fronesis y condenado en *Paradiso*, aunque salvado en *Oppiano Licario* al colocar el placer con la imagen en el lugar del goce de los cuerpos; el Tío Alberto rodeado en la adolescencia por figuras demoníacas que se cruzan con el despertar de la sexualidad. El gran peligro de la poesía es entonces la carne, la inmediatez, el goce que principia y termina en el cuerpo, la idea implícita a esta actitud de que nada existe más allá. A fin de cuentas, la negación de Dios.

> [Labyrinths and erudite allusions, tropological meanderings, convoluted syntax, playing with concepts, actions of characters, a multitude of mythical figures, blurring of meaning, all of this is in service of the written task. From our point of view, we are thus surprised by the violent purity that the body requires in order not to fall into what is seen as an abyss or chaos. Fronesis is pursued by Foción but saved when he transforms his copulation with Lucia into an act of poetry, into possession almost by image; Foción enamored of Fronesis and condemned in *Paradiso* but later saved in *Oppiano Licario* when he replaces the pleasures of the flesh with pleasure in the image; Uncle Alberto surrounded in adolescence by demonic figures that encounter each other to awaken sexuality. The great danger faced by poetry is thus that of the flesh, of immediacy, of pleasure that begins and ends in the body, the idea implicit in this attitude that nothing exists beyond the body. In sum, the negation of God.] (Fowler 1998, 68)

In his analysis of *Paradiso*, Fowler argues that sexuality and pleasure are at the core of the novel. Fowler claims that in Lezama's Catholic representation, the body and the soul are always united by transcending sexuality and reaching the "imago" (the poetic and ontological image of Lezama's symbolic system). He then asks why there is always an excessive presence of sexuality in Lezama that always transcends bodily pleasure. Sexuality leads to pleasure, but it is always a pleasure in words, and not just in the senses. Since poetry (words) and sexuality are one, the fear of pure sexuality is also a fear of words. Ultimately, according to Lezama's Catholic practice, words are the Truth of God. Therefore, the fear of an absence of words actually conceals a deeper fear: that of God's nonexistence. In other words, knowledge and truth are a *horror vacui* that words try to shroud, and Lezama is represented once more as the transcendentalist writer Fernández Retamar "created" in the fifties.

This view of Lezama reflected Diáspora(s)'s anxiety about their political position. The excessive stylistic ornamentation of the early nineties was the symptom of a disavowal. Baroque expresses the subject's unwillingness to recognize that truth is absent. In other words, baroque's convoluted language hid the impossibility of reaching truth. Consequently, Diáspora(s)'s hermeneutic position was as a sign of its members' anxiety about the lack of a political referent. That is, ideologically speaking, Diáspora(s) members did not believe in the existence of absolute truth. Their representation of the world clearly stated this absence. At the same time their poetics was devoid of sexuality, sensuality, or pleasure. Their sober language revealed emotional restraint. We have to remember that some of these writers had developed a baroque poetics in the eighties. Consequently, some of them experienced a pendular movement from baroque to scarcity. They went from the excessive *jouissance* of baroque poetics to the lack of affect. Did this new movement reveal a reaction to biopolitical power and to the sentimentalist and transcendental rhetoric it had produced?

Biopolitical power is the regulation of the soul, which is simultaneously a control of the body. Unlike disciplinary control, which aims to repress and silence sexuality, biopolitics produces discourses to control the practice and representation of sexuality. Why did all critics, of the older and the newer generations alike, reinterpret Lezama as a transcendental writer? In baroque art, as in Christianity, plenitude is always conveyed through sensuality, which does not necessarily imply the revelation of truth. In Christianity, truth and plenitude are reached through the union of the body and the spirit: the body of Christ, which is also the word of Christ. If truth is absent, however, we are left exclusively with the body. The body bereft of spirituality becomes pornographic. Thus, to avoid sexuality qua degeneration, criticism reads Lezama as a transcendental writer. This is also the latest mechanism to control the soul. Sexuality as pornography is what the regime fears the most, because it is also what the market brings forth. But why is this new form of governmentality required? The answer lies in the development of the market economy and its corollary, an independent civil society.

Whereas official critics wished to obliterate the body to foster a politics of reproduction, the new poetics of the eighties, including Diáspora(s), sought to obliterate the word. For these writers, reaching that goal without falling into pornography meant to annihilate the body. Since the baroque transcendental movement demanded the union of the body and the word, by erasing the body, these writers were also erasing the word (baroque poetics). But the members of Diáspora(s) denounced this gesture as insufficient. For them, poetics had to do away with the sexual and physical bliss represented in Lezama's work. These poetics also had to eliminate the sentimentalism that had replaced *jouissance* in their early poetry of the eighties. Diáspora(s)'s rejection of sentimentalism was also a rejection of the bucolic, which is according to Rojas, the genre that articulates the paradisiac imaginary of Marxist utopia (Rojas 1998, 146). Their reaction to sentimentalism and biopolitics was to completely erase the body and affect.

We have seen in previous chapters how the poetics of the sixties also lacked a representation of genuine emotion and affect. These poetics were characterized by artificiality, and I have defined them as melodramatic because of their sentimentality, the strong ethical polarity, and the Manichaeism they conveyed. As in melodrama, the goal was to create a strong bond between the reader and typified heroic characters willing to sacrifice their lives for the cause. Instead, Diáspora(s)'s poetics displays no artificial or exaggerated sentiments, no genuine plenitude or bliss, no dramatic spleen. How does one read this absolute lack of emotional indexicality?

Bare Life and Proyecto Diáspora(s): The Erasure of the Baroque Body

Bare Life or the Schizo

Members of Diáspora(s) turned away from allegorical language in the following decade, becoming increasingly critical of their old baroque-influenced poetics and cultivating what I call barren poetics. Although never metaphorically present, the New Man haunted their work throughout these two decades. The ideological and affective process to debunk biopolitical state power is best understood through the physical and political articulation of subjectivity. If the rhetoric of the eighties was articulated by bodily pleasure, the nineties poetics was devoid of physicality and subjectivity. During the eighties, both official critics and the young poets focused on the role of sexual pleasure in Lezama's work, which had been overlooked during the seventies. But a decade later, these representations of Lezama's baroque bodies disappeared from Diáspora(s)'s criticism, poetry, and fiction.

The project of *Diáspora(s)* testifies to the deformation and defamation of the same bodies that the state seeks to revive. These are bodies that have been divested of subjectivity and that are represented in *Diáspora(s)* by the literary apparition of Agamben's *homo sacer*. What is so interesting about *Diáspora(s)* is that it shows how biopolitics is a politics that both protects life and at the same time creates a space where men can be killed with impunity. In other words, it reveals how biopolitical and sovereign power coexist in the Cuban regime, and how the latter is a consequence of the former. That is, a state that first controls and administers power over citizens' lives, and then over their death (Agamben 1998, 4). This leaves the subject standing always in a liminal space between death and life.

The erasure of the baroque body is a crucial component of the Diáspora(s)'s poetics. This effort consists in the destruction of the materiality of the body and its transformation into its other. As the official revival of Lezama was part of the biopolitical strategy to foster a nationalist and revolutionary reading of the canon, Diáspora(s) read baroque poetics of the eighties as another sign of that politics. As a consequence, Diáspora(s)'s members who had written baroque works at the beginning of their careers now rejected them. The works of Diáspora(s) show how subjectivity, and the body as a corollary, is caught in Cuba's new biopolitical sovereignty. This subjectivity or lack thereof is represented by a figure that Giorgio Agamben calls *homo sacer* or bare life. *Homo sacer* is a paradoxical figure from Roman law designating a convict who cannot be legally persecuted for his crime but who can be killed with impunity. This legal figure is based on one additional premise: *homo sacer* can be killed, but he cannot be sacrificed. *Homo sacer* is thus a figure whose status is neither under legal control nor under divine law. Therefore, *homo sacer* finds himself exposed to violence and to exclusion from both the religious realm and the legal space (Agamben 1998, 82). This means that he is deprived of subjectivity or identity. As a human, he only has one inherent condition, which is "the capacity to be killed" (ibid., 114). The figure of *homo sacer* populates the poems of Pedro Marqués de Armas, Rolando Sánchez Mejías, and Carlos A. Aguilera. For example, "Mandrágora" ("Mandrake"), Marqués de Armas's poem reprinted in *Diáspora(s)* 2, depicts a Kafkaesque and dehumanized being divested of thought or affect.

> En el borde interior de la frontera, que otros prefieren llamar
> callejón sin salida,—B. se mató.
>
> Claro que todas las fronteras son mentales, y en el caso de B.,
> mejor sería hablar de dos.
>
> De modo que B. se mató entre el borde interior y la cresta de
> un pensamiento que ya no se le desviaba.
>
> Para catapultarse, tomó aquellas raicillas de un alcaloide que
> había
> clasificado, y, echándose sobre el camastro de trozos fusiformes,
> al fin
> encontró lo que buscaba: calle de una sola dirección en la que
> todos los
> números están borrados, y los blancos pedúnculos mentales se
> desvanecen en una materia de sueño.[15]

The space represented by the poem, which is simultaneously mental and material, is dominated by dehumanization, madness, death, and its corollaries. There are two barriers, or one that is physical and has become mental, and B. commits suicide when these two spaces become saturated. There is no physical escape, and as a consequence or as a cause (the physical and mental frontiers are logically intertwined) thought is anchored: "De modo que B. se mató entre el borde interior y la cresta de un pensamiento que ya no se le desviaba." B. is dead before he kills himself. Exposed to the violence of the biopolitical regime, and to the double exclusion of the mental and the physical space, B. takes the root of a mandrake plant, best known for its narcotic characteristics. The roots take B. on a one-way trip to an indeterminate zone: a "calle de una sola dirección en la que todos los números están borrados." Again, this trip does not produce in him a different mental state. It just takes him deeper into a state of drowsiness: "y los blancos pedúnculos mentales se desvanecen en una materia de sueño." The effects of the drug take him to a limbo between sleep and waking, death and life. This is the space of exclusion and bare life; a space that founds the sovereignty of the biopolitical regime.

The second issue of *Diáspora(s)* features "La nueva estirpe" ("The New Lineage"), another poem by Marqués de Armas. The poem describes a mental state graphically represented through a dream of sorts. The poem represents a state of mind, but its oniric form resists interpretation:

> Ya viste los monos en la barcaza
> así el delirium de la percepción
> animales brotan de las celdillas
> del cerebro, en ininterrumpida *población*
> y viste alguna roca peduncular
> con la vara de cedro ruso que golpea
> la puerta: mono, rata, lo mismo hombre
> oscuros tejemanejes del anti-Dios[16]

Animals are escaping from the prison of the mind, in an ordered flight, their numbers controlled. Their actions are the work of the anti-Christ, whose acts are ambiguous: Is he liberating them or merely releasing them without saving them?

"Fábula" ("Fable"), a poem by Sánchez Mejías, coincidentally and uncannily represents "the funeral by image" that Agamben discusses in relation to *homo sacer*. When an emperor died in Rome during Antoninus Pius's rule, a wax effigy of him, which was burned on his funeral pyre after the corpse, replaced the dead emperor in his bed during a mourning ritual that lasted several days. Agamben compares the function of the wax effigy and that of *homo sacer*, as both are consecrated to death. In Sánchez Mejías's fable, the conflation of empirical facts and fiction parallels the blurring of the distinction between death and life.

> El muerto es falso, es de cartón. Si el zorro lo voltea (aquel zorro que dio con la máscara trágica en el bosque y se dijo al voltearla: "Qué rostro tan grande para no tener cerebro"), ah, si el zorro lo voltea, dos, tres veces, asegurándose de la sustancia de teatro, diría: "Qué muerto tan grande para no tener vida." (Sánchez Mejías 1994, 25)[17]

The fox thinks that the theater mask lacks a brain because he assumes it is "alive." Similarly, the fox thinks the cardboard corpse is a real body because he makes the analogy with the mask. Ultimately, this means that if one takes fiction as a reality, one equates death with life. This confusion actually clarifies the paradoxical nature of the figure of *homo sacer*. Once we have barred *homo sacer* from being a religious figure by not allowing him to be sacrificed, we can no longer exclude him from the legal world, because by doing that we conflate the spiritual and the legal. And here is where we begin to see that the law is actually empty. This law represents state ideology, and as such it is absent.

Also in *Derivas*, Sánchez Mejías's "Pabellones (II)" ("Pavilions (II)"), takes us to the regimented space of the mental institution, where space is seen as a symbol of dehumanization.

> El hijo suele visitar a su madre y a su hermana. De manera progresiva, ellas se fueron aventurando en la locura y ahora pertenecen a los pabellones. Él no. Es decir: todavía no. De ahí que no use esas ropas blancas que lo formalizarían instantáneamente en el Manicomio. Pero está tan enfermo como ellas. O tal vez más, mucho más. Parece un ajedrecista trunco en plena adolescencia, como si hubiera enloquecido de repente en una situación con demasiadas variantes inesperadas o ante una ficha mal puesta. Usa espejuelos enormes de-fondo-de-botella, tiene el pelo muy corto (a lo militar) y la voz tenaz, inhumana. En ciertos segundos de lucidez, al pasarle una mano por el pelo, la madre levanta entre ellas y su hijo una especie de salvación. Pero enseguida se anula la distancia entre los tres, anudándose en una salvaje santidad. (Sánchez Mejías 1994, 58)[18]

The Weltanschauung represented in the poem is circumscribed to the Manicomio (psychiatric hospital). The hospital is the regimented biopolitical space par excellence. Psychiatry is represented as the set of discourses and medical procedures whose functions are always regulative. These regulations create a normalizing society as an effect of a technology of power centered on life (Foucault 1990, 144). Insanity is a product of these normative effects, and psychiatric hospitals are the places that produce them. It is precisely because society is regimented by medical discourses that the son is not immune to its effects, either. Hence, the poem asks if there is any difference between sanity and madness, a question it answers by positing them as a continuous flow of power that territorializes and deterritorializes discourse. Conceived this way, madness is no longer a pathology that needs to be cured. It is, rather, the medical discourse that needs to be transformed. As a corollary of clinical psychology's general critique, and clearly influenced by Deleuze and Guattari's *Anti-Oedipus*, the poem proposes a more specific critique of psychoanalysis. This explains why the poem negates the existence of an Oedipal relationship between mother and son, as well as the ideology of salvation that this relationship articulates. That is, for example, the type of cathexis between mother and child produced by the fear of castration. Thinking that the mother has been castrated by the father, the child sees the father as an enemy and seeks his mother for protection against the danger of castration.

Instead there appears a third force between them: a "salvaje santidad," which poses an ironic contrast with the religious space of salvation. This "salvaje santidad" results from the blending of their two bodies, and a sudden departure from subjectivity. It could represent bare life, but it could also be a Deleuzian and Guattarian schizo. This hermeneutic difference is essential because it creates two opposite conceptions of the political. On the one hand, the figure could represent the bare life resulting from biopolitical normativity. Like *home sacer*, both the son and the mother are exposed to the violence of a double exclusion: the regulative system of mental institutions and the lack of a spiritual space outside of this ideology. As bare life, they are invisible to society. This figure is expandable because it is no longer socially productive. The psychiatric and religious notions of salvation that regulate the institution and the social are part of a normalizing biopolitical ideology. Hence, there is no space outside of a normative ideology where a new subjectivity could emerge. Bare life is also in stark opposition with *Paradiso*'s representation of being. In Lezama's novel, the body exudes a soul-searching *jouissance*, and there is also a constant interplay between the body's presence and absence. Instead, in this poem the lack of affect erases the body by negating its Aristotelian existence and its Lacanian representation.

The schizo, on the other hand, represents a process of liberation from the normative regime established by biopolitics. Deleuze and Guattari's political ontology has done away with the notion of human subjectivity altogether; theirs is a politics of abstract flows of energy that implement and undo relations of power. The process of liberation is defined as a deterritorialization, and the liberating force is a line of flight or breakthrough. The paradoxical nature of those processes, however, is that the same line of flight can both "deterritorialize" and become a force of "reterritorialization" (repression). Deleuze and Guattari's theory is a critique of Freudian universal categories of analysis, because they create patterns that essentialize behavior by way of mythical figures. Deleuze and Guattari argue that at its core, the Freudian analytical system is based on an essentialist paradigm of family ties that are imposed on the analysand. The schizo is a breakthrough of a repressive method based on the categorization of pathologies as conditions that need to be cured: "Destroy, destroy. The task of schizoanalysis goes by way of destruction—a whole scouring of the unconscious, a complete curettage. Destroy Oedipus, the illusion of the ego, the puppet of the superego, guilt, law, castration" (Deleuze and Guattari 1998, 311). But at the same time that the schizo breaks through the perverse machines, it also produces an opposite movement of reterritorialization, because one cannot exist without the other. The schizo is not only a machine with lines of flight, it also represents and reterritorializes with perversion: "*Psychoanalysis settles on the imaginary and structural representatives of reterritorialization, while schizoanalysis follows the machinic indices of deterritorialization*. The opposition still holds between the neurotic on the couch—as an ultimate and sterile land, the last exhausted colony—and the schizo out for a walk in a deterritorialized circuit" (ibid., 316).

The "salvaje santidad" could represent bare life, but it could also be a schizo, because the mother's stroking of the son's hair provokes a flow of energy that deterritorializes and reterritorializes simultaneously. Identities and subjectivities have dissolved into a flow of energy whose ambiguous condition is rendered through the notion of "savagery." The concept of wildness also points back to "madness," which is—according to Marqués de Armas—an idea that did not exist in nineties Lezamian poetry. Madness as a savage force could thus be a paradoxical form of alienation and liberation. For *homo sacer*, however, madness points to an inescapable space on which the process of sovereignty is founded. That is, the space where the "monarch" or "state" arbitrarily decides who can be killed or treated with impunity. Is this savage force a schizo or bare life? In the case of this poem, the quasi oxymoronic combination of an uncontrollable and nonregimented force, which inhabits at the same time a sacred space seems to point to the figure of the schizo, but as we will see in further examples, that's not always the case in *Diáspora(s)*'s production.

Animality and Humanity

The representation of the human body in *Diáspora(s)* reaches its limit when that form morphs with the animal, as we see repeatedly in Diáspora(s)'s poetics. The group's poetic imaginary is full of rodents, pigs, and insects, the only animals included in their bestiary.[19] These creatures come from the Kafkaesque imaginary that Deleuze and Guattari have incorporated into their analysis of capitalism. These animals are traditionally represented as beings that produce disgust or fear, but not for Deleuze and Guattari or Diáspora(s), who interpret the movements of their packs as lines of flight and deterritorialization: "Plants with roots or radicles may be rhizomorphic. . . . Even some animals are, in their pack form. Burrows are too, in all of their functions of shelter, supply, movement, evasion, and breakout. The rhizome itself assumes very diverse forms, from ramified surface extension in all directions to concretion into bulbs and tubers. When rats swarm over each other" (Deleuze and Guattari 1996, 6–7). In Diáspora(s)'s work, these sorts of creatures seem innumerable and human bodies and subjectivities are in short supply. Animals and humans are no longer represented as two different classes of beings, however. As in Franz Kafka's works, they have morphed into each other. Although the resulting figures call into question the ontological difference between the two, it is not a hybrid being. Hence, we are not in the presence of a transformation of men into animals or vice versa, nor can we speak of a metaphoric process from a rhetorical point of view. It is not a question of mimicry, or one of identification. Unlike in parables, animals are not simply representations of men for ethical or political purposes. Parables conceive of animals and humans as two different types of beings who identify with each other. The creatures represented in this story, on the contrary, are no longer men or animals. They do not have a specific nature or role, and their existence has no particular finality. Like Kafka's animals, they can best be described as what Deleuze and Guattari call "becoming-animal, a being that produces nothing than itself" (ibid., 238). That is, they are beings in a constant process of transformation.

"Zilla," a hybrid piece of verse and prose by Sánchez Mejías published in the second issue of *Diáspora(s)*, clearly describes a "becoming-animal." The story draws on the long-standing tradition of literature about animals, fantastic creatures, and bestiaries. Ultimately, it is a reflection on the ontological representation of animals in relation to humans. In other words, it focuses on the thin line that separates humans from animals, and our disavowal of the fact that, ontologically speaking, there is no clear difference between bestiality and humanity. Deleuze and Guattari's notion of the "becoming-animal" is an ontological response to this question.

In the story, Sánchez Mejías's literary references come not only from Latin American works but also from the larger Western canon. These sources often come from Eastern European dissident literature. This inclusion of non-Cuban works is a clear critique of the political and national notion of a literary canon. Although Henri Michaux and William Gass—the foreign authors evoked in the piece—are part of the canon in the Western literary tradition, their names are absent from the island's intellectual debates. Their works are inexistent in Cuba because they do not fit into the hegemonic discourse that cultural institutions and policies follow and disseminate.

Sánchez Mejías's text functions at a metatextual level as a search for a different language and conceptualization of the nonhuman through its own writing process, while narrating this process through the voice of a fictive author. It is a text with no specific genre that follows a tenuous story line beginning with three characters: Zilla-x-Notata (the spider), Dr. Peters (who is doing research on the weaving of spider webs), and Dr. Witt (his assistant). Very much in the tradition of Virgilio Piñera, the plot is illogical and absurd. But the plot goes even farther than in Piñera by being only ancillary to the conceptual meaning of the narrative. For instance, the first vignettes present Dr. Peters and Dr. Witt trying to solve a problem that is not actually one. It arises from the fact that the spider only weaves at night. The two men decide to solve this "problem" by feeding the spider a stimulant medication for the nervous system, but the spider keeps weaving at night. As Dr. Witt starts imagining spider webs, it begins to become clear that the story line is a pretext to articulate ontological and political questions. More specifically, the text is posing ontological, aesthetic, and political questions about essentialist definitions of subjectivity. Can the subject be conceived beyond the opposition between humanity and animality? Could political action be a nonteleological practice based on individual subjectivities? What type of aesthetic would represent this new idea of subjectivity and the political?

As a correlate to all these questions, the text also portrays the state's subjection of individuals to its power and the type of subjectivity arising from it. What is the rhetoric of power? Sánchez Mejías shows the presence of biopower and its consequences through the representation of subjectivity and life. It becomes immediately clear that bare life is represented by the animalization of humans, an idea already explored by Kafka. As an ideological mode of representation, however, Mejías's text seeks to go beyond Kafka's metamorphosis: "¿Convertirse en 'un monstruoso insecto,' en un grotesco cucarachón al término de una calurosa noche de verano? No. Ya lo hizo K, con mucha efectividad literaria" (Sánchez Mejías 1998, 24).[20] The text is implicitly saying that Kafka's narrative strategy is insufficient to represent the narrator's goal: the specificity of a "becoming-animal." The letter R. refers to the author's first name (Rolando), but, most important, it points to his lack of subjectivity and identity, as he himself is a becoming-animal: "R., miro como tratas de escribir. Te miro a través del ojo de la cerradura. Te montas a la mesa y te mueves a cuatro patas (¿mono?, ¿araña?, ¿mono-araña?, ¿arañamono?), braceando, pataleando entre las hojas revueltas en blanco" (ibid., 25).[21] In his search for a new mode of representation, the narrator realizes the impossibility of his task. After reading William Gass's "Order of Insects," he concludes that one of the characters "acepta, acepta serenamente la imposibilidad de poder pensar en 'el alma oscura del mundo' (¡Ergo: la imposibilidad de representación!)" (28).[22] The narrator defines this impossibility as a "disaster," pointing to the exhaustion of aesthetics, which can only represent reality allegorically: "Por otra parte, en estos tiempos un escobazo no alcanza la emblematicidad necesaria para erigirse en marca del desastre."[23] The "escobazo" (sweep of a broom) refers to the resolution of Kafka's stories, in which the alienated human-animal cannot be redeemed and has to be annihilated. The allusion here is to Kafka's *Metamorphosis*, and specifically Gregor Samsa's sister's sweeping of the food she leaves for her brother, clearly suggesting her desire to dispose of Gregor as well. According to Zilla's narrator, the allegory of death does not suffice to show the "disaster." What does he mean?

The response to this question has to do with representation and aesthetics. How could the limits of sameness and difference between animals and humans be represented? Stylistic recourses such as metaphor or comparisons cannot articulate a relationship that does not involve metamorphosis. This explains why the narrator deems the tropological strategies of Kafka and Michaux insufficient. Michaux's words (translated into Spanish) appear reprinted on the page as the narrator looks at the note in his desk, a detail that adds another visual component to the narration of the story:

> Hacerme insecto para asir mejor
> con patas de gancho para asir mejor
> insecto, arácnido, miriápodo, acárido
> si es necesario, para asir mejor[24]

Like Michaux's collection of poems *Saisir* (*Seize*), Sánchez Mejías's short story is a meditation on representation. Both texts ask how to represent living creatures without utilizing verbal language: "Qui n'a voulu un jour faire un abécédaire, un bestiaire, et même tout un vocabulaire, d'où le verbal entièrement serait exclu?" (Michaux 1979, n.p.).[25] *Saisir* responds to this question with pictorial representations. Sánchez Mejías's story reproduces the same gesture with an ironic tone suggesting that the communicative function of graphic signs is put at a standstill.

What is at stake in this aesthetic choice is the value of allegory as a trope of representation, because the "disaster" refers in part to its exhaustion. Like the body, the power of allegory as a trope of political denunciation has been subjected to the power of state discourse. That is, the "disaster" points to the end of allegorical representation as an aesthetic strategy to confront power. At a metatextual level, writing is thematizing its own destruction, and the text is narrating the process of the quest for its own narration. It searches for a nonmimetic and nonrepresentational language that would be woven like a spider web. Language, like weaving, should be unproductive: "Si destruyéramos los hilos formados en las primeras fases, la araña proseguiría metódicamente con las fases ulteriores de construcción de la tela, aunque el producto final no sirviese a sus fines" (Sánchez Mejías,

1998, 24).[26] Like the spider web, language should not follow a rational logic. Instead it should be an "actividad constructiva que vacila entre el Orden y el Azar."[27] For the narrator, poetics are also the foundation for an ontology and remain largely political. As in Lezama's work, poetics, history, and ontology are woven together, but they are not defined teleologically. It is a quest without an end, a quest that neither awaits nor looks for an answer. The interrelation between ontology, history, and poetics is not one of dependency. Instead, these threads are woven together like a spider web: "La telaraña no se teje en términos absolutos; la elección de las distancias se rige por factores relativos" (ibid., 25).[28] Ontologically speaking, the narrator and the spider are a becoming-animal. The narrator rewrites the history of the Latin American region, a version that unlike Columbus's *Diary* is not idealized. Unlike Columbus, Sánchez Mejías represents his "new world" as a third world without marvels, without cultural comparisons to Spain, without hyperboles, without allegories.

> aguijones/larvas/islotes
> córtex
> surcos
> chips
> nalgas, tetillas y guanches (siempre a tu izquierda)
> boñigaplastadevacaplaff
> oyes campanas y no sabes dónde
> vine, vi
> dale un punzonazo a ese
> rrrrrrrrrrrrrrrrrrrrrrrrrrrrrrrrrrrrrrrrrrrrrrrrrrrrrrrrrrrrrrrrrrrrrrrr
> dime qué ves genovés
> terceros y hasta quintos mundos uy! (Sánchez Mejías 1998, 41)[29]

In a poststructural fashion, the text proposes an antimetaphysical logic based on a post-Kantian genealogy from a tradition including Henri Bergson, Friedrich Nietzsche, and Gilles Deleuze, especially in the latter's departure from Hegel. It is the Deleuzian and Guattarian influence that most clearly demarcates the lack of mediation between ontology, history, and poetics. From a historical point of view, Sánchez Mejías's text points to the lack of freedom of speech in totalitarian regimes:

> Hay un aspecto importante en todo este problema. Y es que, si te fijas bien, Zilla no ha hablado aún. Aspecto que corrobora que nuestro mundo sigue siendo esencialmente coercitivo, en el sentido de que todas sus partes no tienen la misma oportunidad de hablar . . .

> Creemos, a esta altura de los hechos, de que ya es hora de que Zilla habite su página en blanco y que desde ahí nos hable como ella
> quiera. Dejémosla, en el próximo capitulillo, que teja y desteja su urdimbre. ¿Tejerá redes esquizoides o de factura clásica? ¿Tejerá de
> noche o de día? ¿Tejerá? ¿No tejerá? Allá ella con su idea singular acerca del trabajo y la libertad. (36)[30]

Weaving is writing and it is also working, but these two actions are not analogous. The narrator cannot predict the spider's behavior, which might be chaotic (*esquizoide*) or guided by reason (*factura clásica*). It is actually the conceptual possibility of exhibiting order and chaos at the same time that has drawn the narrator to the spider: "R: veo, con placer, que has escogido la posibilidad *arácnido*. Que te fascina esa actividad constructiva que vacila entre el Orden y el Azar" (Sánchez Mejías 1998, 24).[31] Becoming-animal's behavior is schizoid because it no longer follows the Freudian phallocentric narrative of castration as a symbol of repression. Schizophrenia, according to Michaux, is taken as the process that represents the production of desire:

> The striking thing was that it was neither simple nor really complex, initially or intentionally complex, or constructed according to a complicated plan. Instead, it had been desimplified in the course of its carpentering. . . . As it stood, it was a table of additions, much like certain schizophrenic's drawings, described as "overstuffed," and if finished it was only in so far as there was no way of adding anything more to it, the table having become more and more an accumulation, less and less a table. . . . A table which lent itself to no function, self-protective, denying itself to service and communication alike. (qtd. in Deleuze and Guattari 1998, 6)

The schizo defined by Michaux is also the baroque as it appears in Cuban classics such as *Celestino antes del alba* (*Singing from the Well*) by Reinaldo Arenas or *Tres tristes tigres* (*Three Trapped Tigers*) by Guillermo Cabrera Infante. That is, the art of excess that takes the referent through a metamorphosis, transforming its literal meaning. Metaphysically speaking, the narrator chooses baroque as a way of being in the world; but poetically speaking, he rejects the allegorical trope so commonly present in baroque art, and especially the notion of metamorphosis as a trope. The poetics of the story, like the poetics of Diáspora(s), takes the language through the reverse process: no excess, but subtraction; no allegorical metamorphosis, but lack of denotation; no ornament, and no romanticized ruins, but bareness. This is the constant tension that appears in the story: lack and desire. A body that desires bareness.

The body is no longer human, it is a metamorphosis that turns life into death, into a writing that no longer wants to be writing. Its function is no longer communicative. It is the non-voice of *homo sacer*. The political process of the schizo is not teleological and revolutionary; but it is the condition of possibility for a revolution: "The schizo is not revolutionary, but the schizophrenic process—in terms of which the schizo is merely the interruption, or the continuation in the void—is the potential for revolution" (Deleuze and Guattari 1998, 341). Toward the end of the story, the narrator depicts the spider's stroll as she deterritorializes language and space: "Y una tarde se puso en marcha, su cuerpo entre rectilíneo y ebrio por el gozo que le circulaba como un cálido riachuelo de sangre" (Sánchez Mejías 1998, 34).[32] Language undoes itself:

> Hasta que llegó al pie de un árbol, donde descansaba un hombre . . . decía algunas palabras en voz queda . . .
> —Ganancias nulas
> —No obstante tu pelo tan lindo
> —Noches noches noches. (ibid., 34)[33]

Extremely interesting in this vignette is the clear reference to the Lezamian concept of "hipertelia": "Una tarde, Zilla, después de haber atrapado una mosca de proporciones y jugos admirables, decide *ir más allá de sus propios fines*" (ibid.; my italics).[34] Lezama coined the term *hipertelia* to describe the poetics that "rompe[n] la concepción de cualquier finalidad" (Lezama 1975, 764).[35] What does *hipertelia* mean? To explain it, Severo Sarduy describes the behavior of molluscs (Sarduy 1999, 1293). Animals with flagella, he says, swim away from the tides and out of the water; unable to return, they die. They are hypertelic animals because they have surpassed a limit beyond which they cannot survive. In hypertely the end is excess or supplement, but it is also termination or consummation. The supplement is thus the ending or the consecution of the act, but it is also its destruction. This is the paradoxical nature of hypertely: the supplement is needed for the creation of a work of art, but it is also its own destruction. This occurs because the work of art can only reach its end or goal with its own destruction. Like animals with flagella, literature can only be in agreement with its own nature after having exceeded its own limit. Its truth is also the terminus, the end of literature, and at the same time, its death. If the truth of literature is necessarily subordinated to its own death, then truth can only emerge once language reaches its own terminus or excess. Is this not also the moment of *jouissance*? In the story the narrator describes the spider's joy as it reaches its own limit: "Entonces empezó a sentir instintos de nuevo tipo, imantaciones acordadas por una distancia desconocida. Y una tarde, se puso en marcha, su cuerpo entre rectilíneo y ebrio por el gozo que le circulaba como un cálido riachuelo de sangre" (Sánchez Mejías 1998, 34).[36] *Jouissance* leads to death: "hasta que su sombra, una noche se levantara y se fuera, quedando su cuerpo colgado de un hilo de materia lunar, o de seda, o de cualquier otra cosa. Vio las luces repiqueteando en la lontananza, como campanas. Y suspiró" (ibid.).[37]

At this point in the story, one needs to understand how the text conceives desire and *jouissance*. Is desire formulated in a Lacanian way, as the libidinal investment into an object that can never be reached? Or is it expressed as a Deleuzian driving force that destroys and assembles the established order of society? The story ends with the spider's voice and her sound. Not only is the spider finally given a voice, but the latter also takes on a material presence:

> **28**
>
> — ¿No has escuchado el parloteo de Zilla-x-Notata en el caracol de tu oreja?—Te diría al oído un monje zen de algún dojo de París.
>
> **29**
>
> *Arañar*: Raspar ligeramente con las uñas, con un cálamo, con un alfiler, etc. (Sánchez Mejías 1998, 41)[38]

The spider has taken the form of the good conscience that inspires wisdom. In a cinematographic scene that alludes to *The Metamorphosis*, the story closes with the sound of music. First comes the melodic voice of Zilla, then the dissonant sound of the action of *arañar*, a verb that makes reference to Zilla the spider. These two vignettes represent two opposite movements of reterritorialization and deterritorialization. In other words, the story puts into play both an oppressed and an oppressive desire, but it is not clear which one predominates. Which music does the narrator privilege, the melodic and systematic, or the cacophonic? Is desire a negative or a positive force? One needs to recall that the narrator identifies with the spider because through her weaving she represents both order and chaos. The desire to reach that structure through writing remains, however, an impossibility: "Nunca escribirás como Zilla teje sus redes. Ni lo sueñes" (Sánchez Mejías 1998, 26).[39] In other words, what the story represents is the failure to find the object of desire (in this case, representation). Writing has reached its own limit and this is expressed in a metatextual form. Deleuze and Guattari describe Samuel Beckett's style as a nonstyle. In other words, style is still present, but it presents its own death and failure. But this is not the case of Sánchez Mejías's short story or of Diáspora(s)'s overall project. There is not a demolition of forms, or of the body for that matter. The figure of the spider as a becoming-animal could be interpreted as a positive force driven by desire, but it could also be interpreted as a representation of the *homo sacer* that the biopolitical regime has created. Given the impossibility of representing the absence of style that would demolish the institution of literature, I suggest that the body in this story does not carry the positive force of becoming-animal, as the narrator suggests. It is rather the *homo sacer* who has slipped through the margins of a writing articulated by the desire to undo itself. *Homo sacer* remains as the New Man's haunting spirit exposed to the double exclusion of sacrifice and the law. It is only, as Agamben suggests, the actualization of the "capacity to be killed" (Agamben 1998, 114). The *homo sacer* can no longer be sacrificed for the spiritual objective of the revolution, since that type of sacrifice no longer exists; there is no longer a common goal or objective for which the New Man could sacrifice himself. He was sacrificed for the cause. The narrator-spider undoes webs and planes but can go no farther.[40]

The poems and stories we have examined have in common an ambiguous portrayal of subjectivity. The figures they create are neither human nor animal. Their liminality could be due to their representation as bare life, or to the schizo, a body without organs made of flows of power. It is true that the latter is per se an ambiguous notion, since schizos are forces that deterritorialize and reterritorialize almost simultaneously. But this constant transformation and lack of subjectivity is precisely what constitutes them. Their lack of bodies and souls is precisely why they diverge from baroque aesthetics. Like baroque bodies, they are driven by desire. Unlike baroque bodies, however, their desire is not driven by the search for pleasure. While baroque desire constantly seeks pleasure, which it derives from language, the schizo desires "the renunciation of external pleasure, or its delay . . . it is not a question of experiencing desire as an external lack, nor of delaying pleasure in order to produce a kind of externalizable surplus value, but instead of constituting an intensive body without organs" (Deleuze and Guattari 1996, 56). The way the schizo experiences desire is in contradiction with the unending search for a vanguardist aesthetics. In "Zilla," the narrator expresses a constant frustration caused by his inability to come up with a new language. The desire to create a new language posits another premise: If there is a new language, there is also an old one. Language is therefore thought in terms of historicity, but history is scarcely represented in the texts. The poems and short stories that we have analyzed make no mention of time. The stories are developed in an eternal present that has no future or past because ideologically speaking, they are not teleological. And, yet, the past lurks around their edges. Let us take for example the following poem by Marqués de Armas:

> Entre arbusto y piedras mondas, bestias sueltas o enroscadas,
> impasible en lo alto y demoledora, la luna de los campos nos
> seguía . . . Y aún tuviste la inocencia de detenerte y desve-
> larla:
> gesto inútil, como lo lírico es tardío (de ahí el hábito de
> distinguir
> entre verdaderos y falsos alimentos; el hartazgo; gasto
> fútil . . .)[41] (Marqués de Armas 2002, 13)

The scene takes place in an indeterminate time and space, although the moon is clearly marking the passing of time. It is telling us that life is made of cycles. It is also a topos of lyrical literature that the poet criticizes as an outdated mode of expression. The lyrical and useless gesture consists in unveiling the moon ("desvelarla"). By this, the poem is suggesting that the lyrical gesture also carries a utopian message. It tells us that to unveil the moon is also to perform a hermeneutic operation consisting in explaining its core, its essence. The point of this interpretation is to think about time, that is, about history. In this regard lyricism becomes a way of thinking about history as a dialectical process that will necessarily lead to utopia. The poet instead suggests a notion of time that does not differentiate between old and new, false and real. Yet this idea of an undifferentiated notion of time contradicts the idea that lyricism belongs to the past, because it reinstates a notion of temporality. In other words, the past exists and cannot be denied. What is more, the past follows the poet in the form of the moon: "la luna de los campos nos seguía." The past lurks like a specter coming to remind the poet of the importance of history, and the symbolic presence of the New Man as a figure of change and sacrifice. This is why a new ideology will necessarily have to take into account the remains of the past.

Conclusion

The nineties was the first era, since the revolution, in which a whole generation of intellectuals had lost faith in the grand narratives sustaining the nation's ideological cohesion. Although there had been critical writers before, they had never constituted a generational trend. Of course, this was also a sign of the times, and a consequence of the end of the Soviet Union. Cuba had always relied on culture for nation building, and after the socialist debacle it needed a new cultural platform. It needed a movement that would reignite revolutionary ideology by adapting itself to the new political circumstances. In view of the economic reforms, the need for a new cultural discourse became even more imperative. The spirit of the reforms was antithetical to the socialist ideology favored by the government and therefore had to be palliated with a more humanistic doctrine. The new trends of postmodernity, however, in particular those embraced by the younger generations, did not lend themselves to this goal. The solution was a return to the past to revisit the work of writers ostracized in the seventies: Grupo Orígenes, and most specifically, the work of José Lezama Lima and Virgilio Piñera. It was no coincidence, however, that Lezama and Piñera were among the writers who most influenced the generation of young poets. Criticism of Lezama's and Piñera's work became a bone of contention between official intellectuals from previous generations and the nineties poets (as well as intellectuals of the diaspora). Thus began what Rafael Rojas has called an ideological war to reclaim ownership of cultural memory, a vicarious way of continuing the ideological fight that had divided the nation during the revolution (Rojas 2006a, 14).

The revival of Lezama's work was a result of the biopolitical governmentality that proved to be a much more effective form of control. During the seventies, control was imposed through ostracizing techniques (a way to eliminate dissension). In the eighties and nineties, however, this approach was turned on its head. The reintroduction by critics and cultural politics of works previously ignored turned out to be a much more effective technique. The rationale behind this new political strategy was twofold. On the one hand, it was part of the social campaign of acceptance of difference, especially sexual difference. To recognize Lezama's and Piñera's queer identity suited the politics of tolerance that the government was advancing. On the other hand, as I have shown, Lezama's work was resurrected through an ideological matrix that suited the official political agendas. It was precisely the sexual aspect of his work that the critics sublimated. That is, Vitier erased the sexual *jouissance* that can be found in *Paradiso* by sublating it under Catholicism. Prats argued that sexual representation in Lezama always had a reproductive goal. Fowler, a poet of the nineties, read the excess of sexual *jouissance* in Lezama as a sign of his religious doubts. Marqués de Armas read the eighties poetics as the expression of a search for a pastoral idea of pleasure. That is, Fowler and Marqués de Armas began questioning a language representing the plenitude of being by showing that such plenitude was a *horror vacui*. As many scholars have shown, the nineties official narrative about Lezama reified his work. I have analyzed how these teleological readings of Lezama have reinterpreted his work as a biopolitical gesture, subjecting his thought to state power. Most important, these teleological and totalizing readings are the symptom of a discourse that has transformed citizens into docile bodies. In other words, like the baroque and its endless deployment of words, teleological readings about the body are actually hiding its lack, a lack that metaphorically appears in Diáspora(s)'s work as bare life. But the representation of these figures in Diáspora(s)'s texts is also very ambiguous. On the one hand, the figure of the schizo speaks of the endless flow of a desire without goal. On the other hand, as Sánchez Mejías's poetics show, Diáspora(s) constructs itself as a vanguardist movement always in search for a new language. Does this poetic quest not represent an epistemological, and consequently, an ideological desire for change? Instead of reading it as a contradiction, I am inclined to think that it is indicating the resistance of their immanent poetics to acknowledge the excess that poetic language creates. That is, the excess that symptomatically reveals the representation *of homo sacer* creeping into their texts, not only as the docile body that biopolitics creates but also as the specter of a post-Marxism yet to come.

4

Humanism, Irony, and the End of Literature

This final chapter looks at Diáspora(s)'s and Paideia's opposed ethical and aesthetic choices in depth. If Paideia can be regarded as the last humanist project of this generation, Diáspora(s) was the vanguardist alternative that emerged out of the failure of humanism. That is, Paideia represented the failure of the aesthetic representation of emancipatory politics, a failure that Diáspora(s) embodied and performed. Desire and repulsion were the two conflicting forces at the core of cultural production during the nineties. To understand the coalescence of the two forces at play, I call on psychoanalysis, for I am dealing with literature, a form of expression that defies rational logic. In recent decades, two different factors have plunged Cuba into a political crisis of disavowal. The first is the regime's inability to acknowledge the exhaustion of the socialist revolutionary process. The second is the acceptance of capitalism and its paradoxical and simultaneous denial (a disavowal, in psychoanalytic terms). The consequence of this double denial is, on the one hand, what Jorge Domínguez has called the state's "desideologización" (1997, 9). The authoritarian evolution of the current Cuban government largely results, according to Domínguez, from this disideologization of a regime no longer rooted in precepts such as those of the "New Man" and "voluntary labor." Rojas similarly takes up Domínguez's terminology when he affirms that "today the island's regime is no longer ideological, in the fashion of the totalitarian model, which implies a withdrawal from, or at least a weakening of, communist republicanism, potentially enabling the introduction of liberal and democratic principles" (Rojas 2003, 54). Unlike Rojas, I do not believe that the withering of communism will give way to democratic reforms. Instead, I think that the retreat of communism is introducing neoliberalism through market reforms. The fact is that, ideologically speaking, the regime's politics were always defined according to an economist's model of socialism. As one observes in the brief political program Fidel Castro outlined in *History Will Absolve Me*, all the proposed reforms were economic. This program was conceived to attend to the needs of the people: the economy was logically the driving force of change. As a result, the nineties' economic crisis also triggered a severe political crisis.

The crisis is initiated by the lack of the primordial signifier or Law of the Father, that is, the end of socialism and by extension the end of sovereignty. To put it in Lacanian terms, the political crisis of the state points directly to the absence of a primordial signifier, that is, the law of the Father. This lack was neither accepted nor recognized, and this explains its striking similarity to schizophrenia. A defensive pathology caused by trauma, schizophrenia dissolves the differentiation between the imaginary and the symbolic. That is, the law remains within the imaginary without ever reaching the symbolic. The subject's ego is unable to symbolize the law, and the result is an empty law. While a schizophrenic's discourse seems logical to him or her, a different subject cannot make logical sense of it. The patient "symbolizes" everything, and we can also "understand" what he perceives. It actually matters little if his perception is understandable or not. The problem is that the schizophrenic perceives only an illusion. It is a perception that dialectical logic cannot decipher (Lacan 1993, 20).

Never symbolized, the law is thus empty. But by definition, a law cannot be empty, so "a fallen ego-ideal" takes the place of the primordial signifier. If the ideal ego is the ideal of perfection that the ego struggles to emulate, from the position of the ego-ideal, subjects see themselves through that ideal place. If we considered ourselves from a space of perfection we might see our own "normal" lives as vain, useless, and repulsive. We thus have a law (i.e., socialism) that strives to perfection but that is empty, because existing real socialism is disappearing, and no law (e.g., market socialism) has replaced it. This conjuncture provokes a schizophrenic logic of sorts, where the lack of law is filled with a useless and repulsive law (i.e., capitalism). The new Cuba of tourism, *jineterismo* (the "hustling" of tourists, including by selling sex), the black market, blackouts, and precariousness—all of these images were part of a dazzling chain, a new world order in which the island's political leaders were as much suffering subjects as organizing agents. For them, this new image of the nation was simply imaginary, weak, and fallen, an image they could not approach other than to erase it.

This impure socialism was symbolized by the corruption of Division General Arnaldo Ochoa and by the Interior Ministry (MININT) Colonel

Antonio de la Guardia. Immediately after signing the Angola peace accord in December 1989, the Cuban government entered the most serious internal crisis it had faced in thirty years, revealing the weakness of Cuban institutions, especially that of the Cuban Communist Party. In June, the government arrested Ochoa—a hero of the Cuban Republic, a veteran of the wars in Angola and Ethiopia and leader of the Western Army—as well as de la Guardia and twelve other high-ranking officers in the army and state security services. The fourteen military officers, who until then had enjoyed impeccable credentials, were accused of crimes of corruption against the state and drug trafficking. The subsequent arrest of General José Abrantes, interior minister since 1986, was the clearest indication of just how serious the crisis had become. Ochoa and MININT officers were officially accused of having used the Department of Convertible Currency to conceal illegal transactions with Colombia's Medellin drug cartel and were charged with having shipped a load of cocaine to Florida through the military port at Varadero. Judged by a military tribunal, Ochoa, de la Guardia, and their principal conspirators were sentenced to execution by firing squad. The other officers implicated were given prison sentences of ten to thirty years (Gott 2004, 286).

Some observers argued that the executions had political motives, claiming that Ochoa could have been involved in a nascent reformist movement within the armed forces. He had viewed the Soviet reforms of Mikhail Gorbachev favorably and would have been in a privileged position to promote similar efforts as leader of the powerful Western Army. General Rafael del Pino, a veteran of the Angola war living in exile since 1989, affirmed that Ochoa had been arrested to prevent an uprising against the regime. This political purge was mistrusted and viewed with incredulity by many, and if it had not been for the imminent economic crisis, it surely would have had more serious repercussions (Gott 2004, 286). For my part, I see the execution of Ochoa and other members of the government as the first symptom of a schizophrenic crisis. It was the first point at which the government, as the body of the nation, lost control and apparent stability. These images are part of the imperfect present of a socialism infected by a virus whose spread it had to entirely eliminate. The schizophrenic's most coveted ambition is to free him- or herself of all other voices that stand in the way of uniting with the divine. Whatever we make of the claims that Ochoa was executed for political reasons, it is clear that these colonels embodied the image of a capitalism that was being allowed on the island but that could be neither seen nor permitted.

The Diáspora(s) and the Paideia, the two cultural projects that interest us are paradigmatic examples of an era of profound ideological and aesthetic transformations. They have more in common with the visual arts of the time than with literature, because as the former they are deeply invested in articulating an ideological critique. Yet if Paideia was the last humanist attempt at reforming cultural politics, Diáspora(s) was, as Walfrido Dorta has put it, the project of a non-messianic vanguard (Dorta 2013, 45). In other words, Diáspora(s) is caught in what appears to be at best a paradoxical situation. That is, on the one hand, its poetics seek a drastic formal disruption of previous poetic forms by rejecting lyricism and aestheticism, and civil poetry on the other hand. Yet, while their project is counterhegemonic, it is not driven by a messianic force, because it is not based on emancipatory goals. Although this formal upheaval is not at the service of a teleology, one cannot deny that there is a desire for disruption. The paradox to which I referred has to do with the simultaneous existence of a counterhegemonic desire with the refusal to reconquer a space of struggle. I have already discussed their vanguardist position in chapter 2 by arguing that their antisystemic view of the world did not translate into a systematic political agenda. Nor did it produce a prescriptive ideology, nor a systematic poetics. To sum up, their poetics are driven by two strong and antithetical impulses: the desire of disruption (deterritorialization) and a desire to reterritorialize without domination or conquest. In Deleuzian-Guattarian terms, these two irreconcilable demands are actually compatible, and in Diáspora(s) poetics, they formally coalesce as a poetics of irony. Paideia, however represents the last modernist project of the decade as well as the exhaustion of the Gramscian organic intellectual in his role as artistic mediator.

The members of Diáspora(s), on the contrary, display an absolute disbelief in the ethical possibilities of art. Their last works, in particular, bespeak a lack of political engagement. For them, literature is no longer a mode of denunciation; instead, it is pure performance. It is the witty *mise en place* of the joker's jest. But their literature is also marked by the constant *dédoublement* of irony. It is the disruption of an illusion, or of a linguistic code, as well as its own critique (what Gilles Deleuze calls "post-irony"). To illustrate the Paideia and the Diáspora(s) disparaging ideological attitudes regarding art, it is pertinent to look at Daniel Díaz Torres's film *Alicia en el pueblo de Maravillas* (*Alice in Wondertown*, 1990). Alice, the character performed by Thais Valdés plays precisely the role of the organic intellectual in a context characterized by the absence of a law or moral code of conduct. It presents, in other words, the same schizophrenic ambivalence that results from irony. Both attitudes are synthesized in a film symptomatic of the generation's ethical impasse.

Alicia en el pueblo de Maravillas is among the most controversial films of the nineties. Described by many critics as a glasnost film about totalitarianism and bureaucracy, *Alicia* was banned in Cuba after being awarded the jury's special mention at the 1991 Berlin Film Festival. After numerous protests from a group of ICAIC filmmakers, the film opened in ten movie houses in Havana "only to be withdrawn after four days marked by disturbances in the cinemas" (Chanan 2004, 460). The film is a didactic and absurdist satire whose narrative flow is constantly interrupted by scenes from the characters' past. These flashbacks show the immoral actions that led the town's inhabitants to be exiled in Maravillas. Alicia, a cultural officer, chooses to go to Maravillas to support the town's cultural development. She soon finds out that the town is full of odd characters and that it is ruled by a despot, who is also the director of a sanatorium. Allegorically speaking, the sanatorium is where the sinners cure themselves of their immorality. They clean their counterrevolutionary ethos by drinking sulphurous bubbly water. Thus, the cure represents the subjection to the power of the despot. Like Lewis Carroll's *Alice's Adventures in Wonderland*, the film ends by suggesting that its story may all have been a dream. Indeed, the resemblances to *Alice's Adventures in Wonderland* and the dreamlike quality of the images induce us to believe that it is a nightmare, which actually resembles reality. Reality and unreality blend constantly, with everyday life in Havana shown to be as grotesque as it is in the town. The allegories and references to the Cuban regime and government become immediately clear, but the film's originality lies in its confusing mélange of different levels of discourse and truth.

As Díaz Torres wrote in defending his film, Alicia is a revolutionary character.[1] She is actually a cultural reformer who fights to transform the dull and propagandistic plays she is directing, until, like Carroll's Alice, she realizes that she no can no longer recognize the truth: "For, you see, so many out-of-the-way things had happened lately, that Alice had begun to think that very few things indeed were really impossible." The famous line from the opening chapter of Carroll's book introduces us to the different levels of realities spatially symbolized in the film. As if opening a Russian nesting doll, Alicia advances gradually through a space that constrains and imprisons her. She first goes into the bus station, then gets into the taxi, and then enters the town from which there is no return. After she forces her way into the hotel room, another door opens as she stands in the dark. A Chinese cook exits his room and disappears, as Alicia contemplates in awe this first absurd and incoherent appearance. Once in the room, she notices that the stairway has been covered with a wall leaving her no way out. But although she cannot leave her room, others can get in. The armoire door opens by itself, and she sees her neighbor on the other side of the bathroom medicine cabinet. Once she has gone that far, Alicia has no choice but to believe in the new reality that she confronts. In this new space, there are three different narratives with their own truths, and Alicia is forced to believe one of them. First, the film presents Alicia's own narrative as an attempt to rationalize what she sees and reform what she thinks is wrong. Second, it offers the truth of the townspeople, which their odd past actions always call into question. Finally, the film gives us the voice of the sanatorium's director, the despot, whose narrative is imposed on everybody else. He is the only character clearly portrayed as evil. Omnipresent, he appears as a devilish figure in the flashbacks as he tempts people to sin.

But whom do we believe? Whose truth should we follow? Even Alicia becomes unreliable when she begins to imagine that she was also sent to Maravillas for being a sinner. In the Manichean structure of the film, Alicia, is the good character, in her effort to bring back the right revolutionary principles and eradicate corruption. All the other voices say exactly the opposite of what they mean, and this is where the film's irony resides. This is why Rodríguez, one of the cultural officials, tells Alicia not to drink the curative water that the sanatorium director gives her. The film's irony is always set against Alicia's moral standard, which is what makes the film didactic. In other words, all the other characters act contrary to her. Their acts are measured against the right moral law that Alicia embodies.

Alicia's voice represents the Symbolic, whereas all the other voices come from the Imaginary. This is why their discourse is understandable to Alicia, but at the same time she finds it absurd and illogical. They represent the revolution's fallen ego-ideal, so their voice does not articulate a truth. It seems, then, that the film's moral lesson comes from Alicia's truth. But the end of the film shows that Alicia's reformism is not a political choice either. The only "truth" that the film proposes comes at the end, when Alicia tells us that her experience in Maravillas has taught her just one moral: "Con agua de globitos caliente y sin etiqueta no llegarás a la meta [Unlabeled hot fizzy water won't get you anywhere]." The film thus does not embrace reformism. Alicia's efforts at reform have been in vain. Although the people of Maravillas seem content with or resigned to their misery, the film shows us that to be caught up in one's own delusional logic is to be constantly confronted with one's own fallen ego-ideal. This is precisely what happens when the sanatorium patients discover that the water is full of excrement. As one of the characters tells Pérez, who has just taken a mud bath: "Pérez, you stink like shit." Pérez responds to the accusation by acknowledging it as fact: "I don't get your joke. You know that here we're all in it up to our eyeballs [aquí todos estamos cagados]." Once the patients realize the truth about the water, they flee the sanatorium. More than escaping a space, they are fleeing themselves for believing that their sentence and their cure are ethical. Jaded by the failure of reformism, Alicia choses humor and *choteo* (joking), thus embracing her generation's apolitical nature. Humor prevails over ethics.

A similar choice operates in the poetics of authors such as Rolando Sánchez Mejías or Carlos A. Aguilera, as we will see in the following sections. A larger group of authors, however, crafted a revolutionary reformist project. This idea crystallized as a group called the Proyecto Paideia, whose disintegration in turn triggered the creation of the Proyecto Diáspora(s). The writing of the latter reflected and condemned the regime's biopolitical power, as we saw in chapter 3. It also developed a poetics of violence in reaction to the revolutionary tropes of violence and sacrifice. But Diáspora(s) does not cultivate a poetics aiming at rhetorically liberating society from the destructive forces that govern history. Diáspora(s)'s goal is not to support a state practice of terror that demands heroic sacrifices to maintain the law. But the group's poetic is not an attack on state power, either; nor is it a submission to it. At the representative level, violence can also work as an ironic rhetorical operation that reveals the struggle between the fallen ego-ideal and the ideal ego.

Humanism and Paideia

THE ORIGINS OF PAIDEIA

Proyecto Paideia, which I briefly described in chapter 2, was one of the eighties cultural projects that showed how the children of the revolution turned against their revolutionary progenitors. This period was defined by a shift in the cultural dynamics between intellectuals and the state. For the first time, the older generations were no longer interpellated by cultural processes. Younger generations took up the baton and became the crusaders of cultural opposition. The belief that processes similar to perestroika and glasnost could occur on the island led intellectuals to hope for changes in the cultural arena. Inspired by this sense of hope, a large group of intellectuals created Paideia, a project for cultural reform that, while remaining loyal to the revolution's emancipatory project, asked for more intellectual independence. Inspired by the Gramscian vision of the intellectual's active political role, these intellectuals proposed more involvement in cultural decision making and more ideological independence. How did Paideia come together as a group?[2] It is important to note that information about this group is scarce, and the activities of its members are mostly undocumented. The main source of information comes from a special issue about Paideia edited by Los Angeles–based Cuban poet Néstor Díaz de Villegas for *Cubista* online magazine. The issue includes critical accounts by the authors themselves, as well as scanned copies of some of the group's documents and letters. In his book *Proyectos poéticos en Cuba 1959–2000. Algunos cambios formales y temáticos* (*Cuban Poetic Projects 1959–2000: Some Formal and Thematic Changes*), Spanish scholar Jorge Cabezas Miranda has done a thorough and systematic work by processing all these documents, and including some additional interviews with the writers. In what follows, I have tried to reconstruct the evanescent history of a group whose intellectual and political aspirations, partly censored, partly unrecorded, were disavowed by some of its members. This disavowal, more than any other active form of historical erasure, is the main reason for the group's having fallen into undeserved oblivion.[3]

The project, first called Grupo Espirajira, was first conceived in 1986, when it was immediately opposed by cultural officials in charge of neutralizing intellectual autonomy. The earliest document of the group is "Paideia: Proyecto General de Acción Cultural," a December 1988 unsigned manifesto expressing the desire to create an interdisciplinary cultural program with two different lines of inquiry: artistic creation and theoretical investigation.

> Paideia se define como Proyecto General de Acción Cultural dirigido al uso de las Instituciones sobre la base de un programa único e integrado. Dicho programa establece dos direcciones básicas de trabajo, orientadas a la creación artística (literaria, plástica, cinematográfica) y a la investigación teórica (estética, semiótica, científicoliteraria y cinematográfica) y organizadas, respectivamente en dos Talleres: Poesis y Logos.
>
> [Paideia is defined as a General Project of Cultural Action and is based on a unique and integrated program for the Institutions. The program establishes two basic working areas, organized in two separate workshops: one directed toward the artistic creation (literary, artistic, cinematographic), the other toward theoretical research (aesthetic, semiotic, scientific and literary, and cinematographic). Each workshop is to be respectively called Poesis and Logos.] (Proyecto Paideia 1988)

Paideia's goal was to obtain an institutional space to organize debates, workshops, and a series of lectures, which would end up being the Centro Cultural Alejo Carpentier.[4] According to Fowler, it all began at Reina María Rodrígueze's house with an informal meeting of young writers including Rolando Prats Páez, Ernesto Hernández Busto, Radamés Molina, Fowler himself, and Rodríguez (Fowler 2008). Before this, Rodríguez and Prats had organized a project with the same name, Paideia, but a very different focus, a creative and literary emphasis rather than the later project's stress on political and cultural reform (Real Arcia 2011). The idea for the first project was to create a television series about the lives and works of young Cuban artists. The purpose was to desacralize the intellectual ivy tower, to which end the group filmed television documentaries that were subsequently lost.

The definitive Paideia project began its cultural activities on February 16, 1989, at the Centro Cultural Alejo Carpentier. Nine days later, Rodríguez and Prats wrote "¿Qué es el Proyecto Paideia?" ("What Is the Paideia Project?"), a mission statement of their activities at the Carpentier.[5] There is actually an original formulation of the project dating from the month of December 1988, and the aforementioned version from 1989, goes through several revisions until the fifth version of October 19, 1989, entitled "Paideia V. Proyecto de promoción, crítica e investigación de la cultura" ("Paideia V. Critical, Promotional and Research Projects of Culture") (Proyecto Paideia 1989a).[6] It is important to note that Paideia's cultural project always defined itself as a socialist program. As we will see, however, Paideia's socialism veered away from the Cuban hegemonic ideology. From February through July 1989, Paideia organized multiple conferences at the Carpentier, where its members discovered European post-Marxism. For example, they were introduced to the work of Louis Althusser, and several philosophers and historians, including Rafael Rojas and Emilio Ichikawa Morín, lectured about structuralism and Marxism. According to Pedro Marqués de Armas, the meetings were infiltrated early on by members of the Unión de Jóvenes Comunistas (UJC) as well as by hardliners from Asociación Hermanos Saíz (AHS). The tension rose even more when Paideia members found out that the center had closed its doors to them. In July 1989 Paideia held its last "taller" at the Carpentier. The closure of the center to Paideia's activities prompted the August 4 meeting at the Carpentier, where the organizers read a version of the Paideia project. A few months later, on October 19, and as a result of the outcome of that meeting, they would draft "Paideia V" (Proyecto Paideia 1989c). It is important to note that the document created a big controversy among the artists present at the meeting, especially due to the introduction's provocative tone. As a result, the document was approved by consensus without the introduction, which was, among other things, a denunciation of cultural censorship. This was not the only case of censorship, as the state at that time was also silencing visual artists with art exhibit closures, including that of the September 1988 Castillo de la Fuerza exhibition. The introduction establishes the ideological position of the signatories of Paideia in nine different points. It first calls for an analysis of the revolutionary cultural policies with an understanding that the revolution should be taken as a process in constant evolution. The second point demands that the state recognize the organic role of intellectuals, and the third and fourth points disagree with the identification between political power and intellectuals, and the latter with the people. In the following point, the introduction calls for a notion of culture understood in its multiplicity. The final points criticize the reductive use of the popular, the ideological fiction of the New Man, and the teleological understanding of history. Finally, the document also asks for a dialectical understanding of the relationship between art and ideology. With the help of Fowler, by then vice president of the AHS, the Paideia leaders were able to discuss their project again with cultural officials, including Hart.

These discussions, unfortunately, became acrimonious, and the effort failed to win the support of many members of the AHS. Cultural officials regretted their initial approval of the project, and Paideia did not even win the support of the UJC, whose leaders did not agree with the letter. Unable to do anything to convince either of the sides to change its views, Fowler left the AHS and Paideia. He also disagreed with the group's treatment of members with different opinions. Antonio José Ponte, for instance, was ostracized for not agreeing with Paideia's cultural tenets (Fowler 2008). Following Raúl Castro's "Llamamiento al IV Congreso del Partido Comunista de Cuba," the group wrote the "Tesis de Mayo," an undated document that Jorge Cabezas sees as a response to that political event, and which was drafted between March and May (Cabezas 2012, 236).[7] According to Cabezas, in the "Tesis" members of the group "invoke the distinctive signs of their generation, to which different young artists of the period subscribe, including humanism, the ethics of dialogue, pluralism, the democratization of society, and the revitalization of culture" (ibid.). Paideia became increasingly political until in 1991 it renamed itself Tercera Opción (Third Option), led by Prats, César Mora, and Omar Pérez. In a new declaration in 1992, Prats insisted that this group had never been a political party but was rather "an independent movement of opinion with socialist roots"[8] (Prats 1992).

The rest of the group dissolved in 1992 as pressures against it increased. The government was not intent on giving intellectuals any autonomy. After Paideia's disintegration, former members decided to move the debates from the public arena into their private homes, where participants mostly studied and discussed philosophy. Rodríguez recounts how the group began meeting regularly in the Almendares Park offices of the magazine *El Caimán Barbudo* (*The Bearded Alligator*) until it closed in the late eighties (Real Arcia 2011).[9] They also gathered at the house of Ernesto Hernández Busto to discuss critical theory and philosophy and organize workshops that ranged from pre-Socratic philosophy to poststructuralism. Some examples were Marqués de Armas's lecture on the Generation of 1927 and Rojas's talk on José Ortega y Gasset. Hernández Busto, de la Nuez, Rojas, and many others left the country, leaving only a few members on the island (among them Atilio Caballero, Abelardo Mena, Ponte, Fowler, and Rodríguez).

Paideia: A Program for Cultural Politics.

Although Paideia did not identify with Guevara's "New Man," they fought to advance a revolutionary cultural program. Yet at the same time, and probably influenced by the market reforms of the early eighties, postmodernism found its way onto the island. During the second half of the eighties, Alberto Garrandés recalls, European works made their way into these writers' hands one way or the other. They read and discussed works ranging on poststructuralism and post-Marxism, as well as by European authors who had barely circulated on the island (such as Paul Valéry, Jean Genet, Franz Kafka, and Fernando Pessoa).

Disappointed by the literary and ideological narrowness of the state cultural institutions that had formed them, the members of Paideia wanted to create their own cultural space, semiautonomous from the state, for intellectual exchange and creation. Their program, however, also shared some characteristics with Guevarian precepts, especially the common goal to unite intellectual praxis and theory. Like the New Man, Paideia intellectuals were "art soldiers." The revolution had taught them to consider culture as a key element for the ideological formation of citizens, and they used the same principle to propose a reform of the system that would open the public sphere: "Paideia es un proyecto abierto a la colaboración y participación activa de todas aquellas personas e instituciones de la cultura que hagan suyos su programa y sus propósitos [Paideia is a project open to the collaboration and active participation of all people and cultural institutions that subscribe to its program and proposals] (Proyecto Paideia 1989a.) Although they questioned the Guevarian understanding of the New Man, their premises were as melancholic as Guevara's had been. They no longer believed in the sixties differentiation between "bourgeois" culture and a materialist understanding of culture. But for them culture remained organically bound to the idea of *civitas*: "Convicción de que nuestro sistema educacional se engaña a sí mismo si sustituye al hombre real por la ficción ideológica del "hombre nuevo," . . . se impone progresivamente otro método de creación intelectual, *ontológico*, el cual basa su criterio dominante en el *ser* de la cultura, en contradicción con el *deber ser*. . . . La época demostrativa de la cultura cubana ha caducado. Y de la caducidad al carácter conservador sólo media la conciencia de un fin inminente [The conviction that our educational system is fooling itself if it replaces the real man [*hombre real*] with the ideological fiction of the 'New Man,' . . . another method of intellectual creation is progressively establishing itself, an ontological one that bases its dominant criterion in what culturally *is*, instead of what it *should be*. . . . The demonstrative era of Cuban culture is passed. And between its passing and conservatism the only mediator is the awareness of an imminent end]" (Proyecto Paideia 1989b).[10] Culture was still understood as a political and transformative praxis: "Contribuir a superar el concepto de la cultura y, en particular, de la actividad estética, como 'actividad de tiempo libre' . . . su penetración más orgánica en la actividad práctico-transformadora, como componente esencial de la práctica y no como dimensión lúd[i]c[r]a de la misma [To contribute to the concept of culture and, in particular, of aesthetic activity, as a 'free-time activity' . . . its more organic penetration into pratico-transformative activity, as an essential component of practice and not as a ludicrous dimension of the latter]" (Proyecto Paideia 1989b).

Official cultural policies were still based on Fidel Castro's understanding of revolutionary art that he had discussed in his 1961 "Address to Intellectuals." Indeed, culture minister Armando Hart had just defended Castro's ideas during the UNEAC congress of 1988, the same year that Paideia emerged as a group:

> Primero: hemos venido aplicando, de una manera consecuente, los principios enunciados en "Palabras a los intelectuales." Desde luego, no nos debemos llamar a engaño, hay que continuar profundizando en ello. Segundo: el método de masas, presente en la sustancia del pensamiento de Fidel, se promovió ampliamente, lo cual facilitó la acción cultural de las provincias y municipios de una forma y magnitud tales que, de hecho, se convirtió en un elemento innovador de enorme repercusión para el presente y el futuro.
>
> [First, we have been applying, in a consistent manner, the principles articulated in "Address to Intellectuals." Of course, we should not deceive ourselves, we must continue developing this. Second, the method of the masses, substantially present in Fidel's thought, was widely promoted, thus facilitating the cultural action of the provinces and cities in such a way and to such a degree that, in fact, it has become an innovating element with enormous repercussions for the present and the future.] (Hart Dávalos 1988, 1–2)[11]

Paideia was the first intellectual group to openly question the cultural politics in place since the early years of the revolution: "Inconformidad con el margen real de acción política permitido a artistas e intelectuales dentro de los límites de lo que se considera 'revolucionario' [Disagreement with the real room for political action granted to artists and intellectuals within the scope of what is considered 'revolutionary']" (Proyecto Paideia 1989b). The group also rejected the socialist understanding of "art for the masses": "Rechazo al uso reduccionista, paternalista y demagógico del concepto y de la imagen del 'pueblo' y sus aplicaciones al campo de la cultura ('arte para el pueblo,' 'arte elitista,' 'gusto popular,' 'sensibilidad popular,' etc.) [Rejection of the reductionist, paternalist, and demagogic use of the concept and image of the 'people' and its applications in the field of culture ('art for the people,' 'elite art,' 'popular taste,' 'popular sensibility,' etc.)]" (ibid.). For these intellectuals, culture was a praxis of emancipation. In other words, the project's Gramscian mission was to redefine the ties between intellectuals and the state in a way that restored intellectuals' autonomy. Given the important mediation between the state and cultural institutions in Cuba, this became a fundamental goal of the group. The project clearly sought to reform institutional cultural spaces from within.

HUMANISM AND LITERATURE AS PRAXIS IN PROYECTO PAIDEIA

As I have noted, Paideia's project was inspired by postructuralism, but, paradoxically, it was also a modernist project. For example, the concept of *paideia* (education of the ideal citizen) comes directly from Greco-Roman humanism, in which man's virtue came from education. As in revolutionary rhetoric, man becomes ethical through education and culture. As Prats states in his "Palabras de inauguración del Proyecto Paideia," this subject stands in opposition to the uncivilized, who can only become citizens through education:

> La raza de Sócrates y de Protágoras, de Heráclito y de Parménides, de Platón y [de] Plotino—síntesis inicial y no célula pura del cuerpo que anhelamos—nos ha legado[,] en ese nombre, a la vez un proyecto y una clave. Proyecto porque ninguna sociedad de clases ha trascendido la división de la cultura, ninguna sociedad ha superado el viejo desgarramiento entre el púlpito y la plaza. Clave porque sólo en la unidad de la cultura podrá el hombre proyectar la figura y su imagen, la profecía y la pregunta sobre un plano indiviso, hecho de continuas comuniones.
>
> [The race of Socrates and Protagoras, of Heraclitus and Parmenides, of Plato and Plotinus—an initial synthesis and not a pure cell of the body to which we aspire—has come down to us[,] with this name, as both a project and a key. A project because no society of classes has transcended the division of culture, no society has overcome the old conflict between the pulpit and the public square. A key because only through the unity of culture can man project the figure and its image, prophecy and the question of an indivisible plan, made up of continual communions.] (Prats n.d.)

Like revolutionary generations from the sixties and seventies, members of the Paideia also focused on the dialectics between culture and politics. They both asked how to create an intellectual project that could integrate culture and politics and sought a pedagogy. Unlike socialist realist critics from the sixties, they were no longer preoccupied by form. Yet, like those critics, they believed in the emancipatory role of culture. In addition, the three generations also followed the Marxian principle that understands work or culture (i.e., the transformation of nature) as an act unveiling the objective conditions of existence that eventually lead mankind to disalienation and freedom: "haciendo suya la definición marxista de la libertad como comprensión de las necesidades objetivas [making their own the Marxist definition of freedom as the understanding of objective necessities]" (Proyecto Paideia 1989a). Whereas socialist realism is more focused on economic conditions, the Paideia underscores in all its documents the humanist nature of its project. It also clarifies that its members do not have an anthropological idea of humanism. Indeed, in a recent essay about the group, Ernesto Hernández Busto points out their affinity with Martin Heidegger's "Letter on Humanism." Given the obvious Heideggerian criticism of Marxian humanism, and hence the possible contradictions in Paideia's understanding of it, I find it necessary to offer further insight into this issue.

Heidegger argues that we need to liberate ourselves from the "technical" understanding of thinking. This epistemological model comes from Plato's and Aristotle's conception of thinking as a "process of deliberation in service to doing and making" (Heidegger 1988, 240). Since thinking is always a process in the service of praxis, this means that thinking is merely theoretical. For Heidegger this model is part of the "technical" interpretation of thinking. The implication is that thinking for itself is not "practical" but only "theoretical." This is why thinking has always had to justify itself before the sciences. In this regard, Paideia's understanding of culture is not based on the Platonic or Aristotelian understanding of thinking. That is, for Paideia members the sciences and poesis should not be antithetical, and, therefore, thinking is not a process in service of praxis: "Situémonos para ello en una perspectiva gnoseológica-discursiva que tienda a trascender las antinomias, tanto epistemológicas como narrativas . . . entre el llamado pensamiento científico, teorético y sistemático, cerrado a su circunstancia formativa, por un lado, y el denominado pensamiento poético, unitivo y abierto, por el otro [We thus situate ourselves in a gnoseological-discursive perspective that tends to transcend antinomies, whether epistemological or narrative . . . between so-called scientific thought (theoretical and systematic, locked in its formative circumstance), on the one hand, and what is termed poetic thought (unifying and open), on the other]" (Proyecto Paideia 1989b). In other words, they understand thinking as a process involving and accomplishing praxis and poesis simultaneously. But their theories differ from Heidegger's concerning ethics. As we know, Heidegger's ontological project consists of exposing the metaphysical nature of the question about being in the traditional philosophy originating from the Greco-Roman tradition. A non-metaphysical understanding of being is also non-teleological, and thus one that has no effect or result: "Thinking does not become action only because some effect issues from it or because it is applied. Thinking acts insofar as it thinks" (Heidegger 1988, 217). In other words, thinking about being should not be done with a goal in mind. This is why being cannot be considered from an ethical or ontological point of view: "The thinking that inquires into the truth of Being and so defines the human being's essential abode from being and toward being is neither ethics nor ontology" (ibid., 271). Thinking about being does not produce anything and does not create any action. It only pauses to let being unfold. In this regard, it is not causally related to praxis:

> But now in what relation does the thinking of being stand to theoretical and practical comportment? It exceeds all contemplation because it cares for the light in which a seeing, as *theoria*, can first live and move. Thinking attends to the clearing of being in that it puts its saying of being into language as the home of eksistence. Thus thinking is a deed. But a deed that also surpasses all *praxis*. Thinking permeates action and production, not through the grandeur of its achievement and not as a consequence of its effect, but through the humbleness of its inconsequential accomplishment. (Heidegger 1988, 274)

In contrast, the members of the Paideia argue for an ethical humanism: "Un humanismo ético, aunque no antropologizante; polémico con respecto a su tradición, pero vigilante de sus enlaces históricos y sus retos sociales ante la praxis que lo circunda y lo determina y sobre la cual se quiere proyectar; práctico sin ser pragmático; centrado en el hombre histórico, pero gravitando desde su irreductible sustancia hacia la tenaz y renovable utopía de la integración y la libertad necesaria [A humanizing but not anthropologizing ethics; polemical with respect to its tradition but vigilant in its historical connections and its social challenges before the praxis that surrounds and determines it and onto which it wishes to project itself; practical without being pragmatic; centered in historical man but gravitating from his irreducible substance toward the tenacious and renewable utopia of integration and necessary freedom]" (Proyecto Paideia 1989b). Although they reject the anthropological interpretation of ethics, they still have a metaphysical understanding of it. Like Heidegger, they favor displacing the idea of a foundational Cartesian subject. Against Heidegger, their understanding of thinking is still subordinated to a goal. Notwithstanding the metaphysical nature of their manifestoes, they established the conditions of possibility for an anti-metaphysical intellectual space, as I will show in the following paragraphs.

Paideia and Civil Society

Jorge Ferrer, one of the group's former members, argues in a recent article that the Paideia was politically insignificant. According to him, their project was too ambitious and had no impact on Cuban politics. What he does not realize, however, is that he is measuring the project's impact with the same utopian yardstick that he criticizes: "Todo proyecto colectivo . . . sólo consigue rebasar los vastos y nutridos dominios de la insignificancia, si su objetivo se cumple, si concita suficientes voluntades como para que se lo tenga por masivo, o si la fuerza a la que se opone lo aplasta con suficiente saña, como para que perviva en la memoria, siquiera como testimonio de un martirio [Any collective project . . . only succeeds in transcending the vast and well-nourished domains of the insignificant if its objective is achieved, if it brings together sufficient efforts so that it is perceived as massive, or if the force it opposes obliterates it with sufficient fury that it lives on in memory as testimony to a martyrdom]" (Ferrer 2006). Paideia was based on an emancipatory political project, and in that regard its understanding of culture was no different from that of official cultural institutions. Paradoxically, however, it succeeded in displacing its own narrative. I refer specifically to its breaking ground as a civil society movement of sorts. The years that immediately followed the fall of the Berlin Wall saw a renaissance in civil society discourse, especially in the social sciences. Indeed, Paideia's theoretical tenets were much more orthodox and in line with official policies than its real political interventions. The debates introduce the conditions of possibility to think about civil society in antihumanist terms. What is more, the project's failure to establish a semiofficial cultural movement is symptomatic of the limits of political humanism. In this regard, it affirmed itself as an epistemological vanguard. This also proved that the government was right to consider it as a "political party" of sorts, which is something that always remains ambiguous in recent characterizations of the group by former members. For example, Rafael Rojas argues that "Paideia no fue un movimiento o un grupo, sino un proyecto y un espacio de sociabilidad intelectual. Una propuesta, como decíamos, de política cultural autónoma, diseñada por un puñado de escritores y compartida, durante el brevísimo tiempo que duró, por la mayoría de la comunidad artística e intelectual de

La Habana, en la segunda mitad de los 80" [Paideia was not a movement or a group but a project and a space of intellectual sociability. A proposal, as we put it, for autonomous cultural politics, conceived by a handful of writers and shared, during its very brief lifespan, by most of Havana's artistic and intellectual community in the second half of the 1980s]" (Rojas 2006b). But what is the difference between these designations? Unlike Rojas, I think that the Paideia was both a group and an intellectual space, and that although it failed as a group, it successfully established an intellectual space. I believe that it is very important to distinguish the Paideia as a group, for two reasons: first, because this indicates its political character and, second, because this also acknowledges its key role in creating a civil society. In this regard, it is important to stress the political connotation of the movement, because this is precisely what established it as the first *conatum* of civil society.

In the early nineties, as a result of the partial entrance of capital into the Cuban economy and the establishment of foreign NGOs on the island, a theoretical movement emerged based on the belief that Cuban civil society was transforming or at least taking form. Scholars such as Hugo Azcuy, for instance, argued that the state's loss of economic power caused a recuperation of an autonomous social space (Azcuy 1995, 160). Many of these scholars, however, conceived of civil society in a Hegelian fashion as the mercantile society of needs. None of them conceived of civil movements as Gramscian enclaves of resistance that could eventually hegemonize a new historical bloc. In Gramscian terms, civil society is interpreted as the space where new social forces are generated: "We are still on the terrain of the identification of State and government—an identification which is precisely a representation of the economic-corporate form, in other words of the confusion between civil society and political society" (Gramsci 1971, 262). Yet, what made the Paideia even more iconoclastic was that the intellectual space it enabled called into question the same humanist principles that the group brandished, a space also present in the Gramscian concept of civil society that I have just outlined. In other words, the group both enabled the emergence of a civil movement that posited itself as a new hegemonic bloc and, simultaneously, was able to overturn its political nature with an even stronger intellectual agenda. That is, the Paideia was never a new hegemonic bloc, because the intellectual space it opened debunked the Paideia's status as a "group" fighting to establish a political praxis. The Paideia's understanding of "intellectual thinking" ceased being subordinated to a goal, as it was in the group's theoretical manifestos.

Paideia disintegrated under pressure from what Althusser would term ideological and repressive state apparatuses. The political disenchantment and impotence contributed to the creation of the Proyecto Diáspora(s), and especially to the idea of writing a samizdat, as I showed in chapter 2. Irony was one of the ethical responses triggered by the group's political disempowerment and disillusionment.

Irony in the Proyecto Diáspora(s)

Choteo, Irony as Pathos, and Buffo

The work of Virgelio Piñera and José Lezama Lima, both authors ostracized by the regime during the seventies, gripped the attention of the younger generation of eighties intellectuals. This was especially true for members of the Diáspora(s), for whom Piñera became an intellectual icon. It would not be excessive to say that Piñera was one of the strongest voices in *Diáspora(s)*. The presence of his voice was there, even when his writing was not. Its tone and texture, its pitch and gravitas characteristic of his caustic and ironic oeuvre, left an imprint on the Diáspora(s)'s work. Piñera was the only Origenista to whom *Diáspora(s)* devoted a dossier. Aguilera indicates that the journal particularly emphasized Piñera's playful and ironic nature, which in terms of national *costumbrismo* is also what Jorge Mañach called *choteo*:

> De todos los Virgilios que conozco (el narrador, el que sorbía té por las tardes, el que cuchicheaba con Lezama) prefiero el que sentía asco. No hacia una persona o una comida, movimiento común a que suele reducirse el asco; sino el burlón, el tragaespadas de feria, el personajito escatológico. . . . En este sentido, sus cartas también. . . . Cartas lúdicas, pedigüeñas, gozadoras; que caricaturizan lo que están observando y *realifican* la ficción que perversamente se genera (crea) en ellas. Como si después de los cuentos, el teatro, los poemas . . . no quedara otra opción que la risita constante, eso que Gombrowicz llamaba el "sabroso culipandeo.
>
> [Of all the Virgilios I know (the narrator, the one who sipped tea in the afternoons, the one who whispered with Lezama), I prefer the disgusted one. Not with respect to a person or a kind of food, as disgust is commonly reduced to, but rather the mocker, the county fair sword swallower, the scatological character. . . . In this sense, his letters as well. . . . Playful, demanding letters that take pleasure in life, that characterize what they observe and *realify* the fiction perversely generated (created) in them. As if after the stories, the plays, the poems . . . no other choice remains but the constant snicker, what Gombrowicz called "the tasteful dodge (*el sabroso culipandeo*).] (Aguilera 1999a, 26)

In other words, both the Diáspora(s)'s oeuvre and Piñera's belong to a long tradition of works that have cultivated the practice of *choteo* as a unique Cuban trait defining national identity. The difference, however, is that in the Diáspora(s) *choteo* is represented not as a national characteristic.[12] One can see various aspects of *choteo* at play in the Diáspora(s), but also many differences that distance the project's approach from that tradition and bring it closer to Piñera's dry and scathing humor. Mañach defines *choteo* as "tirar todo a relajo," a personality trait consisting in not taking anything seriously and laughing at any type of situation with a slightly teasing attitude (Mañach 1999, 50.) This is in general the journal's prevalent tone on most matters, but Mañach does not consider *choteo* intellectual or witty; for him it is a sincere, lightweight joke (ibid., 51.) Conversely, irony, especially the type we find in *Diáspora(s)*, is "más o menos, una forma de simulación, de doblez, puesto que consiste en decir lo contrario de lo que se siente o se piensa. Pero el cubano es tan sincero—sincero hasta cuando miente, cosa que hace sin escrúpulos—que le repugna toda forma irónica de impugnación. Prefiere el choteo, que es la mofa franca, desplegada, nada aguda generalmente, como que no tiene hechura de dardo, sino más bien de polvillo de molida guasa, que se arroja a la cara de la víctima [more or less a kind of simulation, of doublespeak, since it consists of saying the opposite of what one feels or thinks. But Cubans are so sincere—sincere even when they lie, which they do without scruple—that they hate any ironic form of contestation. They prefer the *choteo*, which is a forthright jibe, openly displayed, generally nothing pointed like a dart but more like the powder of a ground-up ribbing (*molida guasa*) that is tossed in the victim's face]" (ibid., 78). That is, a witty simulation, a Brechtian estrangement, as Rito Ramón Aroche suggests in his review of Lidzie Alviza's work (*Diáspora(s)* 7/8: 94). But *choteo* and irony also have commonalities, in that both can be described as Mañach does the former: "*El choteo es un prurito de independencia que se exterioriza en una burla de todas formas no imperativa de autoridad* [*Choteo* is an itching for independence that manifests in mockery of any nonimperative form of authority]" (Mañach 1999, 62). In other words, both irony and *choteo* indicate a lack of respect for authority and a desire to be above hegemonic power, or at least distinct from it. This irreverent disdain is precisely what *Diáspora(s)*'s ironic tone reveals, and it materializes as a scornful representation of cultural and political state power. This aspect of irony is also a legacy of Piñera. His poem "Lápidas [Tombstones]," for example, shows this ironic irreverence toward the most authoritarian and arbitrary power of all: death.[13]

> ¿A qué no me llamas por mi nombre?
> Son inútiles tus burlas y tus ultrajes.
> Ni siquiera llamarme viejo

y que la muerte me ronda.
De nada vale decirme "carcamal," "baboso,"
"reblandecido," "caquéctico" . . .
Nada me ofendería, nada,
aunque me llamaras "esqueleto rumbero"
mi dignidad quedaría a salvo.
Pero si llegas a llamarme por mi nombre,
si llegaras a decirme Virgilio Piñera,
entonces me ofendería
porque esas lápidas pesan demasiado.[14] (Piñera 1999, 28)

In "Lápidas" the poetic voice playfully personifies death and provokes it in an ironic fashion: "¿A qué no me llamas por mi nombre?" The irreverent tone of the question indicates fearlessness and a willingness to confront the ineluctability of death. Is there any ground to challenge death? By playing with the double meaning of *llamar* ("to call" and "to name"), the poem is pointing to the proximity between life and death, and to a new understanding of the latter. This poem, written in 1971, clearly alludes to Piñera's intellectual persona and to the ostracism that he suffered during the last decade of his life. After having been an early and enthusiastic supporter of the revolution, Piñera grew increasingly uncomfortable with the stifling cultural policies that took place from 1961 onward and fell into disgrace as a consequence of his muffled critiques.[15] Barred from intellectual public life and publishing, Piñera became invisible well before he died. He was like the specter-like figure of his poem who is unafraid of death because, while physically present, he is already gone. This death in life has rendered death more familiar to him and less fearsome: "Son inútiles tus burlas y tus ultrajes / Ni siquiera llamarme viejo / y que la muerte me ronda." But what could be a tragic truth is actually expressed with a playful tone, whose irony is conveyed with the double meaning of "llamar."

The crux of the poem resides in that subtle ambiguity by which in the end death, like the gravestone to which the poem refers, renames us, as it happens, it individualizes us as when we are named (given a name) at birth. This name that we are given at birth symbolizes a new life, a full life, our presence and visibility in the world. The tombstone, in contrast, is what memorializes our life. It is the tribute to our memory and the way to acknowledge the importance of our (now former) existence. In the poem, the gravestone signals or produces an injunction to memorialize the poet's life: "Pero si llegas a llamarme por mi nombre, / si llegaras a decirme Virgilio Piñera, / entonces me ofendería." But it is this type of injunction to celebrate a life after death that the poet fears the most. It is this "renaming" that the poet rejects, "porque esas lápidas pesan demasiado." That is, he rejects the tribute to his memory as a writer, because it goes against his sense of ownership of his experiences. When he was alive he was made invisible by others, but no one could take away his experience of life and the fact that he was actually present, at least to himself: "aunque me llamaras esqueleto rumbero' / mi dignidad quedaría a salvo." Once he is gone, however, he will only be alive through the memories that others fashion of him. What he fears is not that death is calling him but that it will rename him through memory by recreating his persona and the legacy of his thought.

Carlos A. Aguilera's work comes from the same tradition of political irreverence, but poems such as "Mao," for example, introduce us to a much more complex notion of irony. "Mao" recounts the extermination of sparrows during the 1958 Chinese Great Leap Forward. Sparrows were known for eating stocked grain, so the state involved Chinese citizens in their massive killing. The goal was to ensure a high agricultural productivity that would ultimately result in fewer imports of heavy machinery. This campaign turned out to be one of the most tragic events of the Maoist period, because the lack of sparrows brought with it a plague of locusts that caused the Great Famine and the deaths of sixteen to thirty million people. Because the campaign resulted in the opposite of what it was meant to achieve, its representation becomes ironic in Aguilera's poem.

> enemigo radical de / y enemigo radical hasta
> que destruye el campo: "la economía burocrática del arroz"
> y destroza el campo: "la economía burocrática de la ideología"
> con sus paticas un-2-tres
> (huecashuecasbarruecas)
> de todo mao*sentido*
> como señaló (o corrigió) históricamente el kamarada Mao
> en su intento de hacer pensar por enésima vez al pueblo:
> "esa masa estúpida
> que se estructura
> bajo el concepto fofo
> de pueblo"
> que nunca comprenderá a la mao*democratik* en su movimiento
> contra el gorrión
> que se muta en
> *vientre*amarillo
> ni a la mao*democratik* en su intento (casi totalitario) de
> no pensar a ese
> gorrión
> *vientre*amarillo.[16] (Aguilera 1997, 22)

As a *mise en abyme*, "Mao" is actually an irony about an irony. Not only is it a poem about a historical event, it is also a reflection about irony itself. Line after line, the poem represents factual and antithetical events. For example, there is a description of the sparrow massacre in a matter-of-fact form whose aim is to create a suspension of disbelief. But this actually is not what is intended, because immediately after that statement, the poem reveals its falsity by indicating that ideology, like economics, is a matter not of beliefs but strategic planning. The government claims that sparrows eat away the crops and their revenues, but it is actually a planned economy and a stale ideology that does this. The sparrow is a fragile bird and not a menace to the economy. It is fragile, yet "barrueco," original, different, unlike Mao's ideology. Mao despises the masses but uses them. His system calls itself a democracy when it is not one. In the following lines, the poem tackles the question of violence:

> o repito ch'ing ming
> donde el concepto *violencia* se anula ante el concepto *sentido*
> (época de la cajita
> china)
> y donde el concepto violencia ya no debe ser pensado sino
> a partir de "lo
> real" del concepto
> *un*solosentido (como
> aclaró muy a tiempo
> el presidente Mao y
> como muy a tiempo
> dijo: "si un obrero
> marcha con extensidad:
> elimínenlo / si un
> obrero marcha con *in*tensidad: rostros
> sudorosos con 1 chancro
> de sentido")[17] (ibid., 23)

The line "o repito ch'in ming" refers to the April 5 Movement of 1976, when the state violently suppressed demonstrations in Tiananmen Square against totalitarian measures. These protests were held during the Ch'in Ming, a traditional Chinese festival honoring the dead. In totalitarian regimes, state power is stratified and articulated in the form of a Chinese box: "y donde el concepto *violencia* se anula ante el concepto *sentido* / (época de la cajita china.)" Rule is conducted through the establishment of a strong ideology that legitimizes power. Here ideology means reason and the supersession of violence, but that ideology is actually implemented through violence hidden under the concept of reason, as though each were a small box inside of a larger one. Reason in this regard is violence, not a means to a cause but rather the cause itself: "y donde el concepto violencia ya no debe ser pensado sino / a partir de 'lo / real' del concepto / *un*solosentido." Ironically, however, this type of thinking ("*un*solosentido") is intensive, instead of extensive. If intensive thinking, in Deleuzian terminology, is the force that fuels the production of difference, it should not be equated to "*un*solosentido" as the poem does: "si un obrero / marcha con extensidad: / elimínenlo / si un / obrero marcha con *in*tensidad: rostros / sudorosos con 1 chancro / de sentido")." "Mao*democratik*" is actually only the regime of one ideology, and thus one direction (*sentido*: one direction, one meaning, *ex (Latin)*: outside, *tendere (Latin): estirar*): "y subrayando con una metáfora la *no*fisura que debe existir / entre mao*democratik* / y sentido."[18] That is, a worker who wants to deviate from the "un sentido" must be killed; he cannot veer off the path. On the contrary, if he remains on the path (according to state ideology), his process of production is intensive and could potentially create a system of differences. The irony of the poem consists in reversing this process. Instead of creating a system of differences, the worker produces a contagious ulcer (*chancro*) of meaning, that is, a foreign body that corrodes it from the inside ("1 chancro / de sentido"). "Mao*democratik*" is an oxymoron; it creates the opposite of what it means. There is a fissure between tradition and lack of sense, that is, only one ideology can make the tradition, can make history, the rest is outside history:

> "subrayando con una metáfora la *no*fisura que debe existir
> entre mao*democratik*
> y sentido
> y subrayando con la misma metáfora la fisura que existe
> entre tradición y
> *no*sentido: generador
> de violencia y
> *a*orden / generador de
> *no*historia y "saloncitos
> literarios con escritores
> *sin*sentido"[19] (ibid.)

This fissure generates violence and chaos, which at the same time generates "*sin*sentido" writers with no meaning and no trajectory. Aguilera evokes two senses of "un sentido" ("one meaning" and "one way") and plays with the word "violencia." According to the logic of the Chinese state, there is violence when there are different meanings, ways, or ideologies: "(si un obrero marcha con extensidad: / elimínenlo." That is, a worker who does not follow the regime's path must be exterminated, like the sparrow that would dare fly off freely. Yet, the real violence is actually committed by the state, which only permits its citizens to think in one way, thus imposing one tradition and immobility. That is, by walking "inward" (toward "the way"), ideology can become contagious, like a venereal disease: "si un / obrero marcha con / *in*tensidad: rostros / sudorosos con 1 chancro / de sentido." Mao only speaks through metaphors ("subrayando con una metáfora"), and his political discourse is lyrical: "Y sin embargo hoy es famoso por su cerebrito verticalmente / metafísico / y no por aquella discusión *lirik*proletaria entre gorrión."[20] His lyricism is a direct cause of the metaphysical and teleological nature of a political system of thought whose end goal is utopia. In other words, it is lyrical because it is literary, and it is literary because it is mostly articulated through metaphors. This is precisely the aestheticized representation of sixties politics that we studied in chapter 1. The poem thus offers a critique of such discourses and of their metaphorical force that goes so far as to equate violence and reason: "el concepto *violencia* se anula ante el concepto *sentido*." This explains why a metaphor is actually an irony. What other rhetorical figure could dissemble as well as a metaphor? The poem is therefore a metapoetic critique of metaphors because of their potentially ironic use. Paradoxically, however, the poem itself is an irony of the same irony it is criticizing. In other words, the poem chooses to narrate history through irony. At the end of the poem, Qi the copyist of Mao's history gets his finger chopped off, because he accuses Mao of manipulating history. This is how Mao "corrects" history:

> "y como se vio obligado a corregir el (definitivamente)
> civilista Mao al
> coger un cuchillo
> ponerlo sobre el
> dedo más pequeño
> del copista Qi
> (en un tono casi
> *dialektik* / militar
> casi) decirle
> "hacia abajo y
> hasta el fondo
> (crackk . . .)"[21] (ibid., 24)

By "correcting" history with violence, Mao invents his last metaphor. That is, killing is not an act of violence, it is rather a "correction" of history. As a dissemblance, the art of correction is also an irony. The poem shows that violence is always represented as an irony, as something that it is not. From a metapoetic point of view, the poetic voice also chooses irony to narrate the tragic events that led to the Great Famine. If Mao writes history violently, the poetic voice chooses irony instead. Mao's discourse is essentially metaphoric: correction is violence under the guise of reason. The poem clearly attempts, however, to criticize the use of metaphors. We can observe this weariness in the story's narration. The refusal to "metaphorize" the story is also an effort not to repeat Mao's violent gesture. The criticism of metaphors is carried out through irony. The result is a poetic ironic form about political irony, and the first sign of this operation is articulated by the peculiar poem's form, which is actually quite common in Aguilera's poetry. It consists of form where punctuation marks replace words. Not only do punctuation marks replace words, they are also grammatically incorrect. Several linguistic elements are misused or abused: neologisms, incorrect spelling, improper word use, italics, absence of capitalization, slashes, parentheses, character numbers followed by dashes and written numbers, constant enjambments. This linguistic violence also points to a political violence. That is, it's the linguistic representation of an ideology whose economic policies are fraught with violent practices. Punctuation marks can only be irreverently used, but their meaning remains the same. That is, punctuation marks have a grammatical function, but they do not have semantic meaning. When used improperly, however, their function does not change (paradigmatic axis), but the syntagmatic level of the sentence does.

For example, in the "con sus paticas un-2-tres / (huecashuecasbarruecas)" we find both puns and a sign: the number 2, which can be read as a pictogram that resembles the bird. The term "paticas" ("patas" or bird legs) echoes the Cubanism "pláticas" (chats), and "barrueco" (an irregular pearl) is the term from whence "barroco" originates. The line is thus ironically referring to the empty and convoluted arguments that justify the policies to exterminate the sparrows. The repetition of "huecas" ("empty"), joined with "barruecas," produces an alliteration that evokes the bird's pecking sound. Also, the semantical opposition between "huecas" and "barruecas" produces laughter instead of gravitas. In other words, there is not a *traslatio* of meaning as in metaphor. Instead, the punctuation marks add tone. In most cases, as in this example, this tone is one of buffo. Irony in the poem articulates buffo as a tonality. There is a lot of buffo in Aguilera's work, and by extension in *Diáspora(s)*. According to Paul de Man, buffo is what Friedrich Schlegel calls the disruption of an illusion. It is, for example, what happens in commedia dell'arte. "[Buffo] is the aside to the audience by means of which the illusion is broken" (de Man 1996, 178). In the poem, metaphor as a rhetorical figure is displaced by irony as buffo. That is, in political discourse metaphors become ironic because they dissemble and "hide" violence. Instead, poems are ironic because they show dissemblance through the articulation of pathos, or buffo in Aguilera's case. Buffo breaks the illusion that metaphor produces.

Of all the works we have seen, *Historias de Olmo* by Rolando Sánchez Mejías may most clearly show what I call the pathos of irony. The book is a series of Beckettian microfictions about the "absurd" and illogical life of a character named Olmo. Drawing on Piñerian storytelling tradition, the book breaches formal conventions, including those of genre, length, and narrative flow. The reader's expectations are constantly challenged. The absurdity of the stories lies more in the humor they provoke when explanations, space, or time no longer make sense, as in "Viaje a China," for example: "Olmo se abrocha los zapatos, se va a China, vuelve de China y se desabrocha los zapatos [Olmo ties his shoes, goes to China, comes back from China and unties his shoes]" (Sánchez Mejías 2001, 82). The comic effect lies in the inconsequentiality and the incongruence of both actions. The actions of tying one's shoes and traveling to China are made equally important, and there has been an alteration in the cause and effect between them. In *Historias de Olmo*, irony, as we have understood it thus far, is replaced by humor or *choteo*. In other words, what disappears in these stories is the traditional understanding of irony as a trope that posits a *sujet supposé savoir* or an external point of view. Gilles Deleuze argues that in traditional irony an ultimate law always establishes the rule that is broken: "Classical irony acts as the instance which assures the coextensiveness of being and of the individual within the world of representation" (qtd. in Colebrook 2004, 133).

Thus, in irony the subject is always represented as a disempowered victim. Irony reproduces a reality that deviates from an established norm, which is why it always resides in negativity and never empowers the subject. Irony thus conceived comes from the romantic interpretation of irony as an embodiment of the relation between the subject and the Absolute that is later interpreted as negativity in work from Hegel to Kierkegaard. To end the repetition of the negative impact of irony, Deleuze proposes giving up irony and finding an alternative in humor. Thus, for Deleuze irony as a trope must be replaced by something more active and less reactive, and for him that is humor. It is what Deleuze calls superior irony or postirony, a concept that "strives to think all the becomings that lie beyond the subject, all the points of view that lie beyond the grammar and logic of human representation" (Colebrook 2004, 137). Postirony tries to grapple with what we cannot say by delving into the forces that produce subjectivity, rather than with recognition. This is why "humor shows subjects to be collections of sounds, gestures, body parts, and signs devoid of any real sense" (ibid.). In *Historias de Olmo*, humor is also a reversal of irony. There is no subjectivity but rather a perpetual state of becoming as the result of the categorical collapse between bestiality, humanity, and entities.

For Deleuze, change can only occur by cultivating humor rather than irony. Unlike irony, humor does not set a moral standard because it breaks up notions of subjectivity. It no longer presents a point of view looking at us from above. It just disrupts logic, annuls ethics, and deforms bodies and objects. In this regard it is closer to *choteo* and to Piñera's notion of the absurd. This is precisely what "Dostoeivski, libro primero, VII [Dostoyevsky, Book One, VII]" demonstrates:

> A veces Olmo se esconde en las escaleras, saca un cuchillo y desde allí acecha. Que finalmente no mate una mosca no prueba que carezca de talento para matar. Olmo explica que Raskolnikov carecía de talento para matar. Dice: "Era un chapucero. En su obstinación por probar una idea había olvidado las reglas más elementales." Y añade que sobre todo ignoró la regla principal: ¡Cuidado con mujercitas como Sonia!
>
> [Sometimes Olmo hides in the stairway, takes out a knife, and waits. That he wouldn't hurt a fly doesn't prove he lacks talent for killing. Olmo explains that Raskolnikov lacked talent for killing. He says, "He was an amateur. He was so determined to prove an idea that he forgot the most basic rules." And he adds that above all he didn't know rule number one: Watch out for little ladies like Sonia!] (Sánchez Mejías 2001, 59)

This story trivializes Dostoyevsky's *Crime and Punishment* by erasing its moral content. It measures Raskolnikov's crime not according to a moral standard but rather according to his "talent" as a murderer. Olmo's interpretation has a more political twist. His idea, a clear reference to totalitarianism, is that ideas take over praxis, and the latter fails because the idea is no longer adjusted to reality: "He was so determined to prove an idea that he forgot the most basic rules." But immediately, this more serious interpretation is trivialized with a misogynistic popular statement that Cubanizes the Russian novel's context: "Watch out for little ladies [*mujercitas*] like Sonia!"

This type of humor takes us back to Mañach's *choteo*, with which it shares a key characteristic, the irreverence for authority that we also saw in Piñera and Aguilera: "Un mero desorden no es cosa que tenga gracia en sí. El choteo no se la encuentra tampoco, pero se ufana ante una situación semejante *porque comporta una negación de la jerarquía*, que para ciertos tipos de idiosincrasia tropical es siempre odiosa. Todo orden implica alguna autoridad [Mere disorder is not amusing in itself. *Choteo* does not find humor in it either; instead it revels in such situations *because they entail a negation of hierarchy*, which for certain kinds of tropical idiosyncrasy is always despicable. All order implies some authority]" (Mañach 1999, 59). Unlike *choteo*, however, this type of humor is apolitical and nonnationalistic, which is what makes it so light: "Estas dos disposiciones espirituales nuestras—la ligereza y la independencia—han sido, pues, el caldo de cultivo del choteo [These two spiritual attitudes of ours—lightness and independence—have thus been the breeding ground for *choteo*]" (ibid., 71). Most important, this humor has lost the negative connotations that Mañach attributed to *choteo*, because it actually represents *choteo*, but ironically. That is, as in the story "Alas, uñas, o pezuñas" ("Wings, Fingernails, or Hooves"), the narrator teases the reader into identifying with Olmo as the main character, while at the same time ridiculing him and his words. The story shows a categorical disintegration by discussing representation and reality:

> Que parezca un mendigo, que sea un misógino, que confunda a los gatos, no dota a Olmo de profundidad. ¿La poesía en la vida se da por sí misma? Mejor virarse de espaldas mientras el banquero regala unos pendientes a su esposa preguntándose por la naturaleza de los acontecimientos.
>
> Así es la vida. Mejor seguir de largo. Mejor virarse de espaldas mientras una mujer, en la cama, acaricia el omóplato de Olmo. ¿Con qué? Con una plumita. Ella le dijo: "Un cínico, eso es lo que eres . . ."
>
> ¿Pero qué vamos a hacer si la prosa no ama? Entonces Olmo le dijo. . . . ¿Cómo decir en prosa que Olmo la ama? ¿O que no la ama? Y ella, ella, ¿ama a Olmo? Ella le dijo, mientras se pintaba . . .
>
> Veamos, no perdamos el punto de vista. Donde hubo un ala de ángel ahora hay un omóplato vacío. Donde hubo emoción ahora cuelga un bicho en una rama. Donde hubo amor ahora . . .
>
> ¡Pero esto se parece a la poesía! Prometemos que se repetirá pocas veces, por no decir jamás, jamás. Mejor volvámonos de espaldas. Visto en prosa, Olmo duerme. Como un bendito. Profundamente como la superficie de un lago duerme su alma. Le van creciendo alas, o uñas, o pezuñas.
>
> Es un encanto—dice el narrador recogiendo la plumita de la cama.
>
> [That he looks like a beggar, that he's a misogynist, that he couldn't tell two cats apart, doesn't make Olmo deep. Does life's poetry offer itself up on its own? We'd do better to turn our backs while the banker gives his wife earrings, and meditate on the nature of events.
>
> That's the way life is. Better to follow at a distance. Better to turn our backs while a woman, in bed, caresses Olmo's shoulder blades. With what? A little feather. She tells him: "A cynic. That's what you are."

> But what do we do if prose doesn't love? So Olmo tells her . . . How do we say in prose that Olmo loves her, or doesn't love her? And she, she, does she love Olmo? She tells him, as she puts on her makeup. . . .
>
> Hold on. Let's not lose our point of view. Where there was an angel wing there's now an empty shoulder blade. Where there was emotion there's now a bug hanging from a branch. Where there was love there's now . . .
>
> But this sounds like poetry! We promise that this will rarely happen again, or rather, never, never. Better to turn our backs. Seen in prose, Olmo lies sleeping. Like a saint. Deeply like the surface of a lake his soul sleeps. He grows wings, or fingernails, or hooves.
>
> "He's charming," says the narrator taking the feather (*plumita*) from the bed.] (Sánchez Mejías 2001, 68)

The piece poses an amusing paradox regarding poesis (writing) and its relationship to reality as a subject matter. The narrator states that odd characters such as Olmo, as well as unusual events or love scenes, are not poetic subjects in themselves: "That he looks like a beggar, that he's a misogynist, that he couldn't tell two cats apart, doesn't make Olmo deep. Does life's poetry offer itself up on its own?" The comic element comes from the oddity and trivial, inconsequential (and thus realist) absurdity in all the events the narrator represents. In other words, "Alas, uñas, o pezuñas" criticizes realism, its mimetic function, and its objective analysis of reality. An objective analysis seeks to understand the real social conditions, and this is precisely what the narrator is telling Olmo, the writer, not to do: "Better to follow at a distance." In other words, we cannot reproduce an objective image of reality, because there is not one objective point of view. This is why characters are confused and suddenly lose the point of view ("Hold on . . ."). But it is precisely because we lose the point of view, that reality comes together in a sudden poetic representation: "But this sounds like poetry!"

The paradox is that after having said this, the narrator comes up with a poem inspired by the events he has belittled before: "Where there was an angel wing there's now an empty shoulder blade. Where there was emotion there's now a bug hanging from a branch. Where there was love there's now . . ." Once again, the poem has ranked poetry higher than prose: "How do we say in prose that Olmo loves her?" The piece ends, however, with a poetic fragment in prose: "Deeply like the surface of a lake his soul sleeps. He grows wings, or fingernails, or hooves." The narrator is telling us that poetry and prose are indistinguishable. "Alas, uñas, o pezuñas" also shows that poetry is not a social analysis of reality, and that life in itself is poetic. Poetry is actually as inconsequential, odd, alluring, and unpredictable as reality. Writing flows, like the river to which Olmo is compared, as the narrator picks up the "plumita" (or quill in Spanish), which is also the writer's pen.

Irony as Parabasis of Allegory

Allegory becomes a fundamental and instrumental trope to create a utopian political discourse. This fact is so decisive that for the Cuban poetic imaginary, allegory and official discourse have always been indistinguishable. This is what some poets have interpreted as a "usurpation of the language." I am referring specifically to the Diáspora(s) group, whose members have expressed their wish to dismantle the trope of allegory. In "Olvidar a Orígenes [Forgetting *Orígenes*]," one of the most important texts of the group's journal, *Diáspora(s)*, Sánchez Mejías argues that all poetics are susceptible to being appropriated by political rhetoric: "Nunca hubo una escritura tan hermética o difícil que no haya podido ser 'leída' por los imaginarios de la política [There has never been a writing so hermetic or difficult that it cannot be 'read' by the imaginaries of politics]" (Sánchez Mejías 1997a, 18). Commenting on Paul Celan's poetry, Sánchez Mejías argues that history always precedes poetry. He also says that poetry cannot avoid the catastrophe of history, and by referring to Lezama Lima's "poetic extension," he condemns its allegorical nature:

> Incluso si esas palabras bastaran para revivir todos los muertos, no alcanzarían a borrar el horror que circuló entre ellas en nombre de la Historia—esa misma Historia que les concedió la forma de Poesía. Por eso toda extensión poética se vuelve sospechosa. Toda imagen avanzando por una extensión debe sentirse amenazada por los huecos negros de la Historia. Y toda mente fajada con una extensión vacía debe saber reconocer en la blancura una posibilidad del horror.
>
> [Even if these words were enough to bring all the dead back to life, they could not erase the horror that circulated among them in the name of History—that same History that bestowed on them the form of Poetry. As a result, all poetic extension becomes suspect. Any image advancing through an extension must feel itself threatened by the black holes of History. And any mind

tagged with an empty extension must be able to recognize in blankness the possibility of horror.] (Sánchez Mejías 1997a, 19)

By "poetic extension," Sánchez Mejías is clearly referring to Lezama Lima's frequent use of the word in its metaphysical connotation as that which extends itself beyond the letter and into the world. This quotation clearly actualizes Theodor Adorno's paradox between barbarism and civilization: after Auschwitz, poetry has become a barbaric act. A history that has created barbaric acts also fecundates the poetry that negates them. According to Adorno's reading, culture and barbarism have become synonymous; however, culture is subjected to another aporia, namely, the fact that it needs art despite its impossibility.

A poem by Marqués de Armas titled "Claro de bosque (semiescrito) [Forest Clearing (Semiwritten)]," from his most recent collection, *Cabezas* (*Heads*), deals precisely with this issue. Marqués de Armas's poem is a reflection on the historical experience and its representation. The poem suggests that there is a mutual overdetermination between history and its representation. It also proposes looking at history in three different ways: as an experience, as an abstraction, and as a representation. In other words, the poem tries to understand the relationship between universality, particularity, and their representation, taking into account that they have a relation of mutual determination. Universality refers to history and its development, particularity to the experience of being, and representation is the unveiling of being. I will first comment on the representation of history in the poem. In "Claro de bosque (semiescrito)," the act of naming and the experience of historical catastrophe are in constant tension. This conflict is represented in the poem as the margin between the outside as experience and the inside as thought: "las puertas se abren hacia / dentro y / con horror infinito / hacia afuera los pensamientos"[22] (Marqués de Armas 2002, 26). The poem discusses the impossibility of enunciating the historical catastrophe through the act of naming. "Claro de bosque" is a reflection on the conditions of possibility for the unveiling of being in a nonlinguistic or representational realm. The poem's "claro" is thus what Heidegger termed "Die Lichtung," or the unveiling of being: "las puertas se abren / hacia / dentro y / con horror infinito / hacia fuera los pensamientos/ pienso / en una escritura-intensidad / pero no es escritura la palabra exacta / (exacto es claro de bosque)."[23]

Although this nonrepresentational desire is clear, the poem also argues that "el claro," or the clearing, can only happen in the form of a thought. The poem thus emphasizes the paradox behind such nonrepresentational desire: the clearing cannot be made of anything but words, since once it is expressed by thought, it is also already made of words. There is another paradox, however, since language cannot express the experience of the clearing: "en algún punto o claro de bosque / calculado / (en la cabeza) / aunque el término punto también inexacto / y aún, todavía las rayas-excavan / cada uno de esos puntos dispersos"[24] (Marqués de Armas 2002, 26). There is an alternation between the event and the impossibility of its representation, making it clear that words no longer have a performative function. The materiality of language, which is represented by tropes, cannot express what the clearing could express. Materiality is also represented in the poem through reference to Nietzsche's *Thus Spoke Zarathustra*: "molinillos-organillos en Mandelstam, / Nietzsche (¡que crujen!)"[25] (ibid.). The passage in Nietzsche to which this line refers also talks about the difficulty of representing thought with language; the materiality and power of language to represent are thus called into question (Nietzsche 2006, 173–74). At the same time, history resists writing because the event always questions its representation: "pero no es escritura la palabra exacta / (exacto es claro de bosque) / ni siquiera la que más se aproxima / ya que / ninguna palabra es tan intensa / para ser escrita"[26] (Marqués de Armas 2002, 26).

Let us discuss historical experience in the poem, or what I have also called particularity. The "cerebro desenterrado [disinterred brain]" that appears isolated in one of the poem's lines—referring to a poem by Osip Mandelstam—points to the ineffability of history: "ninguna palabra es tan intensa / para ser escrita / en el horror infinito de unos caracteres de tierra / el cerebro desenterrado" (Marqués de Armas 2002, 26).[27] The poem alludes to the earth because these brains and thoughts are also related to a historical event that took place in the gold mines of Serra Pelada in Brazil. The mines are represented through the ravages of a globalized world that takes advantage of an underworld inhabited by dehumanized beings and that produces a history that cannot be narrated: "los caracteres se desprenden / al simple roce de las manos / así también la tierra / al borde de ciertos farallones o mantos de pizarra"[28] (ibid.). Yet, as I have already mentioned, the "cabeza" and "cerebro desenterrado" allude to another historical event that is mentioned in one of Mandelstam's poems. The line "los campus (de ojos) y los campus (de cabezas)"[29] alludes to "Stalin's Ode," specifically the last lines, in which Mandelstam describes Lenin addressing the multitude: "The hillocks of people's heads are growing more distant: / I am diminished in them, won't even be noticed" (Mandelstam, cited in Coetzee 1991, 75). Scholars have traditionally interpreted these lines as pertaining to Lenin, but J. M. Coetzee explains that it alludes to Mandelstam's private mythology. According to Nadezdha Mandelstam, this mythology includes a reference to Genghis Khan. Coetzee argues that the subtext of these lines is the narration of the resistance to Genghis Khan's army, symbolized by the thousands of heads in a mound outside of the city's ramparts, and that this analysis extends to the last line of the last verse in "Stalin's Ode." The narration of two different historical events, one by Marqués de Armas and one by Mandelstam, bears a similitude since both recount those who are at the margins, those who have neither voice nor history.

I can now talk about history as a universal concept, that is, as a science or as a narrative that explains the study of past events. "Claro de bosque (semiescrito)" constitutes a critique of the Marxian epistemological tradition that has determined the interpretation of history in Cuba. The poem thus questions historicism as an epistemological model that is based on the interpretation of history as a scientific event. This critique becomes clear in the poem when the identity of the workers of Serra Pelada is described as a molecular existence in a shattered world. These men have amputated bodies, and it seems as if the writing of the poem, the soil of the mines, and these bodies had all been subjected to neurological surgery. In thus characterizing the historical event as a scientific event, "Claro de bosque" alludes to the supposed scientific nature of history, and also introduces the first ironic element in the poem: "así en las minas al aire libre de Serra Pelada / 400 kms al sur de Belén / donde los humanos (moléculas rientes de negror corredizo) han sustraído / en un corte sagital / la órbita de un ojo infinitamente horrible"[30] (Marqués de Armas 2002, 27). This poem, like the work of the Proyecto Diásporas generally, is also ironic, but in a very de Manian way. This irony, however, is also quite present in its most Schlegelian sense, that is, as self-reflexive poetry and as a paradox: "Irony is the form of paradox. Paradox is everything which is simultaneously good and great" (Schlegel 1971, 266). But, like Schlegel's irony, the poem reveals the break between aesthetic representation and the world. As for Schlegel, for Diáspora(s) there is a fusion between poetry and philosophy. Schlegel wanted that poetry be "in touch with philosophy and rhetoric" (ibid., 175). For Paul de Man, irony is a disruption of the tropological system, in that it calls into question tropes such as allegories and metaphors and their ideological representation of the world. For Schlegel and for de Man, irony is about poetry's inability to communicate. De Man describes irony as the interruption or the permanent parabasis of the allegory of tropes. The parabasis of allegory refers to the interruption of two different codes in the same discourse. By "codes," de Man refers to different types of stylistic elements (genre, subgenre, tone, etc.). The allegory of tropes has its own systematicity, and it is precisely this coherence, as well as the internal dialectics of the allegory, that irony interrupts (de Man 1996, 178). In Marqués de Armas's poem two discursive codes coincide and interrupt each other: the poetic language and the scientific language. Neither can be defined without the other. Science gives a rendering of the physical world through observation and experiment, whereas poetry does not need an experimental justification to be what it is. But experimentation always has limits because it refers to materiality but does not tell us what it means, and as such science is also metaphoric. Poetry evokes a physical or emotional reality with metaphors, but metaphoric language also has limits. The ineffability of reality exposes the limitations of language and opens up different possibilities of representation, one of which is accomplished through linguistic experimentation. The irony resides in the fact that the historical catastrophe cannot be interpreted as a scientific event but is not an unmediated event either. Irony only displaces the two codes to introduce a different representation of history.

This new representation of history needs to be defined through the relationship between thought and representation, a question that, as I have noted, is one of this poem's main driving forces. The relation between thought and representation is also what Heidegger calls the relation between *Denken* (to think) and *Dichten*, which literally means "poetry" or "the act of writing poetry." It is important to note that I am speaking of this Heideggerian distinction in light of Jacques Derrida's comments in his essay "Le retrait de la métaphore" ("The Retreat of Metaphor"). It is also necessary to explain Derrida's reflections on the metaphor to further understand the difference between *Denken* and *Dichten*. For Derrida it is impossible to interrupt the presence of the metaphor (Derrida 1987, 64). Etymologically speaking, the metaphor alludes to the vehicle, to transport. Metaphors are the vehicle of writing. This is why one cannot talk about metaphors without talking through them. Indeed, metaphors do not have a proper name; language itself is a metaphor. This explains the double meaning in Derrida's title. Every time the metaphor retreats, it always leaves the sign of a supplementary stroke, of a *re-trait* (retreat) in the *trait* (stroke) that it had left in the text. The rhetorical margin of this discourse is no longer determined by an indivisible simple line (ibid., 80). Derrida explains that for Heidegger *Denken* and *Dichten* always form a pair and go together. But they run parallel to each other and never meet, and, thus they can never be confused or translated by one another. The paradox is that in spite of these two distinct parallel paths, *Denken* and *Dichten* are so close to each other that at times they intersect and they cut across one another. When they cut across each other, they each mark the other. This cut does not create a wound; rather, it is a cut that opens up their difference, cutting back their own stroke and its supplement. This cut does not belong to either one, nor is it a common stroke, a general concept, or a metaphor (ibid., 87).

The relationship between *Denken* and *Dichten* is expressed in the last lines of "Claro de bosque": "en la intersección / el corte sagital del cerebro / de manera / que / la cabeza y el ojo / el ojo y la cabeza y / así los campus (de ojos) y los campus (de cabezas) / expresen la superficie / (ya, / exclusivamente extirpada) / sólo es, / exclusivamente, / el fondo de la mina"[31]

(Marqués de Armas 2002, 28). The language of the poem resists determination and adjectives. It is also full of "cuts" and "intersections" marked not only by the words that appear isolated in the poem but also because of the cuts (enjambments) in many of the lines. These cuts also represent the moments when *Denken* and *Dichten* overlap, and yet they do not belong to either of them. That is why the poem offers two alternative endings. On the one hand, it offers a scientific representation of the historic catastrophe related to the mine: "(ya, / exclusivamente extirpada)." On the other hand, it gives us an unmediated representation of the historical catastrophe by describing the mine as, "exclusivamente, / el fondo de la mina." What the poem finally reveals is that the *Lichtung* or clearing is also the moment of the "cut" that shows the difference between the scientific history and the unmediated history, or between thought and poetry. This moment does not belong to either one of them, yet it reveals the stroke and the supplement of both of them.

Marqués de Armas's work has abandoned an allegorical interpretation of reality and a scientific explanation of a historic finality, thus creating the "writing of disaster." Although the poem does not theorize about other plausible political answers, it does pinpoint the aporias of art and its representation. This theoretical gesture is a critique of both the aestheticization of politics and the subsumption of art by the market. Far from arguing that contemporary art is futile because it no longer articulates a political message, Marqués de Armas's work underscores the important ethical nature of the writing of disaster. This is not to say that this writing aims to establish a moral injunction as opposed to offering articulations of political utopias. On the contrary, by pointing to the complex relations among thinking, poetry, and history, Marqués de Armas's work lays out the conditions of possibility to go beyond the mimetic or utilitarian function of art and of the political itself.

Schizophrenia and the Proyecto Diáspora(s)

The Limits of the War Machine as a Political Concept

The work of the Proyecto Diáspora(s) is characterized by a paradoxical political premise consisting in desiring both the law's presence and its absence. In Deleuzianguattarian terms, we could understand this paradox as the simultaneity of the flows of energy that configure the structure of power in their theory. This structure consists of the simultaneity of flows of both territorialization (imposition of the law) and deterritorialization (absence of the law). For Gilles Deleuze and Félix Guattari, these two forces always act together by creating a system that is constantly moving from one force to the other and never acquires the nature of either. As I argued at the beginning of this chapter, the political circumstances of the nineties produced a law that is symbolically empty, and that is constituted by a fallen ego-ideal. In schizophrenic logic, the law always oscillates between two positions. It goes from the ideal ego as utopia to the fallen ego-ideal as repulsive. In fact, this logic is very similar to the Deleuzian-Guattarian imaginary that I have just described. That is, in both models the liberating (or utopian) forces and the coercitive (or repulsive) forces become undifferentiated. But a problem arises with this logic.

If liberating and coercitive political forces become undifferentiated, how are we to imagine a politics of resistance? It is true that the Diáspora(s) was not interested in a politics of resistance. Rather, the group's goal was to create a poetics of the war machine. In an interview with the group, Liliane Giraudon asks the following question: "En nuestra entrevista Rolando Sánchez Mejías habla de *Diáspora(s)* como 'una vanguardia enfriada durante el proceso,' una 'avanzada sintáctica de guerra.' ¿Podrían explicar ese concepto? [In our interview Rolando Sánchez Mejías speaks of *Diáspora(s)* as 'a vanguard that cooled off during the process,' a 'syntactical outpost of war.' Could you explain this concept?]" The authors respond by arguing that the journal is a war machine: "Algo de resistencia, por cierto, pero sin esas cantatas misionistas que calcan una pobreza mal entendida, reticente y tan poco moderna. En fin, una literatura que se despliega como maquinita de guerra sin caer en posiciones roñosas o partidistas [An element of resistance, certainly, but without those missionary hymns that sketch out a poorly understood, reticent, and quite unmodern poverty. In the end, (ours is) a literature that is deployed like a little war machine without falling into mean-spirited or partisan positions]" (Giraudon 2001, 58–59). The war machine, however, also articulates an undifferentiated flow of forces of liberation and coercion. Is it the case, then, that the Diáspora(s)'s politics are a reflection of a state politics subjected to the effects of an empty law? Although Marqués de Armas's work is clearly influenced by Deleuze and Guattari's theories, his poems point to the limits of their theoretical system.

Cabezas, Marqués de Armas's collection of highly conceptual poems, use the word *cabeza* (head) as a referent that thematizes thought and representation. Drawing on Deleuze and Guattari's *A Thousand Plateaus*, these poems use botanic or organic imagery to talk about writing and thinking. *Cabezas* focuses on the physiological aspects of the brain, while referencing the ontological and epistemological dimensions of thought. In the following poem, for example, the fields are libidinally connected, like a rhizome. Deleuze and Guattari argue that a rhizome has many entryways, which allows one to access it from a deterritorialized space, and also from a constrained one such as an oedipal formation or a rigid territoriality that opens the way for a transformational operation.

fincas de 1914
de café criollo con seca/
deros de sol y
marmitas de crujiente lepra
                    movimientos
                    parcelarios
o neuro/
bióticos del terreno
            pero adyacente y sin
            solución de continuidad
(númen
voluptas) en la de/
vastada serranía[32] (Marqués de Armas 2002, 35)

The poem takes us on a journey through a rhyzomatic movement, as I will explain. The poem begins with the year 1914, an emblematic date for capitalist formation in Cuba, characterized by the centralization of production and capital accumulation.[33] At the beginning of the twentieth century, the Cuban sugar industry transformed as it transitioned from a slave economy to industrial manufacture.

The poem describes an abandoned and unproductive old *ingenio* soon to be replaced by the more modern *centrales*. With the *central* also came *colonos* or *campesinos parcelarios*, a new kind of farmworker specialized in cane production. In the *Eighteenth Brumaire*, Marx explains that "campesinos parcelarios" [small-holding peasants] were part of the largest working class in Napoleonic France, impoverished and isolated subsistence farmers (Marx 1990b, 123). This class without class consciousness forms the expandable remnants of sacarocracy, a pathologized social body infected with leprosy and inhabiting a dry and unproductive coffee plantation soon to be transformed into a *central azucarero*, thanks to the new flows of capitalism coming from the United States.[34] Paradoxically, however, the poem has replaced a materialist and class-based rendering of society with its post-Marxian version because the text "is opposed in every way to the classical or romantic book constituted by the interiority of a substance or subject" (Deleuze and Guattari 1996, 9). Political subjectivity has no place in this representation of a reality made of machinic assemblages of free-flowing libidinal energy separated from any relation to its cause.

This is not to say that these flows depart from liberating forces. In fact, these forces are produced in the coercitive world of sacarocracy. Hence the paradox that the poem presents: the "serranía" is "de/vastada," both "devastada" (devastated) and "vasta" (vast, enormous). In other words, sacarocracy's ideology has left its imprint in the social and physical configuration of the fields. There are only two liberating forces in the poem: "(númen/

voluptas)" that transform the "serranía" into a "vast" space. Deleuze and Guattari argue that these flows (liberating and alienating) form what they call a "machinic assemblage." Alienating or negative forces are represented as trees (ontologically grounding subjectivity), but liberating forces are represented by rhizomes. In the poem, the fields are affected by rhizomatic forces that have produced the vastness and the greenery of the "serranía." These rhizomatic and positive forces are defined as "(númen/voluptas)." For Deleuze and Guattari, *numen* represents desire, and *voluptas* represents consumption. Desire and consumption (deterritorializing forces) coexist with the alienating forces of sacarocracy (reterritorializing forces). Paradoxically, liberating forces can be produced in deterritorialized or reterritorialized spaces. That is, forces can be liberating (deterritorializing) even if they come from a rigid territoriality (a tree), because they can be produced in a free space (line of flight) or in a space of subjection (territorialization). In political terms, this means that desire is everywhere and can be produced through negative or positive events. If desire can be produced in the coercitive space of sacarocracy, then we could posit that *numen* and *voluptas* come from the economy of sacarocracy. In fact, they cannot come from anywhere else, because as a social and economic space the fields have been determined and shaped by sacarocracy. The poem, however, represents these two forces in parenthesis, which indicate that we are trapped by the laws that create our desires. In other words, in the last instance the social configuration of the fields is determined by the repressive social forces of sacarocracy. The parentheses graphically enclose desire and consumption, indicating that they are repressed forces that strive to be liberated from the law that produces them. For Deleuze and Guattari, the political is conceived as a force or affect whose intensity and direction are successively transformed into territorializing and deterritorializing flows. The poem, however, shows that some of those flows still need to be liberated.

"Hueso de la raicilla [Pit of the Rootlet]" is another poem that calls into question the metaphoric nature of the war machine's theoretical apparatus:

gris
removido
en cuál listón de tierra
pones mi cabeza
la rodante—cabeza—
como artificio de letra falaz[35]

The poem functions at three symbolic levels: the botanical, the epistemological, and the metapoetic. On the one hand, we have the botanical representation, which is the most literal one. The poem refers to the pit of a fruit (*hueso*) as it germinates (*raicilla*). It could be, for example, an avocado pit, which is a very common Cuban fruit. The pit has germinated and is now ready to be planted and grow into a tree—the poem mentions the dividing lines between different plants as a "listón de tierra." This explains the gray color of the pit and its transformation/removal (two senses of the adjective *removido*). On the other hand, the poem articulates an epistemology clearly represented by Deleuzian-Guattarian terminology. The "raicilla," which is originally considered a rhizome, transforms the fruit into a radicle-system as it grows. It reterritorializes as it gets planted to develop into a tree. This also functions at the level of subjectivity, thoughts coming from the "cabeza" (subjectivity) to the nonsubjectivity represented by the "cabeza rodante."

Much like *A Thousand Plateaus*, the poem describes different aesthetic and ideological regimes by drawing botanical comparisons. In their work, Deleuze and Guattari distinguish three types of epistemologies that correspond to different poetics and that they represent with botanical metaphors. First, the root-book, which comes from the Aristotelian and Platonic tradition (Deleuze and Guattari 1996, 5). In this genealogy, representation is a mimesis of nature that results in two different realities. That is, through representation nature becomes a dual reality (artistic and real or essential). The second mode of envisioning the world corresponds to the radicle-system or fascicular root. This system is no longer dual, because the center changes. But there is still an essence, and therefore the system is considered metaphysical. The authors exemplify this idea with James Joyce's *Ulysses*, where the meaning of words is unstable and multiple but still constitutes an overall system, which in this case is cyclical. The radicle-system is still considered metaphysical as it differentiates between subjects and objects, which is no longer the case in their third mode or representation. The rhizome or their last epistemology undoes the duality and systemicity of the other two. It is a heteregenous system without a center and infinite points of connectivity. Meaning is multiple and forms an assemblage where the categorization of the world into subjects and objects no longer applies: "There are no points or positions in a rhizome, such as those found in a structure, tree, or root" (ibid., 8).

The "hueso de la raicilla" is a rhizome which, unlike the radicle-system, is not rooted in metaphysics. It creates words with multiple roots that do not produce mimetic or systemic narratives, but, while the rhyzome is unstructured and without attachments, the radicle gives access to a higher unity of meaning that encompasses all singularities (Deleuze and Guattari 1996, 6). The "rolling head" (*cabeza rodante*) is another Deleuzian-Guattarian metaphor that references their notion of "faciality" (*visagéité*). For them a head that is no longer attached to a body represents faciality, a notion that entails the production of alternative modes of organization (nonmetaphysical and nonpsychological). In the poem the metaphysical mode of organization is represented by the "listón de tierra." The plant's bone (pit) is going to reterritorialize space by anchoring to the earth to grow a new tree. Thus, the rhyzomatic nature of the bone will be transformed into a root.

Marqués de Armas's poem discusses the aesthetics of rhizomes that become radicle-systems. Bones grow roots as poetics grow rhyzomatic literary assemblages, and, like bones, writing is nude and bare. This is also why these poetics do not create subjectivities, and this lack of subjectivity is represented as a "cabeza rodante." When the root of this ryzhome is planted, it reterritorializes the space and becomes a radicle-system that produces subjectivity (a "cabeza"). The same movement occurs in poetics where the word is displaced or trans-posed ("removido") into another word. Words reterritorialize the poetic space to become metaphors. We are interpellated by metaphors, which assign different subjectivities that identify us. Metaphors transform poetics "como artificio de letra falaz." That is, when metaphors are purely ornamental and not conceptual they produce false words that attract us with false appearances. This last line introduces the poem's irony at different symbolic levels. It first criticizes a trope by explicitly using the same trope (the metaphor "como artificio de letra falaz"). The irony at this level would be very simple, since it can only be interpreted as affirming the contrary of what it means. But this also implies that the poem clearly introduces a poetic voice or a subject that clearly establishes an ethical rule in reference to what is false (or "falaz").

It is now up to the reader to find out what creates falseness or fallacy. Is it that metaphors as tropes are always false and deceptive, or is it that false thinking creates deceptive metaphors? In "Hueso de la raicilla," however, the question takes on a different nature because of the ludic tone it introduces. The last line adds a new meaning to the poem, especially as we reconsider the meaning of "falaz." What is false and what is deceitful? Is it the poem itself and the type of thought that it conveys? In other words, is the poem not pointing to the limits of the Deleuzian-Guattarian tropological system? Deleuze and Guattari's philosophical system attempts to create an antimetaphysical space by creating a new vocabulary that neutralizes the ontological dualities identifying subjects, objects, and sciences. Marqués de Armas's poem, for instance, shows how their scientific terminology breaks with conceptual divides (subject/object, law/nature, etc.). But conceptually speaking, their method is purely rhetorical. It consists of borrowing scientific terms and reassigning them new meaning through a metaphorical process. By borrowing Deleuzian-Guattarian vocabulary the poem follows the same process of metaphorization, but it also questions this process. The poem is pointing to its own hermeneutic limit and simultaneously rejecting hermeneutics altogether.

Schizophrenia and the End of Literature: Juan Carlos Flores

Literature of Disaster: Antihumanism—The Parting of History in Literature

The end of literature as a project of social emancipation announces both the birth of postmodernity and the death of representational and allegorical writing. Under this new paradigm, literature reaches its limit once it can no longer fulfill the social function assigned to it by the ideological project of the 1960s governments of national liberation. Thus emerges a literature marked by defeat and by the historical experience of the utopian promise's failure. And yet this writing is not about this defeat but engendered by it. In this sense, literature has become what Maurice Blanchot has called a "writing of disaster" (Blanchot 1980, 25), that is, a literature that is no longer emancipatory, that has no goal and leads to no future. According to Blanchot, the writing of disaster occurs when words are no longer either weapons or means of action and the act of writing has thus lost its urgency and necessity. In this context, the nature of a writing until now marked by its imitation (*mimesis*) of reality begins to change. When the act of writing loses its relevance and its importance, one's relationship to writing begins to be transformed. This is the moment in which language ceases to be sacred. When language is no longer sacred, it is also no longer an offering and no longer a sacrifice in the common interest, as it is in allegorical representations. An antihumanist and antiheroic writing emerges that is no longer one with history. This writing, far from glorifying life and postulating itself as a triumph over death, tells us of the violence inflicted on the writing. But does this violence that gives birth and form to the writing come purely from an outside force to which the writing must submit or is it manipulated from the margins of what it is intended to be a resistance strategy?

This question highlights the main paradox that these poetics must confront. On the one hand, this writing appears to be a demystification of the project of a concluded modernity, representing furthermore an opening toward a deterritorialized space. On the other hand, it is a project constitutionally marked by the experience of an ideological defeat and finds itself facing the void left by that failure. If this project is so deeply marked by the experience of defeat, does this also mean that it also is condemned to this failure? Is there any chance that this writing is not in turn limited by the experience of defeat that engendered it? The poetry published in Cuba during the nineties by an entire generation of young writers raised by the revolution as the New Men imagined by Guevara was created under the ideological and aesthetic conditions that we have been discussing. Specifically, the work of the poet Juan Carlos Flores is a writing of disaster built on a deconstructed syntax in which conventional notions of poetry as an aesthetic and ethical act have disappeared.

Repetition of History: Circularity and Immanence

As the poet Reina María Rodríguez has noted, Flores's writing has the same labyrinthine structure as the Alamar neighborhood in which it is created (Flores 2003, 8). Alamar may be the symbol that best explains the social architecture of Flores's poetics and the conception of history that appears in his work. A housing project in East Havana launched in 1971 as one of the Cuban Revolution's most ambitious social plans, Alamar was conceived as a utopian space that would bring together the different social principles on which the revolution was based, especially the socialization of private property and the chance to obtain housing in exchange for its real value, calculated in terms of labor rather than market value. This project was intended to remedy the shortage of housing for the most needy and promised to be distributed equitably among workers in the microbrigades that were in charge of building them. Intended to be completed in 1981, Alamar was to house 130,000 workers from the area's industrial centers and was to include day care centers, semiboarding schools, theaters, recreation centers, health centers, and new industrial zones (Schuman 1975, 14). At first, it was thought that the buildings would be four stories high, but later this was increased to twelve stories thanks to improved methods of prefabricated construction. This model was never completed as planned, however, and the Alamar complex became an exemplar of the gray style of Soviet architecture associated with socialist realism.

Like Alamar complex, Flores's poems have an apparently circular and symmetrical structure in which the lines—like the gray, Soviet-style buildings—impose themselves uniformly and monotonously. We can see this in the poem "Marina," from his collection *Distintos modos de cavar un túnel* (*Different Ways to Dig a Tunnel*): "El galeón (que bordea la costa) no es un galeón aunque parezca un galeón. / El galeón (que bordea la costa) no es un galeón aunque parezca un galeón. / 'El galeón' es la réplica de un galeón"[36] (Flores 2003, 29). In Flores's imaginary events recur similarly an infinite number of times. This movement of eternal return also takes us back, paradoxically, to the concept of revolution. Hannah Arendt explains that initially the word *revolution* referred to a recurring movement and not to a transformative turn as we currently understand it. The original Latin meaning of the word was later adopted in the natural sciences through the work of Copernicus, coming to designate the regular, cyclic, and recurring movement of the stars (Arendt 2006, 32). That is, if we apply it in the political sense, the term indicates not a type of renewal but a form of government that repeats itself with the same force as that of the stars following their predetermined path through the sky (ibid.). In other words, this type of government does not entail what we mean today by *revolution*, a movement generated by a renewing impulse that in turn is related to the idea of freedom. Through preliminary negations and *mise en abyme*, Flores's poem suggests that the process of identification is condemned irredeemably to failure given the tautological nature of the reasoning it follows. The referent cannot be distinguished from the signified because the former always leads irrevocably to the latter, to the point of rendering the two indistinguishable.

Many of the poems, however, break the circular structure by introducing a sudden and unexpected change of rhythm, as for example in "El ciclista K [K the Cyclist]": "El ciclista K, otro de los segregados convertido en exegeta, todo el tiempo posible haciendo auto-stop entre ciudad y campo, o entre campo y montaña, sin encontrar solución al eterno problema, sin encontrar el necesario reposo del cuerpo negroide, otro de los segregados convertido en exegeta, todo el tiempo posible haciendo auto-stop entre ciudad y campo, o entre campo y montaña, sin encontrar solución al eterno problema, sin encontrar el necesario reposo del cuerpo . . . me ha contado que al mirar allá adentro algo raro notó"[37] (Flores 2003, 61). This poem, like many of the others in this collection, recounts an immobile locomotion through which maximal energy produces minimal travel. This inefficient economy can also be observed in the poem's discursiveness and the long time it takes to tell its story. And yet we should not confuse this verbosity with the linguistic profligacy so characteristic of the Latin American baroque, since although the latter tends toward the production of pleasure and *jouissance* as an alternative to capitalist consumption, Flores's logorrhea instead draws us into an antieconomy in which expenditure produces a consumption that does not transform. The expenditure that points toward a progressive loss of life by what it generates is interrupted in the poem by its coda: "me ha contado que al mirar allá adentro algo raro notó [he told me that after looking inside he felt something strange]." This final rupture of the monotonous and circular rhythm might make us think that some new source of production exists, but the only thing that is broken is the voice and the rhythm. A pause is produced, a transformation that is also a new path in the cyclist's routine. Suddenly three actions occur—looking, speaking, and feeling—and these seem to give the subject a certain autonomy. And yet, rather than a way out, these actions signal the entrance into a new labyrinth, another unknown that brings us again to the point of departure or to the end of a road on which we find ourselves already lost.

The Law and the Absence of the Primordial Signifier

This unproductive economy is also a source of violence generated by the governmental rationality's latest mechanisms of control. In Cuba we are witnessing simultaneous and apparently contradictory political and economic phenomena. If the arrival of the global market has put the island on the path toward economic liberalization, in the political arena the authoritarian model continues to reign. The great paradox is that the model of a society of control, generally associated with neoliberal economies and the utopian doctrine of laissez-faire, has been fundamental to the development of the regime's authoritarianism, such that the new implementation of mechanisms of control has been gradually displacing the functional mechanisms of the disciplinary society. While the disciplinary society model exercises its authority over the body based on the sovereign's prerogative over the right to life, the society of control exercises power based on a rationality that takes into account the population in its multiplicity, its opinions, its modes of behavior, its fears, and so on—all the factors, in other words, that can be controlled through education, political campaigns, or any other kind of state ideological apparatus (Deleuze 1992, 3–4). In the case that concerns us here, the model of sovereignty exercised as power of capture and subjection of life to political control is channeled through the social project of Alamar. In this sense, we can say that for the social unconscious Alamar is one of the utopian projects of the building of the revolutionary nation, when in reality the effect it produces is precisely the opposite: the subjection to political control through a model that seems to leave human consciousness no kind of autonomy whatsoever.

This type of political rationality creates dehumanized, Kafkaesque subjectivity represented as the animalized and monstrous infrahumanity we see in the poem "La mofeta" ("The Skunk"): "Roedor de pequeño volumen, para protegerse de las agresiones de los diversos animales, de miembros y dientes más poderosos que ella, despide un olor nauseabundo, debido a un curioso mecanismo glandular que se articula, en cuanto ella siente la proximidad de un asalto. / En el parque zoológico, cárcel o manicomio donde los animales internados pugnan por un poco de espacio, sobre el cual depositar comidas y heces, aún por entre las áreas destinadas a los mamíferos fuertes veo cruzar a la mofeta, y siento envidia, yo, que con indiferencia he visto cruzar a esos autos que aquí llaman de lujo"[38] (Flores 2003, 64). In this apocalyptic poem creatures are represented as numb and powerless beings. We are faced with what Agamben called bare life, that is, life that can be annihilated with impunity, because it is a life without value (Agamben 1998, 138). The poem ends by posing a false disjunction in a clearly ironic tone, proposing a choice between bare life and nothingness. Why do I refer to the other possibility as nothingness? Because the other possible form of life is that of the consumer, perhaps the communist of the future. And yet the poem clearly makes us understand that the freedom to consume either does not exist or simply does not matter. Apart from this life that does not exist, all that remains is bare life, which therefore is not a choice but an imponderable (since by definition bare life cannot be chosen).

I would like to follow this analysis of Flores's work by returning to the question with which I began: Is the violence of this work a force immanent to the system that generates it and to the poetic representation of this system, or is there any possibility that its aesthetic and marginal representation might produce "an escape valve," as "Visto desde el suelo" puts it: "ex-civilistas, lastre abajo, atraviesan la ley, buscando algún tubo de escape" (Flores 2009, 26).[39] Can this law of subjection to political power be crossed through? The regime's political crisis that resulted from the collapse of the socialist bloc in 1989 is characterized by not only economic debacle but also by the absolute loss of ideological referents. The government's decision not to abandon the revolution's socialist doctrine quickly comes into contradiction with Cuba's penetration by global capitalism and with the regime's gradual disideologization, as reflected in the constitutional changes of 1992. As I have argued, all this means is that at a certain point, socialism becomes an empty signifier that points to the lack of primordial signifier and thus to the existence of a law void of content. To understand this better, we could draw a parallel with psychotic pathology, since in both cases what in Lacanian terms we call the primordial signifier—that is, the law of the Father—is rejected, and as a result this law constitutes itself in turn as the sign of an absence. For the state, this absence is that of a distinct socialist ideology that could have adapted itself to the new economic situation that came into force at the beginning of the nineties, as had happened in the former Soviet Union, but that would not have entailed the loss of the nation. If there is no law, this means that there is no frame of reference enabling a hermeneutic operation of the situation of power. In other words, if there is no law, everything is subject to the most absolute arbitrariness. It is impossible to know when and where the violence of power begins or ends. It is impossible to know the limits of violence with respect to the text, as we see in "Tótem," the poem that opens *Distintos modos de cavar un túnel*:

> B-U-E-Y/ En el centro del poema / comidos los bordes del poema / con ojos de buey mira a la realidad / desde el centro del poema. / "—Doctor, las huellas de sus patas por los surcos eran el poema, donde caía el agua de su nariz abrían sus dedos,

> sus cabezas las flores quemantes del poema—" / B-U-E-Y / Su cansancio es político / ya no se quiere levantar / no se quiere desposar / comidos los bordes del poema / con ojos de buey mira a la realidad / desde el centro del poema.[40] (Flores 2003, 19)

The totem functions in this poem as the sacred law that in this case is the poem itself, writing itself. The ox is also the totem and writing is represented as bare life, as that which can be annihilated with impunity, because it is a life without value. Although Flores's work takes the historical catastrophe as a point of departure, it lacks an ethical dimension. It is an aesthetics that thematizes the nonrepresentability of violence, as well as its own. Unlike Diáspora(s), Flores's aesthetics does not seek to move us, and in this regard it has surpassed the vanguardist gesture of the former. Flores's poetics point to a different understanding of the political, understood in its revolutionary rendition as the classical Schmittian antagonism between friends and enemies. This is precisely where the power of this literature resides.

Afterword

This book has examined the different discursive formations of revolutionary utopia and its withering. The premise of this book is that we live in postideological societies that can no longer be analyzed through a Marxian understanding of social or economic structures. As I argued in the introduction, the concept of ideology no longer holds true. Other post-Marxist theorizations of the same concept, such as Louis Althusser's notion of ideology as the "real conditions of existence," also share a similar *mecanicist* understanding of the "real." Given the relativity of reality as a notion, as well as the need to take race, sexuality, or gender as mediating factors shaping ideology, the "real" is not a useful category. Above all, however, we are in need of a notion that can account for a fragmented (or nonessentialist) view of identity, especially taking into account the unconscious, and the impossibility of knowing which is the object of our desire. In this regard, since we can never really grasp the object of our desire, the notion of utopia is a clear substitute for what remains unknown and inaccessible. In addition, as Slavoj Žižek points out, we are no longer duped by the difference between exchange value and use value. The consequence, then, is that asking what is the goal of literature (political or otherwise) is pointless. It is more revealing, instead, to look at the fantasies that make up for that unknown, and this is why literature is so essential. It is not about having access to that desire; rather, it is about understanding fantasy as a narrative construction that conceals our desire, as an object that belongs to the Real, and that therefore resists symbolization. The book has analyzed these fantasies and narrative constructions, both at political and cultural levels, in an effort to explain the diversity of social discourses and political rhetoric, as well as cultural expressions in the form of literature and film. By analyzing such a large variety of modes of expression, I have sought to show that social reality can be studied as more than a textual symptom. In this regard, the book has shown the various fantasies that have populated revolutionary and utopian discourses.

Beginning with the discursive formation of revolutionary ideology through political discourses and cultural production, I have shown that revolutionary rhetoric has always represented utopia as an emotional ethos based on violence and sacrifice, thereby constantly deferring the enunciation of utopia as a programmatic political discourse. Cuba's political ideology used to be predicated on a stark bipolar division of forces that clearly distinguished friends from enemies, a conception of the political that to all appearances was shattered by the end of the Cold War. Revolutionary discourse, deeply influenced by the melancholic tropology of the New Man and the search for the lost object of desire, formed intellectuals for whom the loss of the object became the loss of self. The influence of this rhetoric, and not so much the fall of the Berlin Wall, was what produced the melancholic ethos among the children of the revolution. The members of this generation had not fought for the revolution; they did not share the initial revolutionary utopian impulse. Yet they had been formed by the double ideological matrix: the discourse of violence and sacrifice. The poets from the two preceding decades were not intellectual referents for them. The children of the revolution were eager to expand their knowledge beyond the *talleres literarios*' nationalist understanding of literature. They had also been assigned the difficult task of creating the truly revolutionary poetry of the New Man, with whom they never identified, especially because this model demanded the elimination of the self for a greater cause. Their initial poetic production resulted from the melancholic understanding of art that demanded an identification with a lost, inexistent self. My analysis has shown the melancholic nature of these literary "fantasies," but I have not been concerned with the political (or ideological) goals of these works.

Unlike their elders, whose war was always against "the imperialist and bourgeois intellectual," the members of Diáspora(s) constituted one of the first intellectual groups to defy the dominant ideology of the revolutionary intellectual community by criticizing the canonical intellectuals who defined the fatherland. The rhetorics of violence and melancholia that they inherited were the roots of their aesthetics, as we observed in the poetry of the eighties. Violence was of particular interest for the vanguardist group of poets who formed Diáspora(s). In what I have called their poetics of defacement, violence became the symbol of a negative dialectics of sorts articulated by a passion of negation that took pleasure in unsettling the baroque and realism.

These poetics opened up an epistemological aporia that demanded thought but disparaged language. It was, in other words, what I explained as a poetics that originated from an experience of dread and a "defacement" of language. That is, the disappearance of language that left behind thinking as a trace.

From the analysis of this initial decade, I have turned to the period encompassing the two decades of the regime's transition to a post–Cold War period. The shattering of utopia's initial meaning explains this chronological leap. The political crisis resulting from the partial capitalization of the economy brought forth a political rhetoric with an apparent desire to insulate life into a dying ideology. Utopia had to redefine itself, but no discourse could be instantiated. The rhetorical strategy was to turn on its head the discourse of the "fatherland or death" proclamation and put the emphasis on ways to keep socialism alive. The emphasis on death and violence that inaugurated the revolution transformed into a biopolitical emphasis on life after the symbolic end of socialism. This new rhetoric, however, did not transform the regime's ideology. It was, rather, a new strategy of political subjection and a new form of administering political control that proved to be no less efficacious than the repressive policies of the past, as well as the present ones. I am saying this because in Cuba sovereign power coexists with a biopolitical regime. Repressive and arbitrary political measures taken against the circulation and publication of a so-called dissident intellectual discourse are the best proof. As the book has discussed, the intellectual persecution of Diáspora(s) and Antonio José Ponte are the most representative examples of this type of censorship.

If one had to die for the revolution in the sixties, one had to live for it in the eighties and nineties. Culturally, this rhetorical turn resulted in the revival of José Lezama Lima, who was consecrated as one of Cuba's national intellectuals and ideologues. Before he had been appropriated by the dominant ideological formation, Lezama had become the children of the revolution's intellectual referent, and many young poets embraced baroque esthetics. For Diáspora(s) this appropriation usurped the younger generation's poetic voice. As Rolando Sánchez Mejías's essay "Olvidar a Orígenes" reflected, Diáspora(s) was the most radical rebuttal of these cultural policies. As in the fifties, Lezama was interpreted anew as a transcendentalist writer, and the sexuality of his works was deemed acceptable as long as it was considered to be of a reproductive nature. The physical jouissance of Lezama's baroque appears in Diáspora(s) as its negative image, represented by docile bodies with no subjectivity. In chapter 3 we investigated whether this image represents bare life or rather a simultaneously conquering and ready to be conquered flow of desire. Diáspora(s) rejected Lezama's baroque period for concealing the concept of the lack, which was actually key to Lezama's understanding of negativity, which Diáspora(s) sought to emphasize.

Lack and negation played indeed a very important role in the political unconscious of the nineties. Without nowhere else to turn, the state suffered a deep political crisis that resulted in the metaphorical disappearance of the law of the father. Because of this political crisis and the lack of a strong ideological referent, the cultural production of those years suffered a schizophrenic split of sorts. Humanist projects such as Paideia sought to reform cultural politics in a way that rearticulated the revolutionary utopian imaginary and the law of the father. Diáspora(s), in contrast, reacted to that emptiness with an ironic poetics. The regime's delirious belief in the power of words was reflected in Juan Carlos Flores's writing as a type of expenditure producing a consumption that does not transform. Together with a discourse of economic liberalization, this produces a life without value and perpetuates the absence of the primordial signifier.

With the end of utopia, or the end of history as it was understood in Marxian discourse, Cuban literature of the nineties reached an aesthetic impasse. The poetics of both Diáspora(s) and Flores testify to this standstill, and Paideia represents the last attempt to reform the revolutionary humanist project. The aesthetic response to this impasse was articulated in Flores by the rejection of representation and in Diáspora(s) by irony. Both poetics show the lack of the law of the father and result from a schizophrenic split, yet there is no political skepticism. Unlike the nineties prose fiction—which, according to Jorge Fornet, came out of disenchantment—these two aesthetics did not engage politics. On the one hand, irony implies the acknowledgment of the lack of the law of the father. On the other hand, it alludes to the revolution's fallen ego-ideal as the disruption of an illusion, the foregrounding of buffo, and what Sánchez Mejías understands as the production of pathos.

At a conference, "Cuba-USSR and the Post-Soviet Experience," held at the University of Connecticut in 2007, Sánchez Mejías caustically denied that Diáspora(s) had any political intention.[1] Instead of ideology, he argued, Diáspora(s) was about pathos. Sánchez Mejías was probably referring to pathos as a communication technique of persuasion. For Aristotle, for example, pathos was the awakening emotion that induced the desired response in the audience. Although in previous centuries, the ethical or epistemic values of this concept had been variously interpreted, in romanticism it was clearly used to refer to violent passions not responding to reason. Pathos thus conceived is a purely vanguardist gesture rejecting, deriding, and mocking conformity to the norm. Pathos in Diáspora(s) lacks any ethical value, but it definitely carries the vanguardist desire to shock captured in the French expression *épater le bourgeois*. Following Aristotle's definition, however, pathos could articulate an ethical value. Is not the desire to shock or move an audience a thought-provoking action leading to a pause, reflection, or different consideration of an issue? As a project, Diáspora(s) is not a response to the ethical possibility of art. It is, rather, the disruption of a tropological system, that is, the disruption of the ideological fantasy that conceals the Real of utopian desire. Like a mirror, however, Diáspora(s) both shows the existence of that social fantasy and simultaneously creates its own. The fantasy displayed by Diáspora(s) poetry is the vanguardist fantasy par excellence, consisting in the creation of a poetics that thinks itself as existing outside of ideology, that is, outside of fantasy. This is why Lorenzo García Vega, in his introduction to *Memorias de clase muerta*, defines the anthology as one where writing is constantly being erased: "Because in the world of droplets of dreams, in the world of splinters . . . there is no valid explanation. So, . . . what has just been said is immediately erased" (Aguilera 2002, 15). García Vega describes writing as an impermanent and ethereal gesture that leaves no trace. Where does such poetics take us? Does it not take us to the end of aesthetics and consequently to the end of literature? This question can only be answered by interrogating the type of poetics that Diáspora(s)'s writing proposes.

The ideological ambiguities of the work of the Diáspora(s)'s members point to the limits imposed by their vanguardist gesture and its aporias. On the one hand, this is an aesthetics that suggests its own desire to disappear; on the other hand, through its constant disruption, it performs a desire to shock (affectivity) and to reflection (thought). This tension breaks the fantasy that the writing of Diaspora(s)'s members articulates, that is, the belief that their aesthetics exists outside ideology. It proves that their aesthetics is bare life and that they exist in that liminal space between literature's end and its new beginning.

After all these years, what is the inheritance of the mighty eighties and nineties? Whither Paideia, Diáspora(s), and Reina's azotea? Were all these aesthetic movements circumstantial to their own times? In his introduction to *Memorias de la clase muerta*, García Vega states that the authors featured in the anthology are not united by circumstances (such as location or age). Rather, García Vega says that these authors share an existential experience, and thus their writing is out of context, hors texte: "No context, then, enables us to approach the poets of the dead class. No context or history" (Aguilera 2002, 14). The writers of Diáspora(s), as well as others from the same generation including Ponte and Flores, have made a point of bringing forward negativity and lack, an aspect of Cuban culture that dominant interpretations of the latter have dismissed. As I have argued, scholars have interpreted this gesture as the simple antithesis of revolutionary poetics, of a group that has been unable to move outside of the revolutionary/counterrevolutionary dialectic. And yet Diáspora(s) never engaged in a political or programmatic war against culture, and their work never fell into a facile political critique of the regime. Instead, their work has always been concerned with language. Like all the other authors I have studied in this book, their work bears an intellectual relationship with language as the only possibility for articulating thought. Theirs is not a nihilistic approach to literature, which places politics before poetics, protest before intellectual thought.

This book has shown that revolutionary discourse is articulated through two main libidinal forces: the pleasure principle and the death drive. These two forces have been at the root of ideological and aesthetic discourse since the beginning of the revolution. These two principles will be in constant opposition, battling each other throughout the entire revolutionary process. In the sixties, the death drive manifests itself as an apology of violence, which takes the form of melodrama in its cultural rendering. It is a defense of violence, and at the same time an incantation of life. This contradiction resulted in the discourse of the New Man in 1965, which reintroduced the clash between utopia and violence, resulting in the melancholic nature of the New Man, as well as the gray man of the seventies. With the eighties came the withering of real socialism, an era of uncertainty that brought back the melancholic New Man. The pleasure principle has regained force through a different aegis. Instead of crafting apologies for violence, the state promises utopia through the protection and preservation of life. The discourse of violence no longer represents utopia, which instead becomes the subjection of life. Biopolitics is the return of a repressed utopia, and it produces the Proyecto Diáspora(s) imaginary and its representation of subjectivity as a space between death and life. The revolution's offspring, like their primogenitors, reproduced the clash between violence and humanism with two different voices: humanism with Proyecto Paideia, and violence with Proyecto Diáspora(s). But the discourse of utopia slowly withers, because it no longer demands the sacrifice of life. The discourse of violence has no utopian dimension, because it has been transformed into an ironic discourse, where the two registers (life and death) become interchangeable. The frustrated desire for utopia, forever repressed, is no longer on the horizon. The same is true in state discourse, with its parallel disavowal of capitalism and its desire. Utopia is capitalism, but it is also violence, and socialism can no longer produce apologies for violence (the market). It can only offer a utopia devoid of an object of desire. An empty signifier, political discourse is absent. This is when the repressed returns, as a sign that points to the end of literature.

Notes

Introduction

1. "Where are you Sir, the strongest? / . . . / In blood, in the dust, in the wound / . . . / Transformed into a saga in the death that I die; / I have become history, madam, I have become history."

2. At the IV UNEAC's Congress, in January 26, 1988, Culture Minister Armando Hart said, "Primero: hemos venido aplicando, de una manera consecuente, los principios enunciados en 'Palabras a los intelectuales' [We have rigorously applied 'the Address to Intellectuals' principles]."

3. Nostalgia both as a Cuban official construct, a market reification, and as a cultural longing for a Soviet Cuba (Ostalgie), have been widely studied. In addition to Quiroga's *Cuban Palimpsests*, see also Esther Whitfield *Cuban Currency*, Ariana Hernández Reguant, ed., *Cuba in the Special Period*, Anke Birkenmaier and Esther Whitfield, eds. *Havana Beyond the Ruins*, Jacqueline Loss, ed., *Caviar with Rum*, and her recently published monograph *Dreaming in Russian*, as well as Odette Casamayor Cisneros, *Utopia, Distopia e Ingravidez*.

4. See much of the recent scholarship: Hernández Reguant, *Cuba in the Special Period*; Whitfield and Birkenmeier, *Havana beyond the Ruins*; and Loss, *Dreaming in Russian*.

5. Cf. José Quiroga, *Cuban Palimpsests*, introduction.

6. This was not the first symposium where invited Cuban intellectuals could not attend, or had difficulties in attending. Past events included the "Stockholm Meeting" (1994), The "Isla entera [Whole Island]" poetry colloquium (Madrid, 1994), the (Cuban Literature Meeting (Berlin, 1995), and the "Festival de Nantes" (1995).

7. "This program, based on a thoroughgoing respect of the specificity of artistic creation, opposed to sectarianism and dogma, established a climate of openness and plurality in which were officially promoted, by official institutions of the revolution, critical, reflective, and disquieting art, the art of heresy and indispensable doubt." This article also appeared in *El País* on February 20, 1996.

8. In his essay "Violence and Literature," Sánchez Mejías accuses the global publishing market of falsifying Cuban contemporary literature's reality. The literary production that gets marketed overseas is just a small portion of the real island's literary production, which, according to him, is caught up in an authoritarian ideology: "The global publishing market has found in contemporary Cuban literature the perfect ally. Europe sells with obscenity an idea more or less stable of Cuban literature by causing thus its new decline" (1999, 7).

9. *Schizoanalysis* is a Deleuzian-Guattarian term created in opposition to psychoanalysis as a nonsystematic and nonontological approach to the psyche and its political analysis. The schizo replaces Freud's schizophrenic as a nonpathological state of being which is mostly a liberating force.

10. "I—This is so confusing / I don't understand anything, anything / about 'Saint Revolution' / Patriotism...Religion... / One no longer knows / if one should applaud God or someone else / so I no longer know / if one should say 'Fatherland or Death' / or one should say 'Amen.' / II—Nowadays the church is 'cool' / and we have merry Christmases; / some people even say / that the earth is no longer round; / and that even if Christ hides / 'he' is still the supreme leader / as a result of this cruel mess / From now on I won't know / if Fidel is Comandante or Father Fidel."

11. According to Jorge Mañach, *choteo* is a national Cuban flaw of taking things rather lightly, and irreverently.

Chapter 1. Sovereignty of Violence

1. Ambrosio Fornet coined this expression to refer to what has now been officially recognized as the most repressive period of the Cuban Revolution: "Inventé la etiqueta por razones metododológicas, tratando de aislar y describer ese período por lo que me pareció su rasgo dominante y por el contraste que ofrecía con la etapa anterior, caracterizada por su colorido y dinámica interna [I invented this term for methodological reasons, and to distinguish this period from the previous decade's colorful dynamism]" (Fornet 2007, 27). There has been a recent debate in Cuba about the length and naming of this period. Some think, for example, that it should also include the rest of the decade. Others believe that "gray period" is a misnomer that doesn't account for the critical and sophisticated literature also written at that time. See Desiderio Navarro, *La política cultural del período revolucionario.*

2. See Fernando Martínez Heredia: "What is certain is that the revolutionary power structure and society are recognized spaces of production and debate for social "thought that would remain or would arise within the revolutionary field, even if these were from diverging currents, and even if they expressed disagreements with others" (2007, 146).

3. "Only where this pathos of novelty is present and where novelty is connected with the idea of freedom are we entitled to speak of revolution" (Arendt 2006, 24).

4. Castro's defense was later published as *History Will Absolve Me* (2007).

5. *History Will Absolve Me* is Castro's written defense for the failed assault on army headquarters Moncada (Santiago) and José Manuel de Céspedes (Bayamo) on July 26, 1952.

6. Militiamen of dawn and blood!
Without source or riverbank
Our eye sees the open image of revolutions
Under a wind that wants to sing
No one knows where these rivers meet
Our blood will not pause
It communicates a level of freedom
The rising of the people
In the deep season of blood.

7. "Unidad dialéctica existente entre el individuo y la masa donde ambos se interrelacionan y, a su vez la masa, como conjunto de individuos se interrelaciona con los dirigentes [existing dialectical unity between the individual and the masses in which the two become interrelated; and in turn the masses, as a group of individuals, become interrelated with the leadership]."

8. "You are in work / in careful attention / in the play of children . . . in the efforts of men of good faith."

9. "Those who think of their neighbor / and help and work for him / are your disciples."

10. "in sweat, / in ignorance, / in the Forgetting Yourself / that is the Material of Reality."

11. "of the air they give you, of the little relief / that their rough, blind hands bring / to the horror of your agony / that does not end."

12. "In truth you wish, / as you die, / that everything were very well done."

13. Those who think of their neighbor / and help and work for him / are your disciples: / it doesn't matter if they ignore it.

14. "The existence of an armed struggle shows that the people are decided to trust to violent methods only. He of whom *they* have never stopped saying that the only language he understands is that of force decides to give utterance by force. . . . The argument the native chooses has been furnished by the settler, and by an ironic turning of the tables it is the native who now affirms that the colonialist understands nothing but force" (Fanon 1963, 83–84).

15. This text was orginally a letter adressed to Carlos Quijano, the editor of the weekly Uruguayan paper *Marcha*, where it was published in March 12, 1965. It was subsequently published in Cuba for the first time on April 15, 1965 in *Verde Olivo*, the Armed Revolutionary Forces journal.

16. See chapter 3.

17. This was the case of Reinaldo Arenas, Virgilio Piñera, and José Lezama Lima, among others.

18. "But what matters is the Revolution / everything else is words / in the background / of this poem that I offer to the world / everything else is my arguments."

19. "planet burning in the sky / the moment comes for my birth / and for my deaths / but in the world I have come to settle . . . / pleased with this Revolution that gives me teeth."

20. "The men of the party should take up this task and seek to accomplish the primary objective: educating the people. So simplification is sought, what anyone can understand, which is what bureaucrats understand. . . . [T]he problem of general culture is reduced to an appropriation of the socialist present and the dead (and therefore not dangerous) past. Socialist realism is thus born on the foundation of the art of the past century. . . . Capitalism in culture has given its all and nothing remains but the advertisement of a stinking corpse. . . . But why look for the only valid solution in the frozen forms of socialist realism?"

21. One of the major challenges facing Marxist theories of art, Thomas Bennett tells us, has been "the attempt to reconcile . . . two sets of concerns: the one consistent with the historical and materialist premises of Marxism and with its political motivation, and the other inherited from bourgeois aesthetics" (104). This is precisely one of the major points of contention between these two groups of intellectuals. Various imprecisions or inconsistencies weaken Aguirre's argument.

22. This letter was signed by twenty-nine intellectuals, including Humberto Solás, Pastor Vega, Tomás Gutiérrez Alea, Sara Gómez, Julio García Espinosa, and Nicolás Guillén. It was subsequently published in *La Gaceta de Cuba.*

23. These consecutive responses were written by José Fraga, Julio García Espinosa, Tomás Gutiérrez Alea, Juan J. Flo, and Sergio Benvenuto. All these essays were published in *La Gaceta de Cuba.*

24. Aguirre's thesis of socialist realism is strongly influenced by Lenin and Zhdanov's theories of realism. See Lenin's "On Party Literature" (1905): "What is the principle of party literature? It is not simply that, for the socialist proletariat, literature cannot be a means of enriching individuals or groups: it cannot, in fact, be an individual undertaking, independent of the common cause of the proletariat" (45).

25. Obviously, what is at stake in this essay is the nationalistic component of revolutionary ideology, as I explain in a different section.

26. It is clear that writers understood the doctrinaire turn of culture, since socialist realism was made official by the Russian Writers Congress of 1934.

27. According to Lenin, truth is both absolute and relative. There is an absolutely objective knowledge in nature that's unconditional, and a relative truth that is conditioned by history.

28. Marx and Engels left an extensive body of short pieces about art and literature that were posthumously collected. In 1993, Mikhail Lifschitz published the first collection. For my purposes here, I have consulted an abbreviated version of their works in Marx and Engels, 1947. For further information, see Salomon.

29. I reproduce here the footnote to the online version of the text, which explains the context of the article: "*Comments on the Latest Prussian Censorship Instruction* was the first work written by Marx as a revolutionary journalist. It was occasioned by the censorship instruction of the Prussian Government of December 24, 1841. Though formulated in moderate liberal terms, the instruction actually not only retained but intensified the censorship of the press. Written between January 15 and February 10, 1842, just after the publication of the instruction in the press (it was published in the *Allgemeine Preussische Staats-Zeitung*, no. 14 [January 14, 1842]; Marx cites from this publication), the article was originally intended for the *Deutsche Jahrbücher* under the editorship of Arnold Ruge (see this volume, p.

381) but because of the censorship restrictions it was published only in 1843 in Switzerland in *Anekdota*, which contained works by appositional authors, mostly Young Hegelians."

30. "I write: / I bite the gray noose of the word / . . . / May those condemned know and remember / Man is not an adjective / In the language of war."

31. "In our hand-to-hand combat / With this death of men / With our nothingness expanded to the point of glory / The green tool of life / Is not the shovel that brings down the leaf storm. / Of the enemy choked on his rotten blood / In his forty-eight stars of vomit / Our words are like our tools / They are not of the future they are the future."

32. "No the masses are not a knot of insects."

33. "A limit of man his word."

34. No the masses are not a knot of insects
Or the black shoes of the powerful
They are a violent dawn
A tree of wings and flags
A bending arc of hope
A tree for which there is no storm
Always green
Mixing earth with blood

35. "Militiaman of the soul / There is no death for you . . . / Your hand uproots the hair of the enemy / Makes him surrender his position / . . . / Advance / Like a contingent of young stars / Trace the lines of the palm / Of men's dreams / And articulate the profound language of the poor in a time of glory."

36. "I have no higher rank than my pen / And my weapon / I sing with you militiaman / I dissolve into guerrilla battalions / My mutilated blood reborn / In a green morning my morning."

37. "Poetry / Forgive me for having helped you understand / that you are not made up only of words."

Chapter 2. Violence and Melancholia in the Eighties and Nineties

1. José Lezama Lima and José Rodríguez Feo began editing *Orígenes* as a project of high modernism involving a group of writers known as Grupo Orígenes. Some of the writers included Cintio Vitier, Fina García Marruz, Eliseo Diego, Virgilio Piñera, and Gastón Baquero. Both the group and the journal were created in 1944 as an independent project whose goal was to revitalize literature. *Orígenes* closed down in 1956 due to internal disagreements.

2. In *Cuba on My Mind: Journeys to a Severed Nation*. Román de la Campa talks about nostalgia as a common feeling among Cubans in exile, which is different from the type of cultural melancholia that this book explores.

3. See my work on this topic in "De la transición y otros enigmas."

4. The grammatically incorrect phrase *Je est un autre* comes from Arthur Rimbaud's letter to his former teacher, "Lettre à Georges Izambard" written on May

13, 1871. The sentence should either be "je suis un autre" or "il est un autre," but the incorrect verb form, serves to indicate that the subject has different selves.

5. "The light dances, darkening his face."

6. "The light dances reconciling / man with his scornful demons. / Both smiling, recounting / the triumphs of universal death / and the tranquil quality of light."

7. "In my country light / . . . / Light / in my country resists memory. . . . And, blind, the light in my country dazzles / its own inviolable heart / without knowing profit or loss"

8. In *El sol a plomo*, the light and the heat represent confusion and hindrance. The novel narrates the political repression of the Batista regime through the kidnapping of a Mexican boxer by an urban anti-Batista commando. The sun introduces a deterministic component to the novel by introducing the scenes of tragic climax. Cuca, the wife of one of the kidnappers, is marked by the tragic flaw since the beginning as the sun blinds her. First, when she is waiting for the arrival of the boxer from Mexico: "The sun beat down hard [*caía a plomo*] and most people squinted" (Arenal 1959, 33). Second, when the sun's presence announces her imminent capture by the Batista police: "The sun came through the window and hit her in the eyes, which she immediately closed. Her father said that in Cuba the sun was very indiscreet, slipping in anywhere it pleased" (ibid., 99).

9. "If, after the bombing is over . . . / you can imagine that you aren't seeing / what's going to be set irredeemably before your eyes . . . / I advise you to set off running right now"

10. Rodríguez will later mentor the younger generation of intellectuals, and as a result, her poetry will also shift. See for example her 1992 work of poetry *En la arena de Padua*.

11. "today I want to write what I need . . . / to go down to my depths alone and naked."

12. "I am simply ugly / with freckles, dreams, and pains."

13. "and many debts / infinite debts to life."

14. "We survivors, / To whom do we owe our survival? / Who died for me in prison? Who took my bullet / the one meant for me in his heart?"

15. Buckwalter-Arias's excellent monograph about posorigenista fiction, brilliantly demonstrates the stylistic contradiction in post-1989 works between the appeal for Orígenes and the return to realist techniques. The author argues that far from producing a contradictory aesthetic, these fiction books show that realism is both necessary and limited. I think that in poetry Lezama's influence was of a completely different nature. First, it produced a modernist language. Second, it was based on a rejection of realism. Although this is true in fiction, poetry embraced neobaroque Lezamian poetics.

16. "There would be more memory if so many deer didn't emerge between the sheets of smoke."

17. "My verse is clear green and fiery red: / My verse is a wounded deer / Seeking shelter in the wilderness."

18. "I leave the spirited horses gasping for breath. / I break bread, the umbilicus."

19. "The murky hoi polloi [or "tunnels"] are afraid. / They fear my soul that rings the brilliant flames."

20. "I am the eye, / Perhaps this island that I walk without memory."

21. "So I'm a child and confuse everything / or I'm a king who forgets."

22. "I beg you, Father, / Let's go out on the terrace and watch the boats."

23. "Tell me if the eternal is a dream—Tell me if memory is not a god, / the cold bench of the oarsman, his oar broken."

24. "Why is it now heavy as the cross someone set in the west?"

25. "The song doesn't return. / Nor does the bird from the ozone. / My reality doesn't return."

26. "I find it hard now to be the inventor of this memory."

27. "How the first things fled knowledge."

28. "Teeth, bones, ashes, ancient salt; / I'm searching for a sign that will clarify this history."

29. This is the same proposition that Franz Kafka explores in many of his works. "There exists a point of arrival, but no path, and there is no escape because one cannot flee from what cannot even be reached" (Agamben 1993, 6).

30. "Where is memory? / Where is he who will be and is innocent / of the forgetting that you scheme to who you were / Will there be another war and you he now that you are dead?"

31. "I went down the icy tunnels of memory / only a spider wove and unwove a gray cloth."

32. "Time is a long falconry / that even in the armor of the greatest knight / leaves chinks."

33. "The angel was throwing into the depths, / what a strange legacy they left me."

34. "For the pious I make way."

35. "I came to sow thyme in [their] brows."

36. "In every serenity / comes a knock announcing the penultimate street / If there were bridges / today we wouldn't see the face of the mistreated angel."

37. "those who were going to set fire to the high towers / keep taking minutiae up the plinth."

38. "I spit in the face of all extras."

39. "But in the kingdom of death light also bursts forth."

40. "Mine was the chaste foot of Antigone."

41. "Today I have lain down among the low flowers. / They are so many songs to the night / like a sea of Antigones, full of naked feet, / of vague bodies that approach until they confound your desires."

42. "You will not go to Troy to deny your shadow / Like love, only this body drips and is collected, and in it you lie down without waking."

43. "a thousand doors that do not flee."

44. "Suddenly the city does not sign with your fever / But love is useless / as is the anxiety of days / that incise the soul."

45. "This night without stars / imitates my desire / flesh of the impossible / This night I wonder / how many feet of Antigone / will I be able to kiss before dying."

46. "It is not the sea of Odysseus, it is expanse."

47. "It is not the sea of Martí, it is jubilation."

48. "It is the nonelusive, nonerrant sea / My flight."

49. "How much sea of naked feet / how much body or mist / toward another unstoppable limit / and finished like desire / Anguish is desire. / It is the woman

who opens by the wound / —what desire cannot attain / while they hide from my eyes / the yellow frame." "The yellow frame [*el cuadrado amarillo*]" refers to a small window in the house in Havana's Calle Amargura where the poet was born.

50. "The lamentable paradox / To its rule you once more bend: 'Know what you do not know / Desire what you do not desire.'"

51. "I have seen the city burned and bodies / burning / the breasts deserts, the accordion mouths / cisterns."

52. "I write these venomous lines and it's like taking / high tide to a hermit / But I am the reef, the eunuch if you like and not what one might suppose / not the county fair singer, who passes out wine and receives / a few coins."

53. "Those who saw the fish on the terrace / saw an oasis in the middle of the war."

54. "my lips, gates of the country, language is not a lake / it is like a clamp / because we lack the great one, the healer."

55. "Yesterday, as I was gathering pebbles on the beach I saw / two birds / burning, the pollen of the sea in their eyes."

56. "A boat. A boat. Boundaries / Cities named with the same love / as one names ruins in childhood / Not only the person who looks to the end remains."

57. "It is not departing [or "parting"] but stroking the water with which you soothe / the limits, stroke it so that the pointer rises and makes a nest / in the wood."

58. "Have you paused, amid the noise of the doors / which no longer mean anything, have you not erased the outside / and noticed the absence of those birds?"

59. "The movement of my skein's hand has the beauty / that lacks in the hand in the forehead's movement."

60. "Poetry in restless sleep / like the bird of resurrection / at every moment is born, is annihilated."

61. "Freedom, rudder toward poetry / poetry, rudder toward freedom."

62. "poetry can transform memory, memory can transform poetry."

63. "Man, woman, island or clot knotted by paradise: between the lines we search, wondering."

64. "The corpse of a king floats in the grass."

65. "In this place I hear the breath of the passing ships and I don't plan on pulling out my eyes like Oedipus."

66. "From my feet I rise up like a statue."

67. "I see time fall stone by stone: what a murky sight is the collapse of fate."

68. "All I could oppose to time was a bay leaf."

69. "Vehemently I would crush this leaf, but sighs of the last ships can be heard. The horizon is a line, another snake uncoils its thousand heads."

70. "Virgil burned his *Aeneid*, I would burn my Rome or we wouldn't have the courage of Oedipus who points at us with his blind hook."

71. "The city burns and I am at its center."

72. "But the smoke also builds. Up there it traces a similar city."

73. "There would be more memory if so many deer didn't emerge between the sheets of smoke."

74. "My verse is clear green and fiery red: / My verse is a wounded deer / Seeking shelter in the wilderness."

75. "Through the hollow reeds stare other deer, advancing quickly like llamas at night."

76. "In my hands a bay leaf."

77. *Los pájaros escritos*, by Juan Carlos Flores, was one of the neobaroque and Lezamian poetic works. The reintroduction of neobaroque sought to emphasize the language and aesthetics that conversationalism had obliterated.

78. "Between the two of them is the void and the bodies turning without touching the salt."

79. I don't look at Paideia until chapter 4, because Diáspora's irony, which I analyze in the last chapter, is in part a response to the failure of humanism that Paideia represents. To show this conceptual concatenation, I have chosen to look at these two epistemological choices in the same section.

80. The AHS was created in 1986 after the fusion of the Brigada Raúl Gómez García (comprised of cultural instructors and promoters), the Brigada Hermanos Saíz (composed of writers and artists), and the Movimiento de la Nueva Trova.

81. Fowler explains that in spite of young writer's demands, cultural supplements were being published elsewhere in the island, except in La Habana. Yet, writers still managed to find creative ways to get their works out: "Lo único, durante meses y en el Pabellón Cuba de la calle 23, una imprenta "para tiempos de guerra" en donde el narrador Radamés Molina se convirtió de modo autodidacta en impresor que publicaba volantes con poemas de los jóvenes de entonces. En otro lugar, en la Casa del Joven Creador, aunque aquí como parte de un trabajo más fino, de arte, los poetas Sigfredo Ariel (imprentero de raza) y Cira Andrés, echaban a andar otra vieja imprenta que entre los tres conseguimos después de mil trabajos y que publicó hermosas ediciones con traducciones de Emily Dickinson y el bello poema "La casa del alibí" de José Lezama Lima, entre lo que ahora recuerdo." (2006).

82. www.habanaelegante.com. /Fall-Winter2002/Verbosa2.html.

83. For a more specific account of all the events that they organized, see interview "Carlos A. Aguilera: para que las ficciones se cuestionen a sí mismas" (Aguilera 2003).

84. On May 24–28, 1994, the Olof Palme International Center hosted a meeting of exiled and nonexiled Cuban writers to discuss the island's future. After many disagreements, participants signed the "Stockholm Document." They could only agree on two main points. First, that the United States should lift its embargo on Cuba, and, second, that the work of exiles was part of Cuban culture.

85. Marqués de Armas first tried living on grants in Portugal and Italy, but he was unable to obtain legal residence. In 1997, he settled in Barcelona, where he works as a psychiatrist. Rolando Sánchez Mejías also resides in Barcelona and teaches creative writing at the Escola d'Escriptura Ateneu Barcelonès. Aguilera now lives in Graz, Austria, with a Grant for International Creation from the Haus der Autoren Graz.

86. In addition to Sánchez Mejías and Aguilera, the two coordinators of the project, the first number's editorial collective is composed of the following writers: Rogelio Saunders, Ricardo Alberto Pérez, Pedro Marqués de Armas, Ismael González Castañer, José Manuel Prieto. All of them were part of the initial Proyecto

Diáspora(s) group, but many of them left the group. Some went into exile, and some quit the group as a result of theoretical disagreements. The chore members who continued the project were Sánchez Mejías, Aguilera, Marqués de Armas, and Pérez.

87. The journal *Pensamiento crítico* (1967–1971) had also played this role at the end of the sixties by publishing Western as well as Eastern revolutionary thought. *Criterios*, the journal that Desiderio Navarro has published since 1972, specializes in translations of essays by well-known critical theorists, work otherwise inaccessible on the island. At the moment, *Criterios* is the only journal that continues the tradition of publishing foreign thought in Cuba.

88. Scholars, as Jorge Luis Arcos considers *Diáspora(s)* group along with Virgilio Piñera or Lorenzo García Vega as one of the few exponents of Cuban vanguardism (Arcos 1999, 11).

89. In an interview in Havana on September 2011.

90. The contributors to *Encuentro de la cultura cubana* were intellectuals and academics residing in Cuba, the United States, or Europe. The idea was to expand the limits of the nation-state by acknowledging the existence of new diasporic communities that were no longer limited to the historic Miami exile and the first generation of Cuban Americans. Various literary anthologies already had questioned the nature of the nation-state and included Miami's cultural production as part of the Cuban canon. Some good examples are "Bridging Enigma: Cubans on Cuba," ed. Ambrosio Fornet, and *Bridges to Cuba*, ed. Ruth Behar. Although Fornet's collection only includes three U.S. scholars, Behar's is a good example of the intellectual presence of Cuban Americans in the United States. Díaz's journal was the first to include a new diasporic generation of young critical intellectuals mostly born at the beginning of the Cuban Revolution.

91. The desire to engage Cubans in a political dialogue is always superseded by a cultural agenda more pertinent to the Cuban American population and their need to assimilate into a U.S. culture predominantly ruled by the white class. This need to assimilate is partly created by the possibility for the first generation of college-educated Cuban Americans to compete for positions among the ruling class.

92. This poem comes from *Trasumar e organizzar*, a collection of poems first published in Italy in 1971 and translated into Spanish as *Transhumanar y organizar* (1981).

93. For example in "Vittoria [Victory]," Pasolini blames the Italian Left for forgetting the revolts of the young peasants, but in "II PCI ai giovani" [The Communist Italian Party to the Young People] he critiques the young 1968 revolutionaries for their bourgeois and conformist behavior.

Chapter 3. Biopolitics and the Revival of José Lezama Lima in the Eighties and Nineties

1. According to historian Julia E. Sweig, "The conventional but unconfirmed wisdom in Cuba is that HIV/AIDS arrived on the island as Cuban soldiers returned from Africa at the end of the 1980s and early 1990s" (Sweig 146).

2. I would like to thank Nikolái Ingistov García for pointing to Sontag as a reference.

3. With a few exceptions, most of Lezama's works were printed in Cuba before and after the revolution, but during the nineties there was an upsurge of reprints and new editions of unpublished works. There were also a vast number of new edited works. These unpublished or newly edited works include *Fascinación de la memoria, textos inéditos* (Havana: Letras Cubanas, 1993); *La visualidad infinita* (Havana: Letras Cubanas 1994); *Los enigmas permanentes* (Havana: Letras Cubanas, 1993); *Diarios, 1939–49/1956–58* (Havana: Unión, 1994).

4. Scholarly interest in Lezama had begun in the eighties. There was an international conference on his work in Poitiers (France) in 1984, and the proceedings became a major reference for Lezamian studies. Minister of Culture and writer Abel Prieto edited *Confluencias: Selección de ensayos* (Havana: Letras Cubanas, 1988). Another precedent was Cintio Vitier's *Ese sol del mundo moral* (Mexico City: Siglo XXI, 1975), not reprinted in Cuba until 1995 (by Ediciones Unión). Vitier's work was an ideological history of the intellectual effort to imagine a teleological construction of the nation. For Vitier, Lezama's vision of the ontological coincidence between poetry (*imago*), history, and creation represented the possibility of achieving this goal.

5. I will reproduce here the endnote in César Salgado's article that traces the publications about Lezama during the seventies and suggests what may have led to the renewed interest in his work:

There were on-and-off signs of rectification attempts in the seventies and eighties with the publication of critical and anthological works that sought to reconcile Lezama's eccentric poetic praxis with the revolution's political line: Pedro Simón's collection of favorable critical essays and testimonies commemorating Lezama's sixtieth birthday, *Recopilación de textos sobre José Lezama Lima* (Habana: Casa de las Américas, 1970); Ciro Bianchi Ross's compilation of Lezama's post-1959 uncollected miscellany, *Imagen y posibilidad* (Habana: Letras Cubanas, 1981); and Carlos Espinosa's biographical assemblage of anecdotes about Lezama from surviving friends, *Cercanía de Lezama Lima* (Habana: Editorial Letras Cubanas, 1986). However, the full rehabilitation of *Orígenes* in Cuba may have been coined in Raúl Hernández Novás's review of the 1989 facsimile edition of *Orígenes* published in Spain; there he contradicts the dismissive official characterization of the group's poetics in state reference publications such as the *Diccionario de la literatura cubana* of 1984. This review appeared in *Casa de las Américas* 30, no. 180 (May-June 1990): 133–42. The *Coloquio Internacional Cincuentenario de Orígenes* (International Colloquium Fifty Years of *Orígenes*) was organized by the independent and now defunct Pablo Milanés Foundation and cosponsored by state agencies such as the Ministry of Culture, Casa de las Américas, and the UNEAC. It took place from June 27 to July 1, 1994, in the Casa de las Américas complex in Havana; Cintio Vitier was president of the organizing commission, Jorge Luis Arcos its secretary. *Orígenes* scholars from Cuba, Spain, Europe, Argentina, Mexico, Brazil, Puerto Rico, and the United States presented more than 80 papers. Although the organizers announced and initiated an edition of the proceedings, it still has not been published. (Salgado 2002, 224)

6. This ideological turn was part of the constitutional amendments of 1992 and the government's decision to privilege a nationalist rhetoric. Although the new preamble of the Constitution does not eliminate Marxism as the ideological foundation of the nation, it places new emphasis on Marti's ideals, stating that Cubans are

"guided by the thought of José Martí and the politico-social ideas of Marx, Engels, and Lenin" (13).

7. *Paradiso*'s first edition was removed from bookstores a week after its publication. José Triana commented that cultural functionaries claimed the work could lead to a diversionary ideology among young Cuban revolutionaries.

8. The two key texts were Roberto Urías's short story "Why Does Leslie Caron Cry?" ("¿Por qué llora Leslie Caron?") and Norge Espinosa's poem "Wedding Gown" ("Vestido de novia") (Alonso Estenoz 2000, 1).

9. A meeting of Youth for Health and Sexual Rights (Jóvenes por la Salud y los Derechos Sexuales) was one of many events CENESEX advertised on its homepage. To exorcize the past, perhaps, this activity was held at Campismo los Cocos, the country estate where the old hospices for HIV-infected patients were located in 1986.

10. As I discuss in another section, Lezama had been an inspiration for young intellectuals, especially in the eighties. His baroque style left an important imprint in the early work of Diáspora(s) and others. For example, Lezama was key for Paideia, a humanist and cultural project created by a group of young intellectuals in the late eighties. Their goal was to open up the cultural mission of the state by conforming to official ideology. In their proposal for a literary journal, Paideia referred to Lezama and Martí as two exemplars of Cuban culture (*Cubista*, "Proyecto de revista," n.d. [c. late 1980s–early 1990s]; http://cubistamagazine.com/050018.html). While Lezama continued being an aesthetic symbol during the nineties, Diáspora(s) rejected their contemporaries' baroque imaginary.

11. Marques de Armas's exact words were: "After this event we still had two or three interventions that year, although these were now controlled by State Security."

12. "The Cuban Revolution means that all the negative spells have been decapitated. . . . The man who dies in the image gains the overabundance of the resurrection."

13. Baroque poetics opened the door to the representation of a signified with multiple signifiers. In the eighties, these young poets read Lezama and borrowed a baroque style whose hermetic form gave them a sophistication that realism did not have.

14. See also César Salgado and his argument about "Catholic pornography," in *From Modernism to Neobaroque: Joyce and Lezama Lima* (Lewisburg, PA: Bucknell Press, 2001).

15. On the inner side of the border, which others prefer to call a blind alley, B. killed himself.

> Of course all borders are mental, and in B.'s case, it would be more accurate to speak of two.
>
> So B. killed himself between the inner border and the crest of a thought that would not leave him.

In order to catapult himself, he took the roots of an alkaloid he had classified and, throwing himself on the pallet of conical strips, finally found what he was looking for: a one-way street on which all the house numbers are erased, and the white brain stems vanish into a material of dreams.

16. You've seen the monkeys on the barge
thus the delirium of perception
animals sprout from the cells
of the brain, in an uninterrupted *population*
and you've seen some conical rock
with the Russian cedar stick that knocks
on the door: monkey, rat, even man
dark schemings of the anti-God.

17. The dead man is fake, made of cardboard. If the fox turned him over (the fox who found the tragic mask in the woods and said to himself as he turned the mask over: "What a big face this is to have no brain!"), ah, if the fox turned him over two, three times, confirming the theatrical substance, he would say, "What a big corpse this is to have no life!"

18. The son usually visits his mother and his sister. They have ventured progressively into madness, and now are in the pavilions. Not him. That is, not yet. That's why he doesn't wear the white clothes that would instantly mark him as a resident of the asylum. But he's as sick as they are. Or maybe more, much more. He seems like a chess player truncated in mid-adolescence, as if he had suddenly gone insane in a situation with too many unexpected variables or before a poorly played piece. He wears enormous glasses that look like the bottom of bottles, has a military-style crew cut, and a thin, inhuman voice. In certain instants of lucidity, as she runs her hand through his hair, his mother raises between her hands and her son a kind of salvation. But suddenly the distance separating the three of them is eliminated, knotting itself in a savage sanctity.

19. See Lorenzo García Vega's introduction to *Memorias de la clase muerta*, Carlos A. Aguilera's edited collection of poems by members of Diáspora(s).

20. "To become 'a monstrous insect,' a grotesque cockroach, at the end of a hot summer night? No. K. has already done that, to great literary effect."

21. "R., I'm watching you try to write. I'm watching you through the keyhole. You climb on the table and move on four legs (monkey? spider? spider monkey? monkey spider?), swimming, flailing with arms and legs among the strewn blank pages."

22. "accepts, serenely accepts the impossibility of thinking of 'the dark soul of the world' (Ergo, the impossibility of representation!)."

23. "Furthermore, these days a sweep of a broom can't attain the emblematicity needed to constitute a framework for the disaster."

24. "Make myself an insect to grab tighter hold
with hooked feet to grab tighter hold,
insect, spider, millipede, mite
if I must, to grab tighter hold"

25. "Who has not wished to create one day an alphabet book, a bestiary, or even an entire vocabulary, from which the verbal would be entirely excluded?"

26. "If we destroy the threads made in the first steps, the spider will continue methodically with the later steps of the web's construction, even though the final product is useless to it."

27. "constructive activity vacillating between Order and Chance."

28. "The web is not woven in absolute terms; the choice of distances is determined by relative factors."

29. "stingers/larvae/isles

cortex
furrows
chips
butt cheeks, nipples, and Guanche Indians (always on your left)
cowdungplaff
you see bells and don't know where
I came, I saw
sock it to that guy
rrrrrrrrrrrrrrrrrrrrrrrrrrrrrrrrrrrrrrrrrrrrrrrrrrrrrrrrrrrrrrrrrrrrrrrrrrrrrrrr
tell me what you see Genovese
third and up to fifth worlds wow!"

30. "There is an important aspect to this whole problem. And it is that, if you pay close attention, Zilla hasn't spoken yet. This proves that our world remains basically coercive, in the sense that all its parts don't have the same chance to speak. . . .

We believe, at this point, that it is high time for Zilla to inhabit her blank page and from there speak to us as she sees fit. Let us allow her, in the next chapter, to weave and unweave her warp. Will she weave schizoid or classic webs? Will she weave at night or during the day? Will she weave? Won't she weave? There she is with her singular idea of work and freedom."

31. "R.: I note, with pleasure, that you have chosen the possibility *arachnid.* That you are fascinated by this constructive activity that oscillates between Order and Chance."

32. "And one afternoon she set off on her way, her body somewhere between rectilinear and drunk with the pleasure that flowed through her like a warm stream of blood."

33. "Until she came to the foot of a tree, where a man was resting. . . . he softly said a few words. . . .

'Nothing gained
'And yet your skin is so lovely
'Nights, nights, nights.' "

34. "One afternoon, Zilla, after having caught an admirably proportioned and juicy fly, decided *to go beyond her own ends.*"

35. "break the conception of any finality."

36. "Then she began to feel a new kind of instincts, magnetizations fixed by an unknown distance. And one afternoon she set off on her way, her body somewhere between rectilinear and drunk with the pleasure that flowed through her like a warm stream of blood."

37. "until one night her shadow got up and left, leaving her body hanging by a thread made of moonlight, or silk, or anything else. She saw the lights chiming in the distance, like bells. And she sighed."

38. " 'Haven't you heard the chatter of Zilla-x-Notata in the cochlea of your ear?' might whisper to you a Zen monk from a Paris dojo." / "*Arañar:* To scratch lightly with the fingernails, with a pen, with a needle, and so on."

39. "You will never write the way Zilla weaves her webs. Don't even dream of it."

40. According to Deleuze and Guattari's analysis of Marcel Proust's *À la recherche du temps perdu*, "the narrator-spider never ceases undoing webs and planes, resuming the journey, watching for the signs or the indices that operate like machines and that will cause him to go on further" (Deleuze and Guattari 1998, 318).

41. "Among the bushes and bare rocks, the loosed and coiled beasts,
impassive in its height, demolishing, the moon of the fields
followed us. . . . And you still had the ingenuity to pause and unveil it:
a useless gesture, like the lateness of lyricism (thus the habit of
distinguishing
between true and fake food; satiety, futile expense . . .)"

Chapter 4. Humanism, Irony, and the End of Literature

1. In an article titled "Sobre el riesgo del arte [On the Risk of Art]," Díaz Torres wrote: "I find myself obligated here to argue for the revolutionary nature of a character like Alicia, who is a simple young girl who doesn't always find answers to problems (as in life), who suffers, who despairs, but who always maintains an attitude of struggle (25)."

2. For a detailed history of the group, please see Jorge Cabeza Miranda, *Proyectos Poéticos en Cuba (1959–2000). Algunos cambios formales y temáticos*.

3. As a matter of fact, Víctor Fowler, one of the group's founders, says the following when he is asked by Díaz de Villegas to write about Paideia: "Lo primero que me ha venido a la mente, aún antes de sentarme a la máquina, es la frase: si escribo realmente de esto. Como yo mismo negando la posibilidad de contar lo que entonces sucedió; de hecho, lo que hasta hoy mismo sucede. Me corto, me autocensuro, me hago sangrar [Before sitting down to write, the first thing that came to my mind is whether or not I should write about this. As if I was denying myself the posibility to tell what happened then; actually, what happens today. I cut and censor myself, and make myself bleed]" (2008).

4. According to *Cubista* magazine (www.cubistamagazine.com), the Centro de Promoción Cultural Alejo Carpentier was inaugurated by Alejo Carpentier's widow, Lilla Estebán de Carpentier, on May 14, 1982. The center was located in Old Havana, in the former residence of the Countess de la Reunión. By then the state could no longer subsidize cultural activities and artists had to rely on private foundations.

5. The original document is available at http://cubistamagazine.com/050004.html.

6. The original document is available at http://cubistamagazine.com/050005.html.

7. In a footnote Cabezas explains that "the Llamamiento [Call], made on the 112th anniversary of the Protest of Baraguá, was issued in Santiago de Cuba, host of the Congress of October 10–14, 1991" (236n). The Protest of Baraguá was General Antonio Maceo's announcement that he would not honor the Pacto de Zanjón, a treaty that ended the Ten Years' War. Maceo's act of rebellion is considered a major event in Cuba's struggle for independence. "Declaración de Principios

del Proyecto Paideia," the document including the response to the "Llamamiento" is not dated. Díaz de Villegas affirms that the document must have been written in 1990, the IV Communist Cuban Party Congress's year, but he is mistaken because the IV Congress took place in 1991.

8. The original document is available at http://cubistamagazine.com/050012.html.

9. The official journal's website states that it was closed during the early nineties as a result of the economic crisis and that it was reopened in 1996.

10. The three last sentences of this citation are a direct quote of Iván de la Nueze's article "El cóndor pasa," *La gaceta de Cuba*, June 1989, 11.

11. "Intervención especial de Armando Hart Dávalos, miembro del buró político del PCC y ministro de cultura en el IV Congreso de la UNEAC (26 de enero de 1988) Año 30 de la Revolución," *IV Congreso de la UNEAC*.

12. In this regard, Mañach says, "*choteo*—a familiar, small, and festive thing—is a way of relating that we consider typically Cuban, reason enough for us to investigate its nature with respect to our social psychology" (48).

13. This poem was written in 1971, but where it first appeared is less than clear. *La isla en peso*, edited by Antón Arrufat, contains all Piñera's published poems. Arrufat, who has been in charge of Piñera's papers, gave the poem to Carlos Aguilera for *Diáspora(s)*. Carlos Espinosa, another Piñera scholar, published the poem as a chapter epigraph in his *Virgilio Piñera en persona* (209). According to his note, the poem appeared in the journal *Lettres nouvelles*, but Espinosa gives no date or page number. Interestingly, these are two different versions of this poem. When I asked Espinosa about the incomplete documentation, he told me that Piñera was not very careful about publication details, and that he could not recall if the poem had a more complete reference.

14. "Why don't you call me by my name?
Your outrageous mockery is useless.
Even if you call me old
and hounded by death.
There's no use in calling me "decrepit," "slobbering,"
"soft," "wasted away" . . .
Nothing would offend me, nothing,
even if you called me a "rumba-dancing skeleton,"
my dignity would remain intact.
But if you went so far as to call me by my name,
to call me Virgilio Piñera,
then you would offend me
because such tombstones are too heavy."

15. "Throughout his final decade of life, Piñera suffered from emotional crises and feared run-ins with Cuban officials who had greatly restricted his freedoms as a writer and a participant in cultural activities. After the publication of his collected poetry, *La vida entera* (*My Whole Life*) and the premiere of his experimental musical comedy *El encarne* (*The Hunting Bait*), both in 1969, none of his works were published or performed in Cuba until nearly eight years after his death. His name was rarely uttered in public, his works were conspicuously left out of anthologies of Cuban literature, and he was gradually removed from official lists and library card

catalogues. According to some accounts, Piñera underwent periodic harassment by military and police officials" (Anderson 2006, 111).

16. "radical enemy of / and radical enemy until
it destroys the countryside: 'the bureaucratic economy of rice'
and demolishes the countryside: 'the bureaucratic economy of ideology'
with its one-2-three chat-feet
(emptyemptybaroque)
of any mao*meaning*
as komrade Mao historically pointed out (or corrected)
in his effort to make the people think for the nth time:
'this stupid mass
that is structured
under the flabby concept
of the people'
that never will understand mao*demokracy* in its movement
against the sparrow
that becomes
yellow*bellied*
or mao*demokracy* in its (almost totalitarian) attempt
not to think of this
yellow*bellied*
sparrow."

17. or I repeat ch'ing ming
where the concept of *violence* is canceled out before the concept of *meaning*
(era of the Chinese
box)
and where the concept of violence should only be thought
beginning with 'the
real' of the concept
*one*uniquemeaning (as
president Mao
clarified in very timely fashion and
said in very timely fashion:
'if a worker
marches extensively
eliminate him / if a
worker marches *in*tensively: faces
sweating with 1 chancre
of meaning')"

18. "and underscoring with a metaphor the *non*gap that must exist / between mao*demokracy* / and meaning."

19. "and underscoring with a metaphor the *non*gap that must exist
between mao*demokracy*
and meaning
and underscoring with the same metaphor the gap that exists
between tradition and
*non*meaning: generator

of violence and
*anti*order / generator of
*non*history and 'little literary
salons with
*non*sense writers'"

20. "And nonetheless he is famous today for his vertically / metaphysical little mind / and not for that *lyric*proletarian discussion among sparrows."

21. "and finding himself compelled to correct the (definitively)
civilian Mao
taking a knife
laying it on
the smallest finger
of Qi the copyist
(in an almost
dialectical / almost military
voice) telling him
"from here and
all way to the bottom
(Crackk . . .)"

22. "Doors open / inward and / with infinite horror / outward beyond thoughts."

23. "Doors open / inward and / with infinite horror / outward beyond thoughts / I'm thinking / of an intensity-writing / but writing is not the right word / (the right one is forest clearing)."

24. "at some point or in some forest clearing / calculated / (in the mind) / although point is also imprecise / and nonetheless, still the rays-excavate / each of these dispersed points."

25. "grinder-hurdy-gurdies in Mandelstam, Nietzsche (how creaky they are!)."

26. "but writing is not the right word / (the right one is forest clearing) / or even the closest word / since / no word is as intense / once it is written."

27. "no word is as intense / once it is written / in the infinite horror of a few earthen characters / the disinterred brain."

28. "the characters come off / when a hand simply grazes them / as does the earth / on the edge of some outcroppings or sheets of slate."

29. "the campuses (of eyes) and the campuses (of heads)."

30. "thus in the open-air mines of Serra Pelada / 400 km south of Belén / where humans (smiling molecules of slippery blackness) have extracted / in a sagittal cut / the orbit of an infinitely horrible eye."

31. "in the intersection / the sagittal cut of the brain / such / that / the head and the eye / the eye and the head and / thus the campuses (of eyes) and the campuses (of heads) / express the surface / (already, / exclusively removed) / is only, / exclusively, / the depths of the mine."

32. "farms of 1914
with creole coffee dry/
ing in the sun and

pots of crusty leprosy
parceled-out
or neuro/
biotic movements of terrain
nonetheless adjacent and
seemless
(*numen*
voluptas) in the de/
vastated mountains"

33. After the beginning of the World War I, American finance capital made its entrance into the island, and with it came the consolidation of the merchant middle class, and the beginning of the labor movement.

34. Sugar production in Cuba rose from 1914 onward as the island became one of the world's main suppliers (Thomas 1971, 536).

35. "displaced
gray
in what slat of earth
do you put my head
the rolling—head—
as artifice of the fallacious letter"

36. "The galleon (that borders the coast) is not a galleon although it seems a galleon. / The galleon (that borders the coast) is not a galleon although it seems a galleon. / 'The galleon' is the replica of a galleon."

37. "K the cyclist, one of the many segregated turned into an exegete, hitch-hiking most of the time between the city and the fields, or between the fields and the mountains, without finding a solution to the eternal problem, without finding repose for his body . . . negroid, one of the many segregated turned into an exegete, hitch-hiking most of the time between the city and the town, or between the town and the mountains, without finding a solution to the eternal problem, without finding repose for his body . . . he told me that after looking inside he felt something strange . . ."

38. "Rodent of small volume, to protect itself from aggression of diverse animals, their limbs and teeth more powerful, it emits a nauseating odor, a curious glandular mechanism used when it was close to being assaulted. / At the zoo, jail or mental hospital, where the animals struggle for a little bit of space to deposit food and feces, I see the skunk cross the areas designed for the strong mammals and I am envious, I who am indifferent to those cars crossing here that speak of luxury."

39. "ex-lawyers, ballast down, cross through the law, searching for an escape valve."

40. "O-X / /In the center of the poem / he eats the borders of the poem / he looks at reality with the eyes of an ox / from the center of the poem./ 'Doctor, the bones of its shins along the furrows were the poem, where the water fell from its nose, its fingers opened, its heads the burning flowers of the poem' / O-X / / His fatigue is political / he will not get up / he does not want to engage / he eats the borders of the poem/ he looks at reality with the eyes of an ox / from the center of the poem."

Afterword

1. Cuba-USSR and the Post-Soviet Experience," conference organized by Jacqueline Loss and José Manuel Prieto and held at the University of Connecticut, May 2–7, 2007.

Works Cited

Abraham, Nicolas, y Maria Torok. 1994. *The Shell and the Kernel: Renewals of Psychoanalysis*. Vol. I. Edited by Nicolas T. Rand. Chicago: University of Chicago Press.

Abreu Arcia, Alberto. 2007. *Los juegos de la escritura o de la (re)escritura de la historia*. La Habana: Fondo Editorial Casa de las Américas.

Adorno, Theodor. 1973. *Negative Dialectics*. Translated by E. B. Ashton. London and New York: Routledge.

———. 1997. *Aesthetic Theory*. New York: Continuum.

Agamben, Giorgio. 1993. *Stanzas: Word and Phantasm in Western Culture*. Minneapolis: University of Minnesota Press.

———. 1998. *Homo Sacer: Sovereign Power and Bare Life*. Stanford: Stanford University Press.

Aguilera, Carlos A. 1997. "Mao." *Diáspora(s) Documentos* 1 (September): 22–24. La Habana. Mimeograph.

———. 1999a. "Introducción Virgilio Piñera Poemas." *Diáspora(s) Documentos* 4/5 (November): 26. La Habana. Mimeograph.

———. 1999b. "Viaje a China." *Diáspora(s) Documentos* 4/5 (November): 38–48. La Habana. Mimeograph.

———. 2003. Interview by Aníbal Cristobo. "Carlos A. Aguilera: para que las ficciones se cuestionen a sí mismas." *Tsé Tsé. Niordenidesorden: Diáspora(s)* (Octubre): 7–12. Buenos Aires.

———, ed. 2002. *Memorias de la clase muerta*. México: Aldus.

Aguirre, Mirta, et al., eds. 1979. *Dice la palma: poesía*. La Habana: Editorial Letras Cubanas.

———, ed. 1980. *Poesía social cubana*. La Habana: Editorial Letras Cubanas.

———. 2006. "Apuntes sobre la literatura y el arte." In *Polémicas culturales de los 60*. Edited by Graziella Pogolotti. La Habana: Ediciones Letras Cubanas.

Alicia en el pueblo de Maravillas. Directed by Daniel Díaz Torres. 1990. La Habana: ICAIC, DVD.

Alonso Estenoz, Alfredo. 2000. "Tema homosexual en la literatura cubana de los 80 y los 90: ¿renovación o retroceso?" Paper read at the XXII Latin American Association Annual Conference, Miami, March 16–18, 2000.

Althusser, Louis. 1971. *Lenin and Philosophy and Other Essays*. New York: Monthly Review Press.

Álvarez, Enrique. 2005. "Islas." *Caminos. Revista Cubana de Pensamiento Socioteológico*. 37–38 Ser cubano. http://revista.ecaminos.org/articles/article/islas/.

Anderson, F. Thomas. 2006. *Everything in Its Place: The Life and Works of Virgilio Piñera*. Lewisburg, PA: Bucknell University Press.

Arcos, Jorge Luis. 1999. *Las palabras son islas: panorama de la poesía cubana siglo XX (1990–1998)*. La Habana: Editorial Letras Cubanas.

Arenal, Humberto. 1959. *El sol a plomo*. 2nd ed. La Habana: Cruzada Latinomericana de difusión cultural. (Comprensión de Cuba, 5).

Arendt, Hanna. 2006. *On Revolution*. Introduction by Jonathan Schell. New York: Penguin.

Azcuy Henríquez, Hugo. 1995. "Estado y sociedad civil en Cuba." *Temas* 4 (October–December): 105–10.

Badiou, Alain. 2007. "The Contemporary Figure of the Soldier in Politics and Poetry." UCLA, January. http://www.lacan.com/badsold.htm.

Balibar, Étienne. 1998. "The Nation Form: History and Ideology." In *Race, Nation, Class: Ambiguous Identities*, edited by Étienne Balibar and Immanuel Wallerstein, 86–106. London, New York: Verso.

Baragaño, A. José. 1979. "Himno a las milicias." In *Dice la palma: poesía*. edited by Mirta Aguirre et al. La Habana: Editorial Letras Cubanas.

Behar, Ruth, ed. 1995. *Bridges to Cuba*. Ann Arbor: University of Michigan Press.

Bene, Carmelo. 1998. "Y bien… ¡Sí, Gilles Deleuze!" *Diáspora(s) Documentos* 3 (September): 19–21. La Habana. Mimeograph.

Benjamin, Walter. 1986. "Critique of Violence," *Reflections: Walter Benjamin Essays, Aphorisms, Autobiographical Writings*, edited by Peter Demetz, 277–300. New York: Schocken Books.

———. 1998. *The Origin of German Drama*. London, New York: Verso.

Bennett, Tony. 1979. *Formalism and Marxism*. New York: Methuen.

Bermúdez, Carmen Paula. 1999. "Eduardo Zarza Guirola: Notas." *Diáspora(s) Documentos* 4/5 (November): 102. La Habana. Mimeograph.

Bernhard, Thomas. 1998. "En busca de la verdad y de la muerte." *Diáspora(s) Documentos* 2: 6–9. La Habana. Mimeograph.

Birkenmaier, Anke, and Esther Whitfield, eds. 2011. *Havana beyond the Ruins: Cultural Mappings after 1989*. Durham: Duke University Press.

Blanchot, Maurice. 1980. *L'écriture du désastre*. Paris: Gallimard.

———. 1995. "Literature and the Right to Death." In *The Work of Fire*. Stanford: Stanford University Press.

Boleto al paraíso. Directed by Gerardo Chijona. 2010. Miami, FL: Kimbara Video, 2012, DVD.

Brooks, Peter. 1976. *The Melodramatic Imagination: Balzac, Henry James, and the Mode of Excess*. New Haven: Yale University Press.

Buckwalter-Arias, James. 2010. *Cuba and the New Origenismo*. Woodbridge: Boydell and Brewer.

Cabezas Miranda, Jorge. 2012. *Proyectos poéticos en Cuba (1959–2000). Algunos cambios temáticos y formales*. Alicante: Publicaciones de la Universidad de Alicante,

Campa Román de la. 2006. *Cuba on My Mind: Journeys to a Severed Nation*. London, New York: Verso.

Canel, Fausto. 1960. *Revolución* (December), Habana.

Cardenal, Ernesto, ed. 1976. *Poesía cubana de la revolución*. México: Editorial Extemporáneos.

Casamayor-Cisneros, Odette. 2012. *Utopía, distopía e ingravidez. Reconfiguraciones cosmológicas en la narrativa postsoviética cubana*. Madrid: Iberoamericana-Vervuert.

Castro, Fidel. 1962. *Segunda declaración de La Habana (febrero 4 de enero 1962). Asamblea General del pueblo de Cuba*. La Habana: MINOP.

———. 1972a [1955]. "¡Frente a todos!" In *La revolución cubana*, edited by Adolfo Sánchez Rebolledo, 77–84. México: Ediciones Era.

———. 1972b [1956]. "Fundación del Mr "26 de Julio." Ruptura con la ortodoxia." In *La revolución cubana*, edited by Adolfo Sánchez Rebolledo, 85–92. México: Ediciones Era.

———. 1972c [1954]. "La historia me absolverá." In *La revolución cubana*, edited by Adolfo Sánchez Rebolledo. Mexico: Ediciones Era.

———. 2001. "Address to Intellectuals." In *Cuban Revolution Reader: A Documentary History of 40 Key Moments of the Cuban Revolution*, edited by Julio García Luis, 76–82. Melbourne, New York: Ocean Press.

———. 2008. *Fidel Castro Reader*. Victoria, Australia: Ocean Press.

Centeno, Miguel Ángel, and Mauricio Font. 1997. *Toward a New Cuba*. Boulder: Lynne Rienner.

Cernuda, Luis. 1993. *Poesía completa. Volumen I*. Madrid: Siruela.

Certeau, Michel de. 1975. *L'écriture de l'histoire*. Paris: Gallimard.

Chanan, Michael. 2004. *Cuban Cinema*. Minneapolis, London: University of Minnesota Press.

Coetzee, J. M. 1991. "Osip Mandelstam and the Stalin Ode." *Representations* 35, Special Issue: Monumental Histories. (Summer): 72–83.

Colebrook, Claire. 2004. *Irony: The New Critical Idiom*. London, New York: Routledge.

Constitución de la República de Cuba. 1992. http://www.cubanet.org/ref/dis/const_92.htm.

Constitución de la República de Cuba. 2010. La Habana: Editorial Política.

Cooper, S. Richard, Joan F. Kennely, and Pedro Orduñez-García. 2006. *International Journal of Epidemiology* 35: 817–24.

Dalton, Roque. 1963. "Poesía y militancia en América Latina." *Casa de las Américas* 20 (September–December): 12–20.

———. 1978. *Poemas clandestinos*. Lima: Ediciones la Sagrada Familia.

Deleuze, Gilles. 1992. "Postcript on the Societies of Control." *October* 59 (Winter): 3–7.

———, and Félix Guattari. 1986. *Kafka: Towards a Minor Literature*. Minneapolis: The University of Minnesota Press.

———. 1996. *A Thousand Plateaus. Capitalism and Schizophrenia*. Translated by Brian Massumi. Minneapolis: University of Minnesota Press.

———. 1998. *Anti-Oedipus: Capitalism and Schizophrenia*. Translated by Robert Hurly, Mark Seem, and Helen R. Lane. Preface by Michel Foucault. Minneapolis: University of Minnesota Press.

Derrida, Jacques. 1987. "Le retrait de la métaphore." In *Psyché: Inventions de l'autre*, 63–93. Paris: Éditions Galilée.

———. 1993. *Spectres de Marx*. Paris: Éditions Galilée.

———. 1997a. "Ché cos'e la poesia?" *Diáspora(s) Documentos* 1 (September): 4–6. La Habana. Mimeograph.

———. 1997b. *The Politics of Friendship*. New York: Verso.

Después de Paideia o el rescate de una memoria. 2011. Directed by Mirian Real Arcia. Miscelaneo, 2011, DVD.

Díaz Infante, Duanel. 2002. "De la casa del *ser* al callejón de las *ratas*: *Diáspora(s)* y la "literatura menor." http://www.habanaelegante.com/Summer2002/Verbosa.html.

Díaz Torres, Daniel. 1992. "Sobre el riesgo del arte." *Cine cubano* 135: 23–25.

Diego, Eliseo. 1973. *Nombrar las cosas*. La Habana: UNEAC.

Dilla, Haroldo. 1994. "Cuba between Utopia and the World Market." *Latin American Perspectives* 21 (Autumn): 46–59.

———, Milena Recio et al. 1998/99. "Controversia: Sociedad civil en el debate cubano de los 90." *Temas. Cultura, ideología y sociedad* 16–17 (October–June): 155–75.

Domínguez, Jorge. 1978. *Cuba: Order and Revolution*. Cambridge and London: The Belknap Press of Harvard University Press.

———. 1997. "¿Comienza una transición hacia el autoritarismo en Cuba?" *Encuentro de la cultura cubana* 6/7 (fall–winter): 7–23.

Dorta Sánchez, Walfrido. 2013. "Discursos postnacionales, política de (des)autorización y terrorismo literario: la poesía no lírica de los escritores del grupo Diáspora(s)." In *Revista Diáspora(s). Edición Facsímil (1997–2002). Literatura Cubana*, edited by Jorge Cabezas Miranda. Barcelona: www.linkgua-digital.com. Print.

"Dossier Proyecto Paideia." 2006. Edited by Néstor Díaz de Villegas. *Cubista* (Summer). http://www.cubistamagazine.com.

Eckstein, Susan. 1994. *Back from the Future: Cuba under Castro*. Princeton: Princeton University Press.

Enzensberger, Hans Magnus. 1999. "América." *Diáspora(s) Documentos* 4/5 (November): 63–66. La Habana. Mimeograph.

Escardó, Rolando. 1980. "Isla." In *Poesía social cubana*, edited by Mirta Aguirre et al. 358–59. La Habana: Editorial Letras Cubanas.

Espinosa Domínguez, Carlos, Luisa Piñera, Virgilio Piñera et al., eds. *Virgilio Piñera en persona*. 2003. Cincinnati, OH: Término Editorial.

Fanon, Frantz. 1963. *The Wretched of the Earth*. Translated by Constance Farrington. New York: Grove Press.

———. 2002. *Les damnés de la terre*. Paris: Éditions La Découverte et Syros.

Fernandes, Sujatha. *Cuba Represent! Cuban Arts, State Power, and the Making of New Revolutionary Cultures*. Durham: Duke University Press, 2006.

Fernández Fe, Gerardo. 2002. "Carta de Gerardo Fernández Fe a la narradora Ena Lucía Portela sobre la antología *Cuba y el día después*." *La Habana Elegante* (Fall–Winter). http://www.habanaelegante.com/Fall–Winter2002/Verbosa2.html.

Fernández Retamar, Roberto. 1974. *Calibán. Apuntes sobre la cultura en nuestra América*. México: Editorial Diógenes.

———. 1994. "A 'Orígenes' como revista." *Thesaurus* 49: 2, 293–322.

———, and Fayad Jamís. 1959. *Poesía joven de Cuba*. La Habana: Editorial Popular de Cuba y del Caribe, Biblioteca Básica de la Cultura Cubana.

Ferrer, Jorge. 2006. "Una escaramuza en las líneas de la Guerra Fría (ya finalizada ésta)." *Cubista* (Summer). http://www.cubistamagazine.com.

Flores, Juan Carlos. 1994. *Los pájaros escritos*. La Habana: Editorial Unión.

———. 2002. "La crítica bicéfala: un nuevo desafío." *La Gaceta de Cuba* 1: 20–25.

———. 2003. *Distintos modos de cavar un túnel*. La Habana: Ediciones Unión.

———. 2009. *El contragolpe y otros poemas horizontales*. La Habana: Letras Cubanas.

Fornet, Ambrosio, ed. 1997. "Bridging Enigma: Cubans on Cuba." *(SAQ) The South Atlantic Quarterly Journal* 96, no.1 (Winter).

———. 2002. "La critica bicéfala: un nuevo desafio." *La Gaceta de Cuba* 1: 20–25.

———. 2007. "El quinquenio gris: revisitando el término." In *La política cultural del período revolucionario: memoria y reflexión*, edited by Eduardo Heras León and Desiderio Navarro. La Habana: Centro Cultural Criterios, 2008.

Fornet, Jorge. 2001. "La narrativa cubana entre la utopía y el desencanto." *La Gaceta de Cuba* 5: 38–45.

Foucault, Michel. 1990. *The History of Sexuality. Volume 1: An Introduction*. New York: Vintage Books, Random House.

Fowler, Víctor. 1995. "La tercera orilla." *Unión* 18: 68–73.

———. 1998. *La maldición: una historia del placer como conquista*. La Habana: Edición Letras Cubanas.

———. 1999. "La tarea del poeta y su lenguaje en la poesía cubana reciente." *Revista Casa de las Américas* 215:11–25.

———. 2008. "Limones partidos." *Cubista* (June 1). http://www.cubistamagazine.com.

———, and Antonio José Ponte, eds. 1989. *Retrato de grupo*. La Habana: Editorial Letras Cubanas.

Freud, Sigmund. 1963. "Mourning and Melancholia." In *The Standard Edition of the Complete Psychological Works of Sigmund Freud*. Vol. 14 (1914–1916). Translated and edited by James Strachey and Anna Freud. London: The Hogarth Press.

———. 1989. *Beyond the Pleasure Principle*. Translated and edited by James Strachey. New York, London: W. W. Norton.

García Espinosa, Julio. 2006. "Vivir bajo la lluvia." In *Polémicas culturales de los 60*. Edited by Graziella Pogolotti. La Habana: Ediciones Letras Cubanas.

Garrandés, Alberto. 2006. "Naranja dulce y la utopía de los saberes." *Cubista*, June 1, 2008, 1. http://www.cubistamagazine.com.

Giraudon, Liliane. 2001. "Diáspora(s): consideraciones intempestivas." *Diáspora(s) Documentos* 6 (March): 58–60. La Habana. Mimeograph.

Gott, Richard. 2004. *Cuba: A New History*. New Haven and London: Yale University Press.

Gramsci, Antonio. 1971. *Selections from the Prison Notebooks of Antonio Gramsci*. Edited by Quintin Hoare and Geoffrey N. Smith. London: Lawrence and Wishart.

Guevara, Ernesto. 1968. *Reminiscences of the Cuban Revolutionary War*. Translated by Victoria Ortiz. New York and London: Grove Press.

———. 1977a. "Guerra de guerrillas: un método." In *Ernesto Che Guevara. Escritos y discursos*, vol. 1. La Habana: Editorial de Ciencias Sociales.

———. 1977b. "Pasajes de la guerra revolucionaria." In *Ernesto Che Guevara. Escritos y discursos*, vol. 2. La Habana: Editorial de Ciencias Sociales.

———. 1977c. "El socialismo y el hombre en Cuba." In *Ernesto Che Guevara. Escritos y discursos*, vol. 8. La Habana: Editorial de Ciencias Sociales.

———. 1997. *Guerrilla Warfare: Che Guevara*. Third ed. Revised and updated with introduction and case studies by Brian Loveman and Thomas M. Davies Jr. Wilmington, DE: Scholarly Resources.

———. 2003. "Carta a Ernesto Sábato." In *América Latina. Despertar de un continente. Che Guevara*, edited by María del Carmen Ariet García. Melbourne, New York, Havana: Ocean Press.

———. 2009 (1962). "¿Qué debe ser un joven comunista?" ("Discurso de conmemoración del Segundo aniversario de la integración de las Organizaciones Juveniles, 20 de octubre de 1962"). In *Documentos de la Revolución Cubana 1962*, edited by José Bell Lara et al., 352–65. La Habana: Editorial de Ciencias Sociales.

Handwerk, Gary J. 1985. *Irony and Ethics of Narrative: From Schlegel to Lacan*. New Haven: Yale University Press.

Hansing, Katrin. 2011. "Changes from Below: New Dynamics, Spaces, and Attitudes in Cuban Society." *NACLA Report on the Americas* 44, no. 4 (July–August): 16.

Hart Dávalos, Armando. 1988. "Intervención especial de Armando Hart Dávalos, miembro del buró político del PCC y ministro de cultura." *IV Congreso de la UNEAC (26 de enero de 1988) "Año 30 de la Revolución*. La Habana: UNEAC.

Hegel, G. W. F. 1997. *Phenomenology of Spirit*. Translated by A. V. Miller, foreword by J. N. Finaly. Oxford: Oxford University Press.

Heidegger, Martin. 1988. "Letter on Humanism." In *Pathmarks*, edited by William McNeill. Cambridge: Cambridge University Press.

Hernández, Rafael. 1999. "Mirar a Cuba. Notas para una discusión." In *Mirar a Cuba. Ensayos sobre cultura y sociedad civil*, 9–30. La Habana: Editorial Letras Cubanas.

Hernández Busto, Ernesto. 2006. "Paideia: Fotos fijas." *Cubista*, June 1, 2008. http://www.cubistamagazine.com.

Hernández Reguant, Ariana, ed. 2009. *Cuba in the Special Period: Culture and Ideology in the 1990s*. New York: Palgrave Macmillan.

Hernández Salván, Marta. 2012. "De la transición y otros enigmas." *Romance Quarterly* 59, no. 3: 145–65.

Historias de la revolución. Directed by Tomás Gutiérrez Alea. 1960. La Habana: ICAIC, DVD.

Ichikawa, Emilio. "Libertad y filosofía: "aplicando" para ciudadano." In *Cuba y el día después*, edited by Iván de la Nuez. Barcelona: Mondadori, 2011.

Jameson, Fredric. 1981. *The Political Unconscious: Narrative as a Socially Symbolic Act*. Ithaca: Cornell University Press.

Kant, Immanuel. 1987. *Critique of Judgment, Including the First Introduction*. Translated by Werner S. Pluhar. Indianapolis: Hackett.

La bête humaine. Directed by Jean Renoir. 1938. Irvington, NY: Criterion Collection, Janus Film, 2006, DVD.

La ola. Directed by Enrique Álvarez. 1995. La Habana: ICAIC, DVD.

"La Revolución Cubana en la generación de jóvenes creadores tiene una fuerza insospechada." *Granma*, Wednesday, March 16.

Lacan, Jacques. 1975. *Encore. Le séminaire, livre XX*. Paris: Éditions du Seuil.

———. 1991. *The Seminar of Jacques Lacan: The Ego in Freud's Theory and in the Technique of Psychoanalysis, Book II*. Edited by Jacques Alain-Miller. Translated by Sylvana Tomaselli. New York, London: Norton.

———. 1993. *The Psychoses (1955–1956):The Seminar of Jacques Lacan, Book III*. Edited by Jacques-Alain Miller. New York: Norton.

———. 1998. *On Feminine Sexuality: The Limits of Love and Knowledge 1972–1973. Encore: The Seminar of Jacques Lacan, Book XX*. Edited by Jacques-Alain Miller. Translated by Bruce Fink. New York, London: Norton.

Laclau, Ernesto. 1990. *New Reflections on the Revolution of Our Time*. London: Verso.

León, Francisco. 1997. "Socialism and *Sociolismo*: Social Actors and Economic Change in 1990s Cuba." In *Toward a New Cuba*, edited by Miguel Ángel Centeno and Mauricio Font. 51. Boulder: Lynne Rienner.

Lezama Lima, José. 1974. *La cantidad hechizada*. Madrid: Ediciones Júcar.

———. 1975. *Obras completas*. Vol 1. Introduction by Cintio Vitier. México: Aguilar.

———. 1996. *Paradiso*. Edited by Cintio Vitier. Madrid: ALLCA XX.

———. 2001. *El reino de la imagen*. Edited by Julio Ortega. Caracas: Edición Unión Ayacucho.

López Lemus, Virgilio. 1988. *Palabras del trasfondo: estudio sobre el coloquialismo cubano*. La Habana: Letras Cubanas.

Loss, Jacqueline. 2012. "Persistent Matrioshkas." In *Caviar with Rum: Cuba-USSR and the Post-Soviet Experience*. Edited by Jacqueline Loss and José Manuel Prieto. New York: Palgrave Macmillan.

Luis, William. 2003. *Lunes de Revolución: literatura y cultura en los primeros años de la Revolución Cubana*. Madrid: Verbum.

Lukács, Georg. 1968. *History and Class Consciousness: Studies in Marxist Dialectics*. Translated by Rodney Livingstone. Cambridge: MIT Press.

Man, Paul de. 1996. "The Concept of Irony." In *Aesthetic Ideology*. Minneapolis: University of Minnesota Press.

Mañach, Jorge. 1999. *Ensayos*. Edited by Jorge Luis Arcos. La Habana: Editorial Letras Cubanas.

Marqués de Armas, Pedro. 1993. *Los Altos Manicomios*. La Habana: Ediciones Poramor.

———. 1994. *Fascículos sobre Lezama*. La Habana: Letras cubanas.

———. 1997. "Orígenes y los ochenta." *Diáspora(s) Documentos* 1 (September): 20–21. La Habana. Mimeograph.

———. 1999. "Virgilio Piñera: entre lúdico y agónico." *Diáspora(s) Documentos* 4/5 (November): 103. La Habana. Mimeograph.

———. 2002. *Cabezas*. La Habana: Ediciones Unión.

Martí, José. 1997. "Nuestra América." In *Política de nuestra América*, 7th ed., introduction by Roberto Fernández Retamar, 37–44. Madrid, México: Siglo Veintiuno.

———. 1997. "Congreso de Washington." In *Política de nuestra América*, 7th ed., introduction by Roberto Fernández Retamar, 145–52. Madrid, México: Siglo Veintiuno.

———. 2007. *Obras Completas. Edición Crítica*. Tomo 14, Poesía 1. La Habana: Centro de Estudios Martianos.

Martín Sevillano, Ana Belén. 2008. *Sociedad civil y arte en Cuba: Cuento y artes plásticas en el cambio de siglo (1980–2000)*. Madrid: Verbum.

Martínez Heredia, Fernando. 2007. "Pensamiento social y política de la Revolución." In *La política cultural del periodo revolucionario: memoria y reflexión*. Primera parte. La Habana: Ciclo de conferencias organizado por el Centro Cultural Criterios.

Marx, Karl. 1973. *Grundrisse. Introduction to the Critique of Political Economy*. Translated by Martin Nicolaus. New York: Vintage Books.

———. 1990a. *Capital: A Critique of Political Economy*. Vol. 1. Introduced by Ernest Mandel. Translated by Ben Fowkes. London: Penguin Books in association with New Left Review.

———. 1990b. *The Eighteenth Brumaire of Louis Bonaparte*. New York: International Publishers.

———, and Friedrich Engels. 1947. *Marx and Engels, Literature and Art: Selection from Their Writings*. New York: International General.

———. 1978. "Economic and Philosophic Manuscripts of 1844." In *The Marx-Engels Reader*. Edited by Robert C. Tucker. 2nd edition. New York, London: Norton.

———. 1999. *The German Ideology*. Edited by C. J. Arthur. London: Lawrence and Wishart.

Memorias del IV Congreso de la UNEAC. 1988. La Habana: UNEAC.

Memorias del V Congreso de la UNEAC. 1993. La Habana: UNEAC.

Michaux, Henri. 1979. *Saisir*. Paris: Fata Morgana.

Mizruchi, L. Susan. 1998. *The Science of Sacrifice: American Literature and Modern Social Theory*. Princeton: Princeton University Press.

Molina, Raúl, et al. 2006. "Conclusión de un debate entre cineastas cubanos." In *Polémicas culturales de los 60*, edited by Graziella Pogolotti. La Habana: Ediciones Letras Cubanas.

Morejón Arnaiz, Idalia. 2006. "*Eppure si muove*: Las transformaciones de la norma poética en Cuba." In *Cuba, poesía, arte y sociedad. Seis ensayos*. Madrid: Editorial Verbum.

Mosquera, Gerardo. 2009. "Cuba in Tania Bruguera's Work: The Body Is the Social Body." In *Tania Bruguera: On the Political Imaginary*, edited by Helaine Posner, Gerardo Mosquera, and Carrie Lambert-Beatty. Milan: Charta.

Nancy, Jean-Luc. 1991. *The Inoperative Community*. Minneapolis: University of Minnesota Press.

Navarro, Desiderio. 2002. "In Medias Res Publicas: On Intellectuals and Social Criticism in the Cuban Public Sphere." *Boundary2* 29, no. 3 (Fall): 187–203.

Nietzsche, Friedrich. 2006. *Thus Spoke Zarathustra*. Edited by Adrián del Caro and Robert B. Pippin. Translated by Adrián del Caro. Cambridge: Cambridge University Press.

Nogueras, Luis Rogelio. 2001. *Y si muero mañana*. La Habana: Letras Cubanas.

Nuez, Iván de la. 1989. "El cóndor pasa." *La gaceta de Cuba*. (June): 1–11.

———. 1991. "Más acá del bien y del mal. El espejo cubano de la posmodernidad." *Plural* 228 (June): 21–32.

———. 2006. *Fantasía roja. Los intelectuales de izquierdas y la Revolución cubana*. Barcelona: Debate.

———, Antonio José Ponte et al. 2001. *Cuba y el día después: Doce ensayistas nacidos con la Revolución imaginan el futuro. Almanaque otoño 2001*. Barcelona: Mondadori.

Padilla, Heberto. 1971. *Fuera del juego*. Río Piedras, PR: Editorial San Juan.

Padura, Leonardo. 2000. *Modernidad, posmodernidad y novela policial*. La Habana: Ediciones Unión.

Pasolini, Pier Paolo. 1981. *Transhumanar y organizar*. Madrid: Visor.

Pérez A., Louis Jr. *Cuba: Between Reform and Revolution*. New York, Oxford: Oxford University Press, 1988.

Pérez-Stable, Marifeli. 1993. *The Cuban Revolution*. Oxford: Oxford University Press.

Piñera, Virgilio. 1999. "Lápidas." *Diáspora(s) Documentos* 4/5 (November): 28. La Habana. Mimeograph.

———. 2000. *La isla en peso*. Edited by Antón Arrufat. Barcelona: Tusquets Editores.

Pogolotti, Graziella, ed. 2006. *Polémicas culturales de los 60*. La Habana: Ediciones Letras Cubanas.

Ponte, Antonio José. 1997. *Asiento en las ruinas*. La Habana: Editorial Letras Cubanas.

———. 1998. "Ceremonial Origenista y Teleología Insular." *Diáspora(s) Documentos* 2 (January): 1–4. La Habana. Mimeograph.

———. 2000. *Cuentos de todas partes del Imperio*. Vauchrétien: Éditions Deleatur.

———. 2002. *El libro perdido de los origenistas*. México D.F.: Editorial Aldus.

Prats, Rolando. n.d. "Palabras en la Inauguración del Proyecto Paideia." *Cubista* (Summer). http://www.cubistamagazine.com.

———. 1992. "Nota de prensa y declaración de Tercera Opción" (February 20). *Cubista* (Summer). http://www.cubistamagazine.com.

Prats Sariol, José. 1996. "Lecturas concurrentes: resúmenes críticos de los capítulos de Paradiso. Cápitulo VIII. Erotismos." In *Paradiso*, Edición Crítica, coord. Cintio Vitier, 2nd ed. Madrid: ALLCA XX.

Price, W. David. 2003. "Thoughts of Destruction and Annihilation in Thomas Bernhard." *The Journal of English and Germanic Philology* 102, no. 2 (April): 188–210.

Prieto, Abel. 1993. "Palabras de Abel Prieto en la inauguración del evento." *Memorias del V Congreso de la UNEAC*. La Habana. UNEAC.

———. 1996. "Ser (o no ser) intelectual en Cuba." *Encuentro de la cultura cubana* 1 (Summer): 93–94.

Proyecto Paideia. 1988. "Paideia. Proyecto general de acción cultural" (December). *Cubista* (Summer 2006) http://www.cubistamagazine.com.

———. 1989a. "¿Qué es el proyecto Paideia?" (February 25). *Cubista* (Summer 2006) http://www.cubistamagazine.com.

———. 1989b. "Paideia I." (July 26). *Cubista* (Summer 2006). http://www.cubistamagazine.com.

———. 1989c. "Paideia V. Proyecto de promoción, crítica e investigación de la cultura" (October 19). *Cubista* (Summer 2006) http://www.cubistamagazine.com.

Quintero-Herencia, Juan Carlos. 1997. "Moralidad y crítica en la *Casa de las Américas* (1960–1971): Notas sobre la *Casa* ante las revistas *Lunes de Revolución* y *Orígenes*." *Revista de Estudios Hispánicos Puerto Rico* 1 (Año XXIV): 85–109.

Quiroga, José. 2005. *Cuban Palimpsests*. Minnesota: University of Minnesota Press.

Rodríguez, Carlos Rafael. 2010. "Concepciones ideo-estéticas en la política cultural cubana de la década del 60." *Revista Universidad y Sociedad* (September–December): 1–7. http://www.ucf.edu.cu/ojsucf/index.php/uys/issue/view/10.

Rodríguez, Reina María. 1982. *Cuando una mujer no duerme*. La Habana: Unión de Escritores y Artistas de Cuba.

Rojas, Rafael. 1998. *El arte de la espera. Notas al margen de la política cubana*. Madrid: Editorial Colibrí.

———. 2003. *La política del adiós*. Miami: Ediciones Universal.

———. 2006a. *Tumbas sin sosiego. Revolución, disidencia y exilio del intelectual cubano*. Barcelona: Editorial Anagrama.

———. 2006b. "Memorias de Paideia." *Cubista* (Summer). http://www.cubistamagazine.com.

———. 2007. "Anatomía del entusiasmo: la revolución como espectáculo de ideas." *América Latina hoy* 47 (December), Universidad de Salamanca: 39–53.

———. 2009. *El estante vacío. Literatura y política en Cuba*. Barcelona: Editorial Anagrama.

Saínz, Enrique. 2013. "Poesía cubana de los noventa: algunas consideraciones acerca del grupo Diáspora(s)." In *Revista Diáspora(s). Edición Facsímil (1997–2002). Literatura Cubana*, edited by Jorge Cabezas Miranda. Barcelona: www.linkgua-digital.com. Print.

Salgado, César. 2002. "The Novels of Orígenes." *CR: The New Centennial Review* 2, no. 2 (Summer): 201–30.

Sánchez Aguilera, Osmar. 1993. *Poesía en claro. Cuba, años 80 (Long Play/ Variaciones)*. La Habana: Letras Cubanas.

Sánchez Mejías, Rolando. 1994. *Derivas I*. La Habana: Editorial Letras Cubanas, Pinos Nuevos.

———. 1995. *Mapa imaginario: Dossier, 26 nuevos poetas cubanos*. La Habana (Embajada de Francia en Cuba): Instituto Cubano del Libro.

———. 1996. "Carta abierta a los escritores cubanos." *Encuentro de la cultura cubana* 1 (Summer): 90–92.

———. 1997a. "Olvidar Orígenes." *Diáspora(s) Documentos* 1 (September): 17–19. La Habana. Mimeograph.

———. 1997b. "Presentación." *Diáspora(s) Documentos* 1 (September): 1–3. La Habana. Mimeograph.

———. 1998. "Zilla." *Diáspora(s) Documentos* 2 (January): 22–41. La Habana. Mimeograph.

———. 1999. "Violencia y literatura." *Diáspora(s) Documentos* 4/5 (November): 1–7. La Habana. Mimeograph.

———. 2001. *Historias de Olmo*. Barcelona: Siruela.

———. 2002. "El arte de graznar." *Diáspora(s) Documentos* 7/8 (February–March): 27–30. La Habana. Mimeograph.

Santí, M. Enrico. 2002. "La invención de Lezama Lima." In *Bienes del siglo. Sobre cultura cubana*. Mexico D.F.: Fondo de Cultura Económica.

Sarduy, Severo. 1999. "La simulación." In *Obra completas* , vol. II, edited by Gustavo Guerrero y François Wahl, 1263–1344. Madrid: Alcalá XX.

Saunders, Rogelio. 2001. "El lenguaje y el poder." *Diáspora(s) Documentos* 6 (March): 1–11. Mimeograph.

———. 2002. "Un gato llamado Adam Smith." *Diáspora(s) Documentos* 7/8 (February–March): 16–21. La Habana. Mimeograph.

Schlegel, Friedrich. 1971. "On Incomprehensibility," translated by Peter Firchow. In *Lucinde and the Fragments*. Minneapolis: University of Minnesota Press.

Schuman, Tony. 1975. "Housing: A Challenge Met." *Cuba Review* 5 (March): 6–20.

Serra, Ana. 2007. *The New Man in Cuba: Culture and Identity in the Revolution*. Gainesville: University Press of Florida.

Sontag, Susan. 1989. *Illness as Metaphor and AIDS and Its Metaphors*. New York: Picador.

Starobinski, Jean. 1963. "L'encre de la mélancolie." *Nouvelle Revue Française* 2, no. 1 (1 March): 410–23.

Sweig, E. Julia. 2009. *Cuba: What Everyone Needs to Know*. Oxford: Oxford University Press.

Techo de vidrio. Directed by Sergio Giral. 1981. La Habana: ICAIC, VHS.

Thomas, Hugh. 1971. *Cuba or the Pursuit of Freedom*. London: Eyre and Spottiswoode.

Triana, José, ed. 1998. *Lezama, cartas a Eloísa y otra correspondencia (1939–1976)*. Madrid: Verbum.

Vatter, Miguel. 2011. "The Quarrell between Populism and Republicanism: Machiavelli and the Antinomies of Plebeian Politics." *Contemporary Political Theory* (October): 1–22.

Vilariño Ruiz, Evelio. 1998. *Cuba: Socialist Economic Reform and Modernization*. La Habana: Editorial José Martí.

Vitier, Cintio. 1976a. "Cara" and "Cara o cruz." In *Poesía cubana de la revolución*, edited by Ernesto Cardenal, 81–82. México: Editorial Extemporáneos.

———. 1976b. "Camilo Cienfuegos." In *Poesía cubana de la revolución*, edited by Ernesto Cardenal, 78–79. México: Editorial Extemporáneos.

———. 1984. "De las cartas que me escribió Lezama." In *Coloquio Internacional sobre la obra de Lezama Lima. Poesía*. Madrid: Centre de Recherches Latino-Américaines Université de Poitiers, Editorial Espiral/ Fundamentos.

———. 1986. *Lo cubano en la poesía*. La Habana: Editorial Letras Cubanas.
———. 2001. *Crítica 2. Obras Completas* vol. 4. La Habana: Editorial Letras Cubanas.
Weiss, Peter. 1968. "Che Guevara." *Pensamiento Crítico* 12 (January): 79–86.
Weiss, Rachel. 2011. *To and from Utopia in the New Cuban Art*. Minneapolis, London: University of Minnesota Press.
Whitfield, Esther. 2008. *Cuban Currency: The Dollar and Special Period Fiction*. Minnesota: University of Minnesota Press.
Zamora Céspedes, Bladimir. "Una ciudad buena para el hombre." http://www.lajiribilla.cu/2002/n80_noviembre/1888_80.html.
Žižek, Slavoj. 1989. *The Sublime Object of Ideology*. London: Verso.
———. 1994. *Mapping Ideology*. London: Verso.
———. 2001. *Did Anybody Say Totalitarianism? Five Interventions in the (Mis)use of a Notion*. London: Verso.

Index